CULTIVATING A NEW SOUTH

CULTIVATING
A NEW SOUTH

Abbie Holmes Christensen and the Politics
of Race and Gender, 1852–1938

MONICA MARIA TETZLAFF

University of South Carolina Press

Published in Columbia, South Carolina, by the
University of South Carolina Press

Manufactured in the United States of America

06   05   04   03   02   5   4   3   2   1

Library of Congress Cataloging-in-Publication Data

Tetzlaff, Monica Maria.
   Cultivating a new South : Abbie Holmes Christensen and the politics of race and
   gender, 1852–1938 / Monica Maria Tetzlaff.
      p. cm.
   Includes bibliographical references (p.) and index.
      ISBN 1-57003-453-2 (cloth : alk. paper)
      1. Christensen, A. M. H. (Abigail Mandana Holmes), 1852–1938. 2. Christensen,
   A. M. H. (Abigail Mandana Holmes), 1852–1938—Relations with African Americans.
   3. African Americans—South Carolina—Beaufort County—Social conditions. 4. African
   Americans—Southern States—Social conditions. 5. Social reformers—South Carolina—
   Beaufort County—Biography. 6. Folklorists—South Carolina—Beaufort County—
   Biography. 7. White women—South Carolina—Beaufort County—Biography. 8. Beau-
   fort County (S.C.)—Biography. 9. Beaufort County (S.C.)—Race relations. 10. Beaufort
   County (S.C.)—Social conditions. I. Title.
F277.B3T48 2002
305.896'073'0092—dc21
   [B]   2002005686

To my family and my teachers

Contents

Illustrations

Abbreviations

Names

AH / Abbie Holmes

AHC / Abbie Holmes Christensen

ACP / Andrea Christensen Patterson

AOC / Arthur Olaf Christensen

AWC / Abby Winch Christensen

FHC / Frederik Holmes Christensen

NC / Niels Christensen Sr.

NC Jr. / Niels Christensen Jr.

RGH / Reuben Graves Holmes

Manuscript Collections

APS / American Philosophical Society, Philadelphia, Pennsylvania

CE / Carroll Eve and Paul Sommerville, Beaufort, South Carolina

CFP / Christensen Family Papers

Pringle / Wyatt and Sally Pringle, Beaufort, South Carolina

SCL / South Caroliniana Library, University of South Carolina, Columbia

Acknowledgments

I begin with thanks to Robert Francis Engs and Joanne Braxton, with whom my work in African American studies began. Bob Engs has been a steadfast mentor and friend without whom this book would not have been possible. Thanks are also due to Drew Faust and Evelyn Brooks Higginbotham, whose excellent scholarship, example, and advice have guided me onward. Robert St. George and John Roberts were my teachers in the field of folklore, which I have happily added to my study of history. The University of Pennsylvania History Department, the Andrew W. Mellon Foundation, and Indiana University South Bend also provided crucial financial support.

Many South Carolinians helped me to uncover the historical riches of their state. I owe a great debt to Allen Stokes and the staff of the South Caroliniana Library, especially Henry Fulmer, Laura Costello, and Beth Bilderback. The Institute for Southern Studies was also a kind sponsor. The Christensen family has been generous with their time and family papers. Frederik Burr Christensen, Niels Christensen III, Carroll and Pinckney Eve, Anne and Rick Pollitzer, and Paul and Anne Sommerville were particularly gracious in their hospitality and storytelling. Hillary Barnwell, Grace Cordial, and Dennis Adams of the Beaufort County Library rendered their invaluable assistance, providing a link with Wilhelmina Barnwell, who offered stories and sparkling wit. I will always cherish the hospitality, memories, and photographs that Thelma Shanklin West and Katherine Doctor contributed to this project. Joseph Shanklin Jr., Inez Singleton, Victoria Austin, and Charles Singleton also added their important remembrances. Helen Shramek pointed to me to documents on woman suffrage; Sally and Wyatt Pringle and Gerhard Spieler added local knowledge of Beaufort. Emory Campbell and Lula Holmes also offered their hospitality through the Penn Center on St. Helena Island. Columbia Friends Meeting, Patricia Montgomery, and Frances Elliott provided a home away from home and more.

Thanks also go to Sue Grayzel, Les Lamon, Deshae Lott, and Kate Wilson, who read portions of this manuscript. Anastatia Sims is the best reader an author could hope for and a superb mentor as well. Lawrence Rowland and Stephanie McCurry also provided insightful readings and Nancy Hewitt, Charles Joyner, and Marjorie Spruill Wheeler gave vital encouragement.

During graduate school, Dana Barron and Tom Sugrue opened up their happy home and read portions of my dissertation, while Komozi Woodard extended his friendship and intellectual companionship. Alexander Moore and Barbara Brannon of the University of South Carolina Press shepherded me kindly and skillfully through the publication process.

Many colleagues and students in South Bend have also been helpful. Mary Satkoski and Cyndy Gehring provided editorial assistance, Maureen Kennedy at Indiana University Interlibrary Loan kept a steady stream of books flowing my way, and Pat Furlong, Pat McNeal, Roy Schreiber, and Les Lamon have been excellent mentors. I am grateful to my sister scholars Rebecca Brittenham, Linda Chen, Louise Collins, April Lidinsky, Betsy Lucal, Margarete Myers Feinstein, Becky Torstrick, and Lesley Walker for their helpful readings and to my Norte Dame friends, Gale Biderman, Richard Pierce, and Elizabeth Van Jacob, as well as the graduate students in my New South colloquium for providing intellectual camaraderie.

I owe more than I can ever repay to my dear friend Mary Boyes, who gave me her wisdom, creativity, and love. Mark Constantine, Bev De Mario, Gail McGuire, and South Bend Friends have refreshed my body, mind, and spirit. I also credit the inspiration and assistance of my family. My late grandmother, Maria Eifert, told me stories of the past and gave me a link to the nineteenth century. My parents, Manfred and Mary Tetzlaff, and my aunts, uncles, and cousins, especially Arthur and Eva Helwing, always supported me in my path. Finally, thanks go to Kurt Hack, who gave of himself and reminded me to play so that the writing of this book became one more adventure along the way.

Introduction

Abbie Mandana Holmes Christensen (1852–1938), a daughter of white Massachusetts abolitionists, began trying to cultivate a New South in Beaufort, South Carolina, as a teenage teacher of black students in the 1870s. Young Abbie became one of the first collectors of African American folklore, married, had six children, and engaged in reform movements such as temperance, woman suffrage, and socialism. Through her publication of *Afro-American Folk Lore* (1892), her work touched a national audience, but her story is mainly a local one—Abbie Christensen played a part in shaping the New South emerging in coastal South Carolina after the Civil War. Her story illuminates the possibilities of interracial cooperation and the tragic limitations of segregation facing a white woman reformer in the New South of her time.[1]

To understand an idea of the layers of history, the hub of activity, and the mixture of regions and races that made up Christensen's life, the reader is asked to imagine a visit to her home sometime in the late 1910s. Standing well back from the street on two acres of parklike grounds covered with rosebushes, fruit trees, palmettos, and live oaks, Christensen's house was a white-columned antebellum mansion in "the Point" area along the river at Beaufort. The home had been built, probably by enslaved artisans and laborers, for a white Methodist minister who conducted a mission to slaves on the Sea Islands' cotton and rice plantations. An African American carpenter and other laborers expanded the Christensen home after Abbie Christensen bought it in the 1880s, adding a new kitchen, a pantry, a bedroom, and a bathroom. Wide porches, or piazzas, wrapped around the two stories of the house, providing a view of the river and marshes where gulls flew across "like flashes of silver." Despite its Confederate past, the house often flew a large American flag. In the gardens around the house John Simmons, an African American gardener, might be working, tending the Cherokee rose vine, apple and plum trees, or the exotic Japanese persimmon tree. In the stable and scattered about the grounds were the animal reminders of nineteenth-century rural life: a cow, a horse, a brood of chickens, and assorted pet cats and dogs.[2]

At the door a visitor might have been greeted by Musetta Lawrence Simmons, John's wife, and then by Abbie Christensen herself, slim and just under five feet tall, dressed in muslin, silk, or broadcloth, depending on the season. Abbie's determined face and alert brown eyes were framed by white hair pulled back into a bun. If she were following her usual routine, Christensen might have risen from sewing or from her desk where she wrote letters to northern and southern correspondents. Moving with her to the library, a visitor could glance past the fireplace to the table and spy a sweet-grass basket, its coils sewn together by a black artist working in the West African style of his or her ancestors. On the shelves of the library sat Christensen's small, red book, *Afro-American Folk Lore,* but she no longer collected tales. Instead, she would probably show her visitor her newest activity in her "Montessori room," where a school of small white children went about their "work," touching sandpaper letters or practicing buttoning and lacing on large frames that made it easy for little fingers. At noon she might check on Mona Brown or another cook, preparing dinner for the household, which included her bachelor son, Fred Christensen, who sometimes left his post at the family hardware and real estate business to join his mother for a meal. In the afternoon Abbie Christensen might be found sitting at a table draped in yellow, the woman suffrage color, taking tea with Mabel Runnette, a white woman milliner and suffrage leader. In her parlor she might also receive another guest, Professor Joseph S. Shanklin, African American principal of the rural black school Christensen had founded. After Shanklin and Christensen talked over the business of the Shanklin School, Christensen might show off that educational project, following Shanklin out of town in her black buggy pulled by her stately gray horse, Presto, and crossing into a landscape with fewer trees and large, flat expanses of cotton and vegetables. Old and New South, North and South, black and white blended together in the Christensen household as they did in Christensen's life.[3]

Women's history, African American history, and other branches of southern history have demonstrated that there have been many Souths and southerners, expanding our vision far beyond W. J. Cash's white, male "man at the center." One of the hardest categories of southerners to place, however, includes those who happen to be northern-born but spend most of their lives in the South. How did these hybrid southerners operate within the ideologies of blackness and whiteness, masculinity and femininity that they encountered in the South? Although a few scholars have tackled the topic of northerners in the South, few have benefitted from the more recent scholarship in women's history that this biography seeks to use.[4]

Abbie Christensen presents an interesting subject for the study of racial, regional, and gender politics precisely because she embodied many contradictions. A white woman in a largely black community, a northerner in the South, Christensen offers a fresh perspective because she forces us to blur what are sometimes artificially rigid divisions of space, as well as time, in the discipline of history. A child of abolitionists and a mother of New Dealers, Abbie lived a long life that formed a bridge between those different generations.

This biography follows Abbie Christensen through the many times that the South was proclaimed "New" after the Civil War. During Reconstruction, African Americans wanted a New South where they would have freedom, citizenship, and land. White northern missionaries such as Samuel Chapman Armstrong tried to create a New South based on white-led education and a capitalist dream of creating self-sufficient black farmers and businessmen. White southerners such as Henry Grady promoted a New South of docile laborers of both races and friendly white businessmen eager for northern investment and reconciliation. Given these many blueprints for the region, one of the tasks of this book is to decipher what Christensen meant when she wrote that she was "of the New South."[5]

Christensen collected and published African American folk-lore from the 1870s through the early 1890s, a time when several different historical plots of gender and race were unfolding. These years in the South witnessed Reconstruction's optimistic promise of equality for African Americans, the violent demise of this dream in 1876, and the steady erosion of African American rights as legal segregation and illegal lynching accelerated in the 1890s. Meanwhile, in the quiet confines of Cambridge, Massachusetts, in 1888, white intellectuals and reformers celebrated the birth of the American Folk-lore Society, which intended to study Negro as well as Old English and American Indian folk-lore. Social Darwinism and scientific racism became the reigning academic paradigm as races were ranked according to their "evolutionary status." Five years later, at the noisy World's Columbian Exposition in Chicago, black novelist and suffragist Frances Ellen Watkins Harper proclaimed that the world was on the threshold of a "Woman's Era." All of these movements affected Christensen and the way she presented her folk-lore collection.[6]

In her folk-lore writing Christensen saw herself as a translator of southern black culture for northern whites. She wanted to share this culture with northern reformers. In the process, however, Christensen depicted African Americans as exotic "others." This portrayal unwittingly aided the southern "white supremacy" campaigns of the 1890s, which drove African Americans out of politics. The folk could be considered picturesque, but folk culture implied backwardness as well.

As a New South reformer with roots in the North, Christensen reveals the similarities in the ideologies of northern and New South paternalism. This paternalism led white people to see themselves in the role of parents who could guide and "uplift" the oppressed of other races. Christensen's aboli-tionist parents and her mission-oriented education gave her a lifelong sense of duty toward African Americans, which she manifested in her education and charity work. Christensen's paternalism differed from that of most other New South reformers, in that she did not promote segregation. However, she did operate within its confines when she created a "black" agricultural school and a "white" Montessori school.[7]

Although there is evidence that prejudice in the United States actually worsened within the white population from the 1890s to 1915—the period in race relations known as "the nadir"—Christensen proved a better ally to Sea Island African Americans as time passed. Quietly defying the social boundaries of segregation in her private life, Christensen helped African Americans to build a black hospital as well as the Shanklin School. Finally, at the age of eighty, when others would expect her to fade softly away, Chris-tensen boldly declared her allegiance to socialism and became a South Caro-lina elector for the American Socialist Party's presidential candidate Norman Thomas. Christensen's life helps make clear the importance of white out-siders, particularly women, who affected her region but who were also restricted by the segregated racial vision of the New South.

Although this history is about a person, for me it began with a place, the Sea Islands of South Carolina. Green and verdant in their beds of salt marsh and reeds, the Sea Islands dapple the blue waters off the coasts of North and South Carolina and Georgia. Coveted for their fertility in the eighteenth and nineteenth centuries, they are now the objects of a multi-million-dollar tourist and resort business, the old rice and cotton fields converted to golf courses and plats of condominiums. But the Sea Islands are about more than plantations and profit. They have been and still are the home of a unique group of African Americans whose creole language and culture are often referred to as "Gullah." Ancestors of the Gullah people were taken from their homes on the Senegambian rice coast of West Africa. These Sea Islanders have retained significant parts of their African cultural heritage in forms such as sweet-grass baskets and spirituals, foods, herbal medicines, and styles of worship, as well as language.[8]

When I visited the town of Beaufort and the surrounding Sea Islands, I breathed in their air of natural beauty, human tragedy, and promise. The weight of history seemed to permeate rural cabins and antebellum mansions, black and white churches and graveyards, giant oaks hung with Spanish moss, and marsh grasses moving with the tide. It is easy to get caught up in the romance of ruins, but in this book I have tried instead to examine the day-to-day struggles and triumphs of Christensen and her black and white neighbors.

I was first drawn to this region because of my interest in the cultural interactions that took place among abolitionist missionaries and Sea Island African Americans during Reconstruction. As a white woman born too late for the civil rights movement, I became conscious of racism in the conservative decade of the 1980s. I hoped to find examples of antiracist Americans and was intrigued with the black/white relationships formed between northern women and African Americans during Reconstruction. I was also curious about what happened after the idealism of Reconstruction faded, a time period more akin to the 1980s and 1990s than to the 1960s and 1970s.

I am particularly interested in the part that women played in this struggle through the public work of their writings and organizations and through the private work of friendships, child-rearing, and teaching. I chose Abbie Christensen as a subject because she was a wife, a mother, *and* an activist, unlike the single "new women" of the region who have received other biographers' attention. Christensen's efforts to influence public life while raising her children bring to light the challenges and compromises faced by mothers who entered public life. Because she was busy raising six children,

Christensen was not able to be a prominent leader, but she stayed involved, sometimes taking her children to meetings and later working with them when they became political leaders. This aspect of Christensen's life reveals the importance of African American women who worked as child nurses and domestic servants, enabling Christensen to do her public work. Christensen's interactions with black middle-class women reformers as well as African American servants show the complex intersection of class and race. Although Christensen cooperated with middle-class black women and treated them as equals in some important respects, her relations with servants were dictated by the boundaries of class.[9]

Abbie Holmes Christensen's life provides evidence of the ways white and black women helped African Americans of the Sea Islands retain some forms of justice and opportunity, while losing others. African Americans retained political power longer and avoided lynching and sharecropping more effectively in Beaufort County than in other areas of South Carolina, a state famous for "extreme racism" during Christensen's lifetime. Part of the reason for this relative tolerance lay in the patrician tradition of paternalist white elite leadership and toleration of some black autonomy, especially landowning, in the coastal regions of South Carolina and Georgia. White elites were not insecure about their status, and they could still find workers, despite the fact that many blacks owned small farms. In Beaufort County an additional factor was the presence of a large and politically active black population and a few strong-minded white women and business-minded white men from the North, who worked together to create this unique New South community. When segregation and disfranchisement overwhelmed this region, Christensen used her influence to try to soften the resulting negative effects on African American fortunes. Christensen's life shows both the power and the weakness of a white woman reformer during a time when African American rights were in retreat.[10]

In this biography I have tried to fulfill the mission issued by a friend of Christensen's daughter: "I wish something of your mother's personality and experiences might be set down for people to read. *She represents so much of America's best in a long and interesting period,* and she was such a unique person herself. . . . It might help other *ardent espousers of causes*—or stir the inardent which is more important."[11]

Biography is a powerful and peculiar sort of historical writing. It can capture the experience of the past in vivid and specific detail, but it can also distort that history, because its point of view is that of a single individual. But perhaps biography's power lies in its ability to acknowledge its limitations openly, refracting time and space through the prism of an individual. I have tried to listen to my subject's words and narrate and interpret her life according to its contours, noting the way these were shaped by her times. It is my hope that the reader will find within these pages a story that will lead us to rethink boundaries of region, race, and time—the story of an intriguing and "ardent" woman and the New South she struggled with and sought to change.[12]

Chapter One

LIFTING THE LATCH

How far back should reminiscences begin? Perhaps the first thing I remember was my triumph of lifting a heavy old fashioned iron latch on the door leading from Miss Kate Sanborn's back kitchen door.

These lines, written in old age, showed the curiosity and will Abbie Holmes Christensen exhibited in early childhood. But although she was strong, Christensen needed and accepted help from others. Her life was lived in a network of care that bound her to friends, family, and servants. Significantly, one of Christensen's earliest reminiscences was of Kate Sanborn, an Irish immigrant who cooked for her family and nursed young Abbie. Working-class and ethnic "others" such as Sanborn would draw her attention as a writer, while they also provided the domestic support that kept things running smoothly at home. The social and moral values Abbie derived from her devout and civic-minded, middle-class New England family would stay with her all of her life.[1]

But Christensen's story begins further back than her reminiscences could reach, on 28 January 1852, the day that Abbie Mandana Holmes was born. On one of the winter days thereafter, while her mother recovered from the labor of giving birth, her father, Reuben Graves Holmes, walked to the Westborough, Massachusetts, town hall and carefully entered his firstborn child in the book of births. The names Holmes told the clerk to write revealed the intricate threads that already connected his newborn baby to her extended family. She was named for her mother's closest sister, Abbie, and for one of her father's sisters, Mandana, who had died in childhood. Thirty-two-year-old Reuben Holmes listed his occupation as grain dealer and his birthplace as West Boyleston, Massachusetts. His twenty-eight-year-old wife was noted simply as Rebecca Winch Holmes, a native of Holden, Massachusetts. By registering Abbie's birth, Reuben Holmes was denoting the importance of his daughter in a way that not every family did. According to one Westborough woman, "Many of us girls were never born, we just grew up in the garden, like a flower. If they did get us entered on the books, the name was not always correct."[2]

Mother

There is little information available about Abbie's mother, partly because women rarely entered the public record and partly because so few of her private writings have survived. Rebecca Winch Holmes was born in 1824, the fifth child and fourth daughter of the prosperous James Winch family. Based on later comparisons with her daughters Abbie and Georgie, apparently Rebecca Winch had a thin face, light gray or blue eyes, and straight, dark brown hair. Her father was a bricklayer, and her mother, Sally, took in boarders and kept a cattle farm. The Winches became the largest landowners in Holden by slowly saving their money and buying piece after piece of real estate.[3]

Rebecca received both religious and secular education from her parents. When his offspring were still young, Rebecca's father wrote a pledge in which he committed "to impress upon the minds of my children the important truths of the bible and to govern them thereby." Just as he had done for his other daughters, Rebecca's father probably sent her to finish her higher education at Leicester Academy, a prestigious coeducational school founded just after the Revolution. Following their education, Rebecca and at least two of her sisters became schoolteachers.[4]

When she met Reuben Holmes, Rebecca was teaching and boarding at the home of her uncle in Holden, Massachusetts. The year 1848 brought many changes in Rebecca's life. In that year her father died and she and Reuben Holmes were married. Rebecca's mother gave the couple a good start in life by lending them three thousand dollars. After her marriage Rebecca stayed in contact with her siblings, especially her younger sister, Abbie Winch, who boarded with the Holmeses during her vacations from teaching school.[5]

Father

In contrast to Rebecca, Reuben Holmes began his life in poverty, the fifth child in a family of nine. Holmes was born in 1820 and spent his early childhood in Amherst, Massachusetts. His father earned a meager living as a maker and seller of "fanning mills" for separating grain, and his mother took in boarders. Reuben Holmes, who was known as R. G., was named for his maternal grandfather, Reuben Graves, who died while a soldier in the American Revolution. Perhaps this naming increased the strong bond between mother and son. R. G.'s mother and his older sister, both named Olive Holmes, were his most important influences. Mrs. Holmes instructed her son in prayer and the ten commandments, and he helped her keep house for their boarders. "It was my supreme delight to help my mother & she kept me at it," Holmes later wrote. At the age of five he began to attend the village school where his sister Olive taught. Soon, however, R. G. had to return home to help watch over his family's newborn twins and an "unruly" cow. All together, Holmes probably never had more than two or three years of schooling, a fact that his creative spelling and erratic grammar readily revealed.[6]

At an early age R. G. showed an acute religious sensibility, and he loved to attend his sister Olive's Sunday school. One can imagine this seven- or eight-year-old boy, with tousled dark blond hair and wide brown eyes, thinking of Jesus as he stood in a pasture watching his siblings and a cow. Holmes later recalled the vision he had at that time:

> Jesus Christ came walking up I remember just how he was dressed & how he looked. he was a tall large man over 6 feet tall & well proportioned with a swallow taled coat on patent leather shews . . . & he says children don't you want to say some verses I at once says yes & lead off in some of the verses we had learned at school & began by repeating Jerusalem my happy home Oh how I long for thee When will my sorrows have an end My joyes when shall I see and repeated the whole 8 verses & while we all were thus engaged we all began to assend up into the clow untill I could look down on the things we had left behind I saw the little waggen on the green & the house we lived in & peeple walking along the road & it seemed to me we were in perfect bliss & this is the last I remember.

R. G. held on to this vision for the rest of his life and sometimes repeated it in letters to his children and grandchildren. Holmes's personal spiritual experience, combined with the religious training from his mother and sister, prompted him to "help those I thought needed help." Later he passed on this sense of personal revelation to his daughters.[7]

In 1831 R. G.'s sister Olive married and he was sent to learn the tanning trade from his new brother-in-law. R. G. found tanning a "tedious and d[i]sgusting business" and greatly preferred helping his sister wash, cook, and clean. Throughout his youth R. G. favored traditionally feminine tasks over labor that was considered masculine. Young Holmes developed empathy and respect for the women who raised him. He later wrote that he "owed everything" to his mother and described his sister Olive Holmes Harrington as "one of the most remarkable women I ever knew[.] She was one who was always Doing for others."[8]

In 1833 young R. G.'s family moved to the wilderness territory of Michigan. They encountered many hardships but eventually established a self-sufficient farm where R. G. spent his teens plowing, tending cattle, and raising fruit trees. At seventeen, R. G. bought his own forty-acre farm and joined the Congregational Church. Soon, however, he had to leave his young orchard to accompany his ailing mother back to the East. Olive Holmes had contracted a skin disease that doctors thought was caused by the lime in the Michigan water.[9]

R. G.'s mother's condition was cured by the healing waters at Hopkinton Springs, Massachusetts, and she and her son settled nearby. In Massachusetts in the 1840s R. G. finally found financial success. He established another farm and used its profits to go into business with a man who ran a small grain store in the town of Westborough. When the county laid a new railroad track, Holmes had the insight to move his grain store next to the railroad, which gave him easy access to outside markets. Soon Reuben added a steam mill and a blacksmith shop, and he began processing and selling lumber to local home builders and nearby sleigh, shoe, and boot factories. In his reminiscences Holmes wrote that on 1 January 1856 his bookkeeper told him that he was worth $50,000. The published tax assessment for the year 1855 lists Reuben Holmes somewhat more modestly as the owner of over twenty-five acres and five houses, a steam mill, a grain store, lumber, a carriage, four horses, a cow, two swine, and bank stock, with a total value of $18,424. Exaggeration or a lag in the town's updating of property assessment may account for this discrepancy. The fact remains that Holmes was a wealthy man.[10]

A New England Girlhood

Abbie Mandana Holmes was born in 1852, a hopeful time when her parents' fortunes and those of the village of Westborough were rising. Situated amid rolling hills "on the beaten path" between Boston and Worcester, the town benefitted from the building of its first railroad in 1834. In 1850 Westborough had a population of 2,371, which grew steadily to reach 3,014 by 1855. In that year farmers on the land surrounding Main Street produced 193,736 gallons of milk, 16,800 bushels of Indian corn, 6,973 bushels of other cereal grains, 2,571 tons of hay, and 19,200 bushels of potatoes. They probably brought much of their grain to Holmes's gristmill to be ground. The town also claimed a straw hat industry and soon developed other fledgling factories.[11]

From an early age Abbie was sharply attuned to her surroundings, noting and enjoying the people, plants, and animals in the world around her. Abbie remembered her family's home on High Street in all its particulars: "Our Westboro home was a fine old place and I was very fond of it, especially the elm shaded street and a very large elm on the east side of the house. There was a little yard fronting the same Main street with roses and lilac bushes. At the rear was a vegetable garden, stable and plenty of room for me to run about in." Rebecca Holmes encouraged Abbie to play outdoors, in part to strengthen her because she was considered "delicate." A photograph of Abbie at about the age of three shows a small girl with large dark eyes, light brown hair pulled back in braids, and wearing a dress embroidered with stars. Through her parents' encouragement Abbie developed an enduring love of nature, which she demonstrated at an early age by embracing her favorite elm tree and promising to write verses for it when she grew up.[12]

Abbie's favorite human companion was Tom Brady, the hired man. She later recalled a family joke about the two of them: "For a number of years an Irishman named Tom worked for us on the place and I used to follow him around hoping to assist. One day mother called from the house, 'What are you doing now?' I answered, 'I am helping Tom.' and 'What is Tom doing?' cried Mother. 'Tom is doing nothing and I am helping him.'" Irish immigrants such as Brady started coming to Westborough about 1850, and by 1855 nearly one-sixth of the town's population was foreign-born. The sense of class and ethnic tension between middle-class Anglo-Americans such as the Holmeses and poor immigrants such as Brady undoubtedly factored into this family joke. Tom Brady married another Irish servant of the Holmes family, Kathleen Sanborn, and the couple lived nearby in a cottage that R. G. Holmes deeded to them.[13]

Besides the Bradys, the Holmes family also employed a black coachman. Although there were few African Americans in Westborough, R. G. Holmes was remembered as an abolitionist interested in the welfare of black people and may have assisted escaped slaves through the Underground Railroad. Neither Abbie nor her father made mention of this activity, but Holmes's later decision to move his family to South Carolina and assist in the struggle for emancipation makes such an earlier interest possible.[14]

During Abbie's early childhood R. G. Holmes's venerable old Georgian-style home, his modern steam mill, and his voluntary participation in the civic and charitable life of the town placed his family at the geographic, economic, and social center of Westborough. Rebecca and R. G. were active in the large Congregational church on Main Street, where Abbie must have joined them on Sundays as she was growing up.

From 1845 to 1858 R. G. also taught Sunday school to boys at the Lyman School, the nation's first reform school, located just outside Westborough. Massachusetts boys convicted of crimes were sent there instead of to the adult prisons where they had previously been housed. Holmes helped to place some of these boys in jobs upon their graduation from the school. Holmes's dedication to these boys showed that he was at the forefront of his generation's belief that individuals, especially children, could be redeemed through a mixture of discipline and kind treatment.[15]

In 1855 and 1856 R. G. Holmes was appointed Westborough's "fence viewer," a position that entailed maintaining the defenses of the town square against foraging animals. Even more important, he was chosen as sealer of weights and measures, an office that required him to give his approval to the scales of all the town merchants. While going down a hill with his heavy sealer's weights, Holmes's wagon dislodged and his horse took off at a run. R. G.'s broken arm never healed properly, and this injury later prevented his enrollment in the Union army.[16]

Holmes's civic pride, his belief in education as a means for reforming character, and his concern for African Americans undoubtedly influenced his daughter. R. G. passed on his sense of duty and paternalism toward the less fortunate. His imprint can be seen in Abbie's later participation in civic projects and her founding of the Port Royal Agricultural School, an African American institution referred to as "the Shanklin School" after its longtime black principal, Joseph Shanklin Sr.

The Holmes family continued to prosper until the Panic of 1857, when the business cycle went into a rapid downturn. The nation was thrown into depression as banks collapsed, bankruptcies doubled, wages and prices declined, and hundreds of thousands of people were thrown out of work. In a dramatic change of fortune, by 1858 R. G. Holmes's only taxable property was a single swine. Greatly chagrined, Holmes looked for someone to blame.

> I was in very prosperous circumstances & greatley prospered & got a good many enemies becaus I was thus prospered perhaps I did get about in to much stile for an ordinary man or rather my family my wife & wives sister who was living with me at that time road out every day with the finest span of horses in the county & a nice carriage which I owned at the time with a collard Driver. I must say it looked bad for a man that could not pay his debts if he did have property enough to pay . . . but as has been allrady stated It was in those days utterly impossible to collect Debts due or sell property for cash & . . . I went into insolvency.[17]

Though he faulted his wife and sister-in-law for spending too much, bad timing and the state of the economy were much more important in leading to R. G. Holmes's downfall. Just before the panic R. G. had decided that the mill was causing him a good deal of "work and care," and he sold it to a company that manufactured chairs. The company failed during the panic, and its owners could not repay him. Also Holmes had done a great deal of his grain business with southerners who were neither able nor willing to pay their debts. In 1859 R. G. Holmes made the untimely decision to go to Maryland and collect thirteen thousand dollars in notes from his southern debtors. He wrote that not only could he not collect anything, but "my life was threttened if I Did not get out of theare." R. G. finally blamed both the Panic of 1857 and the Civil War on the nation's collective sin of slavery. In this way he made sense out of the capricious nature of the business cycle and the nation's violent sectional differences.[18]

In an effort to improve his chances of finding work, R. G. Holmes moved the family to the nearby city of Worcester, where Abbie, with the resilience of a young child, adjusted relatively easily to her family's reduced circumstances. She remembered her family's financial slide as mainly a change of scenery: "When I was six years old father had to sell the place and give up his business there. This was in what was then called 'a panic.' . . . He moved his family into a small brick house in Worcester. There in place of the ample grounds at Westboro I found a small yard about fifty feet square, but it was not without its charms for a small girl." Much as she had done in Westborough, Abbie enjoyed the abundant fruit trees in the neighborhood and found a friendly playmate next door. Worcester was a center for the abolitionist and women's rights movements in the 1850s, with local leaders such as Abby Kelly Foster and liberal ministers such as Edward Everett Hale and Thomas Wentworth Higginson. As she grew older, Abbie may have absorbed some of the abolitionist sentiment from her teachers, ministers, and other adults around her.[19]

Her parents, however, turned inward in their struggle to earn a living. Abbie was old enough to notice that her mother was particularly unhappy. She wrote that her mother "did not care for this house partly because she did not want to live in a city." Abbie also mentioned that the family no longer employed servants, but a woman came once a week to "wash and clean." Though Rebecca must have made her wishes known, Reuben did not move the family out of Worcester.[20]

By the end of 1860 Abbie's mother was more than unhappy. She was beginning to show the first signs of acute mental illness, which would haunt her for the rest of her life. Rebecca was pregnant with her second child, and her husband was traveling in Ohio and Michigan, trying desperately to earn money by peddling rat traps and other assorted goods. As R. G. later wrote, at this point Rebecca Holmes "lost her mind." Although Holmes was able to describe his wife's illness in a plainspoken way, Abbie left no explicit record of her mother's problems. Abbie would only allow herself to remember that "her health was never very good." In addition to mental illness Rebecca Holmes may also have suffered from tuberculosis. Putting the best face on a painful situation, Abbie chose to remember that in the face of her illness her mother was patient, brave, and judicious.[21]

During her daughter's early years Rebecca Holmes modeled charity and instilled a love of learning in her daughter. Though her benevolence was more private than that of her husband, Rebecca was always ready to help her neighbors, even when her own circumstances were depressed. In Worcester a poor family lived down the lane from the Holmeses, and Rebecca regularly sent Abbie to take them gifts of food. Abbie's education was Rebecca Holmes's other great interest. The former schoolteacher "had theories of her own" that led her to teach Abbie at home until she was eight years old. Abbie later wrote, "It was not until we had been in Worcester two years that I went to my first school." When her own children and grandchildren were born, Abbie Christensen would do the same, teaching them at home in their early years.[22]

A copy of an 1854 Boston women's magazine, *The Mother's Assistant and Young Lady's Friend,* and a story she wrote entitled "Abbie & her kittens" are the only other surviving evidence of Rebecca Holmes's early years of motherhood. *The Mother's Assistant* provided Rebecca with sentimental poetry, domestic fiction, and advice about firm but gentle child-rearing tactics as she contemplated her two-year-old daughter. In "Abbie & her kittens," written several years later in Worcester, Rebecca told the story of an average day in the life of her family. She wrote that Abbie had found a kitten under the grapevine and "thought a great deal of it." R. G. Holmes's forgetfulness and inventiveness are featured in the story's next part. "My little readers do you know how Abbie & father & Auntie got into the house?" Rebecca queried. "They could not find the key," so Abbie's father "opened the shuttered window and put Abbie in and she opened the door." Rebecca wrote that in the evening the family ate "as much as we wished" and then put Abbie to bed. The next morning when Abbie awoke, "she jumped up and ran into her papa's room and climbed into bed." Rebecca's story places her daughter closer to her irrepressible papa than to her mother, who played the role of observer, but perhaps this is because Rebecca was the story's narrator. In any case, Abbie seemed certain of Rebecca's feelings when she later wrote that she believed no one ever loved her more than her mother did.[23]

Soon Abbie gained a sister who became her constant companion. In November 1860, when her mother's delivery date drew near, Abbie was dispatched to her Aunt Lucinda in the country. There she dreamed that one of her dolls turned into a baby sister. The real baby, Georgiana Rebecca Holmes, looked very much like the doll of Abbie's dreams. Georgiana, or Georgie, as she was called, inherited her father's features and curly, sandy-blond hair and her mother's blue eyes. Abbie, on the other hand, had her father's brown eyes and now had straight, dark brown hair like her mother. Instead of seeing her as a rival, Abbie liked having a sister for whom she could care.[24]

After the birth of her second child, Rebecca Holmes found that her illness accomplished what her earlier requests had not. "Mother's health was so poor . . . father saw he must move her to the country that she always longed for," Abbie wrote. R. G. bought a farmhouse north of Worcester, and the family moved there in the spring of 1861. Rebecca's health improved, and Abbie enjoyed walking to school, digging potatoes, and visiting with the Holmeses' many cousins in the area. Her aunts, whose concern is shown in letters, filled in during those times when her mother was not able to take care of her.[25]

Meanwhile, R. G. Holmes tried to earn a living as an inventor by drawing on his early experiences doing housework. He patented a wheel-and-paddle-driven butter churn in 1860 and also a rubber-covered clothes wringer. Though his inventions worked, because of the uneasiness over the impending Civil War, he could not find investors to back him in producing them. In an effort to salvage his finances, R. G. Holmes sold his patents for a relatively small sum, left his family in Massachusetts, and went to work as a salesman in Newark, New Jersey.[26]

In December 1862 disaster struck the Holmes family again. While Abbie was at school, a fire burned down their house. No one was injured, but the family home was destroyed. In a letter written "in greatest haste," Rebecca urged her husband to "hasten home immediately and see how you can best provide for us." After a brief stay with relatives, Rebecca and her daughters joined Reuben at a boardinghouse in Newark. R. G. Holmes began selling the hastily written *History of the Civil War* by popular history writer John Abbott. Thereafter, Abbie reported, her mother struggled once again with her undefined illness.[27]

Over time, Rebecca and the girls made friends with the woman who kept their boardinghouse, and the girls led a fairly comfortable existence among the other young people in the home. In 1863 Abbie attended a revival, and at the age of eleven she joined the First Congregational Church. Abbie continued to go to school and was happy with the "lovely teachers" and "worthwhile" pupils in her new home. Not one to give up old ties, she also maintained correspondence with her former teacher and her Worcester classmates.[28]

Abbie was not to rest for long; her father was contemplating yet another move. Because of his abolitionist sympathies, R. G. Holmes ardently desired to join the Union army but was not accepted because of the past injury to his arm. Instead, in 1864 he and Rebecca volunteered to take part in a missionary experiment taking place at Port Royal in South Carolina. R. G.

Holmes first went South alone in the spring, leaving Rebecca, Abbie, and Georgie in Paxton with his sister, Olive. He later took his family with him to the South, hoping that the warm sea air would benefit Rebecca's health.[29]

With this move to South Carolina, Abbie would leave behind the New England world that had nurtured her during her first twelve years. Her extended family, her teachers, her friends, and her church had all shaped her identity, but she was not truly aware of her regional affiliation until she left the North. Although she would never again be a permanent resident there, her formative years were spent in the northern states, and she would always think of herself as a "Yankee." The weight of generations of her extended family pressed this heritage upon her, and she welcomed it, sometimes as a comforting, well-known security blanket and sometimes as a coat of haughty intellectual armor with which to face her southern opponents. In 1864 young Abbie entered a war zone in which she clung to her family and memories of her Massachusetts home, even as her curiosity beckoned her to explore the unfamiliar landscape and peoples of the South.

Chapter Two

A NEW AND BRIGHTER DAY
IN THE SOUTH

May Peace and Prosperity come to our country Wisdom to our rulers and our Congress and Justice and Prosperity to the Freedman.[1]

Even though she was only twelve years old when her family moved to South Carolina, Abbie Holmes understood the significance of the Civil War and Reconstruction and felt a part of the momentous events of this time. "The ending of slavery promised the beginning of a new and brighter day in the south," Abbie later wrote, and her family wanted "to be a part of it." As her father wrote, he wished to be used "in the hand of God for the advancement of the collard race." In 1864, one year after the Emancipation Proclamation, the Holmeses moved to the Union-held territory known as Port Royal. Over the next decade the Holmes family, along with other people, white and black, challenged the idea of racial inferiority and established rights for African Americans. The sense of human possibility and change contained in Reconstruction gave Abbie a lifelong sense that she had a part in creating a New South.[2]

In South Carolina, Abbie and her parents joined the Port Royal Experiment, an abolitionist effort to bring free labor and education to African Americans. The experiment began in 1861 after Union naval forces captured the Sea Islands and white planters fled to the mainland, leaving most of their slave "property" behind. In 1862, in the waters off the nearby city of Charleston, Robert Smalls, a slave and pilot of the Confederate ship *The Planter,* pulled off a daring escape and delivered *The Planter* to Union forces. Born in Beaufort, Robert Smalls was a fitting representative of thousands of enslaved Sea Islanders who longed for a chance to live free and self-sufficient lives. Sea Island African Americans had lived mostly on large plantations farming rice and cotton, with minimal contact with whites. Their creole language, known as Gullah, bound them closely together. Black agriculturalists, carpenters, blacksmiths, cooks, and other skilled workers had made the plantations largely self-sufficient. Often families of several generations lived together, and black communities were only strengthened when whites fled.[3]

A new population of whites including Yankee soldiers, government officials, and missionary volunteers soon arrived to assist and supervise the lives
of these "contrabands of war," who were not yet free. As Christensen later
wrote, "Plantations abandoned by the former owners were worked by the
former slaves under direction of men selected by the government." Northerners sometimes seemed similar to white overseers and masters when they
demanded that African Americans work the cotton fields for little more than
daily rations. On the other hand, most Sea Island African Americans desired
education, and teachers sponsored by the American Missionary Association
and other freedman's aid societies were warmly welcomed. Christensen
described these "evangels" as a "devoted band . . . that carried on this beginning of general schooling of the southern negro." Many of these abolitionists were members of America's oldest elite families. Although the Holmeses
were not in this category, Christensen recalled with pride that the leading
Unitarian minister, Edward Everett Hale, called them "the best blood of
New England."[4]

These Yankees brought with them an ideology that mixed egalitarianism,
"romantic racialism," and paternalism. Most abolitionist missionaries believed
in equal political rights for African Americans after emancipation. As romantic racialists, however, they saw blacks as racially different—more prone to
emotion, religiosity, and musical expression and less gifted in reason and science than white Americans. White paternalists believed that African Americans would be "uplifted" through the guidance of benevolent whites. In their
minds, blacks were temporarily inferior but could advance with the proper
education and moral tutelage.[5]

By 1864, when the Holmeses arrived in Beaufort, massive changes in the
social organization of the Sea Islands had already taken place. On 1 January
1863 over five thousand whites and blacks gathered to celebrate the Emancipation Proclamation. Unlike "contrabands" in several other occupied portions of the Confederate states, African Americans in South Carolina were
unambiguously freed. To add further to the freed people's hope and joy, in
March some abandoned Sea Island plantations were offered for sale. Freedom and land were the two things most sought after by African Americans,
but land was much more difficult to secure. Much Sea Island property was
bought by wealthy white northern investors, some was purchased by African
Americans buying alone or in concert with others, and a large portion remained
in the hands of the government, to be used for "charitable purposes." Such

government land was usually designated a "school farm," which meant that the profits from working the land were used to finance schools and other "charitable" or "police" purposes. While land reform was piecemeal, schools proved to be the one unequivocal success of the Port Royal Experiment.[6]

"The Real Worke of Life"

A school farm on Coosaw Island, about ten miles from Beaufort, was R. G. Holmes's first field of service on the Sea Islands in 1864. As he described it, "I felt my former life had been a failuer, and that I had now been sent to a new field where I could mak myself usefull in Doing to help others to help themselves for this I considered the real work of life." R. G. paid $160 to the government in rent and was allowed to keep whatever profits he could make by raising crops on the land. He joined members of another northern family who were already teaching on the island.[7]

Like many other plantation superintendents, Holmes clashed with the approximately two hundred African Americans on Coosaw Island over the issue of cotton. African Americans wanted to raise food crops and saw cotton cultivation as a reimposition of the old slave system. Though they disagreed with Holmes, the sight of Rebel campfires on the mainland probably encouraged the former slaves to stick with him. Together they raised a "pretty good" cotton crop and an excellent food crop. Holmes had the advantage of having more experience with farming than most other superintendents had. He also made money by peddling goods such as mosquito netting.[8]

Overall, however, R. G. was more successful as a man of God than as a businessman. Like the Perfectionist Methodists who also came with his New York branch of missionaries, Holmes, with his Christ-centered discourse, found an appreciative audience among evangelical African Americans. Over eighty African American scholars came to his Sunday school, and he encouraged them to raise a crop of peanuts to get money for books. Education and religion were areas in which blacks and whites found agreement, though the class resistance of laborers against employers continued.[9]

While overseeing the planting, Holmes fell ill with typhoid fever. He was saved by a friend, who found him in time to ferry him over to the Beaufort hospital. Too weak to speak, Holmes overheard a doctor say that he was dead, but R. G. would not give up. Slowly he recovered enough to return to "the Lord's work." Because of his sickness, Holmes's cotton crop amounted to less than he had hoped it would. Luckily, the prized long-staple cotton that the African American laborers on Coosaw had raised was worth one thousand dollars in 1864 and saved Holmes from debt.[10]

When R. G. returned to Massachusetts, Abbie found her father a ghost of his former robust self—pale, thin, and with a long beard. Quinine and Rebecca's nursing finally restored him to good health. Undaunted, R. G. was ready to return to South Carolina, and Rebecca was determined that she "would not be left behind." She wanted to volunteer her services as a freedman's teacher, and her physician thought that the change of climate would be good for her health. The decision was made.[11]

Abbie was excited at the prospect of journeying to "the strange South." She watched out the train window as the Massachusetts countryside passed by in the moonlight, feeling happy that her family was reunited. In New York they were aided by Frank Holmes, R. G.'s prosperous younger brother. Finally the Holmeses boarded the steamship *Fulton* bound for South Carolina.[12]

A Child of the Experiment

On Sunday morning, 27 November 1864, the *Fulton* landed at Hilton Head Island and Abbie began her new life as a child of the Port Royal Experiment. At the busy army encampment on Hilton Head, the family received passports and Rebecca Holmes was commissioned as a schoolteacher. Luckily Rebecca's position entitled them to rations from the army commissary at Beaufort. "Otherwise," Abbie wrote, "we would have been hard put to it during this period of scarcity."[13]

Abbie's eyes were wide as she and her family made their final one-hour journey "in the golden afternoon" down the broad, smooth river that curved into the bay south of Beaufort. As was their custom whenever they saw a steamer from the North, missionaries and freed people gathered to welcome the ship at its wharf. Ever observant, Abbie noticed the material and cultural differences between her old northern and new southern homes. She wrote that her mother could not bake bread in the manner she was used to because their southern house had no stoves but rather a fireplace in the cabin kitchen for cooking. Missing this familiar staple and seeing it as an emblem of civilization, other northern women taught the mysteries of making wheat bread with yeast to the African American women of the islands.[14]

Abbie was surrounded by unfamiliar people—Yankee soldiers and Gullah-speaking African Americans. She noticed that the officers had their meals brought to them on trays from restaurants or "cook shops" run by African American women and men. Abbie watched in wonder as black waiters walked the streets carrying food trays on their heads as their ancestors had done in Africa. Through the daily necessity of food, the tastes and customs of North and South were exchanged.[15]

While Abbie absorbed her new surroundings, her parents busied themselves in the missionary and cotton fields in which they had come to labor. A week after reaching Beaufort, Rebecca Holmes was given a school housed in Tabernacle Baptist Church, near the center of town. Abbie remembered that the school "was crowded with the old and the young all eager to learn, all of course negroes." Meanwhile R. G. Holmes rented another school farm, bought town property, and set up a cotton gin with money he had borrowed from his brother. In the years following his arrival he added a gristmill and a lumberyard, creating a processing complex similar to the one he had owned and operated in Westborough, Massachusetts. As Abbie later wrote, her father "was always full of projects."[16]

Abbie's time in Beaufort was spent taking lessons from her mother, playing with her sister, and observing the natural and human world around her. Few other northern children were brought to Beaufort, and Abbie must have missed the cousins and playmates she had had in Massachusetts. Rebecca tutored her daughters at home and occasionally took them to school with her.

When they were not with their parents, Abbie and Georgie spent time with their African American neighbors and servants. It was from these Sea Islanders that Abbie heard her first tales of Br'er Rabbit and Br'er Fox. Abbie's girlhood formed the basis for her later writings about the fictional character Alice, who lounged in a hammock or busied herself ironing a dress while she begged the family's housekeeper for stories. Abbie and her sister also explored the countryside, riding horses, gathering moss and flowers, and adopting raccoons, squirrels, and birds as pets.[17]

Abbie's first Christmas in Beaufort highlighted the cultural contrast between northern and southern versions of the holiday. In New England, Abbie had spent this "holiest" season going to concerts, singing carols, and gathering around the Christmas tree with her extended family. In Beaufort, as the Holmes family celebrated a quiet Christmas Eve, they were startled by the noise of firecrackers, torpedoes, pistols, and "considerable disorder." Southerners of both races were making merry. It was not the last time that regional differences would shock the sober northerners.[18]

On Christmas Eve 1864 Abbie also witnessed the incredible spectacle of thousands of African American refugees arriving in the wake of Sherman's March through Georgia. In her recollections Christensen replaced the story of General Sherman sending President Lincoln a telegram offering Savannah as a Christmas present with her own story of Sherman writing to General Saxton on the Sea Islands and sending over seven hundred African American refugees from Savannah as a Christmas gift. Young Abbie was drawn in by the spectacle of "Bay street full of . . . forlorn and weary men in blue." The soldiers sang the abolitionist song "John Brown's Body," announcing the black refugees that followed them. Abbie worried about the fate of people, but she was reassured when the northern officers' wives, nurses, and teachers solicited clothing and money from the North and already-settled African Americans provided shelter and other relief in churches and homes. Abbie remembered her mother coming home from one of her relief meetings and retelling the stories of the refugees' hardships. In this way Rebecca and R. G. continued in a new field the charitable work that had been important to them in Massachusetts.[19]

The horrors of slavery and war became very real to R. G. Holmes early in 1865 when he went to check on the newly liberated mainland. At a plantation he learned that the Rebels had chained together all the able-bodied black men and women and marched them to Greenville in the South Carolina upcountry. The people R. G. found there were the very old, the very young, the crippled, and the sick. They had been left behind without food or tools, not even a hoe. Such was southern paternalism. Holmes saw that "something must be done to save life." He immediately turned back to Beaufort and returned the next day with provisions and tools. Like other missionaries, R. G. was concerned that even refugees with the least capability be put to work without delay so that they would not rely on charity. Such was northern paternalism.[20]

African Americans who had escaped from their masters arrived at R. G.'s farm nearly every day looking for work. Anthony Barnwell, one of the first laborers to work for Holmes, went on to become a successful landowner.

Barnwell, who paid R. G.'s grandson one thousand dollars for building him a house in 1906, remembered that the first fifty cents he made was earned hoeing next to Holmes, who drove a plough on his Coosaw lands. R. G. employed nearly all who came, buying two plantations at tax sales and expanding his planting operations to five hundred acres of cotton.[21]

R. G. encountered problems, but he always managed to find a way out of his dilemmas. When provisions ran low, he solicited and received money from the North to keep his farm going. In addition to setting up a cotton gin, Holmes built a gristmill so that he and others could grind their corn into hominy. After the war ended, he continued to give hominy to the destitute, white or black, who came to him for help.[22]

Making money and doing the Lord's work were intertwined. On his plantations Holmes devised a system to "showe them by example . . . the way to get a living & serve God." He wrote: "I have them work as much or more ground for themselves as they do for me & what I pay them will keep them & I furnish teams to plow their corn & potatoes so as to help them to rase more for themselves then they would without me. This is just what is wanted a good man with a good heart & whole soul to work on every plantation." Of course, R. G. saw himself as such a man. Rebecca and R. G. brought to Beaufort the values of education and industry that they thought would best serve the New South being created on the islands.[23]

As Holmes later wrote, "This was my business after the war for 30 years to furnish land and furnish supplyes to rase crops and takin cotton to pay the bills." Holmes was typical of a class of merchant-planters who would soon dominate the economics of the region. African Americans wanted most of all to purchase land, but if they were unable to achieve this goal, they fell to renting and buying supplies from men such as Holmes. Lacking cash, they performed transactions in cotton or in liens on cotton, as Holmes indicated. His brother Frank kept an account of items such as plates, cups, spoons, coffeepots, pans, and pails, which R. G. sold at a profit in Beaufort. These consumer goods were thought by northerners to be a healthy incentive to hard work for African Americans, and they also helped Holmes earn a living.[24]

R. G. also continued to be a popular preacher. "It would do you good to look into some of our meetings," he wrote to his brother, "& see the earnestness manifested. . . . They say they never had such good understanding [preached] to them before last Sabbath . . . it was two hours before I could close the Meeting. it was go on, wont you say a little more, etc." Holmes's simple message of doing good for others and waiting for Jesus' return found resonance with Sea Island African Americans.[25]

On 9 April 1865 General Lee's surrender at Appomattox brought joy to black and white members of the Port Royal Experiment. While Abbie stayed in Beaufort, her parents joined notables such as William Lloyd Garrison as they cheered the raising of the Union flag over Charleston's infamous Fort Sumter on 13 April. The assassination of Abraham Lincoln, however, threw everyone into confusion. Abbie waited anxiously for her parents and watched as "the negroes walked the streets, weeping and wringing their hands, fearing that freedom would be taken from them, now that Massa Lincoln was dead." The inauguration of Andrew Johnson as president bode ill for African Americans and carpetbaggers.[26]

Uncertainty fell over the Sea Islands as the freed people and missionaries wondered what the return of white southerners would mean. In fields and homes people debated what would happen to plantation lands. Because the Sea Islands had been captured so early in the war, the region was treated differently than other areas of the South. The first legislation regarding land had been the 1862 Tax Act passed to collect taxes from "insurrectionary districts." Beaufort land was assessed at its market value before the war, and when Rebel owners did not pay, it was sold to northern individuals and the few freed people who had already saved some money. The next land auction, held in February 1864, was fraught with controversy. Some missionaries had tried to get the government to allow freed people to "pre-empt" plots of land so that they could buy it at $1.25 an acre. The government, hungry for revenue, sold the land to the highest bidder instead, and many freed people felt betrayed.[27]

The freed people's hopes for economic independence through land were again raised and dashed in 1865. When Sherman arrived with his crowds of refugees, access to land became the key to the survival of thousands of African Americans. To this end the general issued Special Field Order 15, reserving the Sea Island coast from Charleston south to the Johns River for black settlement. Freed people and many missionaries hoped that the "possessory titles" to the land, which heads of African American families received, would be considered legally binding. Their hopes were in vain, for the interpretation of this order eventually fell to a conservative Supreme Court and a new president intent on restoring land to former Rebels. In the end Sea Island planters lost only the land sold outright at tax sales, though in the Beaufort area this was a sizable loss. Tax sales also continued after the war because many of the returning Rebels were too poor to pay the levies on their former lands. Freed people who had bought land at the first tax sales sometimes found themselves in the same predicament as the Rebels a few years later, when they had insufficient cash to pay the government what they owed.[28]

The economic system that began to take shape on the Sea Islands included a combination of contracts between black workers and white landowners, rental by blacks of white lands, and black landownership. The Freedman's Bureau, formed in March 1865, oversaw the implementation of contracts for labor and rental. Slowly, as African Americans were able to save money and whites lost interest as cotton prices dropped, the South's largest base of black landownership grew.[29]

In 1865 Abbie began to keep a diary in which she recorded the family's adjustment to peacetime Beaufort. Her life as a thirteen-year-old revolved around her home and family, but she continued to observe the world beyond it with interest. Sometimes she accompanied her father to the dock where he unloaded goods for his business. Most of her time, however, was spent in a world of women and children. After about a year Rebecca ceased her school teaching and devoted all her time to her household, the care of boarders, and the tutoring of her daughters. Abbie learned both academic subjects and domestic skills such as crocheting. Outside her house she tended a hen, a donkey, and other useful animals and pets. Mother and daughter read literature and history together and practiced arithmetic lessons such as multiplication of decimals. Rebecca Holmes also joined her daughter and friends on horseback rides through the wide countryside and aromatic pine forests.[30]

Besides her parents, Abbie grew to respect certain missionaries who stood above the others in strength of character and temperament. She admired Laura Towne and Ellen Murray, two teachers who founded the Penn School, a long-lasting and successful black institution on Saint Helena Island, five or six miles from Beaufort. Thomas Wentworth Higginson, captain of the first Negro regiment of South Carolina Volunteers, was also a hero in Abbie's and the freed people's eyes. Higginson, an abolitionist, transcendentalist, and supporter of John Brown, encouraged his troops to hold out for equal pay when they were paid less than white soldiers. Many years later Abbie would turn to Higginson for help in starting her own school for African Americans.[31]

In Abbie's world African Americans occupied a prominent place. On Sundays, Abbie became a teacher of a small class of Sunday school scholars, probably grammar-school-age African American girls. She listed their names as Fanny and Sarah Morris, Laura, Hagar, and Clarrisa. Many of Beaufort's churches were integrated, and Sunday school teaching was considered an important missionary activity. When Abbie's uncle Patterson P. Holmes visited the family in Beaufort, he reported his surprise at the ecclesiastical and secular mingling of whites and blacks. In a letter to his daughter Patterson wrote that he was particularly impressed by Abbie's ease and comfort as she sat down between "a colored lady" and "a colored gent" at the Methodist church where she attended Sunday services.[32]

In her own home Abbie listened with interest to the life story of Amelia Godfrey, an African American woman who came to sew for the Holmes family. Godfrey had been enslaved to one of the many white Elliots in Beaufort and had been forced to leave the coast when Yankee troops attacked. She had not been able to escape from her master until the summer of 1865, when she made her way from upcountry South Carolina to the Sea Islands. "She is now learning what it is to be free," Abbie wrote. In her home Abbie also displayed a gracious gift, a branch of an orange tree with twenty-two pieces of fruit, from "Mr. Bithewood," one of her African American neighbors.[33]

The Holmes family's relations with blacks and with newly returned southern whites in the years following the war seem to have been fairly cordial. The Yankees at Port Royal outnumbered white southerners, and their money and political power were forces to be reckoned with. Southerners found it in their own interest not to display hostility. "I am glad you have got along so well with the southern people," Abbie's Aunt Olive wrote to Rebecca Holmes in 1867. She continued, "I am not surprised that the Southern 'Ladies are not inclined to shew themselves among you' in their destitution." Although they may have demonstrated little outward animosity toward the Holmeses, the defeated and impoverished southerners kept to themselves. R. G.'s older sister praised him for his right dealings with African Americans: "I know he has done a great work, if not in making money to himself[,] in feeding the hungry and clothing the naked."[34]

Rebecca must have written to Olive about the corruption of carpetbaggers as well as the dissembling and lack of trust between African Americans and whites. "As far as honesty in business transactions is concerned which is the most guilty of its opposite[,] the white or the black?" queried Olive. "I suppose you would not suffer half as much loss from the blacks were it not for the influence of unprincipled whites."[35]

Unscrupulous whites did indeed serve to reinforce the lesson of slavery that honesty before white people was not a wise course. Even Elizabeth Botume, a characteristically optimistic and cheerful missionary, explained: "It was a long time before these refugees could get rid of their suspicions of white people. Perhaps they never did. Since the beginning of the war they had been time and again deceived by Northerners and Southerners."[36] Abbie would spend the rest of her life dealing with this legacy and with the complicated racial and regional divisions of the town of Beaufort.

Abbie Holmes's experiences as a child of the Port Royal Experiment made a deep impression on her. The abolitionist ethos she absorbed and the historic events she heard about and observed remained in her memory. While many other missionaries returned to the North after the war, Abbie and her family attached themselves firmly to the fate of the freed people on southern soil. At the end of 1865 thirteen-year-old Abbie understood that African Americans were at a critical juncture in American history and that the eyes of the rest of the nation were upon Port Royal. Just before she settled into bed on the rainy evening of 31 December 1865, Abbie Holmes wrote her wishes for the new year: "May Peace and Prosperity come to our country Wisdom to our rulers and our Congress and Justice and Prosperity to the Freedman." Abbie was aware of politics, but what was her part? Her resolution for herself was spiritual: "And above all may I strive to be a better Christian next year than I have been this." At thirteen she was still developing the skills and maturity that would enable her to play a significant role in the race relations of her new region. In the summer of 1866 she returned to Massachusetts to continue her education at Ipswich Female Seminary, where she gained knowledge that she would bring back as a teacher in the reconstructing South.[37]

Chapter Three

PIECES OF CALICO

I went to a box that was filled with pieces of calico and muslin and was laid away in a closet for a long time. . . . I began to stir them up and one of the first pieces that came to view was of that beautiful pink muslin dress you gave Elizabeth when she was at Holyoke. How in a moment it reminded me of all the tokens of love you have bestowed upon me and my children.[1]

These words, written by Abbie's Aunt Olive, her father's sister, speak of long-standing ties among the women of the family. When Abbie Holmes traveled back to Massachusetts in 1866, she reentered a loving and supportive world of women who sought to take care of her while she was away from her mother. Like pieces of colorful cloth that were lovingly given, used, and reused, the support of the older women of the Holmes and Winch families was passed on to their daughters when they left home to attend school. When it became Abbie's turn, Aunt Olive invited her niece to stay with her in Massachusetts during her school vacations, continuing the tradition that Rebecca had begun when taking care of Olive's daughter, Elizabeth. Perhaps because of Rebecca's illnesses, Olive took special care in extending a hand to thirteen-year-old Abbie. While she was a student, many of her New England relatives welcomed Abbie into their homes. When she took leave from her aunts and cousins, Abbie moved into the peer-oriented schoolgirl world of Ipswich. For the rest of her life Abbie Holmes Christensen partook of the "female world of love and ritual," though its presence was never again as intense as during her years of woman-centered education.[2]

Ipswich

The 1864 Ipswich Female Seminary catalog stated that the school's goal was to produce "healthy, companionable, self-reliant women, disposed and prepared to be acceptable and useful in the school, the family, and in general society." Ipswich's promoters were not afraid to say that they encouraged independence of thinking as well as Christian character. If Abbie Holmes were any indication, the seminary succeeded.[3]

Founded in 1824, Ipswich Female Seminary was built up through the far-sighted labors of Zilpah Grant and Mary Lyon, two of the leading women's educators in Massachusetts. The title *seminary* was chosen to connote a place that prepared women for the professions of teaching and motherhood, just as male seminaries prepared men to be ministers. Even though Lyon left to found Mount Holyoke Female Seminary in 1837 and Grant departed a year later, the reputation they established lived on. In 1845 Professor John P. Cowles of Oberlin College and his wife, Eunice Caldwell Cowles, resurrected the school and imbued it with abolitionist sentiment. Blind John Cowles taught the classics from memory, and Eunice Cowles, a former protégée of Mary Lyon, was famous for her morning lectures on such "practical" topics as "table manners, carefulness in dress and the courtesies of life in general." When Abbie Holmes entered, the aging Cowleses taught their young pupils a curriculum similar to that of young men in a college preparatory school.[4]

Writing the Self

Abbie Holmes's 1867 journal tells of her life as a fourteen-year-old schoolgirl, a passionate friend, a budding scholar, and a homesick little girl. Journal-writing helped young women such as Abbie gain a sense of self. The fact that all of the diaries of her younger years began with the admonition "To Be Burned Without Reading Upon My Death" strongly suggests that Abbie wanted to use her journal to express private thoughts as well as describe the events of daily life. After reading over a painful passage, she wrote: "How silly. Well I don't care. It's just as I feel." Although she was sometimes frustrated with her writing, she indicated her reason for keeping a journal: "Tonight . . . I don't feel very amiable and can't seem to agree with anybody and so, dear diary, have come to you because they say it takes two to make a quarrel and I know you will not be one."[5]

One thing Abbie never mentioned in her journal was her mother's mental or physical illness. Perhaps the diaries in which she mused on this were destroyed, or perhaps Abbie could not face this tragedy even in her private journal. Later in life Abbie recalled simply, "I left mother to go to Ipswich." It was the last time she saw Rebecca Holmes alive. In her Ipswich diary Abbie noted a regular correspondence with her mother, and only once did she record a "strange" letter from Rebecca, just before her father placed her mother in an asylum.[6]

Abbie also used her journal to reflect upon her progress as a Christian. She emulated the manner of devotional books and the teachers and preachers who taught her, but she tried to express what was in her heart. On her own she studied the Bible and read books such as *The New Gospel of Peace*. On May Day 1867 Abbie remembered the day she had joined the church in Newark. She prayed, "Oh God help me to serve thee better."[7]

Studies

Abbie had settled into seminary life by the middle of the school year, though she was still sometimes "homesick." In her diary Abbie described her daily routine, beginning with mornings: "I got up at half past six but was about five minutes late to breakfast notwithstanding. After breakfast I spent my time (as it was not my week to do the work) in combing my hair and dressing for school. Went up to writing class at quarter past eight." The "work" Abbie referred to was housework, at which each of the girls took a turn. Mary Lyon, the founder of Mount Holyoke, had introduced this system to lower costs by eliminating servants. It seems that Eunice Caldwell Cowles adopted the method as well. The students also received moral, or "practical," instruction: "At nine class was dismissed and we marched down to General, or opening exercises. Mrs C[owles] gave us a little bit of a lecture, Subject sarcasm. . . . At ten the first series is sent and I can study then and during the next one; but at quarter past eleven I recite in science of common things. The next series I recite in Latin to Miss Parsons. I think I enjoy this lesson more than any other." Although the school was highly concerned with imparting inner discipline and Christian character, Abbie seems to have focused just as much on its academic aspects.[8]

Abbie did not shy away from challenging academic subjects, and she appreciated a good teacher. Her favorite class was botany, which she studied with Miss Parsons. From April through July 1867 she collected and analyzed over 450 flowers. Abbie recounted that botany was "a large and very pleasant class." Together with other young women, she ventured out into the village of Ipswich and the surrounding countryside to "go after flowers till tea. After this sometimes we go again." Botany was considered a proper pastime for women, whereas zoology, with its emphasis on the animal and human body, was not taught. Abbie's introduction to botany inspired her to collect and classify flowers for the rest of her life. An interest in botany may also have influenced Christensen's later practice of homeopathic medicine.[9]

Abbie's strictly regimented routine continued through the rest of her waking hours. She wrote:

> generally dinner is ready (at one). . . . After dinner I have about half an hour to spend on my arithmetic and then hurry over to the seminary to recite at half past two. Then I have one series to study and then comes History. Then closing exercises and I rush home to rejoice that the day is done. There is always something to be done before tea. Some topics to be copied or a letter to be written or perhaps Ida [her roommate] will entice me to play a game of Authors and the Newspaper is always at hand crying Read. Read. After supper there is no more than time for prayers and to get ready for study hours which last from seven to nine. After nine, I pay a visit to you, beloved journal and then prepare to retire.[10]

Ipswich students' days were organized so that they might not socialize frivolously nor neglect to study their lessons. Sometimes, however, study hours did not provide Abbie with enough time to learn all that was expected. At least once she and a friend rose long before dawn and worked for hours on a mathematics assignment. When all of their answers were correct, Abbie felt "bright as a dollar all day." Although mathematics was not her favorite subject, she took pride in a job well-done.[11]

In the year at Ipswich covered by her diary, Abbie did not list any classes in English, although she wrote compositions on a weekly basis. Abbie also read the novels *Jane Eyre* and *Great Expectations* and the plays *As You Like It* and *Romeo and Juliet,* either on her own or with friends. The heroes and heroines of these works of literature provided Abbie with different models of self that she incorporated into her worldview. Abbie's favorite book during her year at Ipswich was *Jane Eyre,* which shaped the sensibilities of many literate Victorian women. Like Jane, Abbie was determined to earn a living and to remain virtuous, despite the temptations of falling in love.[12]

Although Abbie was fairly comfortable at Ipswich, she sometimes wrote that she was homesick. When her father paid her a surprise visit, Abbie burst into tears and longed to go home with him. Still, at another time she wrote that she was happier and, she hoped, "better" than she had been the year before in Beaufort. She prayed with the other students and drank in an emotional experience of God's presence on Communion Sundays.[13]

At the ages of fourteen and fifteen Abbie and her schoolmates wondered a good deal about their futures and enjoyed telling each other's fortunes. Abbie chose to remember the fortune predicting that she would not marry but that she would be "pretty happy" and "do a great deal of good in the world." Abbie wished it might come true but did not indicate why she did not plan to marry. Perhaps Abbie wished to maintain her independence, or perhaps she could not imagine herself falling in love with a man. Other students clearly expected to marry before long. Abbie and her schoolmates signed a pledge to invite each other to their weddings if they became engaged during the next five years.[14]

Loves

At Ipswich Female Seminary, Abbie was enmeshed in an intensely woman-centered community. The pupils lived with female roommates and were supervised by a woman teacher. All of Abbie's classes were taught by women, and there was little contact with the young men of the town. When the school performed tableaux, the students sometimes dressed as men in order to pose for such scenes as "The Jealous Lover." Abbie's circle of friends exchanged notes and confidences, kissed each other good night, and slept together. None of these activities was considered sexual or unnatural, since love between women was considered pure and ideas of sex in the nineteenth century had to include a member of the "opposite" sex. The sentimental atmosphere of the school was heightened by romantic locations in and around the town of Ipswich where the young women could stroll and gather flowers. On a pleasant day in April, Abbie walked with two of her best friends to "Heartbreak Hill" and came home through "Love Lane."[15]

Before long, Abbie developed a crush on Helen "Nellie" Woods, while another girl, Annie Packard, nurtured an infatuation with Abbie. In her diary Abbie's melancholy musings concerned her unrequited love. Abbie wrote that she was "desperately in love with Nellie" and that she would "gladly lay down my life for *her*," though she knew the attraction was "slightly one-sided." When Nellie ignored her, Abbie turned to Annie. "Annie (darling) came and comforted me in her sweet way. She knows what it is to have the heartache."

Both Nellie and Abbie played with the cruel and tender sides of love. After the passions of their teenage years subsided, Abbie and Nellie kept up a correspondence into middle age. Though Abbie later fell in love with a man, her experiences at Ipswich, and later Mount Holyoke, reinforced her attraction to women as intimate friends and intellectual companions.[16]

A Call to Home

In 1867 Rebecca Holmes's mental illness had taken a turn for the worse. Abbie did not write of her mother's mental illness, but through Reuben's reminiscences we know that after a few years of improved health in the South, "soon her old troubles came on her in a much more violent mannar & she soon became perfectly insane & Dangerous & unmanageable so we could not take care of her & I was obliged to take her to [Bellevue] asylum" in New York. Abbie's father called her home because he needed her in Beaufort to take her mother's place. Though her mother's mental illness must have troubled Abbie considerably, her feelings of fear and confusion at her mother's behavior can only be presumed.[17]

As she left Ipswich, Abbie took with her the "book learning" she needed to become a more important part of the Port Royal Experiment as Reconstruction continued in South Carolina. Barely older than some of her students, Abbie would become a teacher in 1870. Her preparation in subjects such as mathematics, English, geography, and history would be translated into instruction for black pupils at the intermediate level. In the meantime, Abbie would have to grow in maturity as she returned home to Beaufort to help her father and sister.[18]

Chapter Four

SCHOOLMARM

I'm a schoolmarm, . . . I teach these little colored children[.] [1]

From 1867 to 1872 Abbie Holmes, a young woman with dark hair pinned up in a bun, could be seen bustling about her father's house and trying to take her mother's place or, later, walking to a wooden schoolhouse by the river to teach. During this time young Abbie struggled with uncertainty and grief as she coped with the loss of her mother and tried to decide the course her life would take—marriage or further education. In Beaufort, Abbie encountered the politics of Reconstruction as the daughter of a Republican legislator and as a teacher in a school system run by black and white supervisors. From 1870 to 1872 she proudly claimed her identity as a "schoolmarm" to "colored children." Abbie at twenty years old emerged from her years of sorrow a woman and was even starting to show a few gray hairs. [2]

When she returned to Beaufort in 1867, Abbie tried to put her schoolgirl days behind her and busied herself with "home duties." Although she did not mention the fact that her mother was away at Bellevue Hospital, she admitted that she felt disappointment and a "dull heartache" after coming home. "How natural and how unnatural everything seems," she wrote. In addition to caring for Georgie and her father, Abbie also shouldered the responsibility of keeping house for long- and short-term boarders, a total of ten people. Assisting her in this task were three African American servants. When a friend of the family later described the atmosphere of the boarding-house as "pleasant" and "home-like," she was proud, saying, "If I can only make the house seem like a home I shall be satisfied." [3]

In her journal fifteen-year-old Abbie poured out wit, passion, and venom as she described the members of her household in 1867:

The family consists of myself (I mention the most important first) father, Georgia, the Doctor (whom I love already, and admire nearly as much as father) Mr. Adams (whom I like) Mr. Wallace (ditto) Mrs. Holmes (whom I don't like. I have always had quite an antipathy to snakes and hers is one of the snakiest faces I ever saw) Annie Holmes (I do like for some things and dislike for others) and lastly Miss C. A. Hamblin. Oh how I hate her. How I despise her. Perhaps I am wrong but I can't help it. I haven't one particle of respect for her and don't know of any one else that has.

While the rest of the boarders eventually faded from her life, Silas Wallace and Carrie Hamblin did not. Wallace became the object of Abbie's love and devotion, and Hamblin, who had designs on Wallace, received her intense disdain.[4]

After she had listed all of the white members of her household, Abbie remembered the African Americans who also shared her home:

> I said lastly Miss H but I should have mentioned Maggie. Good faithful Maggie with always a smile in her sunny brown eyes. She is a perfect treasure. And Robert the cook. Robert the indefatigable (it is cool enough to use a long word occasionally) he should be called I think from his attentions at the table. Never was there such a waiter as Robert. Not a dish on the table that he does not pass you twice at least nor is he ever satisfied unless every one has two cups of tea or coffee. You have only to wish for a thing and Robert will interpret your glance at pickles or hominy and it is immediately at your left hand.

Maggie and Robert provided Abbie with a great deal of help in cooking and cleaning. Abbie was most intimate with Maggie, who combed her hair every morning and helped her plan her day. Rounding out the Holmeses' domicile was a young African American boy named Paul, who helped with the chores—"the most worshipfull St Paul as the Doctor calls him," Abbie wrote. Abbie added that he was "full of mischief as ever boy was before," but she concluded, "He is however always at hand when he is called for and I rather like his mischief and he is truly honest." Though she worked closely with them, these African Americans were separated from Abbie by the gulf of class as well as race.[5]

At the age of fifteen Abbie was learning how to perform the nineteenth-century middle-class role of mistress of servants. As a young child she had observed her mother's interaction with the Irish servants in the family's Westborough home, and later in Beaufort her mother had managed southern African American servants. Letters between her parents and female relatives in the North indicate a constant concern with finding and managing "good girls" or Irish servant women. Still, like most women employers, Abbie operated more by intuition and experience than by any outward guideline. Because she was thrown into the role of household manager at such an early age, Abbie was probably younger and less experienced than Maggie and Robert. They likely had begun their lives as slaves and had been taught to follow the orders of young whites. Despite the differences in class and race between them, common struggles bound Abbie, Maggie, and Robert together.[6]

Abbie and her servants shared the sorrow of bereavement. Although it was not common for mistresses to speak of their servants' personal lives, Abbie took note of Robert's family life because his wife died soon after Abbie returned to Beaufort. She wrote, "Poor Robert. . . . Tomorrow there will be the fourth funeral in his family in a month." Robert's loss affected Abbie as well, because she and Maggie were left to take over his accustomed duties. "We got tea alone with Paul's help," she wrote, but she added that she was ashamed when her shortcake was a failure. When Maggie left for the funeral as well, Abbie's worries over dinner left her so "tired and discouraged" that she wrote lines in her diary that she or someone else later cut out. Unlike some older women who employed servants, Abbie did not try to pretend that she knew more than she did. Although she eventually developed some friendships with northern white women, Abbie was relatively isolated in her father's house. Maggie and Robert, the black "outsiders within" the white household, provided stability to counter Abbie's inexperience. This first, vivid experience of reliance on Maggie and Robert as teachers as well as servants may have helped Abbie cultivate a greater degree of respect for African Americans.[7]

White southerners, on the other hand, were seldom part of Abbie's social circle. Although they worshiped with Abbie at church and passed her on the streets, she usually regarded them as enemies. "To know what a virtue [honesty] is one should live in this *gallant* Palmetto State for a short period," she wrote with bitterness. Sectional feelings still ran extremely high in 1867, and relations between white northerners and southerners were cool at best. When the baby of one of Abbie's northern neighbors died, she experienced the hostility still evident in Beaufort. As Abbie wrote: "Dr. Walker [the Episcopal rector] refused to come and make a prayer. That is a fair sample of the

whole method. They will condescend to allow the Yankees to fill up subscription lists for them but when any small service such as any Christian
owes to another they cooly turn their backs on their benefactors. I could not
help saying when the sweet little thing was carried to the grave without a
prayer even, 'Oh I do hope I shall never die in South Carolina.'" By the time
she died in South Carolina in 1938, Abbie no longer felt this way, but in
1867 even Christianity could not unite Beaufort's Yankees and Rebels.[8]

Within her circle of white northerners and southern blacks, Abbie tried
to balance enormous responsibility and a desire for play. In addition to supervising the household, she wrote letters and taught her seven-year-old sister
her lessons. Pursuing some of the interests of a middle-class teenage girl,
Abbie also played croquet and board games with friends, went sailing in the
bay and riding in the countryside, and attended Sunday school, morning
worship, and weekday prayer meetings.[9]

It was mainly through her father that Abbie maintained contact with the
political world. Although she did not accompany him, she often wrote in her
diary that her father had gone to a Republican meeting. Politics assumed
greater importance for Holmes as success through planting eluded him. On
6 November 1867 Abbie wrote in her diary, "The darkies have been coming
in town today by the score: For the purpose of electing delegates to the convention which is to form a new constitution for S.C. There was a meeting
this evening at the Methodist church for the election. Of the seven candidates three were white men. Father was one." Abbie's use of the term "darkies" indicates the paternalistic attitude she had absorbed from her parents.
Still, Abbie felt that it was an honor that African Americans had elected
Holmes to represent Beaufort at the 1868 constitutional convention. Soon
after the election, Reuben left for a fact-finding mission in the North. He
secured copies of the New York and Massachusetts state constitutions and
looked into the matter of bounties for southern black Civil War soldiers who
had not yet received them. Reuben's interests were clearly with the freedmen
and the Republican Party.[10]

Loss

For sixteen-year-old Abbie, however, her father's absence only meant loneli-
ness and fear. She was left alone to run her father's boardinghouse and had

to rely even more heavily on Maggie and Robert for emotional and domestic support. Abbie's seven-year-old sister, Georgie, was also left in her charge. Abbie had not seen her mother in over a year, and she could not help feeling a sense of dread that something would happen to her father as well. When she received a letter from her father with good news about her mother, Abbie's heart felt "light as a feather." She wrote, "Now we can hope that in three months she will be quite well again." Reuben visited his wife while he was in the North and later regretted not bringing his wife home. He wrote: "When I went up at one time to see [her] she pled with me so [earnestly] to take her back home with me I was persuaded to do it but the [physician] would not allow it he said it would be impossable for me to do any thing with her & utterly refused my takeing her though [she] seemed to be perfectly rational & I told her I would be obliged to let her board there a little longer though in my judgment she was so far recovered that it would be safe to take her home she wanted so much to go. she did not live but a little while after that."

Abbie received the awful news that her mother had died at Bellevue Asylum in New York City on 27 February 1868. Judging from Reuben's description of his last visit with his wife, it is possible that in her despair at her confinement and separation from her family, Rebecca Holmes lost the will to live. In a weakened state, she probably succumbed to tuberculosis, which she had contracted before moving to Beaufort.[11]

The pages of Abbie's diary that encompass the month before and the two years after her mother's death are all carefully cut out, as are other sections that may have contained embarrassing or depressing material. Her "selection book," wherein Abbie and others copied poems, Bible verses, and other quotations, is the only written document that remains from this time. Her choices in February and March 1868 reveal a struggle to accept her mother's death. The following words are an example: "God is almighty— all benevolent; . . . What would he have this evil do for me? What is its mission? What its ministry? What golden fruit lies hidden in its husk? How shall it nurse my virtue, nerve my will, Chasten my passions, purify my love, and make me in some goodly sense like Him Who bore the cross of evil while he lived, Who hung and bled upon it when He died, And now, in glory, wears the victors crown?" Abbie's selection book also included a religious poem called "Led through Sorrow," which was followed by the initials "C. A. H." For a brief moment Abbie and Carrie Hamblin may have patched their differences, though the two young women continued to be rivals for Silas Wallace's attention. More than anyone else, Silas was a comfort to Abbie in this time of grief.[12]

But no one could take her mother's place. On the thirtieth anniversary of Rebecca Holmes's death, Abbie wrote: "She was one of the dearest and sweetest mothers, and no one has ever loved me as she did. The world lost its brightness when she left me, and never has seemed the same since, altho' I have seen many happy years with my family." With the news of her mother's death, Abbie's youth ended.[13]

In their grief Abbie and Georgie had neither the comfort of their father nor the support of other family members. Though he wanted to leave the constitutional convention and attend Rebecca's funeral, Reuben was told he could not be spared and was barred by martial law from leaving the city of Charleston. The girls could not travel alone. Abbie was not to see her mother's grave until 1872, when she went north to attend Mount Holyoke. Until then she managed her sadness as best she could.[14]

The Constitutional Convention

In the meantime, Reuben Holmes attended to his duties as a delegate to the constitutional convention with an awesome sense of responsibility and inadequacy. Holmes was concerned about the dismissive attitude of prominent white southerners toward the convention, and he tried to persuade "some of the leading men" in Charleston to take it seriously, but to no avail.

The former secessionists of South Carolina felt that there was no need for a constitutional convention, and in some white majority counties they made a mockery of the elections. In his reminiscences Holmes cited two cases: one of an upcountry county that purposely elected the most destitute, uneducated blacks in the area and sent them to Charleston barefoot and in rags; and another county that sent an enormous wooden ballot box with a padlock marked "town shithouse." Of the 136 delegates he counted, Holmes believed that less than 10 percent could read and write; he even doubted his own ability, knowing he had little education. Despite his perception, Holmes was wrong both in his numbers and in his evaluation of the delegates. Historians have documented that over 82 percent of the black delegates were literate and ten had acquired a postsecondary education. Many of the 74 black delegates were elected because of their leadership positions in the African American community. Teachers, ministers, artisans, and merchants were more numerous than agriculturalists. The fact that Holmes wrote his reminiscences circa 1905 after the publication of several popular books and articles that ridiculed the supposed ignorance of black politicians may account for his dim view of the proceedings. Holmes's education was probably no worse and certainly no better than the majority of the delegates he joined for the proceedings.[15]

At the convention Reuben Holmes suggested forming a land commission to assess all South Carolina lands and determine the tax they should pay. He proposed that the state government should buy the land of those who could not pay the tax and sell it to settlers at $1.25 an acre. He thought that in this way the large plantations of the old aristocracy would be broken up because their taxes would be too high to pay. South Carolina would become an area of opportunity like the West. Other black and white Republicans shared his views, and Reuben was elected to serve as a land commissioner. His plan, however, was changed to raise the price of land to $5.00 an acre. He refused to accept this change and was removed from the commission. Holmes wrote that after he left, state officials took advantage of the new law and sold worthless land to the government at $5.00 an acre, making themselves rich and causing "the ruin of the state." The land commission was, in fact, crippled by the corruption of its chief officer, R. C. De Large, though he was removed within a few years, and state lands were efficiently sold off to over two thousand landless African Americans by Secretary of State Francis Cardozo and his successor.[16]

Reuben also wanted to pass an educational qualification for voting that would go into effect in five years and apply to the freedmen. While there was prejudice in this distrust of the freedmen, Holmes's view also showed his New England devotion to education and literacy.[17]

After the convention Reuben continued to be active in politics, assisting with the balloting for the presidential election of 1868 between Ulysses Grant and Horatio Seymour. Holmes ran for the state legislature under the reform wing of the Republican Party, but he lost the race. The primarily white missionary reformers were unpopular with black Beaufortonians. They stuck with the Gullah-speaking war hero Robert Smalls, who endorsed the regular Republicans. Although the reformer's platform was concerned with real cases of corruption among the regulars at the state level, vices flourished in both wings of the party. In Beaufort, which was relatively free of corruption, the real issues were race, region, and power. White missionaries had assumed that they would lead the local Republican Party. New black voters, who had observed the white missionaries for approximately six years, were more convinced that one of their own, Robert Smalls, should be their leader, even when the opposing reform Republican was black. In 1872 William Whipper, an African American lawyer from the North, challenged Robert Smalls for his state senate seat. He was soundly defeated. For the next decades Robert Smalls and the regular Republicans had significant power in Beaufort politics.[18]

Holmes gave up on politics, bought a piece of the Port Royal and Augusta Railroad, and purchased several thousand acres of timberland north of Beaufort. In 1869, a year and a half after Rebecca Holmes's death, Reuben married Charlotte Keith, a missionary teacher from Massachusetts. Although her father's fortunes were on the rise, Abbie did not approve of her stepmother, and the remarriage made her feel uncomfortable in her father's house.[19]

Household

By 1870, when the United States census was taken, the Holmes family was among the more prosperous in Beaufort. The Holmeses benefitted from the success of the largely African American community of new farmers, who bought small plots of land, mules, and cows and traded with the Holmeses. In the census forty-nine-year-old Reuben was listed as owning real estate worth seven thousand dollars and a personal estate of three hundred dollars. Charlotte, who was thirty-six, kept house while eighteen-year-old Abbie and nine-year-old Georgie studied at home.

The census stated that the Holmes family shared their household with two other men, Silas M. Wallace (S. M. W.), a white, twenty-seven-year-old miller, and John Phenix, a black, twenty-one-year-old domestic servant. The invisibility of Phenix, except in the census records, speaks volumes about his status within the household. The continual and marked presence of "S. M. W." in Abbie's writings is evidence that it was impossible for her to forget him.[20]

For Abbie, the only flaw in this domestic arrangement was the presence of her new stepmother. Abbie's main concern was that her stepmother would try "to come between" Georgie and her. "Georgie seems a great deal more like my own girl than like my sister," Abbie explained.[21]

No longer needed as the female head of the household, Abbie thought more about her own future. Following in her mother's footsteps, Abbie intended to teach school, save her money, and travel north for further education. On her nineteenth birthday she revealed the tension between her desire for marriage and her wish to be independent: "I must go to school two years more at least and to do that I must teach at least two years more. However I've more time to spare than if I had a diamond ring on my engagement finger with a prospect for a plain gold one by & by." Abbie counted herself among only four single young northern women left in the town. "Alas poor B[eaufort] that you have come to this!" she wrote in mock dismay. Though her thoughts often turned to the possibility of marriage to Wallace, Abbie concentrated hard on her teaching during the months that school was in session.[22]

Schoolmarm

After furnishing "satisfactory evidence of good Moral Character" and passing several academic examinations, Abbie received a teaching position at the "Highest Intermediate" level. Freed people's schools were generally organized into primary, intermediate, and grammar levels. Although public schools were open to both black and white children, all of the students in Abbie's class were African American. During the eight-month 1870–71 school term, Abbie taught a class with an average of thirty students. The class was divided equally between male and female pupils, with a range in age from six to sixteen. Most were engaged in the study of spelling, reading, and writing, and nearly all also studied mental arithmetic and geography.[23]

Teaching school was Abbie's first sustained interaction with African Americans as equals and as superiors. Men and women teachers of both races taught at Abbie's school. Abbie showed respect for the highly educated Mr. Garrett, a black teacher who was the son of a northern Methodist minister, and for young African American Olivia Watson, whom Abbie considered a pleasant colleague. Race seemed not to be a factor in her relations with the man who hired her, Vermont-born Landon S. Langley. Abbie never mentioned the fact that Langley, who had fought for the Union and had labored alongside her father at the constitutional convention, was black.[24]

The power of African Americans was also evident in the fact that they had control over the school building. This medium-sized wooden schoolhouse overlooking the river at Beaufort was fully funded by the state and owned by either "Freedmen" or the Beaufort County School Board, whose members were of both races. Abbie listed both of these parties as the proprietors in her reports, indicating that she was uncertain of the school's ownership. It was not uncommon for individual freed people to donate the use of buildings for educational purposes. For example, Hastings Gantt, a former Saint Helena Island field hand, became such a successful planter that he gave a grant of land to the Saint Helena Penn School, making an important contribution to the advancement of his race.[25]

At eighteen, Abbie was not much older than some of her students, and her first days of teaching were extremely difficult. Without any training in the art of pedagogy, she had to learn solely by experience. A few months into her work she looked back on her painful start: "I think my turning my bad boy out had a very good effect. By the way he has sent word he wants to come back. Well . . . Emily Brown has her geography lesson ready at last so I will depart."[26]

Abbie was candid about the hardships of being a first-time teacher, but she was not alone in her difficulties. Laura Towne, who was many years older than Abbie, and Charlotte Forten, an African American teacher from Philadelphia, also found teaching on the Sea Islands "wearying" and their students "troublesome" upon occasion. Towne, however, grew to love teaching so much that she never gave it up. Abbie had less of a sense of mission than the teachers who taught during the heady days of the Civil War. Nevertheless, she did her best and took pride in her work. The fact that Abbie became "spunky and determined" outweighed her initial frustration.[27]

As Abbie became acquainted with her students as individuals, she came to understand their lives and appreciate their kindnesses. Noah Washington, one of the boys in her class, brought her a note explaining that he would sometimes be late to school because every morning he worked as a milkman for a woman with a small dairy business in Beaufort. Many children, like young Noah, had to assist their parents through paid and unpaid labor. It was just one of the difficulties Abbie's students faced in coming to class on time and maintaining a steady attendance. One of Abbie's happiest moments came when Catherine Frazier, one of her brightest students, brought the young teacher a bunch of flowers. Abbie pressed a few of the blossoms into her diary so that she would always remember this gesture. On the days when her class was smaller, Abbie usually reported improvement in her relations with her students, since she could pay more attention to each individual's work.[28]

By the end of the term Abbie had improved so much as a classroom manager that Superintendent Langley praised her in a lecture to a group of teachers. Much to Abbie's astonishment, Langley said that she had "better order" in her school than anyone else he had visited. Abbie considered this praise "a feather in my cap." Although Laura Towne and other missionary teachers consciously ruled out any physical punishments for former slaves who had been subject to cruel whippings, the freedmen's schools allowed corporal punishment in extreme cases. Abbie established order by keeping her students busy at their work and keeping them after school if they fell behind. Less conscious of the legacy of slavery than older colleagues such as Towne were, she resorted to the threat of a whipping in one case. Expulsion was her punishment of last resort. "Putting out her bad boy," freed her to concentrate on the less troublesome but equally needy scholars. Towne and other missionary teachers also handed down expulsions to keep order. As Langley and most pedagogical experts of the day proclaimed, teaching order and self-discipline was a teacher's highest priority. Once her authority was established, Abbie enjoyed seeing her students learn and found her work interesting.[29]

Like many other teachers, Abbie organized an exhibition ceremony for her students on the final day of the school year to showcase her students' accomplishments. In the spring of 1871 the audience included Mrs. French and Mr. and Mrs. Garrison, who presented the best scholars with prizes. Several children were awarded "handsomely bound" and illustrated books. Abbie said good-bye to her pupils and packed up her maps, her bell, and other supplies, closing a difficult but relatively successful school year.[30]

Bureaucratic difficulties with the authorities who ran the Beaufort school system only spurred Abbie to work harder to stand up for herself. When the Beaufort County School Board paid her thirty-five dollars instead of the forty dollars a month she had been promised, Abbie protested by writing letters and visiting the superintendent. Defending her case, Abbie cited her perfect attendance record and the good order in her school. By the next year her salary was raised.[31]

Besides fighting for a higher salary, Abbie also convinced school administrators to move a teacher she disliked. When she went to check on the appointments to the various schools in 1871, Abbie was shocked to learn that "a person calling herself Mrs. C. A. Wallace" (Carrie Hamblin, the former boarder and her rival for Silas Wallace's attention) would be teaching at the same school as Abbie. Carrie had begun calling herself Mrs. Wallace since the birth of a son, whom she named Silas Wallace for the man she claimed was his father. Silas Wallace Sr. did not marry Hamblin and denied his paternity. Abbie protested that Carrie was not morally fit to be a teacher and that she intended to harass Abbie with "nameless petty annoyances." Abbie's complaints succeeded in forcing Hamblin's transfer to a plantation school so far removed that Abbie no longer mentioned seeing her. Whether motivated by righteous indignation or jealousy, Abbie was showing signs of a forceful adult personality that "got things done."[32]

As Abbie surveyed her new class in 1871, she missed her brightest boys— Daniel Bythewood, Robert Talbird, Edward Bush, and Julius Washington— who had been promoted. "I am sorry for I love them all," Abbie wrote. Her favorite, however, was Daniel. Abbie admired his beautiful eyes and hoped that good influences would come into his life because she believed he could be a powerful leader. She would try to influence him by keeping up a correspondence after she went north. Within the next two years Bythewood married and became apprenticed to Franklin Talbird. He continued in his studies at night and eventually became a leading minister in Beaufort County. Julius Washington became a lawyer and another prominent leader. By teaching and mentoring these students, Abbie played a small role in helping these distinguished African Americans succeed.[33]

Abbie's second year as a teacher (1871–72) was easier than her first. Abbie no longer wrote of troubles in school. On the contrary, she "rather enjoyed it." On Abbie's last day she was sorry to say good-bye to "my children," who gave her bunches of roses as a parting gift. Although this was Abbie's last year as a teacher, the insights she gained would serve her well when she became a school founder later in life.[34]

In 1871, however, nineteen-year-old Abbie was still interested in being a pupil herself. To prepare for further schooling, she and another northern schoolteacher, Miss Noyes, read Italian together. Noyes was assisting Elizabeth Hyde Botume, a Massachusetts "schoolmarm" whom Abbie greatly admired. Botume moved to the Sea Islands at roughly the same time as the Holmeses did. She spoke out as an ardent and articulate advocate of African American and women's rights. Noyes and Botume exchanged social calls with Abbie and encouraged her to read Shakespeare with them. After the loss of her mother, Abbie looked to women like Botume for a vision of the woman she might become.[35]

Teachers Laura Towne and Ellen Murray also continued to be an inspiration. When Abbie and a friend visited Towne's Penn School in 1872, Abbie was impressed by its "really fine readers" and near perfect order. Towne and Murray invited the young women for lunch and treated them to songs from the children after school was out. Abbie heard her favorite spirituals, "Roll, Jordan, Roll" and "Wrestling Jacob." The visitors also observed a ring shout, an Afro-Christian worship celebration of singing and clapping in which the participants moved in a dancelike circular formation. Abbie declared this shout the best she had ever seen. She would later write about shouts and spirituals for the American Folk-lore Society.[36]

Abbie Holmes's career as a teacher of black children lasted two years. She differed from most northern teachers of freed people in that she was young and in that she did not experience a special calling for this work. In these ways Abbie was similar to many young northern women who taught for a few years before getting married. Lucy Stone, the Massachusetts abolitionist and women's rights advocate whom Abbie would meet later in life, followed a similar path. Beginning in her teens, Stone taught school in order to earn money to attend Oberlin College. Her true calling, however, was to be an abolitionist lecturer. Abbie had not found her mission yet, but she never indicated that it was teaching. Older abolitionist teachers such as Botume, Towne, and Murray made teaching black children their life vocation. They had a combination of idealism and a sense of purpose that Abbie Holmes in 1872 had yet to find. Nevertheless, during the time that she taught, Abbie pushed herself to be the best teacher she could be, and her supervisor and many of her pupils were more than satisfied with her work. Perhaps the most important thing Abbie drew from her teaching was working with African

Americans as peers and as superiors and forming bonds with African American pupils, some of whom would later become local leaders.[37]

Sundays, Holidays, Weddings, and Funerals

Relationships with African Americans were also evident in Abbie's social life, though her closest friends were white. In between the lines of her diary the racial and regional outlines of Beaufort's social life become clear. During the early idealistic years of Reconstruction, blacks and whites mingled in public places and neighborhoods were integrated. Federal civil rights laws and Reconstruction acts prevented discrimination, and they were respected for the most part in this Republican bastion. The 1868 South Carolina constitutional convention had also passed antidiscrimination laws opening all public facilities to blacks and whites. In 1870s Beaufort most policemen and constables were black, while the majority of higher local officeholders were white. Beaufort's representatives in the state and federal legislature were of both races.[38]

While members of each group socialized mainly with their own during excursions, sailing parties, picnics, "sociables," and baseball games, Beaufort was still one of the more open places in the nation. Beaufort's centers of belief—the Baptist, Methodist, and Episcopal churches—which Abbie attended, had mixed congregations before and after the war.[39]

The faculty at the school where Abbie taught was also integrated. Abbie was friendlier with her African American colleagues than she was with southern white teachers. In her diary Abbie noted that she was sorry she had missed the wedding of her black colleague Olivia Watson and Tom Hamilton. Abbie slept the next night with a piece of Olivia's wedding cake under her pillow, hoping to dream of her own husband.[40]

When Abbie mentioned race in her journal, it was often parenthetical, as if such things were understood in the town but perhaps needed to be clarified to her diary. For example, when Abbie wrote that Miss Mayo's wedding, in 1871, was the first "white" wedding she had attended since coming to Beaufort, she inserted the word "white" after she had already written the sentence. The other nuptials Abbie had attended had been those of African American couples. In contrast, Abbie wrote explicitly that "almost all the northern people" were at the Mayo wedding. Regional affiliation was never forgotten in Beaufort in the years following the Civil War, and its division was sometimes sharper than race.[41]

During a trip to Charleston, Abbie and her father ran across the isolated home of a northerner far from the closely knit Yankee enclave of Beaufort. Later Abbie learned that this man had been "burnt out by the Ku Klux." Congress found the problem of Klan violence pressing enough to pass a Ku Klux Klan Act in April 1871 to bring individuals before the federal courts if they violated any citizen's civil rights. The Klan's terrorism was a disturbing reminder of the fact that northern families such as the Holmeses were not welcome in most of the South.[42]

A holiday that clearly divided African Americans and white northerners from southerners was Memorial, or Decoration, Day, which honored the Union dead of the Civil War. Women and men worked together to make the annual ceremony at the new National Cemetery worthy of their fallen comrades. Every year Abbie joined other white women who worked all evening to cut and arrange evergreen and floral wreaths for the Union monument and soldiers' graves. Abbie and her family listened to "the usual amount of speeches" and the usual poem, which Henry G. Judd, a lawyer from Connecticut and Beaufort County Clerk of Court, had read since the close of the war. At the 1871 Memorial Day celebration a northern family presented a flag to the black regiment of militia commanded by Robert Smalls. On this day northerners and African American Sea Islanders were united.[43]

The other important African American holiday celebrated on the Sea Islands was Emancipation Day. This was held on 1 January, a day of excursions, speeches, parades, and bands, when the African Americans who lived on the outlying islands, and even in Savannah, would gather in Beaufort to remember their first freedom. Although Abbie did not directly participate in the festivities of this day, she watched the parade of black militia pass by her house, where she sat with friends on the upper piazza, listened to the "speechifying," and "had the full benefit of it all." On nearby Saint Helena Island, African Americans and their white teachers at the Penn School also organized a full day of celebrations.[44]

In addition to happy occasions, death and sickness also brought Abbie and her neighbors together. In August and September yellow fever haunted Beaufort's homes. Abbie complained of mosquitoes during this time, but she and others were still unaware of their connection to disease. Children were especially vulnerable, and Abbie helped nurse her neighbor's daughter, Alice. When the child succumbed, Abbie made her a dress and laid her out in her coffin. Before the days of funeral parlors, this type of service was often performed by women friends of the family. Abbie also tried to comfort another neighbor when he lost his wife to fever. "He did not know how tight he held my hand," Abbie wrote with empathy, having faced her own great loss only a few years before. "I was glad to be able to afford him some little support so. It may be I shall want a human hand to hold sometime." Fever would eventually claim one of Abbie's own children, and she grew to fear the hot months in the Sea Island region.[45]

When yellow fever claimed another northerner, Mr. Newcomb, his death revealed the differences among Beaufort's Yankees. Newcomb had been superintendent of schools for a New York missionary society and pastor of the Methodist Episcopal church until his appointment as a Customs House officer. It is likely that Newcomb, a white northerner, was a regular Republican and therefore a political enemy of Abbie's father and other reform Republicans. Abbie wrote that Newcomb was "generally unpopular" with the white people but that "most of the colored people liked him." To Abbie, Newcomb was "a vulgar, disagreeable man." It is likely that, in this case, Abbie simply followed the loyalties of her father, but it was not the last time she would believe that she and her family knew what was best for African Americans.[46]

When the weather was cool enough, Abbie liked to go off on her own and ride a horse into the countryside, following paths through pine and live-oak woods. Reuben Holmes had unlimited confidence in Abbie's ability "to stick to a horse," and once he even allowed her to ride a mare that had thrown him the day before. Until old age Abbie showed a skill with a horse and buggy that gave her the freedom to go places and observe things she might not otherwise have seen. On one long ride in 1871 she discovered an old Civil War battleground as well as cotton fields, "negro houses," and a group of about a hundred railroad workers toiling in the hot sun. It was a reminder of the war that had brought her to Beaufort and the importance that African American labor still carried after slavery.[47]

In the landscape and social scene that Abbie observed in Beaufort County, whites were deeply divided by region and, sometimes, split by political factionalism within their regional groups. African Americans interacted with whites in a variety of ways. As workers and farmers, they formed the back-bone of the Sea Island region's economy. As teachers, politicians, and church members, middle-class African Americans sometimes stood with whites on an equal footing as leaders. Abbie Holmes noted this situation but did not analyze it. As a young woman moving into marriageable age, her thoughts more frequently centered on romantic love and the agonies and ecstasies it promised.

S. M. W.

Although Abbie continued to have close friendships with other young northern women, her love interest had shifted to the northern man who boarded with her family, Silas M. Wallace. Mr. Wallace, S. M. W., Silas, or "Sidie" absorbed Abbie's thoughts, and she filled her diary with expressions of anxious longing for him from ages sixteen to twenty-two. A young white man of slender build and with dark, curly hair, Wallace hailed from Ohio, where he had left a sweetheart behind. Wallace worked at Reuben Holmes's mill and boarded with the family from 1867 to 1871. Abbie's attraction to Wallace was evident when she confronted him over the attention he gave Carrie Hamblin. Although Carrie had left the Holmes boardinghouse in 1867 for a teaching assignment on Saint Helena Island, on her visits to Beaufort, Hamblin put her things in Wallace's room and waited for him to escort her home. In the parlor Abbie teased Wallace about his devotion to Hamblin. He turned, faced her, and said abruptly, "Abbie do you think I care anything for Carrie?" After they had a heart-to-heart talk about his Ohio sweetheart and his noble intentions, Abbie viewed him more favorably and tried to drive him away from Hamblin.[48]

After her mother's death early in 1868, Abbie and Sidie spent nearly every evening together in the parlor, playing board games, talking, and flirting. Occasionally the two rode out in the moonlight. In 1871, however, one of them decided that their romance could not continue. Although her diary is not clear on which party initiated the breakup, Abbie seems to have rejected Sidie because he was not a converted Christian. Abbie and her friends agreed that Wallace was like the character Richard Hathaway in the novel *Hitherto*. Hathaway was a strong but gentle farmer and a good man, but not a Christian.[49]

Not only was Wallace not a Christian, he was also accused of fathering Carrie Hamblin's child. Wallace denied the charge, and Hamblin lost the paternity suit she brought against him, but she never withdrew her accusation. Sidie celebrated his victory with Abbie over a bottle of champagne.[50]

As a distraction from her woes over Sidie, Abbie mounted a flirtation with a white southern boarder. Despite his interest in her, Abbie was sure that the southerner's racial prejudice would get the best of him. "Mr Tharin if I tell you what my business is I don't think you'll torment me any more about being unsociable. . . . I'm a schoolmarm, Mr Tharin, I teach these little colored children," she told him. Tharin answered that "he should never have believed it," but he then talked with her about teaching school. Abbie's weeklong game of snubbing and attracting the young man ended in an evening of hand-holding, an exchange of Bible verses, and a small amount of increased understanding between members of two recently warring sections.[51]

Still, Abbie reserved her true affection for Sidie. Abbie wondered in her diary if she were making the right decision not to allow their love to blossom. "Am I not too fastidious? It is not wrong to love. Where am I wrong and how far right?" she wrote. "If I only had my mother—but if I had I should have never been where I am today." Abbie realized that she had grown stronger through her adversity but that she missed the advice a mother could give.[52]

No sooner had Wallace cleared himself of his paternity suit than gossip began to circulate about him and Abbie. In response, Abbie's stepmother decided to chaperone the pair in the parlor. This move resulted in a three-way argument that ended with Wallace refusing to set foot in the house again. Abbie was furious at Charlotte and continued to see Sidie outside of her house during the few months that remained before her departure north in the summer of 1872. She would continue to wrestle with her feelings for Wallace from a distance at Mount Holyoke, worrying that she had "learned to love something else better than God" and praying that Sidie would convert.[53]

In many ways Abbie was a typical young, middle-class woman who read novels, believed in romantic love, and was searching for an ideal mate. While Victorian culture was slowly abandoning total devotion to God in favor of romantic attachment, devout women such as Abbie still struggled with this issue. Abbie's tortured romance with Silas Wallace and her ultimate decision to stick with her Christian convictions rather than her emotions showed both weakness and strength. She could not bring herself to give up her relationship, but she refused to let it go further than the boundaries she had set.[54]

Legacy of the Experiment

Abbie and her parents had come to the Port Royal Experiment full of promise and goodwill, sure of the need for their Yankee ways to advance the African American race. Eight years later the Holmeses could say that they had contributed the talents of Rebecca, Charlotte, and Abbie as schoolteachers, and Reuben as a bumbling but well-intentioned plantation superintendent, merchant, real estate speculator, and politician. In return, the family had found a cheaper and less competitive place to call home.

The Port Royal Experiment gave the Holmes family a chance to practice some of their abolitionist and egalitarian ideals by interacting with African Americans with educational attainments and class markers considerably higher than the Holmeses'. Although they did not socialize with the most politically prominent African Americans—the Whippers, the Smalls, Samuel Bampfield, and Thomas Miller—they were not completely cut off from black society.

Tucked within the last pages of Abbie's 1872 diary is a reference that gives a glimpse of the Holmes family's relative openness: "Dr. Webster and Mr. Thompson, the former white, the latter colored—the latter a Methodist minister, the former the presiding elder—were here to dinner." Abbie also wrote explicitly of her admiration for Charlotte Forten, the highly educated African American teacher and writer who had been to the Sea Islands in the early years of the experiment. Forten returned to see her old Beaufort friend Elizabeth Botume in the spring of 1872, and Botume introduced her to Abbie, who wrote: "Slightly colored is she, but very pretty. Some eight years ago while teaching on St. Helena she wrote some article for the Atlantic that mother & I enjoyed very much, called 'Life on these Sea Islands.' I was very glad to meet her and found her very pleasant and entertaining. Miss Brown was there also but I liked Miss Fortin better. Stayed to tea." Abbie wrote glowingly of Forten but showed the racial bias that white northerners still had to overcome when she wrote that Forten was "colored . . . but pretty."[55]

Abbie never lost the sense of mission that her parents imparted to her as part of the Port Royal Experiment. Nor did the schoolmarm forget her

African American pupils, friends, and neighbors when she returned to New England soil. In 1872, when she left Beaufort for Mount Holyoke, perhaps she packed her book of ballads by Forten's friend, the abolitionist poet John Greenleaf Whittier. Men and women such as her parents, Forten, and Whittier would continue to inspire Abbie Holmes in her work as a writer, a folklorist, an educator, and a reformer. Her final years of education in New England would bring these ideals to a fuller maturation.

Chapter Five

WOMAN'S MISSION

Monday is the day set apart here to pray for missionaries. . . . If ever it should seem to me that my work was a mission of that kind I hope I should find the way opened to some field of labor here in our own country.[1]

Twenty-year-old Abbie Mandana Holmes and her eleven-year-old sister, Georgie, steamed out of Charleston Harbor on 12 July 1872. In addition to her bags, her birds, and Georgie's pet squirrel, Abbie took with her a heavy heart full of the events of the past five years in Beaufort. Her mother's death, her father's remarriage, and her persistent attraction to Sidie Wallace weighed on her mind. As she waved to her father she prayed that she would not lose her "place in his heart" and that she would be able to forget her love for Wallace. From a distance Abbie would continue to struggle with these conflicts, even as she immersed herself in the pleasures and challenges of life as a student.[2]

After she arrived in the North, Abbie was buoyed up by the support of her northern family. She and Georgie visited their Holmes relatives in Brooklyn and then went to Worcester, Massachusetts, where Abbie met a gathering of her Winch aunts, Ella (Nellie), Lucinda, and her special namesake, Abbie. "The tears were in all our eyes and I think we all thought of the other sister, whose features mine reflected to them," Abbie wrote. At last she could share her grief and find comfort among those who had loved her mother. Still, her first visit to her mother's grave was difficult. "I was very unhappy indeed," she wrote.[3]

In Worcester, Abbie and Georgie stayed with their aunt Abbie Winch Coes. Mindful of their past, Aunt Abbie took her nieces to visit the State Reform School where their father had taught. Thinking also of her future, Abbie Coes took her namesake to pay a call on her old Sunday school teacher, Miss Pond, a graduate of Mount Holyoke. Pond was one of several Mount Holyoke alumnae who encouraged Abbie to attend the seminary. From the day she went north Abbie was surrounded by strong women. She even managed to visit her old Beaufort mentor, Elizabeth Hyde Botume.[4]

In New England, Abbie also revisited the memories of her childhood and put them in perspective. With her Aunt Nellie, she and Georgie visited her old Westborough home. A new building had replaced the old Georgian farmhouse. Abbie found "nothing the same but the elm trees and some of them were gone. How small the garden looked that I used to think such a wilderness, how low the hedge I once thought so lofty. . . . We went up on a hill to the old Irish cottages to see old Tom Brady who used to be our gardener and my hero. He was not in but old Kathleen his wife came out to the carriage to speak to us. 'Ah, but I nursed ye when ye's a bebby,' said she. She said I looked like my mother but Georgie had her eyes." In this passage from her journal Abbie tried her hand at dialect, an interest she would later develop further through retellings of African American folktales at Mount Holyoke. In addition to developing her literary talents, Abbie's writings about her old home helped her remember her mother.[5]

Abbie's thoughts abruptly returned to Beaufort when she received a letter from Sidie Wallace telling her that her old rival, Carrie Hamblin, had died. Abbie expressed no compassion for her "enemy," writing that she and Sidie thanked God for Carrie's death. This self-righteous view of God smiting their enemy was juxtaposed with Abbie's statement, "I am so glad I had it in my heart to forgive her." She carefully copied down the details of Hamblin's utterly friendless death from a Beaufort newspaper. "The funeral procession consisted of a boy and a wagon that carried the body to the grave. She had no physician but Dr Jones, (a colored quack) and his prescription proved too powerful for she had been pregnant five months," Abbie wrote bluntly. In her writing Abbie did not show the kind of sisterly feeling that female moral reformers of antebellum times had shown "fallen women," perhaps because she considered Hamblin, an educated white woman, a social equal who was not forced into sexual sin. Nor did she concern herself with the fate of Hamblin's child, young Sidie Wallace, who was absent from the newspaper story. Abbie worried instead about the adult Sidie Wallace, whose denials of paternity she (and the court) believed. Her heart was "sore" as she talked alone with Aunt Abbie the next day. Her next trip, to Paxton to see her old aunt Olive Holmes Harrington, helped to calm her spirit.[6]

After the death of her parents, Olive had become the matriarch of the Holmes clan and took pride in her nieces and nephews. Six months before Abbie traveled north Olive Harrington had written to her brother, R. G., congratulating him on the birth of his newest daughter, Almeda. "Perhaps you would have been pleased with a *boy*," she wrote, "but never mind[,] the world could not get along a great length of time without mothers & wives." She closed her letter by saying, "I want to tell Abbie about her ancestors[,] . . . and about my visit to her mothers grave. . . . If Abbie comes North to school I will do what I can in my retired way to help her." Aunt Olive brought back happy memories of childhood by bringing Abbie and her cousins' old playthings down from the attic. Abbie and her cousin Frank Huntington Holmes sat in the shade of a pine tree to write in their journals. Her New England family renewed her strength.[7]

Abbie's visit ended with a second trip to lay a wreath on Rebecca Holmes's grave in the Winch family plot. This time Abbie found words to describe the grave to her father, who had not yet seen it: "In the center is a neat white marble monument with the names and ages of all those buried there inscribed on opposite sides. . . . I liked it all very much, it was so simple and neat. Dear Father, I am so glad to think mother's grave is where it can be green half the year and white with snow in winter. Of all places where she could have been buried I think this was the best, and the one she herself would have chosen." A few days later she decided to incur a large expense to have her mother's photograph copied from a daguerreotype, framing for herself and Georgie an image they could hold. Young Abbie even wore the photograph of her mother as a cameo around her neck. Abbie could feel satisfied that, after her troubled final years, Rebecca was finally at rest and would be remembered.[8]

On 31 August 1872 Abbie said good-bye to Georgie, who was escorted back to Beaufort by their stepmother's sister. Abbie knew that she would miss the sister she called "my little girl." Fortified by her reconnection with her past, Abbie packed her new trunk, marked her clothes, and prepared to go to South Hadley.[9]

Mount Holyoke

Ipswich and Mount Holyoke, the schools for women she attended, gave Abbie a vision of herself as a writer, a reformer, and a political actor. The white world of New England now also made her aware of the unique knowledge she had gained from encounters with the black world of Beaufort. Abbie's schooling pushed her ahead academically, while it also nurtured the bonds between herself and other women. Because she had lost her mother in 1868, the love of her New England aunts and the strong female friendships she made at school were also important.

Abbie Holmes was fortunate that her savings of $40 and her father's contribution of $125 enabled her to attend pioneering Mount Holyoke, the institution that became the model for the nation's first women's colleges. In a coincidence of continuity, Mount Holyoke was also the offspring of Abbie Holmes's former alma mater, Ipswich Female Seminary. In the 1830s Mary Lyon, an Ipswich teacher, began raising funds to build a school in South Hadley, Massachusetts, where serious New England women could find "intellectual mastery, inner system, and the hope of faith." On the train to Mount Holyoke in 1872 it was easy for Abbie to pick out "the South Hadley girls," perhaps because she was one of them. They were mostly middle-class New England women ranging in age from sixteen to their twenties. Many had already taught in rural or town schools, and others intended to do so once they graduated. Reasonable tuition kept Mount Holyoke open even to poor women. Abbie recorded that she paid seventy-five dollars for tuition and board in 1872. An endowment insured the durability of the institution, teachers were paid minimal salaries, and the seminary saved money by employing its students, rather than servants, to perform the school's domestic labors. Even though Mary Lyon died in 1849, the teachers she had trained continued the seminary in her spirit, and Abbie benefitted from the continued vigor of the institution in the 1870s.[10]

The 1878 *Historical Sketch of Mount Holyoke Seminary* sums up the school's mission: "The pupils were to be trained to help themselves mainly for the sake of helping others." During the two years she spent at Mount Holyoke, Abbie Holmes absorbed this spirit of service. Because of her tenuous financial and personal circumstances, Abbie was one of the vast majority of students who enrolled but did not graduate. According to an 1877 survey of 2,341 former students, whether or not they finished, 1,690 had taught school, 1,391 were married, 141 had been foreign missionaries, and an undetermined number were city or home missionaries.[11]

Historian Helen Horowitz argues that Mount Holyoke had a strong impact on its students because Lyon built her school around a system designed "to turn daughters who were acted upon into women capable of self-propelled action." While Holyoke's curriculum was modeled on that of nearby Amherst, its system of rules was much stricter than that of the men's college. By ordering every hour of her students' lives and putting them under the constant oversight of teachers, Lyon constructed a routine that trained her pupils to be "rational, disciplined women oriented to the external world." Even more than when she was a girl at Ipswich, Abbie Holmes was greatly influenced by the mission, the routine, and the teachers of her school.[12]

Still, her experience shows that no system could be so complete as to totally extinguish peer culture or resistance among its students. Although her relationships were less intense than those at Ipswich, Abbie formed solid and affectionate friendships with students as well as with teachers. By the time she left, she had also led a small rebellion in her algebra class and reshaped the curriculum to fit her needs.

When Abbie arrived on 4 September 1872, she was immediately put under the wing of a matron who assigned her to a room and escorted her to dinner. She also met her roommate, Mattie Lamson of North Hadley, Massachusetts. Before she began any classes, Abbie was examined in geography, arithmetic, history, algebra, and "Analysis." She passed all of her subjects except arithmetic and hoped that she would succeed in that on her next try.

Abbie quickly became accustomed to Mary Lyon's system. A few days after her arrival, and again at the start of a later term, Abbie described "the way the days go." Beginning at 6:00 A.M., the young women's days were punctuated by the ringing of two bells, the second of which was a tardy bell. At their meals the young women sat fourteen to a table with one or two teachers. After breakfast Abbie straightened her room and went to "wipe dishes" in the domestic hall. Abbie and all the other students then spent a half-hour in silent and solitary meditation, followed by public devotions in Seminary Hall at 9:15 A.M. Abbie liked this quiet time, which she sometimes spent with her journal.

During her recitation hours Abbie studied or recited in algebra, geography, or ancient history. At midday she put on an exercise dress and bloomers to practice gymnastics, followed by a noontime dinner. On Saturdays the students' chief employment was writing compositions. When the term ended, the students were examined to see if they had mastered their subjects.[13]

Abbie added her own accounting to that demanded by the school. She kept systematic records of time spent working on her domestic chores and money spent on expenses. Though her routine was rigorous, Abbie was usually happy to interrupt her studies to take a walk or talk with a friend in her few unscheduled moments.[14]

If Abbie and a friend wandered outside in the afternoon, they had to be certain to be back in time for their "sectional exercises," a crucial component of the regulatory scheme Mary Lyon had devised. "The school is divided into sections of about [15] girls," wrote Abbie, "& each section has a special teacher." A section teacher was supposed to form a mother-daughter bond with her students and "acquaint herself with the health, habits, intellectual improvement, and moral and religious state of every young lady in her section." During sectional exercises students spent a few minutes reporting failures in holding to the rules, "of which there are many," Abbie noted. This system of self-reporting was intended to make the girls internalize the rules of the institution. Abbie did not report any infractions of her own except being late for supper.[15]

After sectional exercises, all the students met together in Seminary Hall to hear a lecture. Mount Holyoke's lecturers were often male professors. A professor of astronomy gave the same course of lectures he had delivered at Dartmouth College. Seminary-wide lectures were a supplement to the regular curriculum, and students were not tested on lecture topics as they would be in the classes that had recitations.[16]

An hour-long break and then tea or supper followed each lecture. Abbie wiped dishes after each meal and allowed herself to "dissipate" the three quarters of an hour before the 8:00 P.M. "recess meeting" of her section. At each of these meetings the leader, Miss Spooner, gave an inspirational talk or Bible lesson, which Abbie took seriously. At Abbie's first recess meeting Spooner spoke of "the crosses that are put up in dangerous places in the mountains of Switzerland to warn travellers of their danger & point to a safe path." This speech caused Abbie to reflect on her own dangerous relationship with S. M. W. She prayed for "strength daily to fight it out and battle it down." In the evenings following recess meetings Abbie returned to her room and studied or wrote letters or journal entries until the retiring bell at 9:45 P.M.[17]

Self-Reflection

In the private and nonjudgmental pages of her journal, Abbie sorted through painful emotions and affirmed difficult decisions. It is useful to look at

Abbie's journals in the way that Joanne Braxton, a literary critic, has analyzed the diaries of Charlotte Forten. "Although the diaries were intended to be private," writes Braxton, "the diarist's autobiographical act relates to the development of a public voice in the move to objectify and take control of experiences through the writer's craft; in the pages of her diary she gains distance between herself as subject and object." Abbie could use her diary to capture and interpret her experiences in literary form, or she could use her diary to cultivate a persona that she could like and respect. "I do mean to be as jolly as I can," she wrote soon after her arrival. "I won't be either a martyr or a victim at any rate, and whatever heartaches I have I'll keep to myself, and you my sympathetic journal." Although she wisely confided in others as well, her diary was a great help.[18]

When she started school at Mount Holyoke, Abbie was still somewhat self-conscious about her writing and felt an obligation to use her journal to improve herself. She borrowed the popular fictional diary *Stepping Heavenward,* by Elizabeth Payson Prentiss, and contrasted it to her own journal. Katy, the main character in Prentiss's story, progresses from a rebellious girlhood, through loss of a parent and a disappointed love affair, to Christian maturity. Abbie must have found her own life reverberating in its pages. She copied portions of the book into her diary and told herself that she should try to write something more "worthwhile, as Katy did."[19]

A Christian Curriculum

Mount Holyoke kept God and the state of Abbie's soul uppermost in her mind. Devotions, recess meetings, twice-daily public worship, two church services on Sunday, Bible study, speeches by missionaries, and days set aside for fasting and prayer made students acutely aware of the spiritual side of their lives. At the beginning of the term Abbie found it difficult to offer a public prayer. "I have been a Christian eight years. But I haven't lived like a Christian all that time," she wrote ruefully. A few months of Bible study, reflection, and worship transformed Abbie's reticence. By December, Miss Spooner felt so confident of her leadership that she asked Abbie to run the evening recess meeting when the teacher was away.[20]

Evangelical awakening was perhaps the most important of Mary Lyon's aims, and after her death the memory of Lyon was used to inspire students. From time to time Abbie met with those in her section who were Christians, and they prayed fervently for the conversion of all of their friends. Abbie was also comforted by the thought of reuniting with her mother in heaven. In the meantime, she vowed "to make the most of my time here and do the little everyday things faithfully." Her first goal was making peace with her stepmother by writing her a conciliatory letter. This softening of her views toward Charlotte Holmes enabled Abbie to add her stepmother to her supportive cast of female relatives.[21]

Visiting missionary speakers and women teachers provided Abbie with role models who helped her imagine the different paths her life might take. Hearing the account of the life and death of a Mount Holyoke graduate who taught school in New York made Abbie "long for some work to do for Jesus." Abbie also admired a missionary who had established a normal school for Mexican teachers and another who worked at a home for tuberculosis sufferers in Boston. Slowly Abbie changed her mind about single life making one an "old maid." On her botany teacher's birthday Abbie wrote: "I think it would be worthwhile to live fifty one years of such a life as hers has been. I cannot conceive of a more beautiful old age than she is growing to. I don't think anyone would ever dream of calling her an old maid. I think she has a great deal more *motherliness* than half the mothers I've known."[22]

By her second term Abbie had begun to see herself as a Christian leader. When she heard about the case of Mollie Dodd, a student who had gotten into trouble, Abbie wrote a compassionate note. "I know myself both what it is to sin and also how sweet it is to be forgiven," Abbie told Mollie. She was gratified when Mollie responded by calling her down to the south-wing parlor, kissing her, and having a heartfelt talk. Abbie's interest in Mollie demonstrated that she had matured from a concentration on herself to empathy for others.[23]

Abbie continued to widen her circle of friends and acquaintances through walking or sewing and chatting with other students during spare moments. Abbie met her friend Emma Holmes in her section, and the two began asking permission to spend Sunday afternoons together. During Abbie's third term they became roommates. Abbie found her relationship with Emma different from her usual friendships, which had been with "graceful, beautiful, talented" people to whom she did the giving. In Emma's case the situation was reversed. Their relationship partook of the intimacy of "caresses" and quarrels, and the two young women read their journals to each other.

They continued their friendship through correspondence after Abbie left Mount Holyoke.[24]

Women's Rights

Mount Holyoke helped foster a sense not only of women's duties and mission, but of women's rights to earn a livelihood, to vote, and to be considered the intellectual equals of men. During a visit with her Aunt Abbie in Worcester, Abbie found an opportunity to voice her views on women's rights at a church sociable. In her journal she parodied the minister, whom she bested in a contest of wits over women's education:

> Now Dr. Cutler is a conscientious man. He came to the Sociable to enjoy himself to be sure, but that was a minor consideration. . . . [He] began to look about him for the one on whom he could bestow that word of counsel that would be appropriate. He spied me presently and no doubt his reflections were on this wise. "There is a young maiden sitting apart. She is rather intelligent looking and rather sensible too; how deplorable that so many otherwise sensible girls should have such highly improper views of women's sphere. Who knows but I may be able to give this one a bias in the right direction. She looks docile, I think I'll try."

After inquiring about where she was from, Dr. Cutler began to express his views on Mount Holyoke. He "warmly commended the Seminary" but "thought it a great mistake that no gentlemen teachers were employed there." Abbie refuted this point to the best of her ability, and the two had "quite an animated conversation on the 'Woman's Question.'" Abbie wrote, "It was quite interesting to me (and also evidently to two or three young men who sat near by)." She thoroughly enjoyed the battle and thought that it "vexed [Dr. Cutler] a little to see he made no impression on me." She continued, "'Well,' said Dr. C. as a parting shot, 'all the colleges are opening to young ladies, it will soon be time to reverse the order and then I suppose you will open your seminary to young men?'" Abbie retorted, "Ah, Dr. C. that has been spoken of already but we greatly fear it might 'lower our standard.'" Abbie's words showed her belief in the special difference between, as well as the equality of, women and men.[25]

On a visit to the dentist Abbie again voiced her opinion on women's rights. When the dentist asked her what she would do after graduation, she told him: "I wanted to show that I could get a living as well as if I were a young man." He advised her to go "right into business and you'll do well." Abbie found his answer "much more sensible than to say as so many gentlemen I've known . . . 'Oh you needn't worry about getting a living, a girl like you. Do you suppose the young men are going to let girls of your appearance grow into an old maid?'" Abbie had arrived at a confident opinion of her abilities as a woman. "Thank God there is something for girls to think of and live for nowadays beside marrying & giving in marriage," she wrote with relief.[26]

Although the seminary did not say so in its promotional literature, Mount Holyoke led its women students inexorably to the conclusion that women should have a larger role in public life. Abbie recorded such conversational topics as women's clubs, women's education, women as speakers, and "Out-Door Gardening for women." The idea of woman suffrage was not far away, and Mount Holyoke supported it with a mock election staged to coincide with the real election of 1872. "All the girls voted today," Abbie wrote, "221 for Grant, 32 for Greeley." Given her beliefs and her family's situation in Reconstruction Beaufort, Abbie was probably in the majority supporting the former Union general. Mount Holyoke seemed pleased with Grant's victory. To celebrate, the seminary held an "illumination." Abbie wrote, "There was a bonfire in the streets, the bells were rung and a cannon fired so near that numerous panes of glass were cracked and lamps thrown down from the windows." It would have been surprising if this exercise in vicarious democracy did not instill in Abbie and the other girls the feeling that they had a right to vote.[27]

A Small Rebellion

Abbie not only gained the confidence to challenge the patriarchal injustices of her society, but she also began to question the rules of the matriarchal institution she had so staunchly defended against outside attacks. Abbie was probably worried that her family's finances might run out before she had finished learning as much as she desired. Therefore, she resolved to finish the junior studies course of the four-year junior/senior system in one year instead of two. To accomplish this acceleration of her studies, she asked permission to change to a more advanced ancient history class. Abbie prepared herself for this step by studying ahead for a week and doing enough extra domestic work that she could be excused from it for three weeks. Her request was granted. "I felt greatly elated over this small feather for my cap," she wrote. Abbie saw no reason why she should not decide her own fate.[28]

In her attempt to speed her progress in algebra, Abbie touched off a rebellion of other students who were also frustrated with the slow pace of the course. As Abbie described it, her "heroic determination to finish Algebra this term or die in the attempt" was such that her instructor, Miss Hodgson, grudgingly consented to allow Abbie to work ahead. When word of Abbie's special arrangement spread, indignation arose among the other "bright and particular stars" in the algebra class, and they accompanied Abbie to her first "private" recitation. A battle of wills began as Miss Hodgson fired algebra problems at the "meteor shower" of bright students until all had failed. Miss Hodgson seemed to have won the battle, but Abbie still succeeded in completing the course and moving on to study botany and physiology in the next term.[29]

With the way cleared, Abbie threw herself into her beloved botany with vigor. She pronounced her new botany instructor, Miss Clapp, "altogether the jolliest of teachers." Clapp took Abbie and another student into the country to collect specimens. "In waterproofs, rubber boots over gymnastic dresses and old hats we could bid defiance to the rain. . . . We came home with all our botanical boxes full and I was so fortunate as to find the most beautiful bunch of arbutus I ever saw." Abbie enjoyed the outdoor adventure, the beauty of nature, and the spirit of her teacher.[30]

Though she was busier than ever, Abbie was more joyful during her spring term than at any other time at Mount Holyoke. The Monday after her ride in the rain was once again "delightful," even though she had more to do than she thought she could manage. Abbie credited her continued practice of half an hour of silent devotion in the morning with giving her the strength to accomplish all her tasks. She grew physically stronger and more energetic, walking up to seven miles a day in search of flowers.[31]

The longer Abbie stayed at Mount Holyoke, however, the less inclined she felt to follow its strict routine. On 21 May 1873 she stayed at home "just to see how it would seem" and worked all day on her herbarium. The test of

Abbie's success came at the end of the term when she was examined in July 1873. Unfortunately, Abbie's disjointed study of algebra—slow and then fast—did not bring her success. She passed ancient history and physiology and "comfortably disposed" of botany, but not algebra, in which "the whole class did badly."[32]

After she finished her examinations, Abbie closed off her term with "the most trying ordeal of all," a public reading of "The Tar Baby," an African American tale that she had written down as a composition. She had already read her "Negro nursery tale" to a New Year's Eve audience, but the school closing was a much more momentous event. For the occasion she dressed in her "light grenadine" and wore "a bit of coloseum vine in my hair and bosom." When she stood up in Seminary Hall, Abbie did not feel as frightened as she had expected to, and her performance went well. Afterward Abbie received several other invitations to perform tales and "Negro sermons" before smaller groups of teachers, students, and guests. Abbie's distinctive performance was a first step toward her career as a collector and writer of African American folklore.[33]

Tar Baby

Growing up in Beaufort County with its large black majority, young Abbie must have absorbed a good deal of African American culture. There is little comment, however, on this subject in her diaries and letters. In fact, Abbie heard her first African American folktale secondhand, from another white abolitionist. Most of the information about Abbie's folklore collection comes from an article she wrote in 1933 for the *Mount Holyoke Alumnae Quarterly*. In this article, "Folklore on Sea Islands," Abbie wrote that in the 1860s she was in a group assembled in the mission house in Beaufort, South Carolina, waiting for the wedding ceremony of "Mr. Carlton . . . coming from his plantation, nine miles away" and "Miss _____, a Mount Holyoke graduate and teacher in a negro school on our Port Royal Island." While they waited, Dr. A. J. Wakefield, a favorite in Yankee society, told the story of the "Tar Baby," which he had heard from his African American cook. Later correspondence confirms that Wakefield enjoyed retelling "Sea Island legends" to Abbie and her younger sister Georgie as they were growing up in Beaufort.[34]

It was not until late in 1872, however, "during a heavy snowstorm" at Mount Holyoke, that she first wrote down "The Tar Baby." Like so many students, Abbie was sitting at her desk the day before a composition was due, her brain "bare and vacant of ideas." She recalled the inspiration for what happened next in mystical terms: "My habit from childhood, thanks to my mother's thoughtful guidance, had been to pray for help in any perplexity. I did so now, and immediately I recalled quite distinctly the story Dr. Wakefield told . . . the cook's story of the tar baby. I had not thought of it since, but, as I began to write it out, memory restored it to me with all particulars." Abbie's composition met with such success that she was called upon to recite it at seminary assemblies and informal gatherings.[35]

Why were the African American tales that Abbie retold so popular with her northern schoolmates? Perhaps it was their "humor and originality," which their collector later praised. White northerners had never heard such stories before. The depiction of African Americans as humorous storytellers conformed to sentimental racial views of northerners who saw blacks as naturally artistic and happy-go-lucky. The fact that the tales and sermons were rendered in dialect also fit this view. Abolitionist writers had used dialect whenever they quoted African Americans, so Abbie's use of this speech form was not surprising. Dialects of various kinds were also used by writers Harriet Beecher Stowe and Mark Twain to impart authenticity and regional distinctiveness to their work. Dialect, however, set the collector above the "folk" in a way that diminished the teller. The white person who retold the tale or Negro sermon spoke in standard English at all other times and stood out as a person of higher class and education when contrasted with the dialect speaker.[36]

Abbie's recitations of tales in dialect and her performance of Negro sermons were related to a widespread appropriation of black culture by white northerners in the nineteenth century minstrel tradition. Cultural historian Eric Lott has written about this phenomenon, calling the white fascination with minstrelsy a mixture of "love and theft." Whites envied and desired the supposedly lazy and sensual ways of blacks at the same time that they looked down on African Americans for these same qualities. Many elite northern whites with moderate or even abolitionist racial views saw minstrelsy as an authentic American folk form. Since minstrelsy was an exclusively male performance, Abbie probably never even considered literally blackening her face. Still, she took on a black dialect voice in order to present her version of African American culture to her northern friends. When she preached a Negro sermon, Abbie crossed gender and racial boundaries, putting on a black male identity. Indeed, after the publication of Joel Chandler Harris's Uncle Remus tales around 1880, Abbie's friends explicitly called her "The Original Uncle Remus." Playing with alternative identities was undoubtedly a source of pleasure for both Abbie and her white, largely female audiences, given the strict gender and racial roles with which they usually had to live.[37]

Illness

After her "Tar Baby" performance at Mount Holyoke's closing exercises in the spring of 1873, Abbie spent a pleasant summer vacation with her northern relatives. Together with her cousins she sewed, read George Eliot's *Middlemarch,* and went on a sunset row with two gentlemen. Abbie enjoyed her leisure immensely, as she indicated in a journal entry about a picnic outing: "It is a day in which I have done *nothing.* I used to long for such an one, in fact for the last two months it has seemed a desideratum."[38]

Back at the seminary, Abbie worried again about the state of Sidie Wallace's soul. In her prayers Abbie offered her life for his salvation. This method of conversion was one that Victorian literature promoted through heroines such as Little Eva in *Uncle Tom's Cabin,* whose chief power lies in her ability to create remorse in others through her illness and death. Perhaps in an attempt to fulfill her wish, not long thereafter, in November 1874, Abbie became ill and thought constantly of "my heart's wish," although Wallace did not convert.[39]

Until this time Abbie had only had the common ailments of a normally healthy person—occasional headaches, colds, and a toothache. Now, however, she did not specify her illness; she only wrote that she was "tired" and "miserable." Medicines, "2 oz. single zephyr," ammonia, and doctor bills began to appear in her account book. It is possible that Abbie became ill because of her mental anguish over the state of her own and Mr. Wallace's souls. Another factor may have been that she compounded the rigors of her studies by trying to graduate in three, instead of four, years. Her illness could have been mental or physical, a breakdown of nerves, depression, or most likely, a case of tuberculosis, to which her weakened physical and emotional state made her more susceptible.[40]

In any case, events in Abbie's life conspired against a recovery. While she lay ill, she received a letter bearing the news that her stepmother had died of a heart ailment. Charlotte Holmes's death, so soon after Abbie had finally accepted her, must have been hard for Abbie. Abbie's sadness at her step-mother's death was magnified because it was a reminder of her own mother's sudden demise just five years before. Her first thoughts were concern for her father and his "little motherless babies." Abbie immediately wrote to her father asking if she should come home to help him, but he declined her offer. Because her health was not improving, Dr. Ford, a woman doctor employed by Mount Holyoke, advocated that Abbie be taken to Springfield, Massachusetts, after she finished her examinations at the end of the fall term.[41]

From the end of November in 1873 through March 1874 Abbie remained in Springfield under the watchful care of Dr. Williams, a home-opath who was also a graduate of Mount Holyoke. Her father and/or her aunts appear to have paid for her board at a converted farmhouse in Springfield where nurses tended to the patients and servants cooked "bountiful" meals. Although Abbie never stated her diagnosis, she reported that her doctors agreed, "I am in a very critical state and if I ever hope to enjoy health again I must put myself under treatment at once." Because Springfield was close to South Hadley, Abbie was able to receive visits from her friends and teachers at Mount Holyoke.[42]

Abbie's roommate, Miss Nutting, a teacher at Mount Holyoke, also suffered from an unspecified malady. Nutting's chief occupation was compiling statistics for a book, probably *Sex and Education*, edited by Julia Ward Howe, defending the education of women against *Sex in Education*, a widely read polemic by Harvard physician Dr. Edward Clarke, who argued that women's bodies were harmed by education. Even in her illness Abbie was surrounded by the energy of determined women.[43]

Abbie did not specify her illness. She was clear, however, about the other patients' diseases. She wrote, "There are, besides us, two consumptive patients and four sick with the typhoid fever, one Chinese, the other three Irish." This statement probably meant that Abbie and Miss Nutting also had "consumption," or tuberculosis. Her general regimen would have been consistent with homeopathic treatment of tuberculosis. A test she was given in old age indicated tuberculosis in her lungs. Tuberculosis was the leading cause of death in nineteenth-century America, and it carried a stigma because of its ease of contagion. It is no wonder Abbie barely mentioned her disease.[44]

Abbie rested and read Charles Dickens's *The Old Curiosity Shop, The Life of Mary Lyon,* and George Eliot's *Mill on the Floss.* Her girlfriends and Dr. Ford visited her regularly. Abbie wrote that she was grateful God had made her sickness "easy and even pleasant." Her recovery began with this respite from the hard work and mental anguish she had created for herself. Later the sunny climate of Beaufort may also have helped Abbie to recover.[45]

Writer and Collector

While she was convalescing at Dr. Williams's hospital, Abbie had time to concentrate on her writing. On 27 January 1874 she was permitted to spend a week at Mount Holyoke, sleeping at night in the sickroom. As she was "groping about for a place to cry in" after the emotional experience of reunion with her friends, Dr. Ford asked her to perform some Negro sermons for the benefit of a visitor, "a youth in a purple necktie." The request showed the fame she had gained throughout the school for this distinctive brand of knowledge. Abbie began to think once again of how to develop her talents at writing on African American tales or other subjects. She retrieved her old compositions from Miss Bowen, her teacher, and asked for advice. Bowen told Abbie to use her journal to "describe people I meet and tell how they impress me" so that she would learn to develop her opinions more precisely. Her combined interests in writing and in African American culture led Abbie to revise her "Tar Baby" composition and submit it to the *Springfield Daily Republican* after she returned to the hospital.[46]

The *Springfield Daily Republican* printed "De Wolf, de Rabbit an' de Tar Baby" on 2 June 1874, three months after Abbie had left Massachusetts. The *Republican* seems to have been generally sympathetic to expanded rights for women and African Americans, and Abbie Holmes's portrayal of African Americans in her first published story was sentimental but sensitive to the actual cultural circumstances of tale-telling.[47]

Holmes introduced the Tar Baby tale by writing that "the negroes of the South have a literature of their own, although, till lately, unwritten and almost unknown." Abbie connected these tales to the distinctive African American songs of the Fisk Jubilee singers and compared African animal stories to European fairy tales, all positive references. She also described a typical scene in which African Americans told stories to one another, "the old grandmother in her turban, with five or six little wooly heads clustering about her knee, before a blazing fire, waiting for the sweet potatoes in the ashes to roast for their supper." Abbie's description used both wide-ranging cultural references and specific knowledge of Sea Island life to educate her readers.[48]

Then she proceeded to retell, in dialect, the story of "de Rabbit, 'e mos cunnin' man dat go on fo' leg." In this version the Rabbit stole corn and ground nuts from the Wolf, who retaliated by setting up a white scarecrow. Rabbit simply kicked the scarecrow down. Next, the Wolf set out a baby made of tar. The Rabbit became angry when this "gal" did not reply to his questions, and he struck it. Eventually all of the Rabbit's paws became stuck in the tar, and the Wolf was able to capture him. He tricked the Wolf into throwing him into the brier patch by claiming it would be his worst punishment, when, in fact, the Rabbit lived in the brier bush. The Wolf tried to undo the Rabbit once again by pretending to play dead and having Neighbor Dog fetch the Rabbit to "lay um out." Rabbit figured Wolf's trick out, however, by dropping snuff on his nose and making the "dead" Wolf sneeze. As Abbie later noted, "This was the first time the Tar Baby story was ever printed."[49]

Although this story would become the most notable accomplishment for which Abbie Holmes Christensen is remembered today, she did not even bother to mention her submission for publication in her diary while she was in Springfield. Perhaps she did not believe that the paper would publish her work. Like other educated middle-class women in their early twenties, Abbie was trying to decide whether she would pursue the traditional role of wife and mother or try to pursue a career.

Models of Womanhood

Despite her interest in writing, Abbie's greatest ambition had become her desire to be a doctor. A desire to maintain her own health, a love of botany, and admiration of her homeopathic physicians all contributed to this desire. Yet she also admired her aunt Abbie Winch Coes, a wife and mother.

Holmes took advantage of the time she spent under Dr. Ford's care to consult with the homeopathist about the possibility of becoming a doctor. "She says she thinks I might succeed," Abbie wrote happily. "She is a delightful woman and a good friend of mine." Abbie also looked up to Dr. Williams, who seconded her decision to pursue medicine. When her aunt Abbie Coes came to Springfield, young Abbie had a perfect occasion to compare Williams and Coes:

> She and auntie talked of woman's sphere etc, where they met on common ground. But they would never be kindred spirits. What a contrast they presented. Auntie, dark and handsome, dressed in a black silk, very stylish and becoming black bonnet & cloak and necktie *just* her shade of peach blossom pink. The Dr. in her "uniform" of black poplin which bore unmistakable marks of wear and tear, college pin confirming her black tie which according to its frequent custom was somewhat awry. . . . She always gives the impression of strength and self reliance . . . strong in her hates as in her loves. . . . Well as I love my aunt . . . I know that Dr. Williams is the more lovable, the sweeter truer woman of the two.

Holmes would turn out to be a combination of these women. Abbie became a wife and mother like her aunt, but for her, appearance was never as important as action. She was a woman who "branched out."[50]

On 25 February 1874 Abbie's "long-expected draft" arrived in a letter from her father. He wanted Abbie to come home, and she felt well enough to do so. Sarah Keith, her deceased stepmother's sister, was living at the Holmes house, taking care of the new baby and her sisters, and her father needed Abbie as a "chaperone" to stop the gossip circulating about this arrangement. As Abbie prepared to go, Dr. Williams gave her an introduction to the matron at the Homeopathic Woman's Medical College in New York City so that she could visit the institution on her way home. Abbie and her Aunt Martha spent two or three hours touring the college and sitting in on a lecture. Although Abbie never fulfilled her dream of going to medical school, she pursued a lifelong avocation in homeopathic medicine, remaining fascinated by the mysteries of the human mind and body and what kept human beings alive and well.[51]

Legacy

Abbie left New England a more mature and confident woman than she had been when she first arrived. Her extended family had provided love and support, which strengthened her identity as a Holmes, a Winch, and a New Englander. Her schooling at Ipswich and Mount Holyoke had done still more. If not for the encouragement of her teachers and friends at Mount Holyoke, she may not have collected and published African American folklore. If not for the sense of mission and confidence the seminaries instilled in their students, she might not have started a school for African Americans. If not for the ideas of women's equality and special gifts that Mount Holyoke preached and practiced, Abbie might not have taken such a public stance in favor of woman suffrage and equal rights. In a sense, Mount Holyoke reinforced the abolitionist vision she had already inherited from her parents and missionary teachers such as Towne and Botume. But leaving the South helped her to see the significance of her special knowledge of the Sea Islands. Abbie's visionary mind was strengthened at Mount Holyoke, and the school's disciplined daily routine became a lifelong habit. These internal and external resources enabled her to imagine and accomplish much.

On one of her long walks during the two years she was at Mount Holyoke, Abbie had hiked up "Prospect Hill" and viewed Holyoke and the other little towns in the distance. She wrote that "the chief beauty of it, and all New England scenery to me is the many comfortable looking houses and farms and the air of cultivation and thriftiness everywhere apparrint." On the day she left Mount Holyoke she wrote, "I looked my last on the dear old Seminary where I have had such a happy home, and on the beautiful mountain ranges that I shall always remember."[52]

Abbie wrote that she had originally intended to stay in the North forever but that she now believed it was right to return to her southern home. For the rest of her life she would bridge North and South, striving to bring to Beaufort the tidy town life and female activism of New England, while carrying back to New England the African stories and culture of the black southerners who became, once again, her neighbors.

Chapter Six

WIFE, MOTHER, HOMEMAKER

My life work has been that of a wife, mother, home-maker, which has included nursing, teaching children and servants, and the usual varied occupations of a mother.[1]

In March 1874 Abbie Holmes had left Mount Holyoke a single young woman intent on becoming a homeopathic physician. In April of the next year Abbie was wearing a new brown dress; standing in a Baptist church in Beaufort, South Carolina; and marrying Niels Christensen, a man she had barely known a year before. Within another year she had become a mother, and by 1888 she had borne six children and buried one. Years later Abbie Holmes Christensen filled out a "census" form she received from Mount Holyoke College. Most of the blanks were intended for lists of accomplishments in professional work. One can sense Abbie's frustration as the form thwarted her again and again in writing down what she saw as the most important achievements of her life. Under "Work or Position" she wrote "At Home," a designation that some later person crossed out and replaced with "writer." After she squeezed the names of her six children into the three spaces given, Abbie wrote, "Don't some of the alumnae have more than six children?" Under "Remarks," Abbie protested against the form's inability to recognize the contours of her life: "My life work has been that of a wife, mother, home-maker." It was also true, however, that she was a writer, for she made her mark on American culture by writing down the folklore of African Americans for northern readers. Although politics and public work mattered to her, Christensen wished to see women recognized for the labor of bearing and raising children, work that consumed the greatest proportion of her energy and time from 1875 to 1888.

Abbie's private and public decisions during these years were influenced by the regional, racial, and gender ideology of her time. When she arrived in South Carolina in 1874 after a long sea voyage from the North, Abbie noted with pleasure the change of climate, the prevalence of African Americans, and the feminine style of southern women: "How strange it seems to be riding through Charleston streets again. . . . How delightful to see fresh green grass from the carriage window. And the pretty Southern girls in white dresses and lace shawls. Yes, this is South Carolina again. The further to convince me a ragged negro driver opens his door for us to alight." Abbie stepped out of her carriage and into a state that would soon erupt in turmoil over which race would dominate politics. South Carolina men would denigrate the governing capacity of men such as the "ragged negro driver" and fight for white supremacy in the name of the "southern white womanhood" represented by the girls in white dresses. Abbie would find herself outraged by racist politicians, and she would come to join the fight for equal rights, rather than chivalry, for her gender.[2]

Abbie arrived in the waning days of Reconstruction, which ended with gunshots in 1876. In that election year white South Carolinians elected Democratic governor Wade Hampton by invalidating large portions of the black vote through fraud, intimidation, and the violence of white men in "Red-shirt" rifle clubs. Organized by prominent white leaders, these clubs conducted what amounted to a military campaign against Republicans and the black militias that tried to protect them. Not surprisingly, South Carolina, as well as Florida, presented disputed election results, the outcome of which would determine whether Rutherford B. Hayes, the Republican, or Samuel J. Tilden, the Democrat, would be elected president. In the compromise worked out between Republicans and Democrats in Congress, Hayes won the presidency while Democrats were appeased by withdrawal of the last remaining military troops in the South. In South Carolina, Governor Hampton promised "free men, free schools and free ballots" to black South Carolinians, but his promises were conditioned on African Americans allowing white Democrats to govern them. Hampton's rival, Martin Gary, leader of the South Carolina "Straightout" Democratic faction, advocated the complete and violent banishment of African Americans from any role in government. His extreme version of white supremacy triumphed when Benjamin Tillman won the governorship in 1890. Most white northerners acquiesced in this "settlement" of racial affairs, showing little interest in spending money enforcing black civil rights after the devastating Depression of 1873 and practicing various forms of segregation themselves.[3]

America's Gilded Age, from the 1870s through the 1890s, was also the time period historians of race relations have called "the nadir." As the economy went through swings of boom and bust, social reform dropped from the national agenda of the major political parties. Corporate money influenced both parties, and corruption was a factor among politicians at all levels. The United States Supreme Court overturned the Civil Rights Act of 1875 in 1883, and in *Plessy v. Ferguson* in 1896 the court upheld segregation, ruling that "separate but equal" was an adequate guideline for separating blacks from whites in railroad transportation and other public accommodations. As more and more immigrants moved into northern cities, native-born whites became more inclined to advocate limiting the franchise to "worthy" educated, white citizens. In this way many white northerners became sympathetic to white southern efforts to limit black voting. During the 1880s in Beaufort, African Americans tried to counter these forces, but racist policies slowly undermined the victories of Reconstruction.[4]

These events formed the political context in which Abbie Holmes lived. Yet the greatest change in her life was her decision to marry and have children. As historians of women have discovered, the patterns of their subjects' lives do not necessarily correspond to neat historical periodizations dictated by politics. Life-cycle changes such as puberty, childbearing, and menopause often had a greater impact than conventional politics. Still, Abbie Christensen's politics influenced her personal choices. She chose a Danish immigrant, active Republican, and suffragist for her husband, thereby strengthening her ability to stand for equal rights for African Americans and women.[5]

Niels Christensen

The decision to marry is one of the most significant choices a person of any era can make. In the nineteenth century, when divorce was rare, the magnitude of Abbie's decision was even more pronounced. Despite the support at Mount Holyoke for single women, earning a living was difficult, and there was still tremendous social pressure for nineteenth-century women to marry. Looking back on her life, Abbie discounted these factors and explained her decision to her grandson as a positive choice: "I myself believed that if I aimed to do something that would have a real lasting influ[ence] in the world I sh'd marry & bring up children. That c'd not be done unless I sh'd meet an uncommon man, one who was fine in character, and likely to be a fine father—also one that was attracted to me. Such an one I had not seen when I was 22 and I ceased to expect him."[6] Abbie had high expectations for her potential mate. Her first suitor had been Sidie Wallace, but because of his unconverted state and perhaps for other, unnamed reasons, she had ruled him out. Who was the new man who wooed and won her hand?

At five feet, ten inches tall; of average weight; with thick, dark blond hair; blue eyes; and a mustache, thirty-four-year-old Niels Christensen presented a striking physical contrast to petite, dark-haired, dark-eyed Abbie Holmes, who was twenty-two in 1874. Shaped by circumstances far different from Abbie's, Niels was nevertheless a good match in terms of his education and moral views. A Civil War veteran, Niels embodied the war's northern masculine Victorian ideal of self-control. Christensen was well-read, sober, and thrifty; he eschewed drink as well as tobacco and saved his earnings in order to invest them in business ventures. Although Niels lived in Beaufort from 1871 until the end of his life in 1909, he never adopted traditionally southern standards of masculine behavior, such as the code of honor and the use of force to maintain patriarchal power. Niels possessed a great love of family, and the nuclear family he and Abbie created was of particular importance to him because he had no other family in the United States.[7]

Niels was born in Denmark in 1840, the son of innkeepers Frederick and Marie Baker Kristensen. Like Abbie, Niels was the oldest of his siblings. In Denmark, Niels received what he described as a "good common school education subsequently augmented by private studies." Christensen immigrated to the United States at the age of twenty-two in 1862. The Union army needed men to fight the Civil War, and Niels took the opportunity to enroll as a private in the 145th New York Infantry volunteers. Christensen seemed to feel that the army offered him the best opportunity for advancement in the United States, for he reenlisted three times. Niels participated in the battles of Chancellorsville and Gettysburg, was twice wounded, and marched in Sherman's army through the South. His last service in the war was as a captain in the 44th U.S. Colored Infantry.[8]

Niels possessed an excellent command of English and was a talented writer. Christensen's literary and social skills as well as his knowledge of bookkeeping helped him to advance at a time when perhaps a quarter of the Union's enlisted men were illiterate. One of his friends tried to persuade him to publish his "lively and Picturesque description" of a military march. Christensen's skills enabled him to pass the examination required to receive an appointment as captain of colored troops.[9]

Niels's decision to take this position was probably a mixture of self-interest and an open attitude toward African Americans. The U.S. Colored

Troops offered foreigners greater opportunities for advancement because commissions were awarded on a competitive basis instead of local clout. After he passed his examination in 1865, Niels served with the 44th U.S. Colored Infantry in Alabama and Tennessee until 30 April 1866, when it was disbanded. Most of his last year of service was spent in occupation and court-martial duty.[10]

Captain Christensen left no direct record of his views on black troops, but letters from his friends indicate that he must have praised the African American soldiers under his command. Niels's correspondents agreed with him that his regiment was "a Modell of Perfection to equal and excell in drill and discipline that of some White Troops."[11]

Niels's service with black troops in the South gave him an experience in common with Abbie and the rest of the Yankee community in Beaufort. Both Niels and Abbie in their own ways, through school teaching and military service, participated in interracial experiments during the Civil War and in the years thereafter.[12]

During the occupation Niels Christensen, like Reuben Holmes, tried his hand at cotton planting and southern land speculation. He and his partner, Henry W. Meeker, another Union officer, wrote several "share wage" contracts with freed people. The fact that the contract stipulated that more land be planted in corn than in cotton was unusual for the time and may be an indication that Christensen and his partner listened to the requests of the freed people who were anxious to plant food crops.[13]

Christensen encountered business and professional conflicts and bad luck during his two years of planting in Alabama. He was cheated by another officer; the freedman who had signed a contract with him was indicted for grand larceny; and a Freedmen's Bureau agent accused Christensen of stealing a government wagon. Between losing money and fighting with men who were supposed to be his allies, Christensen was fed up. In December 1866 he and Meeker sold a large portion of their lands and returned north.[14]

How did his early years in the South shape Christensen? Economically, he learned that above all, African Americans wanted to own land and be independent of white management. After his return to the South three years later, he usually sold land to blacks instead of renting it. Politically, Christensen joined the minority of white officers of black troops who supported suffrage for African Americans, particularly those who had served in the military. A friend wrote to him:"I accept part of your doctrines as my creed,

particularly that which refer to universal suffrage." Christensen's command-
ing officer had told his troops that after the war they would be regarded as
citizens, and Christensen agreed. Christensen's wartime service with black
troops in the South readied him for Beaufort, a place he might not have ventured had it not been for his earlier southern experiences.[15]

From 1867 to 1870 Christensen served in the peacetime army stationed
at Fort Wayne in Detroit, Michigan, but he wished to transfer to civil service. After passing an examination, he obtained a post as keeper of the
National Cemetery in Beaufort, where he served from 1870 to 1876, caring
for the graves of over eight thousand black and white Union soldiers.[16]

In this post Captain Christensen became identified with an important
symbol of Republican Beaufort. He was also able to express his creative abilities in landscape gardening, a lifelong passion. Christensen obtained federal
funds to employ local African Americans in the transplanting of native trees
to line the cemetery's walks and drives, and he orchestrated the trimming of
grass and weeds around the headstones. In addition, he planted shrubs and
flowers to create four garden spots with overhanging grape arbors. Niels's
dedication to the beautification of the grounds fit in with the burgeoning
"rural cemetery" movement that was given a boost by grief at the huge death
toll of the Civil War. The parklike atmosphere that Christensen created drew
tourists and residents, including twenty-year-old Abbie Holmes, a budding
botanist.[17]

Although Abbie's romance with Niels did not flower until 1874, the
two had already met on an April afternoon in 1872 when Abbie rode down
to the soldiers' cemetery with her stepmother's cousin, Mattie Nye, who was
visiting from the North. They rambled among the graves until Mattie caught
sight of Christensen. Abbie recorded the politely flirtatious encounter that
ensued:

[Mattie] declared her intention of waylaying him and asking to see his silk
worms and peacock. . . . we followed him to the house, a pretty little cottage
just opposite the entrance to the cemetery. He exhibited the beautiful fowl but
could not persuade him to spread his tail, which seemed to be quite hand-
some. Then Mattie asked to see his silkworms, so in we went to a room he had
devoted to them, and there they were at different stages of growth, eating their
way through layers of mulberry leaves on wire frames which covered two long
tables. Mr C. explained a great deal about the process of silk making and

showed us some cocoons so that I understood far more about it than I ever did before. It was very interesting. Then Mr. C. offered to show us his garden and gave us some flowers. He seemed very intelligent and gentlemanly.

Abbie admired the fact that Christensen was interested in the scientific as well as the aesthetic pleasures of gardening and silk making.[18]

When Abbie and Niels's friendship began in the summer of 1874, she lived at home with her father, her sisters, and her deceased stepmother's sister, Sarah Keith. Her favorite pastime continued to be horseback riding, alone or with her friends. Abbie attended church and various social and literary clubs. She assisted a committee of "the Reading Room" in cataloging its books. Abbie was also collecting African American folktales for her next submission to a northern newspaper.[19]

Southern Tales for Northern Readers

Abbie found time to collect tales "here and there" by paying her informants a small sum. She wrote their stories down "verbatim." True to her abolitionist roots, Abbie rejected the offers of southern newspapers and instead sent her tales to the *New York Independent,* "a religious paper taken by my parents for years." This choice showed her political and regional affiliations.[20]

Abbie's work was printed in the "Young and Old" section of the *Independent,* which contained children's stories and poems. This "paper" was actually a weekly magazine printed in tabloid format and had a circulation in the tens of thousands. It featured such prominent writers as Louisa May Alcott and Sarah Orne Jewett. The *Independent's* origins were in the Congregational Church, but it was best known for its spirited editorials supporting, first, abolition and, later, women's rights and Republican presidents.[21]

With each new tale, Abbie experimented with different story-telling frames. Her second tale, "The Story Aunt 'Tilda Told," appeared in the 5 November 1874 issue of the *Independent* and featured an African American woman storyteller and Abbie herself in the guise of Alice. The story reads, "Miss Alice was ironing a white muslin for a croquet party next day, when Aunt 'Tilda came down the back stairs. 'Aunt 'Tilda,' said Miss Alice, 'can't you tell me some of those rabbit stories I used to be so fond of when I was a little girl?'" Aunt 'Tilda was reluctant, so Alice urged her on: "When I was North I used to try to tell your stories sometimes, and everybody was interested in them. And just a little while ago I had a letter from some of the children there begging me to write out some of your stories for them. . . . let me coax you to sit down and tell me a story while I finish these ruffles. 'Sho! I would look fine to sit down an' tell story while you da iron. You lemme finish dem ruffle an' you sit down an' res' you chile.'" Aunt 'Tilda proceeded to iron and tell Alice the story of the Rabbit and the Alligator, in which the trickster fools the reptile into letting him ride on his back across a large river. The scene surrounding this tale showed the class differences between Alice and Aunt 'Tilda quite clearly. Alice had the leisure to listen to stories and write them down, while Aunt 'Tilda knew it would not do for her simply to sit and spin tales.[22]

Except for the references to the North, Abbie's re-creation of the relations between herself and the mammy figure of Aunt 'Tilda could have come from a southern writer as easily as from a northern one, despite her deliberate choice to publish the tales with a northern paper. Later stories and storytelling frames would reveal more of Abbie's views on black-white relations in the New South.

Courtship

When Reuben Holmes and Sarah Keith married in 1874, Abbie's reasons for staying in Beaufort diminished, and she began to make plans to return to the North to study at the newly established coeducational medical school in Ann Arbor, Michigan. Niels Christensen's ardent and purposeful courtship changed Abbie Holmes's plans. He and Abbie became reacquainted in 1874 through Niels's business dealings with Reuben Holmes's lumber mill. At the age of thirty-four, Niels had been ready to marry for some time and had fruitlessly corresponded with several women through a match-making service. These letters reveal that the qualities Niels admired in a woman were independence, self-reliance, and a pleasant disposition. He must have seen some of these traits in Abbie, and he was determined that she would be his wife.[23]

Disillusioned with love, and resigned to a single life at the age of twenty-two, Abbie was not an easy target for Niels's affections. Undeterred, Niels wooed Abbie with flowers, sent witty notes, and took her for buggy rides and evening entertainments given by the Dramatic Society and local lyceum. "He used to send me baskets of flowers about every other day," Abbie recalled. The couple also attended church together, and she expressed no misgivings about the state of his soul as she had with Mr. Wallace. Niels often joined Abbie for card games in the evenings.[24]

When Niels made "a very definite proposal" after a few months of courtship, Abbie accepted and promised that they would marry when the orange blossoms bloomed. "How that man loves me! I see it in his eyes," Abbie informed her diary. "I think I am a fortunate girl, in that I have won the love of so good and so worthy a man," she wrote to her aunt. Niels's respectability, his intellect and education, his morality and right standing with God, and finally his love had convinced Abbie that she should marry him.[25]

By the nineteenth century it was generally accepted that a person should marry for love, and fiction as well as prescriptive literature reinforced this view. At first Abbie doubted that she really loved Niels. In contrast to her lengthy and torturous relationship with Sidie, Abbie's friendship with Niels seemed matter-of-fact and pleasant, though still under Wallace's shadow.[26]

After her engagement, Sidie Wallace called even more frequently than Niels did. Sidie and his brother John often visited the Holmes residence in the evenings to play card games with Abbie, with or without Niels. Others in the community worried about Abbie's and Sidie's continued intimacy after her engagement. Elizabeth Botume's opinion mattered to Abbie, and when she told Botume of her engagement, Abbie listened carefully for her reaction: "In one breath she congratulated me, in the next asked what Mr Wallace thought of it. I exclaimed that I wondered when people would understand that though Mr Wallace and I should always be the best of friends we could never be anything else." Abbie was reassured when Botume told her that she viewed the two as brother and sister, and nothing more.[27]

Abbie's choice of Niels over Sidie may have been more than a religious decision. If Abbie chose Niels because she thought he would be a good companion and parent who shared her values, she chose wisely. If there were anguish in her decision, that was also understandable because so much in the culture of romance gave her the message that she should marry Sidie, however incompatible they might be.[28]

As she made her decision, Abbie missed the advice her mother could have provided in allaying her fears and helping her to arrange a trousseau and ceremony. "A mother would know," she wrote. Abbie told Niels that she would marry him in April and went ahead with her own preparations. She began to sew a brown merino wool dress to wear on her wedding day. Niels and Abbie rented a house and began painting and furnishing it in the weeks before their wedding. Though she did not have her mother, Abbie had her aunts and her old school friends, who sent gifts and letters of congratulations.[29]

Marriage

Almost until the last moment Abbie Holmes agonized over the wisdom of her decision to get married. Two days before her wedding Abbie became filled with fear. She prayed: "I will put my trust in my God now and for all the future. Oh, if only He will only give me the grace to be all that I can be, as a wife, and in every other relation to which I may be called,—if I may make such a home as I have dreamed of—then I know not what more I have to ask. . . . Yes—I can hardly see to write it through my tears—but there is one more prayer very dear to my heart. . . . That all the souls I have loved and prayed for . . . might be saved in Christ at last." Abbie believed that Niels was a Christian and that they could serve God together. Her last prayer was probably for Sidie Wallace. There is no more record, after this date, of Abbie's thoughts on Wallace. Eventually Sidie married his Ohio sweetheart, and the two couples continued on as friends.[30]

After a simple ceremony on 13 April 1875 in Beaufort's Charles Street Baptist Church, Abbie's love for Niels grew as the couple began the intimate life of husband and wife. Niels was a genial and obliging partner who fit the masculine ideal of a good provider. Abbie worked to make the marriage succeed, taking care of the household and providing companionship for Niels as he went about his daily work. Abbie might have doubted that she could be an "ideal wife," but she was a supportive and assertive spouse.[31]

In the nineteenth-century North, as industrialization and urbanization moved men's workplaces outside the home and household production decreased, middle-class married women's main work became the nurture of children, cooking, and housekeeping. Women acquired more authority in child-raising and decisions regarding the family. Still, while equality was the ideal, most men had the upper hand economically and legally. The fact that the Christensens' marriage was a relatively balanced partnership resulted from a combination of Niels's restraint and respect for his wife's wishes and the economic power she gained from an inheritance she received in 1882.[32]

A few months after she was wed, Abbie discussed her marriage to Niels in a letter to Emma Holmes, who had been her closest friend at Mount Holyoke. Abbie informed Emma that she was "about the same girl you knew" but that she was happier since her marriage. Abbie also described Niels:

> He's ever so much like you, you dear child, honest, conscientious, dreadfully in earnest about everything, if it's only a game of Whist. Don't he look like one "born to command"? and—shall I confess it? I am finding out to my great astonishment (but this is the strictest confidence) that I seem to be admirably suited to that other part said to be so appropriate to my sex! But yet I get my share of the management of things. Don't you believe it? — Niels is one of those who improve on acquaintance. I knew he would, that's why I married him. He is so *comfortable* to live with, and we do have so much fun, good times every day. Best of all he really loves me, yes, I do believe, almost as much as I do him. He says *more.* That was true once, but not now.

Like Emma, Niels had started out loving Abbie more than she loved him. Like Emma, he won her love through his persistence and devotion. Abbie's preference for those with whom she had the upper hand in love indicates her desire to be the one in charge, the adored rather than the devotee.[33]

A woman was wise to look for such emotional power in a marriage, for society gave men the lion's share of authority in the North and the South. This was certainly true of a man who had been a military officer, a captain who was "born to command" and whose family nickname became "the Commander." In her admiration for this quality Abbie sounded much like young southerner Ella Gertrude Clanton Thomas, who praised her husband in 1855 for having "just such a master will as suits my woman's nature." On the other hand, the young Mrs. Christensen felt ambiguous and expressed her feelings only in "the strictest confidence." While Niels's masculine demeanor may have given Abbie a small thrill, she made certain that she got her "share of the management of things" and retained her autonomy within the marriage.[34]

Niels's finest and enduring quality was his sense of humor, which lightened their days together. For example, Abbie told Emma that in their parlor was "a bust of Shakespeare to which Niels always refers as authority for any preposterous slang!" Niels's playfulness was evident in elaborate notes in which he addressed her as "Goosie." In their letters the couple adopted the custom of addressing each other in Danish as "din kyere husbunde" and "Dein lille Kone." Abbie went from great fear to making her peace with marriage.[35]

At home in Beaufort matrimony enabled Abbie to have her own household with all the trappings of middle-class, Victorian domesticity. In a letter to Emma, Abbie described her surroundings. First in importance was the parlor, the showpiece of middle-class homes where the couple spent their evenings by the fireplace. The parlor contained a profusion of objects with sentimental attachments—a photograph of Abbie's mother, a basket from Abbie's sister, and a stuffed incarnation of the peacock that had brought the Christensens together. A landscape painting, the bust of Shakespeare, and "books lying about" testified to the couple's educated and cultured status. Outside the parlor the objects of greatest sentimental and status value were the pieces of silverware Abbie had inherited from her mother. These were the material contours of Abbie's private indoor life.[36]

Publicly, Abbie's life continued as it had before, with the added benefit of respectability that her married status gave her. Besides taking care of her household, Abbie maintained her membership in the Round-About Club, a mixed-sex social and literary society; attended church; and occasionally collected charity for the "motherless." She also continued her work as an author of black folktales.[37]

Business, Politics, and Race

Because her time was occupied with childbearing approximately every two years from 1876 to 1887, and because women were largely excluded from party politics, Abbie was primarily an observer in the public male world of politics and economics at this time in her life. Abbie attended a Beaufort campaign meeting in 1876 and maintained contact with the political world by reading newspapers and magazines. She also participated in symbolic ways, such as hanging out the American flag to celebrate the inauguration of Republican James Garfield in 1880.[38]

A year after their marriage, Niels turned his commercial skills to the founding of a hardware store and lumberyard in the town of Beaufort. In 1878 he was relieved of his duties at the cemetery because he and Abbie refused to live on the cemetery grounds, which they considered unhealthy. As well as running his hardware store, Christensen became deeply involved in the real estate business, buying land at low prices at tax sales and selling it, mostly in small parcels, to African American families. Finally, Niels also became a general contractor, using his access to land and wholesale building materials to his best advantage. Niels commented to Abbie about the state of the economy and his business. "Business in Beaufort dull, Hotel depleted, [phosphate] mines closed, cotton prices low, prices on everything else going up, no money and plenty of debt on my hand," he wrote her in 1879. Not surprisingly, Niels's chief difficulty was collecting money owed him. He expressed this problem in terms that defied racist stereotypes: "the white are as bad as the colored, could I collect from the white that are considered good all that there is coming me I would feel easier."[39]

Despite his complaints, Niels's real estate and lumber businesses prospered, and by 1881 he was able to buy one of the finest antebellum homes in Beaufort, a large, white, columned mansion on the river in the genteel area known as "the Point." A large natural area surrounding the house gave Niels the opportunity to design a garden with a huge variety of flowers, shrubs, and trees. Undoubtedly this "dream" home did much to anchor Niels to Beaufort. In 1885 an unnamed Beaufort resident described Niels Christensen as "a wealthy, prominent and enterprising merchant" who had "the sympathy of all classes of people."[40]

"All classes of people" probably meant all races as much as all income levels. Race was a constant topic of discussion in Beaufort in 1876–88. Because of its large black majority, Beaufort County remained a political anomaly when South Carolina restored white supremacy at the state level in 1876. Black Beaufort Republicans were threatened during the election that year. However, they held on to most offices and shared others with Republican and Democratic whites in an arrangement known as "fusion" through the 1880s. Large numbers of black voters were a key factor in Beaufort's difference from other areas of the South. The town of Beaufort, which had a population of 1,739 in 1870 and 2,549 in 1880, was variously represented as being from two-thirds to nine-tenths African American. Beaufort County's black majority stood at around 90 percent during these years.[41]

Robert Smalls remained the most prominent black political leader in Beaufort, but he was under constant attack from white Democrats beginning in 1876. In 1877 the Democrats set out to prove that there had been corruption among Republican legislators in previous sessions. Smalls was a prime target. Based on the testimony of a clerk who was given immunity from prosecution, Smalls was charged with taking a bribe to vote for an appropriation to the Republican Printing Company. Smalls was convicted but was later pardoned by Governor Hampton in a deal designed to obtain freedom for white men charged with election fraud and violence. Even his enemies conceded that the evidence against him was slim, but Smalls's reputation was permanently damaged. Moreover, his effectiveness as a legislator was hampered by the fact that he spent a good deal of his time fighting vote count challenges by Democrats and proving that his Democratic opponents had used fraud. From 1876 to 1882 Beaufort County was part of the Fifth Congressional District, which included Edgefield, Barnwell, and Aiken counties, where whites were the majority. In those areas Robert Smalls and his black Republican followers faced violence at the hands of the followers of his white Democratic rival, George Tillman, whose brother would later be governor of South Carolina. In 1878 and 1880 Tillman took the congressional seat despite well-substantiated charges of voter fraud, until the Republican Congress of 1880 finally seated Smalls in 1882.[42]

The fact that Niels, a Republican, was chosen by Wade Hampton, a Democrat, as commissioner of elections for Beaufort County in 1878 may have meant that he was trusted to be fair, as his son later recalled, but missionary teacher Laura Towne was outraged by his doings. She mistook him for a Democrat and wrote that he had appointed Democratic managers at polling places throughout the county, including a notoriously cruel former slaveholder on Saint Helena Island. In that same election campaign Towne wrote that the Democrats arrested black county commissioners for not maintaining the roads properly and intimidated African American Renty Greaves into resigning from the board of jury commissioners. In Gillisonville, a town on the mainland outside of Beaufort County, eight hundred Red Shirts surrounded a meeting of Robert Smalls and other African Americans and shot at them when they retreated. There is no evidence that Niels Christensen either approved of or condemned these Democratic actions, and in the end the African American voters in Beaufort County elected three black Republicans to the state legislature. Elections were quiet and fair on Saint Helena Island, where black committees monitored the proceedings of the Democratic election managers. In many South Carolina counties other than Beaufort, Red Shirts, rifle clubs, and fraud made election results invalid in 1878.[43]

In the decade that followed, Beaufort alternated between Republican and Democratic representation in the state legislature and other offices. White Democrats had gained enough strength and there was enough disunity among the embattled Republicans in 1886 to elect William Elliott, the first white Democrat to serve since Reconstruction. In 1888 Beaufort politicians struck a compromise, putting together a fusion slate of white Democrats and black and white Republicans that stayed together until 1895. Beaufort County was constantly at odds with the Democratic government of the state, particularly after the 1890 gubernatorial election of Democrat Benjamin Tillman, who referred to the county derisively as a "niggerdom."[44]

During the latter part of the 1880s Niels Christensen took part in Beaufort politics, serving on the town council and briefly filling in as intendant (mayor). Niels was a Republican reformer who saw himself as an independent fighter for "clean government." He was wary of Robert Smalls after his 1877 conviction for bribery, but he was critical of white officeholders as well as blacks. In 1884, Niels denounced "the suppression of a free ballot in the South" by white Democrats whe helped elect President Grover Cleveland.[45]

Niels commented on competition between blacks and whites within the Republican Party, but this was not the only kind of factionalism Beaufort faced. In 1879 he complained to Abbie that "Wheeler, Smalls and that gang hates white people and don't want whites to hold office or give them employment of any kind." Like all other ethnic groups in the United States, African Americans expected their officeholders to favor them in patronage posts. The white minority, on the other hand, expected the lion's share of government jobs because of what they perceived as their superior qualifications. Competition between reform and regular Republicans did not break down on racial lines. Instead, black reformers such as Julius I. Washington joined whites such as Christensen in opposing "ring rule." In 1889 Niels Christensen joined whites and blacks who signed petitions opposing Smalls's appointment as collector of the Port of Beaufort. Smalls, however, persevered in gaining this appointment and performing his duties for nearly twenty years. Though Smalls and Christensen were often at odds, the two powerful men were relaxed enough to exchange pleasantries and even jokes on occasion.[46]

During his involvement with local politics, Niels was also concerned with protecting women from abuse. When Amelia Sanchez, the Christensens' cook, took a man to court for trying to choke her, Niels wrote of his fear that "being before a Democrat she probably will get the worst of it." Christensen worried that the judge would be unsympathetic to a black woman. When Niels served as acting Intendant, he showed solidarity with women by imposing high fines on men who beat their wives. In that year he criticized the former Intendant, a Republican, for being lenient in order to win votes.[47]

Within the regional and racial politics of Beaufort, Niels Christensen made friends with several white southerners, including Democrats. Christensen demonstrated his respect for his former Confederate enemies by improving the gravesite of a Beaufort general who had fought against him at Gettysburg. Nevertheless, Christensen never went so far in reunion as to forget the principles of freedom and universal suffrage for which he had fought.[48]

Niels most clearly articulated his philosophy in an article he wrote titled "The Sea Islands and Negro Supremacy." This passionate and fact-filled essay refuted racist statements by the Reverend Dr. Charles Cotesworth Pinckney of Charleston, grandnephew of his namesake, the early American diplomat and signer of the Constitution of the United States. Christensen wrote in response to a lecture by Pinckney titled "Our Blighted Sea Islands." The former captain of colored troops argued against Pinckney's claims that blacks were reverting to a state of "barbarism." He also took issue with an article by Wade Hampton, then a United States senator, that expressed "doleful views with reference to the political status of the colored race in general." Niels quoted extensively from the 1880 census showing an increase in the majority black population of Beaufort County and the large amounts of crops grown and taxes paid. He stated emphatically that most blacks in Beaufort were home owners, taxpayers, and contributing members in churches, schools, and charitable associations. Christensen wrote: "To maintain under these circumstances that the negroes are 'Retrogressing toward the worst phase of African life' is to contend that they are morally and mentally incapable of improvement, and that in the State of Slavery alone was there hopes, and in it the means that pointed to their elevation. The Falsity of the premises is made clear by the deduction that necessarily impresses itself upon the mind as a result that follows a thoughtful perusal of the figures herein produced from official records." Christensen sometimes criticized individual black politicians who might be corrupt, but he found them no worse than white politicians. Though he decried the "dirty business" of politics in general and urged African Americans to concentrate on commercial business (as he did), he praised Beaufort's black sheriff, school commissioner, and coroner. "The Sea Islands and Negro Supremacy" makes it clear that Niels Christensen Sr. defended the rights of African Americans to vote and hold office.[49]

Niels and Abbie discussed the racial and political situation of the 1880s and 1890s at home and in their correspondence. Abbie was even less willing to accept white southern racism than her husband was. For example, her husband joined other Beaufort residents in promoting white Democrat William Elliott as a circuit judge. Abbie disagreed and censured Elliott for unjustly "starting the report of a riot among the colored people." Still the couple was united in opposing the violent white supremacist tactics of the 1890s. "I return you the clipping 'Brute Rule in the South' which is a strictly correct statement of the *Denmark affair with Tillman's part in it,*" Niels wrote to Abbie in 1893. A black man accused of attempted rape had been hanged and shot by a mob of "unknown parties" in Denmark, a small South Carolina town. Governor Tillman had written a letter to the state senator from Denmark's district, expressing his hope that the accused would be lynched before the law intervened. Less than a year earlier Tillman had announced, "Governor as I am, I would lead a mob to lynch the negro that ravishes a white woman." Niels wrote to his wife, "I am sorry that the name of my native country should have been given to such a disreputable burough." By marrying Niels Christensen, Abbie Holmes gained a partner who shared her abolitionist ideals and spoke out publically for black rights.[50]

Motherhood

From 1876 to 1888 Abbie remained aware of politics, but her scanty diary entries from these years revolve around the fact that she bore six children, and caring for these babies and toddlers was her chief occupation. Abbie became pregnant in the first year of her marriage and gave birth to Niels Christensen Jr. in April 1876. The birth of her child was a mixture of joy and anxiety as she waited for his first cry. Christensen wrote that when she heard it, she "deeply felt that the child would grow and be a loving and faithful servant of his mother's God." In the diary she began a month after her son's birth, the child assumed primacy and she referred to herself in the third person. Perhaps Abbie was trying to distance herself from the intensity of her first experience of motherhood, or perhaps she considered this diary more public than her earlier volumes. In her later diaries, when she had more children, she resumed a more confident and comfortable first-person narrative.[51]

Both Niels and Abbie took part in decisions regarding their first child, but Abbie had the last word when there was a conflict. In the nineteenth century young children, especially infants, were seen as the province of mothers, so it was not entirely unusual that Abbie would win out. Their first conflict occurred over the treatment that six-week-old "Nielie" should receive when he had a cold. Abbie tried homeopathic remedies, but Niels Sr. wanted to take his son to a conventional physician. Abbie refused, and when he seemed better the next day, she congratulated herself that she had "persevered" with her homeopathy. Other than this incident, Abbie recorded few disagreements. Later she wrote that having children was good for her marriage, since care for their child had made both parents "grow thoughtful and unselfish."[52]

Niels Jr., Frederik, and James

Abbie's responsibilities multiplied with the birth of Frederik ("Fred" or "Fritz") Holmes Christensen in 1877 and James ("Jamie") Winch Christensen in 1880. With much of the drudgery of housework taken care of by servants, Abbie could concentrate on the education of her young children. Despite the fact that she had never received any formal training as a teacher, Abbie Christensen showed great interest in the theories of early childhood development and began her children's education when they were young. In 1881 Christensen set up a kindergarten for her two oldest boys, who were four and five years old. "Tis surprising how much can be learned from the 1st gift of 6 worsted balls," she wrote. Inspired by the ideas of German educator Friedrich Froebel, the kindergarten movement had begun in the United States in the 1850s. Though it had caught on in the urban areas of the North, kindergartens were rarer in the South, and Abbie forged ahead alone when teaching her sons. She would continue her interest in early childhood education when she set up a Montessori school for her grandchildren in the 1910s.[53] Abbie's belief in gender equality was evident in her choice of toys. Christensen wrote that on a shopping trip with her boys, "Freddie teased so hard for a doll that I got them both a doll at Odells." She asked, "Why shouldn't we cultivate the *fatherly* instinct in boys as well as the *motherly* ditto in girls?" Abbie's move was unconventional, but her view was shared by a leading advocate for gender equality, Frances Willard, president of the Woman's Christian Temperance Union.[54]

Christensen looked to her children's spiritual education and frequently quoted the youngsters' voices in their questions regarding God. "What is God doing now?," Fritz asked after he had gone to bed. Little Niels asked even more difficult questions. When Abbie read her children the biblical story of Joseph and his jealous brothers who sold him into slavery, Nielie asked, "What made Joseph's brothers be so bad?" Even when she stayed home alone one Sunday, Christensen heard Christ's words "Lovest thou me? Feed my lambs" ringing in her ears. "And with these words Jesus gives to all parents—as to St. Peter—the keys of Heaven and Hell," she wrote. It was an enormous responsibility.[55]

As a nineteenth-century father, Niels's primary responsibility was working outside the home and supporting his family. "Papa has to be down in the lumber yard and sell lumber," he wrote his sons when they wanted him to come north in 1879. Still, his letters to his children indicate an active interest in their doings, a sense of humor and playfulness, and an attempt to support Abbie in admonishing them to improve themselves in their studies and their relationships with one another.[56]

Niels Jr., the eldest, excelled in school, and Abbie pinned great hopes on her son. "You have the capacity to grow to be a good scholar and a good man, for God has given you a good head and a good heart, that you may fit yourself for your part in His world's work," she wrote him. While he was in boarding school in 1888, Abbie wanted to know all the details of his life. "Are you doing well this week in your lessons? Your music? and especially in the company you keep?" Christensen quizzed her son. She also gave him spiritual advice she hoped he would internalize: "Love the teachings of God's love for my sake because your mother before you, and her mother before her, found their greatest help and comfort there, and by and by you too will find them just as much to you."[57]

In contrast to Niels Jr., Fred was less of a scholar, but he was a hard worker with a greater sense of humor and humility. Fred's left arm was injured or congenitally weaker than it should have been, and Abbie fretted over his health. Nevertheless, he was a calm and obedient child. "You are a good boy," Abbie wrote him when he was twenty years old, "and I am proud of you, 'sof' heart,' level head, self-denial, clear grit, and your other noble traits." Christensen credited her second son with having more of "the sterling qualities of your father" than any of her other children, but she pushed him to cultivate a "greater reverence for the sacred."[58]

Jamie seems to have been the darling of both his parents, but he only lived to the age of five. Their memories of his sweetness were surely romanticized after Jamie died of diphtheria on 13 October 1885. Jamie's aspirations to be a soldier made him especially dear to his father, and mourners at Jamie's funeral sought to comfort Niels Christensen by burying his son at the National Cemetery. Niels planted flowers at the grave and watched the spot with "tender care." In the years that followed, the ways in which each parent dealt with sorrow over their son's loss pushed them apart. Niels wished to remain near Jamie's grave, while Abbie wanted to move north.[59]

A Choice between North and South

Unlike her immigrant husband, who was happy to find a new home and community in Beaufort, Abbie missed her New England friends and family. She responded to the loss of her son by clinging more closely to Addie Barrows, "a mental healer," whom she had met when she visited Boston earlier in 1885. Abbie considered Addie her "most devoted and true friend" and desired to move the entire family to Massachusetts within reach of Barrows's constant care. The Barrowses practiced "mind cure," a form of healing that resembled Christian Science. Barrows's husband explained that he and his wife harnessed the placebo effect apparent in experiments with "bread pills." In the Barrowses' version of mind cure, the healer and the patient cured disease through concentrated positive thinking. Abbie easily added this method to her practice of homeopathy, seeing both as a better alternative to conventional medicine. Barrows did not charge for her services, but she depended on Abbie and other patients for gifts of room and board. Her husband, Charles Barrows, assisted her and wrote about her cures. Niels, who was skeptical of mind cure, thought that the Barrowses were taking advantage of Abbie. When Abbie admonished her husband for not assisting his son Freddie with positive thoughts, Niels retorted that Abbie was "a little cranky." When his wife and children were in the North, Niels also wrote that he was "familysick," "pining away," and "forsaken."[60]

Conflict over the Barrowses turned into a conflict over where to live. Abbie undoubtedly felt more at home with New Englanders who shared her intellectual and spiritual interests in reform and women's rights, but the reasons she gave publicly were that she wanted her children to receive a bet-ter education. Niels, on the other hand, found friendship and success in Beaufort. He preferred not to leave.

Abbie resolved the situation by living in Massachusetts, apart from her husband, for extended periods of time. Her disagreement with Niels would not have carried much weight if she had not had the economic power to carry out a move to the North. In September 1882 Abbie's uncle, Alden Winch, died and passed on cash and assets worth over seventeen thousand dollars to Abbie, along with an equally large sum for her sister Georgie. Winch had been director of the American News Company of New York, and Abbie received a sizable share of stocks in this company. This inheritance gave Abbie power in her marriage and in her community. Abbie lent twelve thousand dollars to her husband, keeping some cash and stocks and buying property in Beaufort for herself. In 1887 Niels deeded their stately Beaufort home to his wife, possibly in repayment for his debt. For the rest of her years Abbie Christensen was able to manage her investments shrewdly to provide her with substantial independence.[61]

In this respect Christensen was unlike the average nineteenth-century married woman; most wives were completely dependent upon their husbands' income. Abbie Holmes Christensen was the beneficiary of a law granting mar-ried women's property rights in the 1868 South Carolina Constitution. Abbie's father, R. G. Holmes, and others had passed this law to prevent scoundrels from marrying women and squandering all their property, and also to protect families from creditors who seized married women's property to pay their husbands' debts. Although the law gave her some power, Niels's ability to maintain their Beaufort household and his respect for her right to use her property as she saw fit were just as important in securing her inde-pendence.[62]

In 1888 Abbie came close to convincing Niels to trade his hardware store for a house in the North, but he was hesitant, and the deal fell through. Abbie was prepared to sacrifice servants and other aspects of their "extrava-gant outlay" in the South, even the presumption that her husband would sup-port her. She wanted her children to grow up with northern, not southern, influences. Abbie wrote: "Let *me* buy a home here with my own money and I will promise to live on $100.00 per month. . . . I think I can be strong enough in this climate to do my own work if I can not afford help . . . I wish my income would allow you to give up business altogether, I would be only too glad to support you if I could." Abbie's bold offer went completely against nineteenth-century gender expectations, and Niels's pride would not allow him to take it. He did not want to move to a place where he was unknown and his livelihood was uncertain. As a result, the Christensens established what today would be called a "commuter marriage." From 1886 to 1888, from 1890 to 1897, and from 1900 to 1902 Abbie used her inheritance to live in Boston part of the time. Reversing the usual coastal South Carolina pattern of leaving the swampy area during the fever days of summer, Abbie and her children resided in the North during the fall and winter months of the school year.[63]

Although it caused them considerable pain, the couple's willingness to disagree but live with a compromise can be seen as a sign of strength and equality in the marriage. The fact that Abbie persisted in pursuing paths that her husband opposed showed her tenacity and strong sense of self. It would not have been remarkable if a wife sacrificed elements of her happiness for the sake of her husband, but for a husband to do so for a wife was unusual. Though they were often apart, in their correspondence the couple sent one another kisses, affection, and "a great deal of love."[64]

Arthur, Andrea, and Winnie

Because the care and education of children was expensive, many urban middle-class families began to restrict their family size in the late nineteenth century. The Christensens were undeterred and seemed to welcome their large brood. After Jamie, Abbie had three more children: Arthur Olaf in 1882, Andrea Rebecca in 1884, and Abby Winch ("Winnie") in 1887.[65] Jamie's death and Abbie's decision to live in the North thereafter adversely affected Abbie's "difficult" son, Arthur Olaf, or "AOC," who was three at the time of his brother's death. Arthur was gifted athletically and in mathematics and science. While he had a great capacity for love and loyalty, he had difficulty getting along with others. Abbie wrote that he possessed both her and her husband's worst traits, with stubbornness chief among them. The son's relationship with his mother began inauspiciously when his birth in 1882 interrupted her negotiations with a potential publisher of her collection of folktales. Abbie seemed to resent his arrival and may have treated him differently from the start. After Jamie died, both parents were depressed and must have had difficulty responding to Arthur's needs. Jamie's death also robbed

Arthur of his closest playmate. Family legend has it that Abbie asked God for two matched sets of boys and one set of girls so that each child would have a companion. When Jamie died, Arthur became the odd child, not fitting with either pair of siblings. He later recalled that he fought with his youngest sister, Winnie, for the attention of Andrea, who was closest to him in age.[66]

Lost in the middle of this relatively large family, Arthur drew attention chiefly through his misbehavior. "What he will do next is a constant problem," Abbie wrote to her husband in 1888, relating that six-year-old Arthur had poured ten empty cartridges from a revolver into a saucer next to his breakfast plate. Abbie seems to have attached some of her frustrations with her husband onto Arthur. She wrote that Arthur "appreciates just treatment" but "*never* remembers a kindness." Because he was separated from his father from the time he was six or seven years old, Arthur also missed the attention and understanding he might have received from Niels, to whom he was a "beloved" son.[67]

Abbie's eldest daughter, Andrea, was considered to be the child most like her mother in appearance and personality. A close friend of the family described Andrea to Abbie as "the most sensitive child you have. . . . She has a delicate, spiritual organization." Intelligent and artistic, Andrea excelled in school and extracurricular activities such as drama, art, and volunteer work through the Unitarian Lend A Hand Club. Abbie's older daughter looked to her mother for guidance in religion, manners, and health and later gave advice of her own. Mother and daughter remained close all their lives.[68]

Winnie, or "Winsome," Abbie's youngest child, grew up to be an adventurous woman who remained single and became a companion to her mother in her old age. Perhaps because she was the youngest, she received less scrutiny than Abbie's other children. Her aunt Georgie described Winsome as a "sweet-tempered child." Highly intelligent, but less introspective than Andrea, the youngest Christensen was nevertheless her sister's constant companion in childhood, and they were known collectively as "the little girls."[69]

What kind of mother was Abbie Holmes Christensen? Her writings and those of her children indicate that she was attentive, conscientious, loving, and firm but somewhat prone to favoritism. She seems to have fulfilled the standards she set for herself to provide her children with the best environment, education, and moral guidance that she could. It is unfair, however, to judge her by the way her children "turned out," because their individual personalities and societal influences beyond Christensen's control were also crucial in shaping her children's lives.[70]

Because of their varied personalities, Christensen had a different sort of relationship with each of her offspring as they grew and developed. With all of them, however, she was an involved and sometimes overprotective parent. Her extensive correspondence with her children indicates that she entered into and enjoyed their world, commenting in detail on their pets and games. Abbie was also a strict disciplinarian, but she used a variety of rewards and punishments, such as giving presents and withholding privileges. Christensen was similar to other nineteenth-century middle-class mothers who were moving from force to persuasion in child-rearing methods but who still relied to some extent on corporal punishment. Her children seemed happy with her as a mother, except Arthur, the son with whom she constantly sparred.[71]

Abbie Christensen saw herself as a wife, a mother, and a homemaker, but she did not act through her husband or her adult children; they were not her puppets. For example, Arthur disagreed with Abbie on almost every issue, and Winnie was often neutral. Christensen encouraged and admonished her children, making sacrifices for what she saw as in their best interests. Not only her parenting style, but her choice of location had an impact on her children. Abbie's decision to raise her children in the North and the South kept them from developing into true southerners, but they all identified with the South more than their parents did. After she became a mother, Abbie Christensen's life was intertwined with the lives of her children. When they were young they limited her public work, but as they grew older they could expand her field of influence, though not always in ways she could control.[72]

Servants

Like most middle-class white women in the South, Abbie was able to concentrate on her children's moral guidance and education because African American servants took on many of the mundane burdens of child care and household work. A baby nurse named Nancy who had cared for Alma and Lottie, Abbie's half sisters, came into the Christensen household in 1876 to "help take care of Nielie." After the birth of Freddie and Jamie, Abbie's reliance on Nancy was even greater. As her husband's wealth increased and her family grew larger, an ever-increasing number of black servants cooked, cleaned, and maintained the gardens and grounds of the house on the Point. In choosing her workers, Christensen was most concerned with their ability to get along with her children. Cooking skill ranked a close second.[73]

Abbie's high standards of housekeeping must have kept her servants busy, but her letters to them do not indicate conflict over this issue. Christensen's demands for cleanliness probably derived in part from her experience of her mother's housekeeping and in part from her keen interest in matters of health. "Keep everything sweet and clean about the house, especially in the basement, for the house can't be healthy unless you do," she wrote her housekeeper in a four-page letter of instructions in 1888.[74]

A sense of class and racial distinction characterized Abbie's relationships with her servants. Christensen treated educated, middle-class African Americans differently than she did her cooks and nurses, whom she saw as being of a lower class. She had learned this paternalism from her parents, whom she observed in their dealings with white servants in the North and black domestics in the South. Abbie had had an Irish nurse when she was a small child, but she had become accustomed to African American servants while living in the South.

Perhaps the chief and most dehumanizing aspect of the servant-mistress relationship was the invisibility of domestic workers. Although she was probably present every day, Abbie only wrote of Nancy when a Christensen child was involved in a crisis. Nancy left Nielie in his carriage for a moment to open the door, and the carriage slid down the steps and turned over. Nielie was saved from injury by a patent carriage strap (a kind of seat belt) that his mother had bought for just such an instance. Abbie did not seem to blame Nancy. Neither did she see her as being as important as herself in insuring her child's safety. In Abbie's 1881 diary Amelia Sanchez, her cook, was conspicuous only by her absence when she had to attend to a family emergency. In family photographs servants such as Amelia and Nancy sometimes appear as whole human beings, but at other times one or the other is represented by a black arm or a lap, while the white child is the focus of the photograph. Niels expressed this same partial representation when he wrote that his son Fred would only look at his grandfather "from behind Nancy's dress or a chair." While Abbie Christensen's later correspondence reveals a closer relationship with African American servants such as Mona Brown, a cook in the household for over ten years, Abbie usually left them out of her daily recollections in the 1880s.[75]

In the late nineteenth century many African American servants "lived in" with their southern employers, and this was true of the Christensen household as well. Nancy and Amelia had to give up much of their own family life in order to serve their "white family." The extent of this sacrifice usually was not a great concern for their employers. Abbie excused Amelia from service for at least a day because Amelia's "sister-in-law Clara Sanchez was dead and she must go to lay her out & take charge of the four little children." Christensen showed concern for Amelia's nieces and nephews, offering them some old clothing, but it was up to Amelia to find homes for the children so that she could continue to live with the Christensens. Cook Mona Brown's daughter, Victoria, rarely saw her mother during the years when she was a child. Victoria resided on Saint Helena Island with her aunt, while her mother lived at the Christensens' seven days a week. As soon as they could, African American women gave up this kind of arrangement in favor of working days and at least spending their nights with their own families, but they did not have this option in Christensen's time.[76]

Although Abbie saw her lifework as "teaching children and servants," the black workers who toiled in her home did a share of teaching themselves. African American servants' influence on the Christensen children could be heard in the children's distinctly southern grammar in their early years. These women and men relieved Abbie's burdens and enabled her to take on public work as a writer and reformer. Still they remain, largely without last names, almost totally invisible and unknown.[77]

Writer

As busy as she was with her large family and her moves south and north, Christensen had not lost her interest in and ambition for writing. When this ambition conflicted with her responsibilities as a mother, Christensen chose motherhood and privately and publically stated that she was happy to do so. Still, a twinge of ambiguity and even regret can be detected in her statements as to the way this conflict played out.

In the late 1870s and early 1880s Christensen gathered more African American animal stories, and one of the editors encouraged her to publish them in book form "before some one else should bring one out." She planned in the spring of 1882 to produce a book by the fall, but, as she later wrote, she was "prevented by the coming of my fourth son" during negotiations with her publisher.[78]

The reason for her prolonged negotiations with the publisher, D. Lothrop & Co., seems to have been the high cost of the firm's work. In July 1883 the publishers wrote that they would charge one dollar per electroplate of each page of the book. Since she was not willing to pay this price, they returned the manuscript she had sent them. Perhaps she could have tried again, but the care of her small children must have seemed a more pressing concern than the search for a publisher within Christensen's means.[79]

Later in life Christensen regretted her missed opportunity and made oblique reference to the inequality of the sexual division of labor that favored the public productivity of men. She wrote: "Being now a married woman, busy and happy with husband, home and three little sons, [publishing a book] was difficult for me to manage and my negotiations with a Boston publisher were interrupted by the advent of a fourth son. About that time Mr. Harris published his first volume of negro tales, and captured the market."[80]

After Joel Chandler Harris published two books of Uncle Remus's animal tales in the early 1880s, Christensen's work would always be in Harris's shadow. Christensen's dilemma was similar to that of many other nineteenth- and twentieth-century women. As long as the gendered division of labor placed men in the role of provider and women in the role of caretaker of the home, it would be difficult for a woman who was a wife and mother also to be a public woman.

Although Christensen did not say so explicitly, perhaps her burgeoning interest in the women's rights movement was kindled in part by the handi- caps she faced as a woman writer. But other sparks from an abolitionist back- ground and her woman-centered education also ignited this flame of reform. As a wife, mother, homemaker, and writer, Abbie Christensen entered into the public world of women's associations.

Chapter Seven

MY KNOT OF WHITE & YELLOW RIBBON: TEMPERANCE AND SUFFRAGE

On 4 July 1892 Abbie Christensen wrote a letter to her two oldest sons:

> I've forgotten something I want very much. What do you think it is? Just as Arthur broke the little table I had dropped my knot of white & yellow ribbon & I forgot to pick it up. Fancy how I feel up here among strangers without my declaration of independence on a 4th of July! Cant you send it to me by return mail?

What was this "knot of white & yellow ribbon" that Abbie Holmes Christensen called her "declaration of independence"? Christensen's white ribbon was the symbol of the Woman's Christian Temperance Union (WCTU), the largest women's organization of the day and a growing force against alcohol abuse. Her yellow ribbon was the symbol of the National American Womans Suffrage Association (NAWSA), a smaller but crucial movement that promoted votes for women and recognition of their other rights as citizens. Abbie's responsibilities as a mother made her want to make a better world for her children, but her duties also placed limits on her public work. The story of Christensen's temperance and suffrage activity shows that her public and private life were intertwined as tightly as her knot of white and yellow ribbon.[1]

Christensen's participation also reveals aspects of regional relations within the temperance and suffrage movements. Abbie joined branches of the NAWSA in the North and the South, befriending important leaders in both sections. In this way she was part of the process of regional reconciliation among white women. Christensen's moves between the North and the South offered her different opportunities to pursue political activism. In the South, Abbie lived with her husband, her children, and an array of African American servants, but in the North she kept house alone with her children or with boarders and one white servant. As a consequence, Abbie had more leisure time to pursue her political interests in South Carolina. In Boston in the

1880s and 1890s Christensen was surrounded by like-minded women in several thriving reform organizations. One of these women, the venerable suffrage leader Lucy Stone, realized that Christensen could be important in South Carolina, where suffragists were few. Abbie's contact with both regions made her part of a national suffrage strategy, but her efforts in South Carolina bore little fruit. South Carolina's conservative resistance to changes in social relations was certainly as much to blame as Christensen's outsider status.

This conservatism had its roots in antebellum times when the subject of women's rights was taboo because of its association with abolition. After the Civil War, abolition of slavery was no longer an issue. Many middle- and upper-class southern women shed their isolation as their lives began to resemble those of their northern sisters. More of them moved to towns and cities and joined in women's voluntary associations—mostly church societies, but also the national WCTU. Through the WCTU woman suffrage began to gain a foothold in the South in the 1880s. As a supporter who continually crossed the Mason-Dixon line, Christensen facilitated the 1880s process of reunion between the sections of women reformers.[2]

Christensen's participation also points out the racism in the temperance and suffrage movements, a racism that was in keeping with the times. Abbie's entry into interest-group politics in the 1890s coincided with the nadir of race relations in the United States, when segregation of blacks and whites became accepted legal practice as well as custom in the South and much of the rest of the nation. In 1890 South Carolinians elected as governor one of the nation's most extreme white supremacist politicians, Benjamin Tillman. Although he was a wealthy landowner, Tillman posed as the representative of average white farmers and the defender of white women against "savage" African Americans. Tillman bragged about his role in a white riot in Hamburg, South Carolina, where at least five African Americans were killed in cold blood during the 1876 Red Shirt campaign. As governor, his major accomplishment was an 1895 constitutional convention that disfranchised African Americans through a complex system of poll taxes, primaries, and registration procedures controlled by white Democrats. Not surprisingly, given the racist animus generated by Tillman's demagoguery, frequent news of lynchings haunted African Americans beginning in 1889. From 1881 to 1940, 170 blacks were lynched in South Carolina. A third of those lynchings took place in the 1890s. When Abbie Christensen joined the WCTU and suffrage movements, their attitudes mirrored the national mood on race.

The WCTU slighted black women members and refused to take a stand against lynching, while the NAWSA actively tried to keep African Americans away. Like many others, Christensen was silent on black suffrage, although she attended a protest meeting against lynching in 1894 in the North. In that year journalist Ida B. Wells found evidence of 134 lynchings of African Americans throughout the nation. White women's silence on race was a logical but unjust position in a nation bent on complete white supremacy.[3]

Like many American women, Abbie entered civic life through her church. Religion was an acceptable social arena for nineteenth-century middle-class women and one to which they were seen as uniquely suited because of their emotional nature and sheltered position away from the evils of the marketplace. As it had done at Mount Holyoke, Abbie's religion gave her a mission and a place to exercise it, first through an interdenominational Protestant church in Beaufort and later through the Unitarian Church of the Disciples in Boston. The latter church connected her with others in the temperance and suffrage movements.

In addition to drawing strength from these churches, Abbie was also emboldened by her belief in the mind-cure movement and its denial of material obstacles. This thinking gave her confidence even when the odds were against her, especially in suffrage work in the South. "No one approves your course—everyone deems you unwise even cranky," Christensen wrote in 1895. When she felt isolated, Christensen relied on her faith in the Divine Power to sustain her. Abbie's devotion to "the progress of mankind" came from a combination of transcendentalism and spiritualism that met in the branch of the Unitarian church to which she became affiliated. Christensen's spiritual beliefs strengthened her will to devote resources, time, and energy to increasingly public causes, most notably temperance and suffrage.[4]

A Union Church

Abbie Christensen entered the public world of community building in 1883 when she tried to found a nondenominational "Union church" in Beaufort. The movement for a Union church was led by H. G. Judd and John Conant, two white northerners who were old acquaintances of Abbie. Sidie Wallace and his wife, Cuta, were also among the founding members, an indication that perhaps Sidie had become a Christian after all. Through this church Christensen sought to obtain the northern theological and political influence she desired for herself, her children, and her community. The idea for a Union church grew out of the services Abbie had attended as a child. As she later wrote, "Mr. Conant had been one of the leaders in simple services held by the dissenters, as they might be called, held for nearly all the years since the Union Army first appeared in Beaufort." Abbie sought advice on establishing this church from missionary teacher Elizabeth Botume and her Brookline congregation, the Unitarian Church of the Disciples.[5]

After the end of the Civil War, Abbie had attended interracial services at a Beaufort Baptist church, but white and black congregations had since separated, and the Christensens did not feel comfortable at the predominantly southern white Episcopal and Baptist churches. It seems that the family did not consider joining an all-black church or attending one full-time, as missionary teachers Laura Towne and Ellen Murray did on Saint Helena Island. The Christensens identified more with the other white northerners in Beaufort, while Towne and Murray, who were practically the only northern whites on Saint Helena, identified with the black community. Black congregations went their own way because of white prejudice toward blacks and because of African Americans' desire to form autonomous religious institutions. This separation marked a gradually widening social distance between whites and blacks in Beaufort.[6]

For white and black women new churches functioned as quasi-public spaces, where they learned how to form associations and practice protopolitical procedures such as establishing a quorum and voting. Christensen gained this experience when she and other Yankee women formed a Ladies Aid Society and raised $150 to furnish the interior of the church. Christensen had charge of the carpet and chairs, and she spent several months corresponding with merchants. With a carpet from Augusta, Georgia, and chairs from Boston and Cincinnati, its furnishings certainly symbolized a "Union" church.[7]

With her 1882 inheritance Abbie quietly purchased and donated a lot on Carteret Street where the church could be built. Niels Christensen was appointed contractor, and the building went forward in 1884. A surprise announcement by Conant and Judd that the church was to be Presbyterian sent the organizers into a tumult. On a moonlit night they held a meeting to decide what to do. As Abbie recalled: "A number of speeches were made but none of them announced anything definite. Finally, Mr. James Crofut rose and asked the question, 'Who is the owner of the lot?' Mr. Clark replied, 'Mrs. Christensen has purchased the lot on which the building is being erected.' Mr. Crofut replied, 'Well the question is settled then.'" For a time Abbie's choice of an interdenominational church prevailed, and in all likelihood she was the "Congregationalist woman" appointed to the committee that sought a pastor for the new church. The committee secured a Lutheran minister, but he left after one year because the congregation could not pay him enough to support his family. The church members decided that they needed denominational backing to survive and voted to affiliate with the Methodists.[8]

Christensen had not felt confident enough to speak on her own behalf, but she was determined enough to use her money as power to influence the outcome of the first vote to make the church nondenominational. When the second decision was made, she did not have a trump card to play and apparently remained silent. In her later years Christensen would write and rewrite her version of the history of the Carteret Street Methodist Church, finding a dissenting voice on paper even though she had not been able to raise it at the age of thirty-two.

The Carteret Street church was a good example of how the Christensens worked together in building the New South. Niels worked as contractor in constructing the church—a small, white, wooden building with fish-scale siding, gothic details, and a short steeple. Abbie and the Ladies Aid Society took responsibility for the interior space of the church, much as Abbie had taken charge of decorating her home. The result was a cozy space where light filtered through pointed arched windows onto the wooden chairs and carpet that Abbie had purchased. But Christensen had also entered the "male" realm when she asserted her ownership of the church property and used her economic power to try to insure that the church would be interdenominational. Abbie's power of the purse was not complete, but it is significant that she felt entitled to exercise it, despite her second-class status.[9]

Mind Cure and New Thought

Abbie Christensen also began to assert herself when she advocated Addie and Charles Barrows' mind cure, a mixture of religion and medical practice, beginning in the 1880s. Below her mainstream Protestant surface flowed a river of "harmonial" belief, which combined faith with mental healing. Historian Sydney Ahlstrom defines harmonial religion as "those forms of piety and belief in which spiritual composure, physical health, and even economic well-being are understood to flow from a person's rapport with the cosmos." Mental healing, alternative medicine, and harmonial religion (or "New Thought") provided inner strength and community for Abbie Christensen and other reform-minded women who shared her beliefs.[10]

Christensen's adoption of mind cure was not unusual. Just as Abbie had done with homeopathy, many other women of her time looked to alternative therapies for the power to heal and be in control of their own and their children's lives. Health reform literature, often written by women, elevated their roles as mothers and gave them basic information about their bodies, which was left out of ordinary conversation in middle-class Victorian life. Abbie was probably better trained in science than most antebellum homemakers were. Nevertheless, without a mother or any significant elder woman near her in Beaufort, Abbie turned first to her *Homeopathic Primer* and then to Addie Barrows, who took on a motherly role in Christensen's life.[11]

Barrows was particularly important to Abbie during her two youngest sons' illnesses and Jamie's death in 1885. "Rest in that deep calm which comes to us by a firm belief that our real self can know no trouble," Addie wrote to Abbie in the weeks after her loss. Addie spent hours "holding" Abbie and her family members, though she was thousands of miles away. "I held you and Arthur until twelve o'clock last evening. I woke at four this morning and have been with you for quite a while. I do so hope my visits help you," Addie wrote. This constant epistolary and, as Abbie believed, telepathic attention must have been a comfort to Christensen, isolated without extended family or close friends in the South.[12]

Mind cure and Abbie's belief in spiritualism softened the blow of death for her, as they did for other nineteenth-century mothers. The deaths of children were a favorite theme in Victorian literature. For example, in Eunice Cobb and Sylvanus Cobb's *The Memoir of James Arthur Cobb,* children revisited their old haunts and brought messages back from above, converting the reprobate and consoling the grief-stricken. After Jamie's death Abbie sent her husband verses "with tender sentiments on the hope of immortality." She wrote, "I think really J. is nearer to you now than to the rest of us. He feels he has you more to himself now and he always was so fond of you and so affectionate I suppose he enjoys it."[13]

Spiritualism and mind cure attracted such prominent New England transcendentalists as Margaret Fuller. Charles Barrows quoted Ralph Waldo

Emerson in support of clearing the mind of fear, although Emerson was skeptical of spiritualism. Like transcendentalism, mind cure advocated the principle of mind over matter. Through hypnotism, massage, and telepathy the Barrowses tried to get their patients to heal themselves. "Thought is able to correct whatever is abnormal in the body," Barrows wrote. A final cure restored moral wellness as well as physical health.[14]

Mind cure has been criticized as a selfish indulgence of leisured New England ladies who had lost the Puritan work ethic. In Abbie's case, this characterization is not correct and a newer interpretation is more appropriate. As historian Gail Parker writes, the adherents of mind cure "sought to find a new synthesis of being and doing, of hard work and spiritual ease, worthy of the twentieth century." Christensen's mystical experiences never detracted from her engagement with the world around her. From her teens until her death she faithfully performed the "woman's work" of caring for children, the sick, and the elderly, and of managing a household. She also engaged with the "male" public world of newspapers, politics, reform, and creative activity. Mental healing validated a view of God as both male and female, enabling her to slough off the strictures of patriarchal forms of Christianity. Mind cure helped Abbie conquer her fears, and she believed that she could draw on the "Absolute Energy" of the universe. After her immersion in the "mother seas of God," Christensen found herself "eager to get back to work."[15]

Unitarianism and the Church of the Disciples

Christensen was also inspired to become a reformer through her involvement with liberal Christianity, specifically Unitarianism. Abbie discovered Unitarian Ralph Waldo Emerson's essay "The Oversoul" in 1882, the year Emerson died. She regarded it as "the most inspiring writing outside the New Testament," quoting it to her son Arthur years later. "All goes to show that the soul is not an organ but animates and exercises all the organs, . . . is not the intellect or the will, but the master of the intellect and the will . . . From within or from behind a light shines through us upon all things and makes us understand that we are nothing, but the light is all." When Christensen lived in Brookline, Massachusetts, she was drawn to Boston's Unitarian Church of the Disciples. Sea Island teacher Elizabeth Botume, who had long been a member, probably introduced her to the church, which supported Botume's Beaufort County school. During the flowering of New

England transcendentalism, the Reverend James Freeman Clarke established the Church of the Disciples as a place of worship that featured group discussions for "the intellectual part of the mind, prayer for the spiritual part, and community reform for the moral faculty." In the 1890s, when Charles Ames was its pastor, Abbie Christensen attended the Church of the Disciples regularly, and she and her two oldest sons joined the church in 1895. Abbie found Unitarianism more comforting than the torturous ambiguity and self-abnegation of her earlier Calvinist Christianity. She was much more comfortable with the "social gospel" of the Church of Disciples, which encouraged its members to emulate Christ's life of service. Communion with the "Oversoul" prompted her to seek reform, and the Unitarian Church provided a community of like-minded people to encourage her efforts.[16]

In 1895 Christensen summed up her ideas of health, spirituality, and morality in a paper titled "The Duty of Being Well," which she delivered to the Church of the Disciple's Moral Education Association. Addressing these busy middle-class women, Christensen explained her beliefs. She told them that they needed to pause and listen to the "life current" or "Truth" speaking to them through intuition. Much of her speech concentrated on a woman's taking care of herself, resting when the "Divine Power" led her to do so. It was her belief that women should not always sacrifice for their children or children for parents if doing so resulted in ingratitude or injury. She qualified some well-known maxims: "We must allow that altho' it is more blessed to give than to receive, still the greatest blessedness is found in mutual giving and receiving."[17]

Yet hers was not a self-indulgent belief system. In every course of action, she believed, "the minority must be considered also, and . . . the only perfect scheme is that which includes the well being of every child of earth." Christensen advised against too much agonizing over decisions instead of obeying the Absolute Energy. Too much thinking could lead to selfish fear. She stated: "We persuade our friend not to raise her servants['] wages lest ours become discontented. We vote against the public-spirited man on the school committee fearing appropriations may be made and our taxes increased. Or, if we be so minded, we remonstrate against municipal suffrage for women lest, if it come to pass, our conscience may reproach us for neglect of unwelcome duty." For Abbie, spirituality and politics were linked. Christensen drew strength from other women who believed in mental healing and "New

Thought." Together they summoned the forces of universal love and well-being to aid them as they stepped into the male-dominated world of politics.[18]

Temperance

In 1888 Abbie Christensen joined tens of thousands of other American women whose public and private concerns were woven together in the temperance crusade for "Home Protection." Nineteenth-century women saw it in their interest to keep their husbands and sons from becoming alcoholics or heavy drinkers who abused their families and drank away their paychecks. The crusade's roots were in the evangelical churches of the Midwest, where groups of praying women had shut down saloons in the early 1870s. By the time Christensen joined the WCTU in the late 1880s, the movement embraced woman suffrage and a variety of other reforms. Christensen's belief in women's special mission to society made the WCTU and Frances Willard's "Do Everything" slogan attractive. Christensen became a teetotaler and plunged wholeheartedly into temperance work.[19]

Penn School founders Laura Towne and Ellen Murray were the first temperance crusaders on the Sea Islands. In 1870 they organized a WCTU Band of Hope for African American young people, hoping to save them from "the whiskey-shop influence." The organization, with its songs and speeches, proved popular on an island with little entertainment. Adult African American women organized a branch of the WCTU on Saint Helena Island, and the island's organized temperance advocates numbered over fifteen hundred by 1898. Local WCTUs were segregated, which may have accounted for Christensen's lack of contact with their work. In the area of temperance African Americans had taken the lead and white Beaufort women followed.[20]

Although the *Savannah Times* described Beaufort as a place where the white "ladies" formed "tightly drawn" social circles for northerners and southerners, women's reform activities in the WCTU began to bring them together. A white Charleston WCTU organizer, Sallie Chapin, seems to have been the catalyst for Christensen's entry into temperance circles. Chapin visited Beaufort in 1886 and gave her main lecture at the Carteret Street church. Miss Mary Hamilton, a white southerner, and Mrs. George Waterhouse, a white northerner, soon organized a Beaufort WCTU. Christensen seems to have joined the organization in 1886, and she entertained Sallie Chapin in her home when she visited Beaufort in January 1888. By that year Christensen was running a chapter of the WCTU's Band of Hope that included ninety-eight white Beaufort children. Abbie served as the group's president, while Mary Hamilton served as vice president. Hamilton and Christensen's long friendship was the beginning of Abbie's sectional reconciliation through women's reform activities.[21]

Abbie drew on her experience as a teacher to lead the Band of Hope. She enrolled her oldest sons and their white neighbors and organized them into smaller groups under the leadership of other Beaufort matrons. The boys and girls carried banners and marched in processions; they prayed and read Bible verses; they recited the temperance pledge and other mottos. Christensen's sons and the other children signed a printed "anti-treating pledge," promising never to enter a saloon, accept liquor, or offer liquor to anyone else. Like the Saint Helena Band of Hope, Christensen's group operated on a parliamentary basis, and the members voted on large and small issues.[22]

In 1888 Christensen gave more time, money, and energy to the WCTU than to any other entity outside her family. The WCTU permeated her public and private life. In November 1888 she wrote Niels Jr., who was away at boarding school, that "Callers & a W.C.T.U. meeting & sewing" had taken up her time on a typical day. Christensen's letters to her husband and her son were written on WCTU stationery that read, "For God and Home and Native Land." Abbie organized a fund-raising drive for a Band of Hope Hall in Beaufort and planned to attend the state convention of the WCTU in Charleston in 1889. She followed the fate of Prohibition Party candidates endorsed by the WCTU in the newspaper. Most significantly, in the fall of 1888 Christensen gave a large sum of money to the Woman's Temperance Publishing Association (WTPA), which operated its own presses.[23]

Being a woman of independent means gave Abbie the power to materially support the causes she believed in. And her support made a difference. Christensen's willingness to risk five thousand dollars to become the WTPA's largest investor was important in furthering the independence and efficacy of the WCTU in promoting women's causes. For example, in 1889 the WTPA published social reformer Florence Kelley's *Our Toiling Children,* a comprehensive pamphlet on child labor. In addition, having members as investors helped to keep the organization under women's control. The WCTU's *Union Signal* noted that Christensen was sacrificing the higher dividends she had been receiving from her previous stock. "I like the class of literature you sell, and shall be glad if this investment helps you to increase your business," Christensen said matter-of-factly.[24]

In 1889 Frances Willard, president of the Woman's Christian Temperance Union, cemented Abbie's devotion to the WCTU. Willard, a magnetic speaker, was probably the most famous woman of the nineteenth century. Like many others in the 1880s and 1890s, Christensen and Willard shared a belief in spiritualism and Christian love as a solution to society's problems. "Saint Frances" captivated Abbie when she stayed at her home during a visit to the Sea Islands, which included a speaking engagement at the Beaufort Arsenal. "She is beautiful in her character and every one who heard her admired and loved her," Abbie wrote to her son. "I know of no one in the world whom I w'd feel more honored to have in my house except Mr [John Greenleaf] Whittier." Abbie praised the quintessential American woman of the late nineteenth century, never forgetting her loyalty to the abolitionist generation of her parents. Her comparison to the abolitionists did not stop there. She wrote: "I never heard a speaker to equal her—no not Phillip Brooks even[,] for she speaks with such *love* for humanity in every look, gesture & tone. Not only 'Home & Native Land' but the whole world she carries in her great loving heart." And Christensen was not the only one who was moved. "If she had spoken here three times instead of once she w'd have made Beaufort a Prohibition town—there is a very great change in public sentiment here," Abbie asserted. Many of Willard's southern audiences had never heard a woman speaker and were wary of her, but Willard won them over by her strong, sweet voice, her softly feminine dress, and the evangelical Christian language she used on behalf of her reform interests.[25]

Willard described Christensen in glowing tones when she reported back to the *Union Signal,* saying, "She is a Massachusetts lady, living South twenty-five years; progressive, keen, true-hearted. Our society and enterprises have no wiser or more steadfast friend." Willard also lauded the two white southern sisters who presided over the WCTUs of Beaufort and Port Royal. By praising them all, Willard promoted her agenda of uniting the North and the South for her cause. The WCTU was particularly successful in such North-South unification and was the first cross-regional organization to which Abbie belonged.[26]

At the same time, Willard managed to visit and write about the black temperance activities on Saint Helena Island without offending white southerners. Temperance was popular with the white middle class of the South, and in the 1880s an attitude of paternalism prevailed over the virulent white racism that erupted in the 1890s. Christensen accompanied Willard to the island, where they were greeted by the singing of African American pupils at the Penn School. Buried within Willard's praise for the school's white principals is a simple statistic that spoke volumes about the place of blacks in American society. "Here are a thousand in the Band of Hope," Willard wrote of Saint Helena Island. Abbie's group had only fifty children, but she and her white southern sisters received more attention because of their money, power, and status.[27]

Home and family were Willard's touchstones, and she praised Christensen's home life. "What a 'good talk' we had with her, and that 'noble Dane,' her husband, and how refreshing was the atmosphere of that home and the presence of its many bright, teetotal little ones," she wrote. Christensen encouraged her oldest son in Massachusetts to hear Willard when he got the chance. "If you can speak to her & tell her whose boy you are I know she will be glad to see you. She saw your picture," Abbie informed him. Christensen's status as a wife and mother made her an acceptable nineteenth-century leader.[28]

With the purchase of WTPA stock worth five thousand dollars, Christensen became a sort of celebrity to the *Union Signal*'s readers. In 1890 Christensen was elected to the board of directors of the WTPA, taking the place of Sallie Chapin as a southern representative. Christensen remained on the board for two years, although there is no evidence that she attended any meetings of the WTPA in Evanston, Illinois. Her place on the board was an honor, rather than an active duty.[29]

Abbie remained a temperance supporter for the rest of her life, attending meetings of the WCTU in Massachusetts as well as in South Carolina. In later years Christensen and many other WTPA investors became concerned when the association stopped dividend payments after a massive downtown office building was built and suffered from declining rents during the depression of 1893. Eventually she moved her investments to safer quarters. In 1901 Christensen still corresponded with Mary Hamilton, the Beaufort WCTU leader. Both Hamilton and Frederik Christensen discussed Carrie Nation's "drastic" and "unlawful" attacks on saloons with Abbie Christensen that year. In 1905 state senator Niels Christensen Jr. took up his mother's cause when he exposed corruption in the South Carolina Liquor Dispensary. He succeeded in closing down the dispensary in 1907, much to Abbie's pleasure.[30]

Suffrage

In 1891 Abbie's contacts with the WCTU led her into the South Carolina Equal Rights Association, mostly a group of WCTU women who stood for woman suffrage. For many American women, joining the WCTU led them to advocate woman suffrage as a means to achieve temperance legislation and other societal reforms designed to protect women and children. Christensen's views were a blend of belief in women's special place in the home and equality based on individual rights. She paid homage to gender difference but also believed that women should have equal access to education, the vote, and property rights on the same terms as men.[31]

The United States women's rights movement began a few years before Abbie Holmes was born. The birth of the movement is traditionally traced to 1848 in Seneca Falls, New York, when Elizabeth Cady Stanton and Lucretia Mott called the first woman's rights convention, which drew approximately three hundred attenders. These abolitionist women had come to see the parallels between African Americans' and women's inferior statuses in the American polity. Lucy Stone, Abby Kelley Foster, William Lloyd Garrison, and other abolitionists organized the next women's rights convention, which was held in 1850 in Worcester, Massachusetts, near Abbie's birthplace. This time over a thousand people crowded the convention hall, and many more had to be turned away. With orators such as Stone and, later, Susan B. Anthony speaking across the North and Midwest, the movement spread, drawing tens of thousands of supporters.[32]

After the Civil War an acrimonious debate erupted over whether to allow the word *male* in the Fifteenth Amendment to the U.S. Constitution, which guaranteed black voting rights. Breaking with their abolitionist allies, Stanton and Anthony started the first independent woman suffrage organization, the National Woman Suffrage Association (NWSA). Lucy Stone, Henry Ward Beecher, and other abolitionists who supported the Fifteenth Amendment fought for women's right to vote through the American Woman Suffrage Association (AWSA). The AWSA was led by men and women and worked closely with the Republican Party, while the NWSA was led by women only. Neither group had a large following until the two mended their differences, merged into the National American Woman Suffrage Association (NAWSA), and engaged in large-scale organizing efforts in the 1890s. It was at this point that Christensen became an active suffragist, working with the NAWSA in the 1890s and later in the 1910s to build a national consensus on the issue.[33]

Many in the abolitionist generation, which so greatly influenced Christensen, partook of women's rights sentiment. In 1866, when Abbie was thirteen, her aunt Ellen Winch Lovell wrote a stirring letter on the subject to Abbie's mother. Lovell could hardly contain her excitement after hearing a speech by the eminent Henry Ward Beecher:

> One assertion pleased me *hugely* partly because no other man in my hearing ever had the *chivalry, gallantry,* or the *justice* to assert that women had a right to vote,—and partly because I have always met with so much opposition when I have made this same assertion, also he confirmed my still further prophesy, that the time was not far distant when women *would* vote and with the *consent* and *approbation* of the *Lords of Creation,* and still further that these same Lords *would be obliged to own that instead of the bad effect of this measure upon our sex, we should see the ennobling effect upon both sexes.*

When Abbie visited her aunt later that year, they may have discussed women's rights. Ellen Lovell went on to become president of the Worcester, Massachusetts, WCTU, giving Abbie another example of a woman who linked her reform interests. On the Sea Islands, Laura Towne, Thomas Wentworth Higginson, and Elizabeth Botume promoted women's suffrage. After imbibing these views, Abbie received a strong infusion of the concept of women's rights at Mount Holyoke. In 1889 Christensen purposefully entered one of the most liberal white enclaves in America when she purchased a home in Brookline, Massachusetts, and began attending the Church of the Disciples. It was most likely at this church that Abbie met veteran women's rights activist Lucy Stone.[34]

Lucy Stone, born on a Massachusetts farm in 1818, was one of the first graduates of coeducational Oberlin College and one of the first women orators on behalf of abolition and women's rights. Despite illnesses, migraines, and conflicts with other suffragists who were less committed to the rights of

African Americans, Stone worked tirelessly for the cause of women's rights. Keeping her name after her marriage to Henry Blackwell, she supported his business ventures and worked together with her husband and daughter on their women's rights newspaper, the *Woman's Journal*. At seventy-one, in 1889, she was a plump, white-haired matron whose Dorchester home and garden were peopled by her wayward nieces as well as women's rights organizers from around the nation. Stone's motherly concern and her espousal of both African American and women's rights in the AWSA must have made her attractive to Christensen.[35]

Lucy invited Abbie to her large home for a meeting of the Massachusetts Woman's Suffrage Association. "We will talk over the work at the South," Lucy wrote her. Christensen participated in several activities of Stone's suffrage group and began subscribing to the *Woman's Journal*. Stone encouraged Christensen to be a suffrage leader despite the fact that Blackwell and Anthony were bypassing carpetbaggers to court native southern white women such as Laura Clay and Belle Kearney. Though Stone and Christensen were never more than acquaintances, her contact with the famous suffragist from 1889 to 1893 was undoubtedly an inspiration to Abbie. When she returned to the South, Christensen continued to lead Beaufort's Band of Hope, but her most daring work in South Carolina in 1890 was on behalf of woman suffrage.[36]

Virginia Durant Young

In the 1880s and 1890s the issues of temperance and woman suffrage were increasingly linked, though not without controversy. When Frances Willard endorsed woman suffrage as a right and a necessity for women to achieve their goals, she was opposed by WCTU women who wanted to rely on personal persuasion and stay out of politics. Willard prevailed, however, and the WCTU endorsed woman suffrage. Willard, Stone, and others influenced Christensen, but Virginia Durant Young, a white southern woman, became Abbie's most important personal link to the suffrage cause.[37]

Young was born in South Carolina in 1842, making her ten years older than Christensen. Like Abbie, Virginia lost her mother as a child and grew up close to her father, who was a state legislator. In another parallel, her father remarried and started a second family of daughters. Virginia married at the age of sixteen and began publishing short stories while her husband served in the Confederate army. When he died in 1879, she was thirty-seven and had no children. In 1880 Virginia met and married William Jasper Young of Fairfax, South Carolina, a twenty-nine-year-old physician. She called him her "Prince," and he was devoted to her. The two believed in women's equality, and she had sole title to their house and managed her own money. Historian Barbara Bellows describes Young as "ebullient, a great lover of people, and a habitual 'joiner' of organizations. A very plain woman, the doctor's lady wore her hair pulled back into a small knot that failed to hide her protruding ears. The severity of her hairstyle was broken by abundant curls on the top of her head. . . . She loved lavishly plumed hats and brilliantly colored, large bustled dresses of material that rustled when she walked. . . . she was a tiny woman, less than five feet tall and weighing under ninety pounds." This physical description of Young paralleled that of Christensen, who was also slim, was under five feet tall, and wore her straight brown hair in a neat bun on the top of her head. Unlike Young, Christensen tended to dress in darker, subdued colors, paying little attention to fashion. Both women were part of the "leisured" middle class. A staff of two servants and the fact that she had no children enabled Young to devote herself full-time to temperance and suffrage. Like Christensen and Willard, she combined a traditional image of domesticity with advocacy of women's rights. Young and Christensen were both writers, and the two women shared a belief in harmonial Christianity.[38]

Like Christensen, Young became involved with the WCTU in the second half of the 1880s and moved from temperance to suffrage. She began to write temperance articles and later bought a paper, the *Fairfax Enterprise,* which she used as an organ for woman suffrage as well as temperance. Young probably first met Christensen at the state WCTU convention in Charleston in 1889. Sallie Chapin, who brought both women into the WCTU, was a firm antisuffragist, but Young became more and more convinced of women's inherent right to the ballot. In 1890 she was elected corresponding secretary of the state WCTU, a position that put her in contact with a large number of the Union's constituency. In the same year she and a few other dissident WCTU women in Greenville, South Carolina, formed the South Carolina Equal Rights Association (SCERA).[39]

In the hours before she gave her first speech for woman suffrage at a WCTU meeting in Beaufort in 1891, Young was encouraged by Christensen, her hostess for the event. When she spoke, Young smoothed over the sectional differences between an old Rebel such as herself and Yankees such as the Christensens by pointing to Niels Christensen's improvement of the grave of his old Confederate enemy Gen. Richard Anderson. With the way cleared for the topic at hand, Young stated that she "plunged in *medias res* of that topic presumably so abhorrent to the average Carolina lady. My first sentence seemed to thrill them to a deeper interest for it was couched in these amazing terms: 'My husband said to me the other day . . . "Why don't you tell the women they will never get prohibition till they vote?"'" Noting Christensen's supporting presence, Young began her career as a suffrage speaker. From this time on, the two women were fast friends.[40]

Christensen came to the South Carolina suffrage movement during its second phase, at a time when suffrage was gaining nationally but not in the South. Southern African American and carpetbagger women began the South Carolina suffrage movement in 1870, but it was never supported by more than a few Reconstruction legislators. In the 1890s a core group of veterans of the temperance crusade and missionary societies revived the movement. They saw the ballot as a means to accomplish their humanitarian ends. *The History of Woman Suffrage* lists Abbie Christensen as one of a dozen or so South Carolina women who were "devoted workers in the cause of suffrage." As a worker and supporter of Virginia Young, Christensen played her part.[41]

In 1892 Young wrote Christensen that after a confrontation with Sallie Chapin, she started sending out woman suffrage leaflets, writing about it in her newspaper, and speaking out to people she knew. Christensen and her husband signed on to Young's list of supporters for "the doctrine of Equal Rights." Virginia kept Abbie abreast of their progress and was pleased when membership reached about fifty South Carolinians. Abbie tried to recruit members in Beaufort and paid for the *Woman's Column,* a shorter version of the *Woman's Journal,* to be sent to fifty South Carolina women. Young wrote Christensen long letters about the persecution she suffered in the WCTU at the hands of Chapin, and Christensen wrote to the *Union Signal* in Young's defense.[42]

Female friendships of the type that Abbie and Virginia shared were important in sustaining activists such as Young. Political women who lived without such relationships often felt lonely and were less effective in their work. Virginia Young frequently thanked Christensen for shoring her up during times of insecurity. The two women's friendship was a same-sex version of the "romance of reunion" between North and South during the 1880s.[43]

Abbie introduced Virginia to mind cure, and the two women tried to use their "powers of attraction" to persuade wavering suffrage supporters. Young's third novel, *The Blue Hen's Chickens,* is largely concerned with mind cure, and she employed a southern psychic healer. Virginia wrote to Abbie of her husband, of the work of being an author, and of course, of suffrage and temperance activism. Young bared her deepest fears of inadequacy and seemed relieved by her unburdening. "It quite rests me to sit down for a little talk with you on paper," she wrote in 1892. Abbie's "sweetly serious face" and her "sincere voice" were a comfort to Virginia. The language used by this woman of fifty years carried the same intensity as the intimate and religiously charged friendships of Abbie's youth. In the same year Virginia wrote: "I clasp your hands and *thank God* for your love and for the *strength* He imparts to me *through you.* For oh! You do communicate to me even at this distance something of your quietness and courage." In 1905 Virginia wrote that Abbie's "words of approval of my speech give me joy." In a state with as little suffrage sentiment as South Carolina, such a friendship could mean a great deal.[44]

Perhaps the most important and complex question about Christensen's friendship with this white woman who identified strongly with the South was how it affected Christensen's views on race, especially black suffrage. It is likely that Christensen favored educational qualifications for voting, but not racial discrimination. Suffrage with an educational test was the position of many of her white northern friends and family, and even some African Americans such as suffragist Frances Ellen Watkins Harper. Abbie's father, her sons, and Virginia Young were all in favor of educational qualifications. At the same time, Harper and Christensen's abolitionist friends Laura Towne and Ellen Murray were dismayed by the disfranchisement of African Americans through the manipulation of literacy and property requirements. Abbie's husband, Niels Christensen, defended "Negro Supremacy" in Beaufort and cooperated with a mixed-race government in the town. No record of Abbie's views survives, so the best way to learn them is to map out the constellation of views around her and guess where her star might have stood.

It seems improbable that one woman could have been influenced by suffragists as different as Lucy Stone, the abolitionist, and Virginia Young, the Confederate widow. Yet by the 1890s Stone's commitment to black rights had been pushed behind her husband's "southern strategy" of arguing for woman suffrage as a means for establishing white supremacy in the South. Using statistics, he showed that there were more southern white women than the entire black population of the region. In 1890 the NAWSA began to broadcast this argument widely as part of its southern campaign. Usually the argument carried with it the caveat that black women who met property and educational qualifications would be allowed to vote. However, the goal was white supremacy. Stone disapproved, but like Christensen, she did not disagree publicly.[45]

Young voiced this argument and others when she spoke to the South Carolina Press Association as its first woman member in 1892. Christensen possessed several copies of Young's speech, "A Star in the West," which was reprinted by the *Woman's Journal.* Young took her title from Wyoming, the first state to pass woman suffrage. She cited natural rights and the Declaration of Independence as the foundations for her belief in women's right to the ballot. Young also wrote that suffrage with an educational qualification would add 76,000 educated white women to 96,000 white men, which would add up to a majority of 34,000 over the 118,000 black voters of South Carolina. Young tried to appeal to southern men's "generous chivalry," arguing that the ballot would protect their daughters, wives, or sisters if their men died. Young aimed her campaign at the 1895 state constitutional convention, which was designed to undo the 1868 constitution and its guarantees of African American rights. Aware of Young's reasoning, Niels Christensen Sr. explained to Abbie that a property qualification "would exclude practically all colored women." Her reply has not survived. The end result in South Carolina in 1895 was that Young's arguments garnered woman suffrage a respectable number of votes at the convention, but not enough to win them the ballot.[46]

Frances Ellen Watkins Harper

Abbie was also influenced by Frances Ellen Watkins Harper, the African American writer and speaker whom she had met at an 1889 Massachusetts WCTU convention. Christensen heard Frances again in 1894 at a "colored people's meeting" against lynching and in 1897 at an Anti-slavery Memorial

Meeting in Boston. Though the two women differed in looks, Harper had as much in common with Christensen as Young did. In addition to her leadership in the temperance and suffrage movements, she had been an abolitionist, lived in the Northeast, belonged to the Unitarian Church, and was a widely published author and a mother. After listening to Harper's 1889 speech, Christensen obtained her Philadelphia address along with that of her friend William Still, author of *The Underground Railroad.* When Harper spoke in the African American churches of Beaufort in 1893, she stopped to pay a call on Niels Christensen. Harper toured the South as a lecturer from the 1870s to the early 1890s, encouraging African American audiences to strive for education, temperance, and economic and political success. To white southern audiences she spoke of the need for reconciliation, toleration, and respect for black rights. In the 1890s, in addresses to northern women, Harper made some of her strongest statements against disfranchisement and lynching. Frances asserted that it was women's duty to speak out against these evils, in addition to the other social ills they were already critiquing.[47]

Harper and other prominent black women such as Anna Julia Cooper and Ida B. Wells tried to convince white women to swim against the prevailing racist current of the late nineteenth century. In an address to the National Council of Women in 1891, Harper outlined the way she thought white American women should view African Americans: "I deem it a privilege to present the negro, not as a mere dependent asking for Northern sympathy or Southern compassion, but as a member of the body politic who has a claim upon the nation for justice, simple justice, which is the right of every race, upon the government for protection, which is the rightful claim of every citizen, and upon our common Christianity for the best influences which can be exerted for peace on earth and good-will to man." Harper praised suffrage leader Susan B. Anthony for her personal dislike of prejudice, but criticized her and Frances Willard for keeping their causes "safe" from the unpopular issue of discrimination against African Americans. The same criticism could have been applied to Christensen, who never spoke out against black disfranchisement.[48]

In an exchange of letters with Christensen around 1892, Harper put the matter of black women's rights bluntly: "You asked if I expected to come to the Massachusetts WCTU. No[,] unless I am invited. The colored superintendency has been abolished and I scarcely ever get a call from

WCTUs for a lecture. Are you not going to fight this thing as a white woman's fight. In all the lynching burnings and murders in the South, do you think that generally speaking Northern women feel scarcely any interest?" There is no record that Christensen answered Harper's question in the affirmative by speaking out in the WCTU or the NAWSA, although she joined the Southern Women's Campaign against Lynching in the 1930s. Abbie's attendance with her children at meetings against lynching in Boston indicates that she agreed with Harper, but she chose not to speak out on her own. While living with his mother in Brookline, Abbie's sixteen-year-old son Fred expressed his views when a lynching occurred in 1893: "There was another colard man linched in the South (South Car.) they say for having murdered a white man. I tell of these linchings so that if this diary ever comes to light in after years one may see the brutal and unsettled state of the south. One notices that a white man is never linched no mater how cruel he is, and that those who take part in the linchings are never arrested." Fred's diary indicates a steady interest in the topic of racial injustice and attendance with his mother at events promoting black education. It seems that Christensen was in favor of black rights and concerned about injustice but was fearful or thought it unwise to speak out.[49]

Aside from her encounters with Harper, Christensen rarely addressed the relationship of suffrage and race or ethnicity. Many northern suffragists feared immigrant voters and used the argument that native-born women deserved the vote more than foreign-born men did. Abbie, who married an immigrant, left no record of her views on the Irish, Italians, Germans, and others crowding into turn-of-the-century Boston.[50]

In 1892, the year Abbie forgot her yellow and white ribbons, the wife and mother of five took on yet another task. She began writing to Frances Willard and others to secure government recognition and compensation for Anna Carroll, a Maryland woman who had devised a strategic plan used successfully by the Union army on southern rivers. Her friends began to worry that Abbie was doing too much. Lucy Stone, who had experienced some of the same pressures, advised Christensen in 1892 not to take on yet another cause. Lucy wrote: "I have not done a thing about Miss Carroll. And I cannot and you might not to[o] because your own [work] is too much for you. I did not see you at the meetings. so concluded the children needed you. I will send reports of the meetings." During the school year, when Christensen and her children resided in Massachusetts, she probably missed meetings because she was attending to her children's needs. Her husband was in Beaufort, and she did without servants in order to afford the expense of maintaining her Brookline household.[51]

Addie Barrows, Christensen's friend and "healer," tried to suggest other areas that Abbie could let go: "I hope you will not try to get your house [in order] tonight—if you do you will come back tired. The spirit—not house always needs to be kept in order." When Abbie expressed a desire to affect reform on a return visit to the South, her friend admonished her: "Do not try to regulate Beaufort." Christensen followed such advice for a few more years, but when she returned to Beaufort on a more permanent basis, her efforts at reform resumed.[52]

Christensen's friendship with Addie Barrows and her mystical beliefs in mental healing led her to see women, including herself, as powerful beings who could defy mainstream expectations. Frances Willard, Lucy Stone, Frances Harper, and Virginia Young connected Christensen with the temperance and women's rights movements in the North and the South. These leaders provided Christensen with an example and an ideological basis for continuing her public work despite her family responsibilities. The women's rights movement and its support of literary women may have encouraged her to enter into her most public venture, the collection and publication of African American folklore.

Reuben G. Holmes ca. 1848, copied from a daguerreotype. From the Christensen Family Papers. Courtesy of the South Caroliniana Library, University of South Carolina.

Abbie Mandana Holmes as a child. From the Christensen Family Papers. Courtesy of the South Caroliniana Library, University of South Carolina.

Captain Niels Christensen, 44th Regiment, United States Colored Troops. From the Christensen Family Papers. Courtesy of the South Caroliniana Library, University of South Carolina.

Abbie Holmes Christensen as a young woman. Carte-de-visite by George S. Cook. From the Christensen Family Papers. Courtesy of the South Caroliniana Library, University of South Carolina.

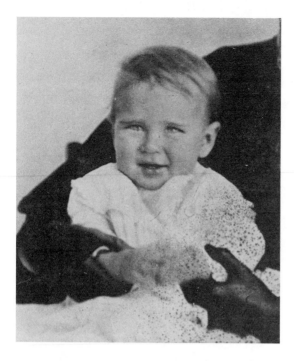

Tintype of a baby (possibly Niels Christensen Jr.) being held by a nurse. From the Christensen Family Papers. Courtesy of the South Caroliniana Library, University of South Carolina.

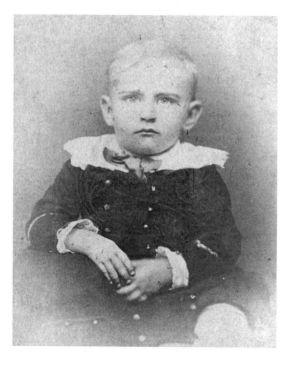

James "Jamie" Winch Christensen Abbie's third son, Beaufort, South Carolina. From the Christensen Family Papers. Courtesy of the South Caroliniana Library, University of South Carolina.

The Holmes Family, including, Needham, Massachusetts, 1888. Seated second row from left, Andrea Christensen (age 4), Abbie Holmes Christensen (with baby Winnie in her lap). Standing far left, Arthur Olaf Christensen (age 6), and standing second from right, Frederick Holmes Christensen (age 11). From the Christensen Family Papers. Courtesy of the South Caroliniana Library, University of South Carolina.

The Christensen home, Beaufort, South Carolina, ca. 1890. From the Christensen Family Papers. Courtesy of the South Caroliniana Library, University of South Carolina.

Port Royal School class, ca. 1902. From the Christensen Family Papers. Courtesy of the South Caroliniana Library, University of South Carolina.

Students with teacher, Port Royal Agricultural School, 1906. From the Christensen Family Papers. Courtesy of the South Caroliniana Library, University of South Carolina.

Christensen family and friends at Bay Point beach, ca. 1910; Abbie Holmes Christensen seated with portfolio. From the Christensen Family Papers. Courtesy of the South Caroliniana Library, University of South Carolina.

Abbie Holmes Christensen in coastal sand dunes. From the Christensen Family Papers. Courtesy of the South Caroliniana Library, University of South Carolina.

View from Abbie Holmes Christensen's upstairs sleeping porch, Beaufort, South Carolina. From the Christensen Family Papers. Courtesy of the South Caroliniana Library, University of South Carolina.

The Montessori School, Beaufort, South Carolina. From left, Joe Lipsitz(?), John Morrall(?), Stratton Christensen(?), Minnie Harms(?), Sarah Wilson(?), Pinckney Eve. Second row, Abbie Christensen, unidentified teacher. From the Christensen Family Papers. Courtesy of the South Caroliniana Library, University of South Carolina.

Niels Christensen Jr. and Niels Christensen III. From the Christensen Family Papers. Courtesy of the South Caroliniana Library, University of South Carolina.

Arthur, Lillian, and Cornelia Christensen at Beaufort, South Carolina, 1923. From the Christensen Family Papers. Courtesy of the South Caroliniana Library, University of South Carolina.

Andrea Christensen Patterson and Lawrence Orr Patterson, ca. 1930.

Abby Winch "Winnie" Christensen, ca. 1930.

Frederik Burr Christensen and his grandfather, Harry Porter Burr, ca. 1930. From the Christensen Family Papers. Courtesy of the South Caroliniana Library, University of South Carolina.

Oil portrait of Abbie Holmes Christensen holding a copy of her book, Afro-American Folk Lore. *Courtesy of Paul Sommerville, Beaufort, South Carolina.*

Joseph H. Shanklin and his family, with an inset photograph of Foch Shanklin. Courtesy of Joseph S. Shanklin Jr., Foch B. Shanklin, and Thelma S. West, Beaufort, South Carolina.

Portrait of India Shanklin. Courtesy of Joseph S. Shanklin Jr., Foch B. Shanklin, and Thelma S. West, Beaufort, South Carolina.

India Shanklin Library at the Shanklin School, Beaufort, South Carolina. Courtesy of Joseph S. Shanklin Jr., Foch B. Shanklin, and Thelma S. West, Beaufort, South Carolina.

Joseph Shanklin with his classmates at Tuskegee Institute class reunion. Courtesy of Joseph S. Shanklin Jr., Foch B. Shanklin, and Thelma S. West, Beaufort, South Carolina.

Catherine DeVeaux, detail from her Hampton School of Nursing class photograph. Courtesy of Katherine P. Doctor, Beaufort, South Carolina.

Photograph of Catherine DeVeaux. Courtesy of Katherine P. Doctor, Beaufort, South Carolina.

Chapter Eight

THE ORIGINAL UNCLE REMUS

In Boston some of my friends amused themselves by calling me "The Original Uncle Remus."[1]

When Abbie Christensen had her portrait painted in 1928, she posed in an elegant black silk dress with a matching ribbon at her throat, and a small smile played about her lips. Christensen looked up at the painter as if she had just been interrupted while reading *Afro-American Folk Lore,* a small red book that lay open in her hands. Written during the 1870s and 1880s and published in 1892, this book is the most important public work for which she is remembered. Christensen's pride in this work shows in her decision to include it in her portrait. She also took pride in being called "The Original Uncle Remus," a reference to the fact that her folktales were published earlier than the Uncle Remus stories of Joel Chandler Harris. Recent scholars have been able to use the folklore Christensen collected to re-create a part of the cultural life of enslaved Africans. While *Afro-American Folk Lore* can be read as a record of black culture, its meaning and message are complicated and compromised by the introductory frame that Christensen set before the stories she retold. This frame encompassed her own blend of abolition, New South paternalism, and a plea for gender equality. The historical circumstance of Christensen's participation in the world of American folklore, the ideological work of writing about African Americans, and the content of the tales are all worth examining.[2]

Abolitionist Roots

The motivations for Christensen's work in folklore grew out of her connections with the Gullah people of the Sea Islands and the abolitionists who were her mentors. In her writing Christensen carried on and modified an abolitionist legacy that already existed in African American folklore collections. Older abolitionists, whom she knew from her childhood on the Sea Islands, had been drawn to slave songs and spirituals since their first contact with the "Contrabands." Abolitionists chose to highlight this portion of

African American experience because they wanted to present African Americans to white Americans as humble Christian folk deserving of support. Whites such as Quaker Lucy McKim collected slave songs at Port Royal in 1862, and teacher William Francis Allen did so in 1865. Charlotte Forten, a black abolitionist teacher on the Sea Islands, was also greatly impressed by slave songs and religious rituals. In fact, Forten's letters inspired poet John Greenleaf Whittier, her friend, to write his "Song of the Negro Boatmen at Port Royal," which Christensen used as the foreleaf to her 1892 book. Christensen's selection of this poem showed her conscious connection to these abolitionist forebears.[3]

Two abolitionists whom Christensen knew well, Thomas Wentworth Higginson and Elizabeth Hyde Botume, discussed spirituals, folk life, and African-influenced customs in a positive way in their reminiscences of the Civil War. These writings presented a "romantic racialist" view of African Americans whose nature was different from that of whites—less rational and more musical and religious—but who nevertheless deserved freedom and citizenship. Abbie Holmes became an adult and began to write down African American folklore after many of the political goals of these abolitionists seemed to have been achieved. Without their abolitionist purpose, her aims as a collector were not as clear as Higginson's and Botume's. However, their influence never completely faded.[4]

New South Paternalism

In addition to her abolitionist roots, Christensen was also influenced by the New South paternalism she encountered in South Carolina in the late 1870s and 1880s. Paternalism, whether southern or northern, cast whites into the role of parents and blacks into the role of children, who would be "uplifted" through the guidance of these benevolent whites. New South paternalists such as Uncle Remus's creator, Joel Chandler Harris, advocated industrial education of African Americans and limited suffrage. Christensen's portrayal of African Americans was similar to Harris's, but her historical antecedents were northern white missionaries.[5]

When she was writing in the mid-1870s, not long after her own experience of being a teacher of black pupils, Christensen did not seem particularly worried about the fate of African Americans. Perhaps this was because Reconstruction was still in place and her circle of white Republicans shared power peacefully with black Republicans. Christensen's aim seems to have been mainly to entertain her white readers, but whether she wished it or not, her representations of African Americans carried political import as well. Negative impressions of African Americans could lead white northerners to abandon their support for Reconstruction. In the fall of 1875 Abbie Christensen published two folktales in the *New York Independent*, "Negro Folklore: The Elephant and the Rabbit" and "A Story-Teller." While "Negro Folklore" continued the sentimental but culturally accurate depiction of Christensen's earlier tales, "A Story-Teller" created a derogatory stereotype.

"Negro Folklore" portrayed Christensen's fictional character Miss Alice "swinging in her favorite hammock on the broad, shaded veranda." Alice begged Aunt 'Tilda for a story, but she was too busy with housework and instead sent Uncle Scipio. Christensen described him as "a very ancient specimen of ebony humanity." They conversed, and he told her that the stories came from his grandfather, an old African. He also related the context in which animal stories were usually told: "In slabery times I knowed a heap. When I b'longs to ole Marse Heywood, down on Red Ribber, 'e worked us so hard, 'bout all de comfort we had dose days was tell story. When we got in from cotton-fiel' at night, an' done git our supper, we use ter sit roun' de fire an' tell story. But sence de Union come in an' we all hab summuch odder ting for study 'pon I ain't ben practice um so long I mos' done forgit all." By including the words of her storytellers, Abbie informed her readers that the tales came from Africa and were associated with slavery—two points that she and later folklorists would return to over the years.[6]

In the previous piece Aunt 'Tilda had been a "captive" storyteller when Alice caught her at work. Uncle Scipio, on the other hand, consented to relieve Alice's boredom because he was indebted to her through the bonds of paternalism and reciprocity. He told her: "I 'member you, jus' biggin for walk an' talk, come out to da cabin for see ole Uncle Scipio dat winter, when de rheumatism fight me so hard; always bringin' something for poo' ole Scipio. So, when Tilda tell me, I tuk my stick an' start right off; an' as I come 'long I ben study 'pon dis story I gwine tell you now, same as how my ole gran'-daddy use to tell us chilluns 'bout 'How the Rabbit Rode the Elephant.'" As he had done before, the rabbit in this tale employed trickery to outwit the larger, more powerful elephant. Her later writings indicate that Christensen understood that the rabbit represented black people under slavery, but she did not comment on this meaning at this time.[7]

Christensen's next work for the *New York Independent,* "A Story-Teller," introduced a new African American informant, Prince Baskin. She highlighted his connection to the North and the ideals of the Civil War by relating that he wore a coat of "faded army blue," the Union uniform. In the next part of her description Christensen switched from her earlier warm characterizations to a harsher view of African Americans that drew on the scientific racism of her day. Christensen wrote that seeing Baskin tell his stories would "send a true disciple of Darwin into ecstasies" since "he look[ed] much less of a man than a monkey, with his absurd gestures." It could have been just a description, but Christensen must have known that it was not complimentary.[8]

Why did Christensen make a reference to Darwin? Charles Darwin's 1859 book, *Origin of the Species,* influenced other folklorists as well. Many nineteenth-century folklorists believed that they were preserving romantic survivals of the premodern folk that revealed the evolutionary path from savage to civilized. Darwin opposed slavery and did not see his work as supporting in any way the repression of nonwhites. In fact, reformers such as Florence Kelly used Darwin to argue for progressive legislation to protect future generations from the debilitating effects of exploitation in the workplace. In her views of Darwin, Christensen joined the New South paternalists in viewing African Americans such as Baskin as quaint and temporarily inferior but "upliftable" through education. Historian Robert Bannister has called the New South paternalists' program "outrageously conservative" by present-day standards, yet it was more temperate than the later racism of such whites as Thomas Dixon Jr., the author of *The Clansman,* who interpreted social Darwinism to mean the permanent and bestial inferiority of African Americans.[9]

In her description Christensen lamented that Baskin and many other African Americans admired the Rabbit and his treachery. Later, in *Afro-American Folklore,* she blamed slavery for this preference for dishonesty. In 1875 she allowed Baskin to explain the situation in his own words: "You see, Missus, I is a small man myself; but I ain't nebber 'low no one for git head o' me. I allers use my sense for help me long; jus' like Br. Rabbit." Baskin's identification with the trickster rings true when placed in the context of African and African American history. Folklorist John Roberts writes that tales in which the trickster obtains food by stratagem were relevant in African countries where there was often a scarcity of food. The hero of these stories would trick the gods into giving him something, or he would cleverly deceive an authority within human society. In slavery, the importance of the trickster tales became magnified because stealing was the only way to provide good things for one's family, and acts of trickery were usually the only form of resistance open to slaves. Sometimes, however, the interpretation that the Rabbit is trickster and role model is not adequate. For example, the Rabbit's pretentiousness in his insistence on genteel address in the Tar Baby story is meant to be cautionary, not exemplary. Christensen may have had some understanding of the utility of the trickster figure in slavery, but her main comment in 1875 was disapproval of the cruel "treachery" of the trickster.[10]

From 1875 through the end of 1877 Christensen published four more trickster tales in the New York Independent: "The Rabbit, The Wolf, and the Keg of Butter"; "The Rabbit Desires a Long Tail"; "The Reason Why Brother Rabbit Wears a Short Tail"; and "The Rabbit and the Wolf Plant Potatoes and Hunt Honey." These later tales were presented without any introduction or commentary by the collector, allowing them to stand on their own merits.[11]

Afro-American Folk Lore

Between 1877 and 1891 Christensen's publications ceased. Although Christensen had tried to publish her tales as a book in 1882, her motherly duties and her reform interests turned her attention away from this goal. In the midst of the rich intellectual milieu of Brookline in 1891, however, Christensen experienced a renewed desire to participate in the literary life of the nation. Responding positively to her inquiries, the Boston firm of J. G. Cupples agreed to publish 250 copies of a collection of stories entitled Afro-American Folk Lore.[12]

Christensen's small red book of 116 pages contained a foreleaf, a preface, the stereotypical description of "A Story-Teller," the blue-coated Prince Baskin from Christensen's 1875 article, and eighteen animal tales. Typewritten copies of the tales in the book seem to indicate that Christensen's editors crossed out her scenes with Miss Alice and Aunt 'Tilda. In addition to the eight stories already published, she added "De Tiger an' de Nyung Lady"; "De Reason Why Dog Hates Cat an' Cat Hates Dog"; "De Rabbit an' de Elephant Tushes"; "De Rabbit, de Bear an' de Locus' Tree"; "De Reason Why de 'Gator Stan' So"; "De Rabbit, de Wolf, an' de Alligator"; "Br'er Rabbit an'

Br'er Wolf Go to a Party an' Hunt de Deer"; "De Wolf, de Hog an' de Lion"; "De Rabbit an' de' Partritch"; and "De Wolf, de Rabbit an' de Whale's Eggs." The only story she changed from the magazine to the book version was "The Rabbit and the Elephant," which became "Br'er Rabbit Gone ter de Weddin' in Style." In the first version the Rabbit rode the Elephant; while in the second he rode Br'er Wolf.[13]

Her full title, *Afro-American Folk Lore As Told 'Round Cabin Fires on the Sea Islands of South Carolina,* informed her readers of the setting and region in which these African American tales were usually told. Christensen's use of the new word *Afro-American* indicated the connection she saw between the United States and the continent of Africa in her collected animal stories. She noted in her preface that these stories were "verbatim reports from numerous sable story-tellers of the Sea Islands, some of whose ancestors, two generations back, brought parts of the legends from African forests." The book's two illustrations showed a black family entertaining themselves in front of their fireplace as well as a scene of an African American woman crossing a footbridge to reach a one-room log cabin, reinforcing the images of the title.[14]

In her preface Christensen wrote, "The colored people of the South have a folk lore of their own, . . . rich in humor and originality." She indicated that most people had not known of these African American tales until "Mr. Harris's delightful volumes wherein we are introduced to that kindly 'Uncle Remus.'" Though she deferred to Harris's greater fame, Christensen immediately noted that she had published the Tar Baby story first. Christensen set her tales apart from Harris's by pointing out that the Sea Island versions of animal stories were distinct from the middle-Georgia variety that Harris retold.[15]

Joel Chandler Harris

Because the stories they collected were so similar, a comparison of Christensen and Harris is useful in determining the political agendas and historical circumstances behind Christensen's work. Both collectors were paternalists, but their views on slavery and the Civil War differed. Like the white missionaries who had come to the Sea Islands in the 1860s, New South paternalists of the 1880s believed that benevolent whites should aid and educate African Americans. This paternalism acknowledged the humanity of African Americans and left open the possibility that blacks and whites would one day be equal. The relatively benign quality of New South paternalism can be gauged by judging it against the virulent racism of men such as South Carolina governor Benjamin Tillman and women such as the Georgia WCTU activist Rebecca Latimer Felton, who raged against "black beast rapists." It was this argument for black degeneracy that Niels Christensen had refuted in his article "The Sea Islands and Negro Supremacy." Though Christensen published her work in the 1890s, it was written in the late 1870s and 1880s and shared many aspects of Harris's work.[16]

Harris was born in Eatonton, Georgia, in 1848, just four years before Abbie Holmes. He began his life more precariously, however, as the illegitimate son of a poor white woman. Harris obtained his main education as an apprentice for a Georgia planter, Joseph Addison Turner, who ran his own newspaper. On Turner's plantation young Harris heard animal tales told by elderly slaves and learned to write journalistic prose.[17]

In 1873 he married Esther LaRose, a French Canadian woman, whom he had met while working for the *Savannah Morning News.* Harris worked his way up in journalism, and in 1876 he became an associate editor at the *Atlanta Constitution.* He was fortuitously given the assignment of writing Negro dialect sketches when the journalist who had previously been writing a dialect column took a leave to campaign for the 1876 Democratic presidential nominee, Sam Tilden. Harris used black characters, including Uncle Remus, to expand on the *Constitution's* perennial theme of black and Republican "misrule" and the necessity of returning white Democrats to power.[18]

But by 1879 white southerners seemed to be securely in charge once again, and both ex-Confederates and white northerners were ready to forget politics and soothe themselves with a new romantic view of race relations in the South. In that year Harris turned away from overt political themes in his writing for the *Constitution* and began a remarkably successful African American folktale series. He put the fictional Uncle Remus in the plantation setting he remembered from his youth and had him tell Br'er Rabbit stories to a young white boy. Harris's facility with this new voice may have come from his memories of enjoying the company of African Americans, who were probably not as concerned with his lowly boyhood status as were whites. Harris's white southern audience responded enthusiastically. The harmonious race relations between Uncle Remus and the little boy to whom he told his tales distracted his readers from the unpleasant reality of recent violent clashes over black political rights. Like Christensen's Rabbit stories, Harris's careful rendering of the adventures of Br'er Rabbit and his friends conveyed the universal appeal of fables and fairy tales the world over.[19]

Uncle Remus's animal stories were so successful that Harris quickly assembled and published them in 1880 as *Uncle Remus: His Songs and Sayings.* This book was followed in 1883 by *Nights with Uncle Remus* and several other books of dialect tales. Harris's work sold well in the North and even internationally. Christensen was certainly correct when she wrote that by the time her book appeared, Harris had "captured the market."[20]

While Harris seems to have waxed nostalgic about slavery times, his paternalism did not always conflict with that of white abolitionists. In fact, he paid a backhanded compliment to abolitionist Harriet Beecher Stowe in his first *Uncle Remus* volume. Harris praised Stowe for her "wonderful defense of slavery as it existed in the South," arguing that it had created the character Uncle Tom, whom he thought similar to Uncle Remus. Harris suggested that the finer points of both Uncles could be attributed to the paternalistic side of slavery.[21]

Harris has been criticized for romanticizing slavery as well as for stealing and warping African Americans' cultural legacy, while other Harris scholars have defended him as a white writer who argued for the "ultimate irrelevance of race." Harris's close friendship with Henry Grady, who argued for the necessity of permanent white political dominion over African Americans, seems to give credence to those who criticize his lack of respect for blacks. On the other hand, Harris's defenders argue that it was the "black world" of the slave cabin and not slavery that Harris was nostalgic about. These scholars also point to editorials by Harris against lynching and for black suffrage, as well as the subversive quality of the Uncle Remus tales. It seems clear that Harris saw himself as an ally, not a foe, of African Americans. Nevertheless, his paternalistic writings can be seen as harmful to blacks because of the stereotypes they perpetuated.[22]

Abolitionist Legacy

Despite their similarities, Christensen's abolitionist roots set her work in a different historical context than Harris's. Christensen foregrounded *Afro-American Folk Lore* with these lines from John Greenleaf Whittier's poem "Song of the Negro Boatmen at Port Royal":

Rude seems the song; each swarthy face
Flame-lighted ruder still;
We start to think that hapless race
Must shape our good or ill;
That laws of changeless justice bind
Oppressor with oppressed
And, close as sin and suffering joined,
We march to fate abreast.

The selection of this poem shows the responsibility that Christensen felt white Americans had to black people because of the sin of slavery. Whittier's path to the noblesse oblige of paternalism differed from Harris's because he acknowledged the wrongs of the past.[23]

Christensen also put a harsh cast on slavery and, by extension, on the African Americans who had been affected by the peculiar institution. In her 1892 book she reprinted her earlier Darwinian references to Prince Baskin without alteration. Although Christensen had originally published her tales in the children's section of the *New York Independent,* she now added the warning that "we of the New South cannot wish our children to pore long over these pages, which certainly could not have been approved by Froebel." Others had also alerted Christensen to the moral dangers of African American trickster tales. Before she published her book she had sent a story about Br'er Wolf to *St. Nicholas* magazine. As she wrote later, "It was returned— being too cruel for young children—I agreed. Many of the negro Folk Tales were cruel, so are German Folk Tales—and others." By the 1930s Christensen grouped folk cultures together, rather than ranking them on a hierarchy. Her change was in step with an antiracist shift in anthropology led by the liberal and innovative Franz Boas.[24]

Christensen's 1892 preface moderated her description of the Br'er Rabbit tales with a sophisticated view of the environmental forces that led to the trickery of African Americans. "The negro, without education or wealth, could only succeed by stratagem," she wrote. Christensen rightly understood that the circumstances of slavery had produced dishonest relations between owners and bondspeople. What she did not see so clearly was that such relations continued between African Americans and European Americans in Boston as well as in Beaufort. The gap between Christensen and her informants' experience kept her from fully understanding the double meaning of the African American culture she presented.[25]

Though she usually identified herself as a Yankee, Christensen wrote in her preface that she was "of the New South." The idea of the New South had been advanced by Henry Grady, the editor of Harris's paper, the *Atlanta Constitution,* which welcomed northern capital and industry to the region. In order to sell this idea to agrarian southerners, Grady relied on Harris's plantation stories to provide the approval of the "Old South." John Roberts writes that Harris was the first to use a depiction of black folk to advance the white paternalist agenda of southerners. The character of Uncle Remus aided this agenda because his relationship with a young white boy on the plantation and the content of the tales presented a picture of black people as "simple childlike, mischievous." On the other hand, the term "New South" also had abolitionist roots. African Americans and white missionaries who came to Port Royal with Christensen's parents had named one of their first newspapers the *New South.* Although they came from different backgrounds, both Christensen and Harris ultimately shared a belief in a New South and in an attitude of paternalism toward African Americans.[26]

A more radical commitment to gender equality can be seen in Christensen's mention of "De Tiger an' de Nyung Lady" as the most interesting tale in her 1892 volume. In this story the haughty young lady refuses to marry the Tiger because he has a "scratch" on his back. The Tiger fools the young woman by disguising himself as a well-bred man, marries her, and makes her a prisoner in his cave. She is rescued by Sambo, a brave hunter who finds her and sets her free. The tale ends with the young woman's mother saying, "I tol' you that you always speak too venomous. God had nebber made a woman for be head of a man." Christensen interpreted this story as "a masculine protest against the prevailing inequality of the sexes" in ancient Africa, where "the modern European order was reversed and the supremacy of woman in the home was well established, the mother being sole guardian of the children, the property-holder and the bestower and perpetuator of the family name." Although Christensen overstated the power of African women, she was, of course, opposed to the patriarchal situation in the "modern European order" and made her point subtly, with humor.[27]

Tales from the Inside Out

While Christensen framed *Afro-American Folk Lore* with her own ideas, her retelling of these tales can also be read "against the grain," so that it is possible to hear the voices of the African Americans who retain a claim to their language. By looking at the collector and then stepping away from her, it is possible to read African American folklore "from the inside out." Christensen's material needs to be viewed as part of an African American vernacular tradition formed in response to the specific historical conditions of Africans in the New World.[28]

For example, in *Afro-American Folk Lore,* the tale "De Reason Why Dog Hates Cat an' Cat Hates Dog" demonstrates the value and importance of "free papers" in a world of slavery. "Now de Dog he ben a free man always. He min' de yard," the story begins. Br'er Dog asked Sis' Cat to "tek charge" of his free papers while he went for a walk. She laid on top of the papers to keep them safe and fell asleep. When she saw a rat, however, she forgot about the papers and chased it. While she was up, the wind blew the dog's "free papers" away. He was so angry with Sis' Cat that all dogs have chased all cats ever since this incident. This tale is pointedly specific in its message to guard the written evidence of freedom in a land of slavery.[29]

In addition to Christensen's reading of "De Tiger an' de Nyung Lady" as a tale of gender inequality, this story could be read as a vernacular warning to African American women and men not to slight their fellow slaves because they had a "scratch," or the marks of a severe whipping, on their backs. While slave owners might have viewed such a scar as the sign of a dangerous slave, African Americans had to look out for one another and view signs of resistance with respect. These differing interpretations show how malleable the text of *Afro-American Folk Lore* could be.[30]

Another way of looking at trickster tales is through the transformation of Pan-African symbols in the New World. Literary critic Henry Gates focuses on the figure of mischievous and powerful deity Esu-Elegbara in the Yoruba and Fon cultures. Esu-Elegbara became the "signifying monkey" upon transference to the United States. The trickster monkey and Br'er Rabbit engaged in "signifying" upon the larger animals. African American storytellers might be doing the same. It adds another layer of meaning to think of informants such as Prince Baskin "signifying," or producing double meanings, even as they talked to Christensen. She may have interpreted Baskin literally when he told her he was a trickster during slavery times, but he might still have been playing the trickster even as he spoke to her.[31]

It is also significant that black people were reluctant to share their tales with Christensen. In 1875 she noted in her diary, "staid at home from the

Reading Circle because Jack Snipes was coming to tell me stories but he didn't [come]." As Christensen explained later in an article for *Mount Holyoke:* "It was no easy task, for I found that the old negroes felt that those tales belonged to a bygone era. 'Fo de war I ben use for tell dem story to de chilluns, but sence Freedom come I done forgit all,' one old mauma told me. But here and there a story teller could be found who would accept a small sum in exchange for a story." This reluctance may have arisen in order to keep white people from gaining even more power over African Americans through knowledge of their attitudes toward them. It may also have been a savvy tactic to get Christensen to pay. Or it is entirely possible that the old woman who explained the situation to Christensen was being candid. Sea Islanders' silence may have come from the sense that the trickster tales applied to slavery more explicitly than they did to the New South and that new vernacular strategies, such as the blues, as well as new rhetorical strategies, such as the "New Negro," would have to be devised to deal with changing economic and political situations.[32]

Folklorist

Since Christensen did not consider these African American trickster tales appropriate for children, for whom was her book intended? Christensen wrote in her preface that "such legends must always be interesting to all students of folk lore; and as a simple study of the legends of Afro-America this unpretending little volume is presented." In the end it was mainly students and scholars of folklore who were interested in Christensen's work. Christensen's slim volume won her the respect of leading folklorists and others in Boston's intellectual and reform community. Her friends gave her the wry nickname "The Original Uncle Remus," and as Christensen proudly wrote, "an editor of the *Boston [Evening] Transcript* paid me the compliment of inviting me to join the Author's Club, to which he belonged."[33]

American folklorists in the 1890s were divided into two camps, the anthropologists and the literary folklorists. At its founding in 1888, the aim of the American Folklore Society had been to transform the study of folklore from an amateur pursuit into a scientific discipline. Its founder, William Wells Newell, called for the collection of "Lore of Negroes of the Southern States of the Union" along with English, American Indian, French Canadian, and Mexican lore. In 1891 literary folklorists, under the leadership of Fletcher Bassett, a retired naval officer, split off from anthropologists and formed the Chicago Folklore Society "for the purpose of collecting, studying, and publishing traditional literature."[34]

Although Abbie Christensen would have been considered an amateur rather than a professionally trained anthropologist, she was courted by both folklore societies. Shortly after the publication of her book in 1892, Christensen began receiving letters from Helen Bassett of the Chicago Folklore Society and from Newell and his American Folklore Society. Bassett asked Christensen to present a paper on "the work done in Afro-American Lore in the States" at the International Folk Lore Congress of the World's Columbian Exposition in July 1893. Christensen declined this offer, although she accepted membership in the Chicago Folklore Society and sent a copy of *Afro-American Folk Lore,* which Bassett presented at one of the society's meetings. Bassett also requested that Christensen send in "charms or objects that belong in a folklore collection" and legends from her South Carolina friends. Christensen seems to have attempted to fill these requests through her husband, who sent Christensen a rabbit's foot and wrote that he was trying without success to collect African American tales. "I probably could get you some stories," Niels Christensen wrote, "but the negroes give the bare outlines of them, a skeleton story as it were and I can't dress them up." Later he did send a tale, although he did not "think there is much to it."[35]

Shortly after she ended her correspondence with Bassett, Christensen began to communicate with Newell. He promised that he would call on Christensen and published a notice of her book in the *Journal of American Folklore.* The convenience of its Cambridge address and the presence of abolitionists, especially her friend Thomas Wentworth Higginson, drew Christensen into the American Folklore Society. Finally, her training as a botanist may have made her more inclined to follow the greater emphasis on science in the anthropological wing of the folklorists.[36]

Afro-American Folk Lore was reviewed favorably by Newell in the *Journal of American Folklore.* Newell reprinted large portions of Christensen's preface on "the ethical character of the tales" and then went on to use the review to discuss trickster tales of various cultures. His assessment of Christensen's work was brief and polite. "This pleasing and welcome little volume contains seventeen tales, for the most part variants of those already given by Uncle Remus, but in some cases original," Newell wrote. Even though he added in the next sentence that Christensen had actually published some of her tales "before the advent of Uncle Remus," it seemed that "The Original Uncle Remus" would never escape from Harris's shadow.[37]

Folklorists had expressed interest in Harris's collections from the time of the first publication of *Uncle Remus: His Songs and Sayings*. Harris, in turn, became a founding member of the American Folklore Society. Although he engaged in the comparative study of tales when he wrote *Nights with Uncle Remus*, he soured on the controversies over the African origins of his material and ended up parodying scientific ethnographers in his 1903 book, *Wally Wanderoon and His Story-Telling Machine*.[38]

Christensen steadfastly maintained that the animal stories she collected originated in Africa. She later recalled that at the time her book was published, "a scholarly friend . . . objected to the title 'Afro-American' etc.; he said the term was inaccurate—unscientific." Newell and other folklore scholars, however, seemed to agree with Christensen in 1892. Christensen followed this debate with interest, marking on a preliminary American Folklore Society program a paper by Adolph Gerber on the relation between the Uncle Remus tales and the animal stories of other nations. Attacks on the African character of the stories grew stronger in the decades after *Afro-American Folk Lore* was published, but Christensen did not change her mind. Informants such as Baskin had told her that older slaves from Africa had borne the tradition of the animal stories along with them. Several of the tales she collected contained African words, and for Christensen, this evidence seemed to settle the matter.[39]

Christensen and Harris both influenced the study of African American folklore by emphasizing dialect and animal tales. Perhaps they chose to write in dialect because northern and southern white writers before them had often represented black speech in this way. Both collectors claimed that they were simply repeating the tales they had heard "verbatim." African American animal tales seemed to appeal to their audiences, and storytellers seemed relatively willing to tell them, perhaps because their messages were more oblique than the messages in stories with human characters. Enslaved Africans had also created the more explicitly confrontational "John and the Old Master" cycle of human trickster tales in the New World, but did not record them.[40]

When Newell wrote to Christensen a second time, he seemed particularly interested in hearing what animal tales revealed about the character of African Americans. Newell invited her to speak at the 9 December 1892 meeting of the Cambridge, Massachusetts branch of the American Folklore Society. Perhaps thinking of the "amoral" character of the tales, he suggested that she discuss "the ethics, and the original and improved or changed character of these negroes." Newell later referred to the same theme when reviewing Elizabeth Botume's *First Days amongst the Contrabands,* published the same year as *Afro-American Folk Lore.* Because Botume's memoirs dealt with "racial character," Newell believed that they had a connection with folklore. Given the difficulties of their situation, he wrote, "the progress of the negro race in the Southern States is extraordinary."[41]

These explicit references by Newell confirm John Roberts's argument that African American folklore was used in the debate over African American character waged between the North and the South after the Civil War. Newell, Christensen, and Botume seemed to look forward to progress and evolution for African Americans, while apologists for slavery predicted devolution. Since Africans or African Americans were not considered sufficiently authoritative to speak for themselves, scholars would have to be consulted. Newell added that he also expected "to have a negro, the son of an African chief," at the meeting. Newell invited Christensen because "this negro will not be sufficient in himself to ensure the success of the meeting." Neither Christensen nor the son of the African chief seems to have complied with Newell's request, since the 9 December 1892 meeting's minutes in the *Journal of American Folklore* makes no mention of the appearance of either guest.[42]

In the same issue of the *Journal of American Folklore* in which he reviewed Christensen's book, Newell sounded a cautionary note regarding the feud among folklore societies, strongly suggesting that readers should not participate in the International Folklore Congress planned by Fletcher and Helen Bassett for the World's Columbian Exposition. Newell argued that because this congress was connected with the Department of Literature, which was subject to "loose theorizing," folklorists should go instead to the Department of Anthropology, which he regarded as "sound science." Perhaps Christensen was under the influence of Newell's advice when she decided to offer a paper to Frederic Noble of the African Ethnological Congress instead of aligning herself with the Bassetts' International Folklore Congress.[43]

Noble sent Christensen "Suggestions for a Program for The African Congress" indicating that her paper would be in the literature section along with those of writer George Washington Cable and J. E. Rankin, a poet at How-ard University—leading literary lights who took a stand against racism. Other sections covered by the African congress were the arts, philology, his-tory and geography, religion, science, and sociology and political science. Proposed papers at the congress included such topics as "Did American Slav-ery Contribute to the Civilization of Africa?," "What Can America Do for Her Afro-Americans in Reparation?," "The Negro and the Amendments to the Constitution," and "The Results of Twenty-five Years of Education for the Negro." Christensen was not able to attend the World's Columbian Exposition in person, but her paper on "African and Afro-American Folk Lore" was read by "a leading Swedenborgian minister" on 16 August 1893 at the African Ethnological Congress. Perhaps once again it was her respon-sibilities to her children that kept her from sharing her knowledge of African American culture and interacting with others with similar interests. The African congress might have furthered her cause in intellectual and antiracist work. Through the printed word, however, she continued to read and write for those interested in African Americans and reform.[44]

An excerpt from Christensen's paper was published in the June 1894 issue of the *Journal of American Folklore,* in the "Notes and Queries" section under the heading "Spirituals and 'Shouts' of Southern Negroes." In this excerpt Christensen showed a knowledge of Sea Island African American culture greater than could be seen in her stories of "de bestises," as she referred to the animal tales. She also moved back to the older abolitionist emphasis on spirituality, rather than the supposed immorality of African Americans found in the animal tales. Christensen wrote that "sperrichels" were sung by African Americans "at night on the plantations when they held what they called the 'shout,' a kind of religious dance." Though Christensen referred to the shout as a dance, African Americans Baptists who forbade dancing were adamant that it was not. Participants in a shout were careful never to cross their feet, which is considered dancing. Christensen wrote correctly that shouts were held in "Praise Houses," small, plain wooden buildings where the residents of each former plantation met to pray and offer praise. She hypothesized that the shout originated from "African dances used in fetish or idol worship." On the Sea Islands, the Praise House or cabin room floor was cleared for the worshipers, who formed a ring that increased as onlook-ers joined the circle. The best singers and clappers led the shout. Christensen wrote that "the fascination of the music and the swaying motion of the dance is so great that one can hardly refrain from joining the magic circle in response to the invitation of the enthusiastic clappers." This admission was unusual for Christensen and connected her to her informants. In the almost obligatory manner of so many folklorists, Christensen also warned (incorrectly) that the shout was dying out and would soon be a dim memory. Christensen's turn toward spirituals, which were more consistent with the abolitionist outlook of her parents, signaled the move she made in later years toward promoting charity and education for African Americans.[45]

Christensen did not remain long in folklore circles, maintaining her membership in the American Folklore Society for only one year, 1894. She envisioned a larger appeal for *Afro-American Folk Lore* within the reform-minded network of Boston and South Carolina friends to whom she sent copies of the book. Christensen's publisher wrote her that the North would be "the more important section," and Christensen submitted the book to the *Woman's Journal,* the suffrage magazine run by Lucy Stone and Henry Blackwell. Blackwell reviewed the book and compared it favorably to Harris's because its tales were "free from any impress of the author's own personality." Blackwell took the analogies of the animal tales further than any other interpreter had, suggesting explicitly that Br'er Rabbit was "the typical negro, while Br'er Wolf is the typical white man." He hoped that the "gifted compiler" would publish more tales for "young and old . . . for instruction or amusement."[46]

Christensen also gave copies of *Afro-American Folk Lore* to abolitionists William Lloyd Garrison and Lucy Stone. Garrison wrote to Christensen, thanking her for her gift and telling her, "it is always interesting to recognize old friends in new garbs." Like Blackwell, he compared Christensen to Harris, but he preferred her work to his. Garrison wrote: "It is evident that Harris has served up Uncle Remus with much of his own humorous sauce which while adding to the piquancy of the dish changes its severe original flavor. As an accurate portrayal of the tales as told by the colored people themselves your unadorned transcript will doubtless be adjudged the palm." Lucy Stone found "added interest" in *Afro-American Folk Lore* because it gave her "a fresh introduction" to Christensen as an author.[47]

Drawing on her hybrid regional allegiances, Christensen thought that *Afro-American Folk Lore* might also have a southern market. She asked her friend Virginia Young to inquire regarding the chances for "*Folk Lore's* having a good sale in Charleston" upon her next visit to that city. Young was too busy explaining her suffrage views to curious Charlestonians to fulfill Christensen's wishes, but she sent her friend the names and addresses of several booksellers in the old city. Later in 1892 Christensen sent her book to A. J. Wakefield, whose retelling of the tales had originally inspired her to write them down. Christensen's warnings in the introduction notwithstanding, Wakefield loaned the book to a young mother and referred to it as "a book for children." He tried to persuade the largest bookseller in Jacksonville, Florida, to stock *Afro-American Folk Lore* but did not meet with success. In an unconventional move, Christensen's publisher employed an African American woman as an agent to sell her book in the South, but her efforts were also fruitless.[48]

The most intriguing person Christensen wrote to regarding her book was black novelist Frances Ellen Watkins Harper, whom she had met through her WCTU activity. In a move that indicated a willingness to cross racial boundaries, Christensen asked for advice on how to reach an African American audience. Harper voiced no direct objection to Christensen's presentation of African Americans in *Afro-American Folk Lore*. Rather, she politely declined her help and offered her opinion on how African Americans probably regarded her book.[49]

Harper wrote that she could not help Christensen because she was "getting my book through the printer's hands and have been engaged to weariness in the work of rewriting and rearranging." She doubted that *Afro-American Folk Lore* would appeal to African Americans because it reminded them of the "sad past" of slavery, which they were trying to forget. She also advised Christensen to market the book in a cheaper edition since "poverty is one of our race inheritances." In light of this circumstance, Harper charged one dollar when selling her book to "the colored people." Christensen's volume was probably within this price range, since her publisher wrote that he sold copies of *Afro-American Folk Lore* to a Beaufort bookseller for seventy-five cents.[50]

Christensen intended her book to sell, but *Afro-American Folk Lore* was not a financial success. Because her original publisher, J. G. Cupples, went bankrupt, Christensen did not have the assistance of a firm in promoting her book. More important, Joel Chandler Harris had already "captured the market." Charles Colcock Jones, another collector of African American stories in the Gullah dialect, could well have said the same. His *Negro Myths of the*

Georgia Coast, published in 1888, also did not sell as well as Harris's Uncle Remus tales. Like Christensen's Gullah stories, Jones's dialect versions of the myths were difficult to read. They both also lacked the secondary plot of storyteller and child that personalized and bound the Uncle Remus stories together. Finally, Christensen sabotaged her own success by pronouncing her work unfit for young children and alienating her potential black audience with the insensitive Darwinian references in her introduction.[51]

When Christensen decided to republish *Afro-American Folk Lore* in 1895, her new Boston publisher, Lee and Shepard, advised her to create two different versions of the book—one with the abolitionist poem by John Greenleaf Whittier for the North and one without the poem for southern whites. When Abbie told her husband of this plan, he wrote that he would do "nothing of the kind for the sake of the few copies that could be sold in Charleston." Abbie went ahead with the two versions, but copied the poem by hand into the front of the copy she gave to Niels Sr. It is clear that she had become used to moving between the North and the South, making chameleon-like changes to fit into each region. These two 1898 versions of her book represented a division of her loyalties. With the deletion of Whittier's poem, southern paternalists could enjoy the pleasures of reading dialect tales with few hints that they had been written by a carpetbagger. Abbie Christensen was of the New South at the same time that she was of New England.[52]

The Legacy of Afro-American Folk Lore

The publication of her book and the presentation of her paper with a similar title seemed to close this chapter in Christensen's life. In the fall of 1893 her attention was turned to the immediate physical needs of the black and white people of Beaufort by the disastrous hurricane that struck Beaufort in September 1893, leaving death and destruction in its wake. Christensen was in Boston at the time of the disaster, and she used all the resources in her power to raise funds and materials for the hurricane victims. This use of Christensen's talents in writing and organizing was of direct benefit to over a thousand destitute African Americans whose homes and crops had been wrecked.[53]

Once Christensen moved from collecting tales from African Americans to collecting funds from whites, she continued her work in this direction. With the money she earned from the publication of *Afro-American Folk Lore,* Christensen began in 1898 to try to relieve some of the poverty she had seen among African Americans in the remote rural parts of Port Royal Island. As she later wrote in her *Alumnae Quarterly* article: "After paying all the bills for publishing, I kept the small surplus from the sales to swell a fund we were gathering for our project—a Tuskegee branch school on our Port Royal Island." Although she did not say so explicitly, Christensen may have felt a responsibility to give something back to the African American community whose creativity had helped her achieve a small modicum of fame. Christensen turned her book into a fund-raising device for the school and sent it to people whom she thought likely to make donations. Her daughter Andrea recalled, "When I was small, she would take me along to homes in New England in her search for funds. I would read the stories, many of which were in Gullah." Christensen was occasionally consulted by later scholars of linguistics and folklore, but collecting tales was never again her main pursuit.[54]

Instead, Christensen tied her interest in African American culture to a concern for the welfare of black people in her community. This development in Christensen's consciousness following the 1893 hurricane could be seen in the Port Royal Agricultural School and in a narrative she wrote about a camping trip to Bay Point beach, near Beaufort, in April 1903. This letter, which she sent to the "Listener" column of the *Boston Evening Transcript,* connected African American folklore with Christensen's thoughts on the fate of Africans on both sides of the Atlantic. The paper's revision of her letter shunned controversy and included only a description of the beach and its sea turtles and alligator, but Christensen's draft, titled "Glimpses of Bay Point," contains rich musings on the subject of race.[55]

Christensen described Bay Point in Beaufort County, an undeveloped island beach, where she and her friends sat around a driftwood fire listening to the thunder of waves breaking on the shore, while stars illuminated the night sky. Despite the deserted setting, reports of a "negro riot" in Beaufort were on Christensen's mind. She believed that the supposed riot had been reported with "foolish exaggeration." African Americans had massed to protect two Hampton County debtors whom they feared were in danger of being lynched. Abbie wrote that she took pride in the fact that a lynching was prevented by Beaufort's black and white citizens who cooperated to see that the law was enforced without incident.

Christensen turned to the subject of folklore when she described the talents of the African American couple who worked for the white campers on Bay Point. Cupid Polite was a gifted storyteller, according to Christensen. She wrote: "Actors we had seen, but never one who could mimic and personate animals to such perfection. Br. Rabbit with Br. Wolf for his 'Grandaddy ridin' hoss,' 'Sis' Partridge who lef' her head home fur ten' to her business,' 'Deer an' Cooter on de ten mile track[,]' 'Br Crane in do cou't at de trial of Br. Rabbit'[—] these and more he made to speak and move before us in vivid action. How we wished to show him to northern friends." Christensen had improved on her description of Prince Baskin, but she still saw Polite as a person she wanted to "show," not introduce, to northern friends.

Her portrait of Cupid and Chloe singing plantation songs for their white audience was more romantic and drew Christensen into broader, more political themes. She wrote: "Chloe's voice is rich in quality . . . and listening to its cadences, earnest, plaintive, tender, how could one choose but muse on the possibilities in her exotic race? Our forefathers planted them here for their own use and behoof, and they have served us faithfully for nigh three hundred years. Do not we, proud Caucassions, owe it to ourselves to give to them opportunity for development and progress?"[56]

With this passage Christensen summed up a philosophy that encompassed both African American folklore and education. Folktales did not inspire her as much as the creative expression in spirituals, but the sum led Christensen to muse upon the undeveloped talents and long-suffering of African Americans. Even though she was not the daughter of slave owners, she did not exempt her ancestors from the part they had played in introducing slavery to the New World. As she wrote she may have been thinking again of the collective "sin" in Whittier's poem "Song of the Negro Boatmen at Port Royal." Earlier in 1903 the gunning down of Narciso G. Gonzales, the moderate editor of the (Columbia) *State*, by Ben Tillman's nephew outside the state capitol building had prompted Christensen to look to slavery as an explanation for this violence. As she explained to her son, "There is naturally much feeling throughout the State about the cowardly murder of editor Gonzales by the brutal Lieut. Gov. James Tillman. . . . All such cowardice and brutality seem to be the direct legacy of slavery, which trained the whites to cruelty and cowardice (i.e., attacks on the defenseless) as surely as it trained the blacks to dishonesty and deceit." Christensen's differences with those who romanticized slavery were obvious in this analysis.[57]

In "Glimpses of Bay Point," Christensen connected Africa and "Afro-Americans" as she had done in her folklore work. She wrote, "Africa is calling to the world today, 'Come and help us,' but to us in America the cry is not from afar, it is at our doors." She celebrated the "exotic" yet "faithful" nature of African Americans, distancing them from proud Caucasians, whom she called to take responsibility for the fate of blacks. While she depicted African difference in a positive way, her attitude was still paternalist. The continent of Africa was only calling for help in the form of colonization and "civilization" in Europeans' imaginations, and if blacks had been granted true equality in the United States, they would not have needed as much "help." Christensen, however, did not call for charity; she asked that whites grant African Americans "opportunity for development and progress." She was probably thinking of the newly founded Port Royal Agricultural School as she made these statements. "Development and progress" were the watchwords of this institution.[58]

Over the next several decades, while Christensen raised money for what became known as the Shanklin School, *Afro-American Folk Lore* became a reference point in the body of coastal "negro dialect" material imitated by white writers such as John G. Williams and Ambrose Gonzales in humorous pieces in South Carolina newspapers. Gonzales mentioned Christensen in the introduction to his collected Gullah stories, and Williams autographed his pamphlet *De Ole Plantation* for Christensen. The dialect material of these two journalists was more of a burlesque than Christensen's "unadorned" tales and made no reference to "students of folklore."[59]

George Philip Krapp of Columbia University and George Armstrong Wauchope and Reed Smith of the University of South Carolina wrote to Christensen in the 1920s in order to obtain copies of her book for their studies of Gullah. Although Christensen had never used this term, it became increasingly popular among white scholars, from the 1920s on, as a way to describe the African American culture found on the Sea Islands. "Gullah" and "Geechee" were terms used occasionally by African Americans to describe the type of language spoken on the Sea Islands. The word "Gullah" may have come from the country name Angola, although most Africans brought to the Sea Islands were probably from the rice-growing region that is now Sierra Leone and Liberia. "Gullah," which is now considered by most scholars to be a creole of several western African languages and English, became even more fraught with controversy over its linguistic origins than black folklore had been a generation earlier. Most white scholars saw the language as a corruption or "baby-talk" version of the Old English spoken by white slave owners. Not until 1949, when Lorenzo Dow Turner published his *Africanisms in the Gullah Dialect,* did scholars begin once again to accept the African origins of this creole.[60]

Wauchope regarded Christensen's *Afro-American Folk Lore* and Williams's "Coteney Sermons" of "great importance in a literary and linguistic study of a new type." He planned to write an article for *The Southern Magazine* on "the Gullah in Literature," in which he intended to use Christensen's work. Christensen disagreed with Krapp and Gonzales, who argued that African languages played no part in the Gullah dialect. Smith may have offended Christensen because of his clash with the folklorist Christensen most admired, Elsie Clews Parsons.[61]

Although Christensen did not object to being associated with Williams and Gonzales, her interests and style of presentation were much closer to those of Parsons than to theirs. Parsons, a northern feminist and anthropologist, visited the Sea Islands in 1919 to gather African American folklore. She stayed for two weeks, collecting mostly at the Penn School on Saint Helena Island and making occasional trips to more remote black communities. Parsons also listed among her informants ten pupils at the Port Royal Agricultural School, which Christensen had helped to found. Abbie Christensen probably directed her there after her introduction to Parsons through Grace Bigelow House, a principal at the Penn School.[62]

Parsons was mainly interested in gathering as many tales as possible, although she also included folk customs and superstitions among the material she collected. After she visited South Carolina, she wrote an article critical of Joel Chandler Harris's African American folklore collection. In a review of his posthumously published *Uncle Remus Returns,* Parsons pointed out that Harris's settings, Uncle Remus and the little boy, and a "developed" animal community owed more to Harris's literary talents than to an accurate recording of African American folktales. She also noted that African Americans would generally not share their folklore with whites because of the air of condescension and bigotry with which whites treated blacks. She wrote, "It takes something of an artist to listen to a folk-tale as well as to tell it, and between artists theories of social inequality do not obtrude." Parsons would probably have included Christensen in the select community of listening artists. The anthropologist's preference for Christensen's and Jones's "unadorned" tales made the "dressing" of Harris's stories seem all the more overpowering and unnecessary.[63]

From the hours she spent with Christensen, Parsons drew new knowledge of Sea Island African American folklore, and Christensen found "a kindred spirit" to whom she expressed feelings that she seldom revealed. In a note thanking Parsons for sending her *Folk-Tales of Andros Island, Bahamas,* Christensen wrote: "*Please* keep Beaufort in mind, and some day come back. Let me know *when* for I meet few kindred spirits—please don't mind if I imply you're one—I'm a free lance myself by nature, with only a streak of conservatism." Christensen must have felt a kinship with Parsons because of her feminist ideals, folklore interests, and independent lifestyle. Her brief meeting with Parsons also made her aware of her longing for like-minded intellectual companionship, which she could find little of in Beaufort.[64]

Christensen, a pioneering folklorist, now aged sixty-seven, and Parsons, a forty-four-year-old star in the field of anthropology, each had an influence on the other. Parsons later wrote back that she had enjoyed her visit and thanked Christensen for sending her a copy of *Afro-American Folk Lore.* In her 1923 book, *Folklore of the Sea Islands, South Carolina,* Parsons thanked Christensen in a footnote and praised her for being "long since esteemed among the most faithful of pioneer recorders of American Negro folklore." Parsons also revised some of her lectures on African American folktales to include Christensen's material, which she became aware of through her meeting with the older folklorist.[65]

Though the two strong women *were* kindred spirits, Parsons saw at least one generational difference between herself and Christensen. In her preface to *Folklore of the Sea Islands* she made this difference clear in a discussion of "vulgar tales." One of her informants would stop when he got to parts of tales he considered indecent. She wrote: "'I leave it dere,' he would say. White story-writers, like Harris or Jones or Christensen, have left it there, too, I infer. Indeed, Mrs. Christensen has told me that, faithful recorder as she was, on this point she has been selective: the stories she found 'vulgar' she had not taken." Parsons was part of a generation whose norms were not as Victorian as Christensen's. Like her contemporary, African American folk-lorist Zora Neale Hurston, Parsons debunked the scientific validity of racism and Victorian judgment of the morality of other cultures. Through Parsons, Christensen may have become more attuned to the idea that cultures, including African and European, were equal. Parsons, whom Franz Boas described as his "fellow in the struggle for freedom from prejudice," may have influenced Christensen's radical universalism in politics as well as culture in the 1920s and 1930s.[66]

The conflict between Parsons and southern male scholars had racial as well as sexual overtones, which Reed Smith emphasized in a loaded reference to Parsons, who had criticized his praise of Gonzales's work. He wrote: "I have met Dr. Elsie Clews Parsons, . . . [but] we aren't as mutually attracted to each other as you and she seem to be. What do you think of her attempt to get indecent folk-tales direct from Negro men?" Parsons's distaste for Gonzales's work showed the starker differences in the political agendas of northern anthropological folklore collectors and southern literary folklore collectors in the generation after Christensen. Although she favored Parsons, Christensen never publicly took a stand between these two versions of African American folklore. This ambiguity probably came from Christensen's unique position as a hybrid Yankee-Southerner. Just as she had printed copies of her *Afro-American Folk Lore* with and without Whittier's poem, Christensen sought to please both sections, a predilection that could only have been heightened by the use of the book in fund-raising.[67]

Although Christensen's folklore collecting ceased in 1893, she saw her interest live on in a different form in her children. These children of the New South were not as interested in using folklore as part of the project of African American uplift. Frederik Christensen collected bits of African American dialect and used them to entertain whites with "Negro sermons" at social gatherings. It may have been Frederik who made political use of Negro dialect to discredit African American politicians who opposed Niels's political ambitions. In 1908 a column called "Kumbee Brown on Election Matters" featured comments such as: "Seem like de wite pipple try fur hold de nigger down abry side 'e tun. When I stan fur run fur Kongress I tink shore I gwine hob some sort exchange fum de context. . . . Dem pipple onderstan berry well you kin git nigger fur swear enny fashun you tell um pervidin you cash up same time." This use of dialect portrayed African Americans as ignorant and undeserving of the franchise, while the words themselves conveyed this message even more clearly. By introducing them to African American folklore, Abbie Christensen may have indirectly aided her sons' efforts at disfranchisement. It is likely that she knew of these dialect columns since she was writing "stroller" articles for the *Gazette* in the same year. It is unlikely that Abbie authored the "Kumbee Brown" columns, because the style of dialect differed from *Afro-American Folk Lore* and she had shunned the degrading term "nigger" in public and private writings. Nevertheless, the *Gazette*'s misuse of black dialect was the most negative legacy of her folklore collection.[68]

In a different twist on her mother's legacy, Christensen's youngest child, Abby Winch Christensen, or "Winnie," became attracted to Old English folklore and southern white folk culture. Winnie joined the English Folk Song Society and the Appalachian Club while a student at Radcliffe College. The passion of her life was English folk dancing, which she taught at summer camps and at the Pine Mountain Settlement School in Harlan, Kentucky. By teaching at this school during the 1920s, Winnie Christensen combined folklore with "uplift" for poor mountain whites.[69]

In the 1930s Christensen briefly revived the rivalry between herself and Harris in order to assist the Rag-Bag Alley Puppets, a Georgia troupe that performed Br'er Rabbit stories. Harris's son Lucien was trying to contend that his mother, Esther LaRose Harris, "own[ed] exclusive rights to Br'er Rabbit, Br'er Fox, the Tar Baby and probably some others." Christensen wrote the troupe's leader, Kathryn Dallas, informing her of her earlier publication of the Tar Baby tale and suggesting that the puppets perform *Afro-American Folk Lore*. Dallas thanked Christensen but stated that the puppeteers created their own material, with African American folklore serving as inspiration.[70]

At the age of eighty Christensen was able to reflect upon her connection with African American folklore in the early years of her life. She used her reminiscences to promote the Shanklin School in her 1933 *Mount Holyoke Alumnae Quarterly* article, "Folklore on Sea Islands," which explained so much of her career in folklore. The magazine's editor condensed most of the information about the school, focusing on Christensen's years at the seminary and her folklore collection.

Christensen ended her article as she had originally begun her book, with the lines from Whittier's "Song of the Negro Boatmen at Port Royal." She also referred back to the thoughts she had had while writing her letter from Bay Point Beach. Years of reflection and work with African Americans had sharpened her understanding of these earlier lines, which she rewrote to say: "Is it still true that 'close as sin and suffering joined, we march to fate abreast'? At any rate our Caucasian race that held the Africans as bond servants for over 200 years has not yet paid its debt to the former slaves. So let us 'not be weary in well doing, for in due season we shall reap if we faint not.'"[71]

In her handling of African American cultural knowledge, Christensen referred to herself as "of the New South," but she retained some of her abolitionist roots. Christensen criticized slavery and felt she owed a debt to black Americans. On the other hand, in her book Christensen portrayed African Americans in a less than dignified manner. To her, trickster tales were evidence that black people needed assistance in the form of education, which she sought to help them obtain. Christensen's later emphases on spirituals and black education were a clearer return to her abolitionist past.

Like her rival, Joel Chandler Harris, Christensen did not see all the subtleties in African American animal tales, although she was motivated by an appreciation for their "humor and originality." Because of her abolitionist parents, because she wanted to share the tales of southern African Americans with her northern friends, and because she enjoyed collecting and gaining the power of knowledge, Christensen crafted her version of African American culture and made her mark on the study of the "others" all around her.[72]

Chapter Nine

THE SHANKLIN SCHOOL

In August 1897 Paul Watson, an African American minister in Beaufort, wrote an intriguing letter to Abbie Christensen:

> According to my promise I went out into the country and examined very carefully the tract of land to which I called your attention when you were here. ... Would to God that some of our Northern friends would interest themselves in the purchase of this place for the industrial education of our young people.[1]

Christensen took hold of Watson's industrial education idea, rallied northern friends, and started what would later be called the Shanklin School, an important part of African American life on Port Royal Island. Because of differences between them, Watson moved on, but Christensen remained an essential backer of the school for the rest of her life. In the 1900s, when most white women reformers in the New South concentrated on improving schools for white children, Christensen remained committed to carrying on her abolitionist connection to African Americans. Building the Shanklin School was Abbie Christensen's most important act in shaping the race relations of her region. Like many black schools based on Booker T. Washington's Tuskegee model, it embodied both accommodation to whites and black autonomy. Like Christensen, it was a mixture of missionary paternalism and egalitarian idealism.

When forty-six-year-old Abbie Christensen returned to Beaufort on a permanent basis in 1898, her desire for reform did not allow her simply to run her household and take her place as a Beaufort matron. Those who had depended on her care made fewer demands as time passed. Christensen's husband and her two oldest sons, Niels Jr. and Fred, had managed without her in Beaufort for years. Even though Niels Sr.'s Bright's disease had prompted her return in order to nurse him, her husband continued to work as a hardware and lumber merchant along with his oldest sons. Abbie's teenage children, Arthur and Andrea, boarded with one of Christensen's suffragist friends in Brookline as they finished their schooling. Winnie remained with Christensen for a short time in Beaufort until she too went to boarding school in Massachusetts. Arthur and Winnie went on to Harvard and Radcliffe College, while Andrea alternated between Beaufort and art school in Massachusetts. Although Christensen entertained and instructed her children with a steady stream of letters and summertime visits, she had time to "reform Beaufort," with a particular focus on improving conditions for African Americans. In 1906 Abbie's father, R. G. Holmes, died, leaving Abbie to carry on his mission "to make the world better."[2]

In the Wake of a Hurricane

What had happened to African Americans in Beaufort County since Reconstruction? For a time the sale of land in small plots, funds from federal school farms, high cotton prices, and good phosphate industry jobs had enabled African Americans to be independent farmers. Then in 1893 a depression drove crop prices down and a hurricane ravaged the island destroying crops as well as the phosphate industry. Real and metaphorical waves crashed on Sea Islanders for years thereafter. In 1896 the Supreme Court had declared segregation legal, and when the United States gained colonies in the Caribbean and the Pacific through the Spanish-American-Cuban-Filipino war of 1898, people of color around the world came to be seen as a "problem" and "the white man's burden." White southerners also suffered from poor economic conditions, and lacking a solution to their problems, white politicians kept the issue of racial enmity alive, making acceptable the expression of cold hatred and contempt toward African Americans. Even though there were no lynchings in Beaufort County, a young white resident had told Abbie's son in 1895 that "it would be a good thing to kill off half a dozen 'niggers.'" Abbie had attended protests such as a "colored people's meeting" against lynching in 1894 and the Anti-Slavery Memorial Meeting hosted by the African American Woman's Era club in 1897. Such occasions spurred her to make an effort to help African Americans in this time of need.[3]

Christensen's response to the hurricane of 1893 marked her transition from an abolitionist daughter with an interest in black culture to a reform leader intent on improving conditions for Sea Island African Americans. Safe in Boston during the time that the hurricane hit, Christensen received daily reports from the newspaper as well as dramatic letters from her husband.

The Christensen home and business suffered over eight thousand dollars in damage, and saltwater flooding killed every plant in Niels's garden, but this was not as severe as the complete destruction of small wooden cabins, belonging mostly to blacks, on outlying islands. Christensen wrote that along the Sea Island coast over a thousand people were drowned and disease threatened the rest. Abbie wrote three letters to the *Boston Evening Transcript* asking for donations, exclaiming on 9 September 1893: "Oh! For words to portray the condition of those seven thousand homeless, starving poor. . . . With all the fruits of their labor for the thirty years since emancipation carried away in one night, nothing left but the land, what can they do during the next nine months till the crops begin to ripen again?" Christensen distributed appeals at all the Brookline churches, organized collections, and packaged and sent materials to the Sea Islands. Her efforts helped to draw the attention of the nation. The well-known Red Cross leader Clara Barton came to Beaufort and worked with Niels Sr. in aiding survivors. Sea Islanders began to recover, but with low cotton prices and the end of the phosphate industry, most remained poor. In the years that followed, Abbie Christensen looked for other ways to assist them.[4]

Instead of tackling segregation, disfranchisement, and white violence head-on, Abbie focused instead on black children's poverty, an issue that raised sympathy rather than controversy. Although the town of Beaufort still hosted a healthy community of black artisans and businesspeople, children from the nearby rural areas of Port Royal were in need. As she later told her readers in an article for the *Mount Holyoke Alumnae Quarterly:* "Groups of hungry and ragged children used to come into town bearing in their hands bundles of lightwood which they had cut from the pitch pine stumps. After walking from five to ten miles with a lightwood bundle on his head a boy or girl would feel well rewarded to receive ten cents for it. These children, barefoot, ragged and forlorn were pitiful to see." As Abbie watched these children with her own, more fortunate daughters by her side, she wondered how to help them.[5]

At first Christensen tried the traditional forms of charity. She continued to solicit barrels of clothing and supplies from her Brookline neighbors and church sisters and distributed them to poverty-stricken Sea Islanders who came to her door. Abbie also donated vegetable seeds to encourage African Americans to take up truck farming, which was becoming successful in the region. Part of the problem in the Port Royal area, however, was that some white landowners who wished to engage in large-scale vegetable farming had brought in poor African Americans from other regions precisely because they wanted laborers who did not have their own farms.[6]

In a close echo of her father's paternalist words during Reconstruction, Abbie described the African Americans of the area as being "as peaceable and well behaved as such ig[norant] people can be, but they know nothing of thrifty liv[ing] & wise ways of cultivating of the land." For a variety of reasons Christensen came to the conclusion that improved education would teach self-sufficiency and eliminate the need for piecemeal charity.[7]

An Agricultural School

To begin with, the rural Port Royal area maintained woefully inadequate schools for African Americans. Black teachers received half the salary of white teachers, and their schools were open for only three months of the year. "We talked of these conditions with friends and neighbors, and a committee was formed including my husband and me," Abbie wrote. Drawing on Watson's idea (but not acknowledging him), the committee decided to start an agricultural school.[8]

Outside of the need for a school and Watson's plea, there were other factors that led Christensen to choose education as her cause. She had watched the women she admired, her mother and Elizabeth Botume, devote themselves to African American education. Laura Towne's Penn School on Saint Helena Island, the northern-based American Missionary Association's Avery Institute in Charleston, and Philadelphian Martha Schofield's vocational Institute in Aiken all enjoyed a good reputation for producing prosperous black citizens and leaders. Christensen was a former teacher of black students, and she had continued to read and study pedagogical theory during her years as a young mother. For Christensen, the abolitionist legacy was real, and improved education for the next generations seemed the best way to continue it.[9]

Industrial education, the kind of schooling she chose, was the most popular approach to the training of black children at the turn of the century. Abbie had washed dishes and performed other chores at Mount Holyoke Female Seminary, but this labor was touted in only a minor way as character-building, not as a crucial part of the academic curriculum. At black industrial schools, however, vocational training in trades, agriculture, and "domestic science" became the central mission. But this format could also be applied to poor whites. In 1898 the *Charleston News and Courier* featured a positive article on a black minister who promoted twin public industrial schools, "one for white and one for colored children." In the years that followed, white South Carolina club women also supported the formation of industrial schools for poor white children.[10]

The specific industrial school program that Christensen came to follow was begun by white missionary Samuel Chapman Armstrong at Hampton Institute in Virginia in 1868. As Armstrong's educational philosophy for freed people evolved through the turbulent 1870s and 1880s, it could be distilled to "agricultural self-sufficiency through land-ownership, and abstinence from politics" as the black path to the American dream. Armstrong's paternalistic mission to uplift "backward races" would have made sense to Abbie Christensen. So too would his selection of Booker T. Washington, a Hampton alumnus and Armstrong's protégé. Washington, as a black man at the head of a black institution, Tuskegee Institute, gave Armstrong's ideas legitimacy. Many black graduates of Hampton and Tuskegee became teachers who brought their training in industrial and agricultural education to schools throughout the South. In the 1880s and 1890s Washington's fame grew as he courted northern industrial philanthropy and southern conservative goodwill. The "Wizard of Tuskegee," as Washington was known, accepted segregation and tried to make a virtue out of necessity.[11]

Industrial education became hardened into an inflexible policy through the formation of the philanthropic General Education Board by John D. Rockefeller in 1899. Because of the influence of this fund, it was almost impossible for a southern black school to receive funds without subscribing to its program. The Saint Helena Island Penn School made the transition in 1900, changing from an academic to an industrial curriculum, to gain funds from the General Education Board's subsidiaries, the Peabody and Slater Funds.[12]

Abbie was familiar with Hampton Institute and Tuskegee because the schools' faculties and students regularly came to New England for fundraising. In Brookline in the 1890s the Christensen family heard speakers and singers from Hampton and Tuskegee, including Booker T. Washington, in 1894. Christensen had also helped Carey Gray, a young man from Beaufort, obtain financial help to attend Tuskegee. In 1897 Christensen had had Margaret Murray Washington, Booker's wife, to dinner at her home in Brookline. "We had corresponded with Booker Washington and I had met

Mrs. Washington and secured her interest and a promise of their help to start a school on the Tuskegee plan," Abbie later wrote. Abbie's special connection with other women reformers, regardless of race, was the crucial link in helping to start her school.[13]

Abbie also drew inspiration from teachers Laura Towne and Ellen Murray of the Penn School. In 1897 Christensen visited the school and pressed her sons to do the same. Fred was favorably impressed, writing: "After lunch we went across the road to a brick church, built in antebellum days, and there watched a temperance meeting of the school. The scholars sang some spirituals for us. The people seem better off on St Helena than on this island. They have better houses. The crops look well." Better houses and crops were the marks of success for which Abbie and her sons were aiming. These goals were in harmony with those of the black community. Future visits and the friendship between Christensen and Murray sustained the ties between Penn and the future Shanklin School.[14]

Beaufort's Mather School, founded by northern Baptist missionary Rachel Mather in 1868, was another local model. Abbie did not mention it, but her husband and sons were well aware of the institution since they were the contractors constructing its new school building in 1901. Mather died in 1903, but teachers from the Women's American Baptist Mission Society carried on its work, teaching reading, writing, arithmetic, and "industrial" skills such as cooking and sewing to African American girls until well into the 1950s.[15]

In 1898 Abbie wrote her son Arthur that Daniel Bythewood, a favorite former student and now the minister of Beaufort's prestigious Tabernacle Baptist Church, had been to the house twice to "talk school business." She wrote, "They have asked your father and a colored man to act as trustees," and they asked her to act as treasurer. She replied that she would rather be "what the colored people call a selecter–collector" and raise funds for the school. Among the 1898 founders there were three black and four white trustees. In a bow to gender conventions, Abbie remained behind the scenes of this biracial group.[16]

Somehow Paul Watson had slipped out of this picture. The reason is unknown. It is clear, however, that starting a black school in 1898 involved a frustrating negotiation between African American needs, aspirations, and initiative and the dependent position of the black community in a town, a state, and a nation controlled by whites. While Watson and Bythewood had the desire to found a school, they did not have enough money and hoped for help from sympathetic whites. Help, however, usually meant struggles for control.

Watson and Bythewood had both received their college degrees from Lincoln University in Pennsylvania, one of the oldest historically black institutions in the nation. They were pastors of the two most prominent black Baptist churches in Beaufort. Bythewood led Tabernacle Baptist, while Watson preached at the First African Baptist church, or "F.A.B." Watson had first worked with Abbie in 1897 on the organization of a reading room for African Americans. This socially concerned preacher started benevolent societies and other social projects wherever he pastored, and he eventually went on to head the agricultural and industrial department of Benedict College, a black Baptist school in Columbia, South Carolina. Bythewood went on to become a superintendent of schools in Beaufort and a trustee of Morris College of Sumter, South Carolina. It is hard to imagine men of such talent and drive subordinating all their wishes to the white trustees of the new school. When it became clear that this is what they would have to do, they probably left the project to the Christensens.[17]

Although she did not indicate the reasons for their split, Abbie feared that Watson would found a rival school in 1901. Her son Fred tried to reassure her and reminded Abbie that there were already three other schools for blacks operated by white women in the county. He believed that all could coexist without conflict. Abbie's fears illustrate that she was not satisfied with just anyone putting up a school on Port Royal; she wanted it to be *her* school. In addition to wanting to help the people of Port Royal, Abbie also wanted control.[18]

The greatest control came from the power of the purse, and that may have been one reason Abbie wanted to be a "selector." This role would also enable Abbie to be a spokesperson for southern African Americans in the North, a role she had enjoyed as a folklorist and as a fund-raiser after the 1893 hurricane. Unfortunately, soliciting funds was an uphill struggle in 1898. Most of the contributions were small sums. Christensen blamed the United States' racist and "foolish" war with Spain for draining interest away from her cause, and she and the others temporarily gave the project up until the war ended.[19]

Education and Black Suffrage

When Abbie took up the project again from 1900 to 1901, controversy swirled around the issue of black suffrage and the school's relationship to this issue. Ellen Murray of the Penn School, an Englishwoman and steadfast radical abolitionist, and Abbie's son Niels held opposite opinions, and each of them tried to sway Abbie.

In 1900 Murray and Saint Helena African Americans were fighting a losing battle to retain their political rights. In 1898 the Penn School had instituted a special class on the South Carolina Constitution so that young African American men could pass the state's new requirements for voting. But when Laura Towne died in 1900, the school's new teachers and northern supporters reorganized it along industrial and nonpolitical lines. Ellen looked to Abbie as an ally and wrote her with some confidence, "I wonder what you think, or rather I know what you think of this southern disfranchisement of the negroes." Ellen argued, "The law making being entirely in the hands of the whites, the laws will be made more and more oppressive and burdensome to the weaker race." Murray cautioned Christensen about accepting the Tuskegee program wholesale, writing: "Booker Washington advises them to devote themselves to commerce, but that, I fear would end as it is at Port Royal, in numbers of little stores with no one to buy. Farmers intelligent and educated, on their own land is what I think the very best life for them." If Murray assumed correctly, Christensen fully agreed with the justice of black political rights and the goal of farm ownership.[20]

When the Penn School changed to an industrial format around 1900, the goal of independent landowning was not lost, though the school ceased to be a center of black political activity. Agriculture became its centerpiece, and the younger Christensens followed this lead. "If Miss Towne's school can be run on the same lines with Hampton," Fred Christensen wrote his mother, "I should think the benefits would certainly extend beyond St. Hel. Isd. perhaps through the whole lower part of the state. . . . However education of the right kind can't be put on too thick." For Fred, "education of the right kind" was industrial education without politics, but it is not clear that this program was entirely what Abbie Christensen had in mind. She never became as friendly with the new principals, Rossa Cooley and Grace Bigelow House, as she had been with Murray. As late as 1910 Christensen was passing on materials salvaged from Miss Murray's days to be used at the school Christensen founded.[21]

By 1902 white supremacist South Carolinians had drastically restricted black voting by means of the property and educational "understanding" requirements written into the state constitution in 1895. Under this system white registrars, whose offices were infrequently open, were allowed to use their discretion to determine whether potential voters "understood" selected portions of the South Carolina Constitution. White South Carolinians' attitudes can be gauged from an 1890s *Charleston News and Courier* article describing the difference between blacks and whites: "Their racial peculiarities sharply differentiate them from all the other and practically homogenous elements of the people among whom they live, and must continue always to exclude them from recognition as 'Americans' in any other than a forced, artificial and narrow sense of the term." The paper argued further that deportation would be a fitting solution to the "problem" of this "hopelessly unassimilable element." Extremely punitive solutions to the "race problem" were by no means out of vogue in the1900s, when Benjamin Tillman moved from the United States Senate to the national lecture circuit on the strength of his racist speeches. "The negro must remain subordinate or be exterminated," Tillman insisted. This was the political climate in which Christensen sought to found her school.[22]

Christensen's oldest son, Niels Jr., entered into this political climate when he decided to run for the South Carolina State Senate. Not surprisingly, Niels supported the exclusion of blacks from political office. Niels told his mother that he had been discussing the prospects of an industrial school with a white southern friend who asked how Niels would "keep an intelligent majority of negroes from attempting to govern their locality" if they received a good education. White southerners refused to have black officials govern them, Niels explained. Advising Abbie to forget black suffrage for the time being, he wrote, "Educate your negroes to be moral, self supporting and intelligent, then will be the time to discuss the admisability of allowing them the suffrage, then and surely not till then will the whites *perhaps* be willing to think of allowing them to vote and hold office." This was a bleak but "moderate" view. Having said this, Niels tried to reassure his mother, "But be all this as it may[,] it is necessary and conceded by all to be wise, to educate the negro to be intelligent breadwinners and we want an industrial school here now."[23]

Educated, propertied African Americans presented a threat to the legal disfranchising measures whites had adopted. White southerners who were comfortable with an industrial school believed either that they could hold on to power through extralegal means or that the industrial school would convince African Americans that they did not want the vote after all. Ironically, Niels had been disfranchised in 1900 through legal means; he had misplaced his registration certificate and therefore could not vote.[24]

Abbie probably did not agree with her son's opposition to black suffrage. The Spanish-American-Cuban-Filipino War, which she viewed as racist and imperialist, had pushed her to a position on race that was more, not less, egalitarian. More than once she tried to convince her sons that race was not the determining factor in a person's character and habits. In 1898 Abbie admonished Fred for assuming that thieves of fruit from the family yard were black: "Don't think that any disappearance of said fruit are chargeable always to Afro American citizens. Arthur says his mates in Mr Barnwell's school told him that they often went there for pears and things." Abbie's use of the term "Afro American citizens," an uncommon usage during her time, indicated her recognition of the rights of citizenship granted in the Fourteenth and Fifteenth Amendments to the Constitution.[25]

During the years when Thomas Dixon published his influential racist novels, *The Leopard's Spots: A Romance of the White Man's Burden* (1902) and *The Clansman: An Historical Romance of the Ku Klux Klan* (1905), Abbie Christensen defended African American political participation during Reconstruction and refused to tolerate any apology for racism and injustice. In 1903 when Benjamin Tillman was reelected to United States Senate, she wrote her sons, "What's the use saying he don't represent S.C. when all his meanness and rascality only endear him to a constituency so large that they elect him to any office he demands." In a pointed comparison, she made her views clear: "Please notice that the reconstruction era or time of negro ascendency never produced so notorious a pair as Ben and James Tillman . . . they belong to the day of the white man's government." In the same letter Abbie pushed her sons to read "DuBois' book," which in 1903 was probably W. E. B. Du Bois's *The Souls of Black Folk*. Abbie was aware of Du Bois's eloquent and radical arguments for equality, and she agreed with some of them. Her view, however, was distinctly in the minority, and it would have to be kept hidden if plans for the school were to go quietly and smoothly.[26]

Although Niels Christensen Jr. became part of the movement for black disfranchisement, he was a moderate by the racist standards of his time because he did not call for mob violence against African Americans. Antilynching was an area on which the Christensens were in full agreement. When white "regulators" shot at a group of blacks in Beaufort in 1901, because of a letter they perceived to be insulting to a local white woman, Niels and Fred persuaded the Beaufort Board of Trade to issue a statement against "mob law." In the same year Niels Jr. wrote a column against lynching in the *Beaufort Gazette*.[27]

In 1900 Niels Jr. had taken the political pulse of white South Carolina. No school that endorsed black political participation stood a chance of getting funding. Not only were politics to be strictly verboten, but black trustees also became out of the question. The institution that emerged from these constraints was the Port Royal Agricultural School, run by a board of white northern and southern trustees who met for the first time in November 1902. The black ministers who had originally appeared as trustees were now relegated to the back pages of the school's brochure as members of a "Colored Farmer's Conference," which was certified as being "in no sense a political organization." Once the school was established, these anxieties remained. In 1911 the principal of the Port Royal Agricultural School, Joseph Shanklin, wrote to Abbie Christensen, reassuring her that, "as you say, we don't care to have any politics in the work."[28]

Instead of politics, the Christensens put their faith in agriculture as the best hope for southern African Americans. Little did they know that they had hitched their wagon to a falling star. Eclipsed by large-scale commercial agriculture, the family farm would provide little security in the twentieth century. But Booker T. Washington and the Christensens could not see the future; they could only see the world they knew. The United States had a rural majority in 1900 and would retain it until 1920. The South was even more rural than the rest of the country, and the site the Christensens chose for their agricultural school was in a completely rural district. Local African Americans were in harmony with the Christensens' goals of promoting landownership and greater prosperity for their farms. They were not asked if they wanted more.[29]

Port Royal Agricultural School

Although the board of trustees was all-white, some black leadership was called for in the form of an African American principal and teachers. In order to make sure that the school conformed to Booker T. Washington's model and also to maintain control, the Christensens recruited a Tuskegee graduate, an outsider, to head the new school. Margaret Washington, Abbie's contact in the "Tuskegee Machine," sent Edinburgh Mahone to interview with Abbie for the position of school principal.[30]

Mahone had graduated from Tuskegee Institute and had in 1898 secured a place as a teacher in the small rural town of Denmark, South Carolina. In a letter in 1900 he introduced himself to Abbie as a "race man," an African American who was devoting his life to advancing his race: "I feel that much good can be done for my people and I am willing to do what I can toward making the Race what it should be. I have not had much experience in farming but am willing to do what I can along that line[.] I know something about it. I think that much good can be done for my people by teachers doing all they can in the homes, churches and Sunday Schools." Abbie was impressed with Mahone's ability and his values. She also liked his wife, a graduate of Tuskegee's nursing and domestic science program. "She is well fitted to work among the women and girls," Christensen wrote.[31]

The Mahones remained behind the scenes until the Christensens and their collaborators signaled that they could make their move. Niels Jr. persuaded the Beaufort County School Board to give Mahone a position in the public "country school" located in a church ten miles from Beaufort. Abbie paid the five dollars to transport him to Beaufort.[32]

Mahone's mission was daunting. "I am very glad to inform you that the School you so much desire has been started. . . . I have been informed that the attendance is about two hundred when all the children are in," he wrote to Abbie in November 1901. Mahone tried to get the support of the community. "I held a meeting last night and asked the people for their cooperation to make this a successful school year. I shall have them know that they will only get help by helping themselves," he wrote, stressing the gospel of self-help.[33]

Questions of control soon surfaced. Abbie wanted to help Mahone with his fund-raising, but her husband and sons objected. They argued that Mahone was "better posted and better able to talk" and that she was "not strong enough to give up [her] time and strength." Fred reminded her that the project was to be "self-help": "Remember he is to build and found the school not us. He is in a small way our Washington. We can merely advise, see to it his funds are not wasted or foolishly spent. Assist him to meet the people who are able to help him. Use our influence to remove obstacles here, which might be put in his way by the whites or blacks. Get as much assistance from public funds here as possible etc. But he must do the soliciting the teaching etc." Despite her sons' advice, Abbie found it impossible to accept a limited role. She continued to solicit donations for the school for the rest of her life, advertising in the *Boston Evening Transcript,* sending copies of *Afro-American Folk Lore* to potential contributors, and talking and writing to wealthy friends. When Fred told Edinburgh that Abbie doubted his ability to solicit donations, he "looked incredulous for a moment, laughed and said he supposed that as you . . . were on the spot you were better able to judge than he but he felt sure he could raise the money." It must have been an awkward moment for Mahone, and it began a fissure in his relationship with Christensen.[34]

Abbie made the Port Royal Agricultural School a family effort. Her wealthy sister Georgie and her equally well-to-do aunt Abbie Coes provided financial support. Even Abbie's youngest children contributed to the school in small ways. Arthur composed a school motto, while Andrea and Winnie crafted Beaufort souvenir books and gave their profits to "mother's school." Niels Jr. and Fred, who were the eldest and also permanent Beaufort residents, played the greatest role. Niels provided contacts with influential southern politicians and shaped public opinion through his newspaper, the *Beaufort Gazette,* while Fred took care of administrative details such as obtaining a state charter.[35]

While he was alive Niels Sr. was always featured prominently because his name carried respect, but he rarely participated in the affairs of the school. Niels Sr. was in declining health after 1895, and he died in 1909. Joseph Shanklin Jr., son of the longtime principal of the Port Royal Agricultural School, recalled the Christensens this way: "Her husband wasn't interested in the school. He was interested in the cemetery, money and land. That was her area. He didn't fool with her. She had her own transportation. . . . Niels, Jr. was her man. He took care of her projects." As they had done for most of their marriage, Abbie and Niels pursued their own independent paths.[36]

Despite her energy and vision, Abbie and her sons chose to downplay her leadership role in the school. "You would be competent alone if it were not for the looks of the thing," Fred wrote to his mother in 1902. Perhaps he meant that according to gender conventions of the day, it would not do to have a woman in charge. But several area schools were run by white women. It is just as likely that Abbie's liberal racial politics were the reason she had to stay in the background. Behind the scenes, however, Abbie held the greatest power. She was the most active person in each of the first meetings, suggesting that the board issue an illustrated prospectus, reporting donations gathered in Brookline, inquiring about mortgage payments, reading letters from donors, conveying Mahone's request for a fixed salary, and taking the minutes of the meetings.[37]

In the few disagreements that arose, her opinion usually prevailed. Fred urged her to "drop the notion of many trustees," but Abbie continued to add board members, calculating, perhaps, that trusteeship conferred a feeling of obligation and that contributions flowed not only from the trustees but from those who recognized familiar names on the school's letterhead. The names on the letterhead kept changing, but from 1902 on, Abbie Holmes Christensen's name appeared in one form or another at the top of every sheet.[38]

Still, Christensen's more conservative sons stopped some of her plans, significantly her attempt to add Septima Bennett Bythewood, a black woman, to the board of trustees. Fred vetoed the idea of including Reverend Bythewood's wife but thought that "perhaps Rev. B. as an influential interested colored minister might be of help to us." Gender sometimes formed a bridge in Abbie's relationships across the color line, and Christensen had a long-standing relationship with Daniel Bythewood. It was her last try. No woman besides Abbie was ever on the board.[39]

"The trouble will be to get any money," Abbie had written in 1898. The General Education Board (GEB), which promoted black industrial education, seemed the best hope. The board was amply funded by John D. Rockefeller's millions, but most of its contributions went to white colleges. Nevertheless, Niels Christensen Jr. tried to win favor with Wallace Buttrick, the board's secretary. The Christensens also submitted a report outlining the economic and racial conditions in Beaufort and concluding pointedly, "The hope of our section . . . IS IN THE EDUCATION OF THE NEGRO ALONG THE LINES MORAL INTELLECTUAL AND INDUSTRIAL." Still, no money was forthcoming.[40]

Undaunted, Abbie Christensen and the other founders worked tirelessly to piece together a package of support from a collection of friends representing the Christensens' northern and southern ties. Abbie recruited old New England missionaries such as Thomas Higginson, Charles Ware, and Helen Philbrick, as well as newer suffragist friends from Brookline. In 1902 she even sent a copy of *Afro-American Folk Lore* to the nation's First Lady,

Edith Roosevelt, although it is unclear whether she solicited her financial support. Meanwhile the Christensen men pulled in white educators from South Carolina. Finally, Mahone secured a key player, Port Royal landowner W. H. McLeod, as president of the board of trustees.[41]

Abbie described the new school to her son Arthur, who was attending Harvard in 1903. Mahone and the schoolchildren had cleared a large field for cotton and another for sweet potatoes. They planted a cabbage patch, a turnip plot, an onion bed, green peas, corn, and potatoes. Abbie praised the Mahones' flower garden and the "neat and orderly" appearance of their house and the school. "The children most of them wore clean clothes, tho' sometimes ragged," she wrote, attesting to the poor but proud nature of the students.[42]

Gradually the African Americans of Port Royal began to accept the school and the Mahones as part of their community. In February 1903 Mahone organized a "Farmer's Conference" working along the lines of Tuskegee Institute's extension or "rural settlement" work in the Alabama countryside. He was joined by Professor Dawkins of the Penn School and Reverend P. P. Watson. The constitution that the all-African American Conference wrote was a mixture of radical and conservative elements. One of the first things the farmers wished to do was "abolish and do away with the mortgage system," from which real estate investor Niels Christensen Sr. had benefitted enormously. This system was certainly preferable to tenant farming, but members of the conference may have seen it as exploitive or risky in comparison to buying with cash. They exhorted those in their community to raise their own food and own their own homes. More conservative measures were opposition to "standing around," drinking on Saturdays, and "the Excursion and Campmeeting"—all of which were seen as distractions from work. Finally, the group disavowed politics. Within these constraints the farmers vowed to improve their lot.[43]

From 1903 to 1904 the school grew. Four women teachers taught more than 150 students reading, writing, arithmetic, and geography for a full six months. Applications began to exceed spaces, and the board hired Joseph S. Shanklin, another Tuskegee graduate, as the school's agricultural instructor. Profits from the school farm, individual contributions, and a three-hundred-dollar donation from Rockefeller's Slater Fund enabled the trustees to make substantial payments to relieve their debt. The Port Royal Agricultural School was finally beginning to look secure.[44]

Everything appeared harmonious, but below the surface a storm began brewing between Mahone and Shanklin. Shanklin, who had more farming experience, groused under Mahone's direction. Their rivalry broke into argument, and Mahone insisted on Shanklin's removal in the fall of 1904. "For some time [Mahone] had been discontented, full of complaint," Abbie wrote in the minutes of an emergency board meeting. Mahone left the school and moved his family from the farm. In effect, Mahone had quit, but the board moved to discharge him officially and appointed Shanklin as principal in his place. Booker T. Washington managed to salvage a little of Mahone's dignity by inviting him to Tuskegee to "recuperate."[45]

The change in the school's leadership strengthened Abbie's role within the board of trustees. Christensen marshaled the board through the crisis. Her record of trustee meetings in 1905 shows that mortgage payments were made on time, crops were planted, and Joseph Shanklin was dispatched to the North for fund-raising. Abbie Christensen also continued to act as a fund-raiser, but to avoid the issue of "social equality," each traveled separately and visited different audiences. No longer adding caveats such as "secretary pro tem" behind her signature on the minutes, the school's founding mother signed herself, with gender-neutral initials, A. H. Christensen.[46]

The Shanklins

The African American institution that Christensen had begun planning in 1897 eventually outlived her. The school's official name changed with the ongoing trends in African American education—from Port Royal Agricultural School in 1902 to the Beaufort County Training School in 1920. But local blacks and whites called it "the Shanklin School."

Joseph Shanklin's background had prepared him well for heading the Port Royal Agricultural School. Joseph was born into a farming family in Alabama in 1872 and knew firsthand the struggle of poor, rural African Americans for an education. "After my mother's death, there were four of us left with our father, who was a very good man, and did what he could to have us go to the country school which was about three months a year," Shanklin told the editor of the *History of the American Negro*. He also related the sense of mission that pushed him to become an educational leader: "In the year 1892 I became a Christian and after that I always felt that there was something for me to do. What it was I could not tell. I wanted to go to school but had no means." Shanklin worked as a janitor at the People's Village School in Mount Meigs, Alabama, and he credited a teacher with informing him about Tuskegee and preparing him to enter Booker T. Washington's famous institution in 1895. After six years of hard work, Shanklin graduated and went to the Port Royal Agricultural School.[47]

In June 1905 India Gordon, a Tuskegee graduate, married Shanklin and joined him at the Port Royal school, serving as its "Matron" and unofficial cosuperintendent. She was born in Abbeville, Alabama, in 1868, a few years after the end of slavery. Although she was raised in a family of poor farmers, probably sharecroppers, there was pride as well as oppression in her background. Family members believed that with a higher education, their daughters would go on to lead in the progress of their race.[48]

The women students of Tuskegee Institute were taught that they were especially important. Following the missionary idea that the advancement of a race could be judged by the moral and legal status of its women, the school instructed women students to uphold strict standards of sexual purity, manners, and morals. Both married and single women graduates were urged to provide moral and mental guidance to family members as well as the less privileged. As Margaret Washington, Booker T. Washington's third wife, wrote, "There is always a spirit of learning, that she may be of service to others."[49]

India Gordon held degrees in several women's departments, including midwifery, and had previously taught in an industrial school in Tennessee. She ran the domestic science component of the Port Royal Agricultural School, and under her direction sewing classes provided all of the school's children with clothing. With her gracious talents in correspondence and conversation, India also provided an important female link to Abbie Christensen and the white women donors to the school. Abbie described India as "very capable" with a "gentle, quiet, but firm manner." When Joseph Shanklin left on fund-raising trips, India ran the school alone, supervising both the boys' and girls' summer programs. "Miss India" was in charge of the boarding department and took many troubled young children under her wing. Charles Singleton, who attended the school for many years, remembered her as, above all, "a mother" to the students. Like the wives of black college presidents in the 1900s, India Shanklin served as "first lady" of the Shanklin School.[50]

The Shanklins became pillars of the Port Royal community later known as Burton, and they were recognized as leaders in the town and county of

Beaufort as well. They joined the Allen A.M.E. church, and the congregation became an unofficial sponsor of the school. India Shanklin started a chapter of the Lady Knights of King David, a self-help and service-oriented African American society. Joseph Shanklin Sr. became president of the Royal Knights of King David. The group bought a hall and met once a month, providing a grocery store for the community on the first floor. The Shanklins petitioned for and eventually received from the Port Royal Agricultural School a gristmill, a rice mill, and a sugar-cane mill, to which members of the community could bring their food crops to be processed. In the 1920s they added a canning facility.[51]

Following the lead of other Tuskegee graduates, Joseph Shanklin tried to bring his faith in scientific farming and cooperation with the white community to his black South Carolina neighbors through weekly Thursday night meetings. India Shanklin tried to inculcate the pride and values of the new educated middle class in her local community, as Margaret Washington and other African American women had done. Using the school as a sort of rural social settlement that modeled right living, India organized "Mother's Meetings" that would "give the mothers some ide[a] of keeping a home in order and how to prepare the food."[52]

Abbie Christensen and India Shanklin shared a common vision of Christian missionary service to African Americans. Christensen had inherited this missionary ethic from her abolitionist parents, and it had been reinforced as "woman's mission" at Mount Holyoke. Shanklin's training at Tuskegee impressed upon her that she should serve her race and promote positive relations between the races. A shared understanding of mission and manners united Shanklin and Christensen.

Friendship across the Color Line

Christensen shared close friendships with the Shanklins. Although white privilege and class privilege created an unequal power relation between them, they were able to maintain a relationship that defied many of the boundaries of segregation. Christensen violated the southern practice by which whites did not grant African Americans the dignity of titles and last names. In their letters both women addressed each other formally as Mrs. Christensen and Mrs. Shanklin. Christensen also wrote of "Mr. and Mrs. Shanklin" in her private diary. Whenever they visited, Christensen entertained the Shanklins and other middle-class African Americans in her parlor or even the more informal and intimate space of her porch or piazza. When Christensen visited the Shanklins, she dined at their table. Although northern white women teachers at Avery Institute defied social segregation and visited socially with the families of their black students, they did so at the price of total exclusion by white society in Charleston. Even "progressive" white South Carolina club women in the 1900s barred black women's clubs from their federation because they dreaded meeting and dining under conditions of "social equality." Given such attitudes, Abbie Christensen's simple acts of good manners and reciprocity were the bravest and most defiant actions she took as a white woman in the segregated South.[53]

Although Abbie had worked closely with Joseph Shanklin in the North, her ties to India were more intimate because of her gender and the fact that she reached out to Abbie as a friend. Of course, an inequality of power existed between them, but as much as was possible in the segregated South, these women cultivated a friendship. In her diary in 1910 Abbie recorded a visit with India Shanklin on a clear, sunny March afternoon. She wrote, "Mrs. Shanklin called, came upstairs and we sat on the piazza talking over a book of notes Miss Murray used for her class of oldest girls." One can imagine the two women sitting next to each other in the sunshine, looking at the book of notes, then looking out at the flowering trees and shrubs, and breathing in the fragrance of the purple *Akebia quinata* flowers on a vine that reached up thirty feet to the second floor. India Shanklin's visits with Christensen were rarer than her husband's because, like most women with young children, she had many responsibilities at home. Christensen visited her more often, riding her horse and buggy into the countryside to the Shanklin School.[54]

When the two women wrote to one another, not only did Shanklin tell Christensen about the happenings at the school, but she also wrote of her personal life. "I have spent a very pleasant summer with my people," India wrote upon returning from Alabama with her firstborn child. "He has six teeth and is trying to walk" she reported. As she did with other friends and family, Abbie sent India, clippings, books, and dried flowers. "The little blossoms were pressed nicely," India wrote her in 1921. Abbie even entered India's dreams. Shanklin wrote that she was relieved when she learned of Christensen's safe arrival home in 1932 because she had dreamed of her death.

Christensen addressed her 1936 letter to "Mrs. Shanklin" and signed it
"Your Friend." Shanklin's daughter recalled that the two women were "good
friends" and that their friendship was a "continuation, proved over many
years."[55]

India told Abbie of needs at the school and hoped that she would find the
money to address them. "There has not been any aprons bought for the girls
this Summer. . . . A few more sheets will be needed also for the school. Also
night shirts for the boys. You know boys are very hard to keep in shirts" she
wrote, emphasizing their common bond as mothers. India always brought
the concerns of women's work before Abbie, pointing out the need for a new
laundry room, informing her of plans for "Mother's Meetings," and asking for money for a new sewing machine. India had to ask Abbie to fulfill
these needs because Abbie held the power of the purse. Nevertheless, Shanklin equalized things whenever she could, sending Christensen presents of
fruit, pecans, and other homegrown produce, which she knew the health-
conscious older woman enjoyed.[56]

Abbie Christensen's equal treatment of the Shanklins was challenged during one of her trips to the North for solicitation. In 1922 Christensen and
Joseph Shanklin both took part in a fund-raising talk at the home of Niels
Christensen Jr.'s in-laws in Petersham, Massachusetts. As usual, it was an
extended family affair, with Fred giving his mother advice about her speech
through the mail. Shanklin, however, was not treated as part of the family
during this visit. Niels's wife Nancy had written to ask Abbie if it would be
all right if Shanklin ate in the kitchen with her servants and stayed in the
chauffeur's quarters. Niels had already been criticized for being too liberal in
starting a school for African Americans. As a southern politician, he did not
want to be accused of promoting social equality by entertaining the principal of the Shanklin School in his family's home. Therefore Joseph Shanklin
was not afforded the dignity and consideration a white person of his position would have received.[57]

The ease with which Abbie Christensen's racial liberalism could become a
target for Niels Jr.'s political enemies is best illustrated by an incident that
took place in 1914. In that year Abbie visited her son Niels as his special
guest in the chambers of the South Carolina Senate in Columbia. The South
Carolina governor at that time, Cole Blease, addressed the house on the day
of her visit. Blease, who carried the violent, racist political style of Benjamin

Tillman even further than the former governor had, won campaigns by behaving in the extreme style of masculinity that one southern observer called the "hell-of-a-fellow" style. He endorsed lynching for the crime of rape, openly cursed, gambled, and bragged of drinking bootleg liquor. Although Blease appealed to white mill workers with anti-aristocratic rhetoric opposing reform-minded businessmen such as Christensen, his actions in office did not better their lot. Rather than solving economic problems, Blease preferred to raise racist fears, and Niels and Abbie Christensen's involvement with the Shanklin School gave him a chance to do so.[58]

While Abbie watched from the gallery of the South Carolina statehouse, the governor attacked Niels Christensen Jr. for being a trustee of a school that used a black person (Booker T. Washington) as a reference. "I can hardly believe this, . . . that white people, would, in South Carolina, give a negro as a reference," the governor said. Blease also criticized the school for printing a card for its students stating "Do not be ashamed of your race, rather be proud to be as the Lord made you." As part of his campaign to outlaw white teachers in black schools, he asked the legislators to investigate whether "white men and women are teaching along side by side with negroes and negresses" at the Shanklin School. Although they were not, Blease needed merely to insinuate this; the symbolism was what counted. Falling back on his favorite tactic of raising the specter of black male sexuality, Blease warned that the next step at the Shanklin School was "negro men marrying white women." Although he never mentioned Abbie Christensen by name, his attack on the day when she sat in the gallery indicates that he intended to needle Niels Christensen by making insinuations about his mother and her school. Most of Blease's remarks were considered so offensive that they were stricken from the record as the senate later rallied to protect Niels Christensen's offended honor as well as the honor of his mother. A few days later Blease continued the attack, impugning Niels Christensen Sr. for serving as a captain of colored troops during the Civil War.[59]

Niels Jr. weathered this attack and others, but they show the constraints that his political career put on Abbie Christensen. Nevertheless, Abbie continued to defy some of the customs of segregation. Abbie's grandson Niels Christensen III remembered asking black visitors to his grandmother's home to go around to the back of the house, as was the southern custom. Abbie corrected him and told him to direct their guests to the front door. She received her black guests in the parlor just as she did her white guests. Her grandson recalled, "She had no hesitation. . . . There was no color line as far as she was concerned. But her son was a political power in the county. She was pragmatic enough to know there was just so far she could go." When she visited the Shanklins at their home in Port Royal, blacks and whites ate the homegrown food of the school at the same table. To a point, Abbie was willing to stare down the disapproval of white neighbors. It was a small but significant courtesy.[60]

Shanklin School Life

Joseph Shanklin's background as an agricultural instructor strengthened the school's agricultural/industrial focus but maintained its basic academic function. The Port Royal Agricultural School's 1905 pamphlet announced: "With regard to instruction for day scholars, it is our aim to confine it to practical elementary lines. This school is not endeavoring to furnish a higher education that would carry individuals away from their homes, but to provide enough practical education, and cultivate habits of cleanliness, thrift, and industry, to enable the average child to go back to his home fitted to make a good living off the land." Timeworn Yankee values were echoed here, as well as the reassurance to white southerners that African Americans would not leave the land. Still, the Shanklin School was not merely a mechanism for holding black farmers in the South.[61]

W. E. B. Du Bois had criticized schools on the Tuskegee model for failing to educate African American youth "according to ability," but in the Shanklin School the existence of gifted African Americans who sought higher education was acknowledged. The Port Royal Agricultural School's 1905 letter stated that "children of exceptional ability will be furnished, as far as possible, means to continue elsewhere the higher branches for which each seems best adapted." For most talented Shanklin students, higher education, in practice, meant attendance at Tuskegee or State College in Orangeburg, South Carolina. Several went on to become teachers and businesspeople. Still, for most, the dream of owning and living off the land in the relatively safe and comfortable black community of Burton was their highest aspiration in a segregated society that thwarted so many of the ambitions they might have had.[62]

By 1906 the Shanklin School received enough in donations to expand the cultivated acreage and infrastructure of the institution substantially. Shanklin managed to raise fifteen bales of cotton worth one thousand dollars in 1907, and the school farm consistently brought in a modest profit. The five hundred acres of drained and cleared woodland proved to be the "best land in Beaufort County," according to Joseph Shanklin Jr. Vegetables became more important after 1918 when the boll weevil destroyed cotton cultivation. In addition, a barnyard of cows, pigs, chickens, mules, and a horse helped the students with plowing and the production of eggs, butter, and pork. The Shanklin School also became famous for the nuts from its thriving pecan orchard.[63]

Most important, the Shanklin School offered facilities and an educational program superior to anything the poor black public schools could provide. Parents were willing to pay tuition for the children to stay in school longer. From November to April 1906, for example, the school received a total of approximately $48.31, the hard-earned savings of the families of two hundred pupils.[64]

Letters from students to Abbie Christensen describe the girls' daily routine: "washing, ironing, cooking and sewing, and some time work on the farm." India Shanklin's young seamstresses made linens, napkins, pillows, bedclothes, and denim uniforms in the Tuskegee style. Student Julia Fripp wrote of canning, cleaning the buildings, and varnishing the chairs and floors. The girls took care of the school's poultry and garden, sowing turnips, beets, cabbages, and beans.[65]

Shanklin's young men were between the ages of twelve and eighteen, and they went to school half the day and worked on the farm the other half. They were taught "crop-raising of grains, cotton, and vegetables, care of stock" and "how to run the grist mill and the sugar can[e] mill." The boys did not write letters or do housekeeping chores; instead they spent a great deal of time on the farm. In August they cut down corn and gathered hay. Both boys and girls participated in two hours of summer-school classes. School was certainly not an escape from labor, but it did offer more knowledge and peer companionship than just working on the family farm provided.[66]

Leisure was rarely mentioned in any official or even unofficial school papers; the emphasis was on a strict work ethic. No child's life could have been completely devoid of play, however. The younger children played with donated toys or concocted their own games, while the older students passed time at baseball, which was popular on the islands. They played against the other "colored schools" of the area, engaging in day-long picnics and socializing. The Penn School was the Shanklin School's main friendly rival, and students enjoyed their excursions to Saint Helena Island as much as the other school's reciprocal visits.[67]

The Shanklin School provided mentors and even substitute families for some children. "I love out here very well and I love the girls and boys too and also the farm," wrote Wilhelmina Kaintuck. Joseph Shanklin told Christensen that Kaintuck had been considered "one of the worst girls in the section where she lives" before she attended the school. Perhaps Wilhelmina was able to make a fresh start at the new school, where the children and teachers had no prejudices against her. Kaintuck described her teacher as "very nice" and Mr. Shanklin as "very kind."[68]

Yet, because of its limited financial resources, the Shanklin School fell short of what it could have been. Although Mary Clayton wrote, "We have plenty of food to cook an[d] also to eat" in 1907, another student recalled feeling hungry in the 1930s, even though she worked in the kitchen preparing meals for the teachers. It is possible that the amount of food available depended on the time of year. In the summer food was more plentiful and students fewer. Like the farm families around them, Shanklin School students lived through feast and famine, depending on economic and agricultural conditions.[69]

Pressure from the General Education Board and local white school boards caused the school to emphasize agriculture and "domestic science" to the detriment of academics in some cases. Its mission was always constrained by the prejudices of northern philanthropists who wished to keep blacks on southern farms and the anxieties of white southerners who did not want to educate African Americans "out of their place." On at least one occasion Abbie Christensen expressed an opinion indicating that she held her black women students to a different standard than those she set for herself and young white women. Christensen reported in her diary that she was conferring with "a black brother Rev. Frazier concerning his daughter Victoria," a recent Shanklin graduate. "He desires a public school for her. I had an amusing time . . . Mrs. G. and I trying to convince him that home work is much better suited to a girl than 'public life.'" Although it is possible that she was joking because she and her friend needed servants, it certainly seems that Christensen was blind to the aspirations of this young woman, not to mention the fact that she might be vulnerable to rape or sexual coercion as a servant in a private white home. Fortunately, Christensen was not usually in the business of advising students, leaving that responsibility to the Shanklins, who tried to push their young students to the highest levels of character and achievement they could muster.[70]

African American Culture and Black Pride

Although economic advancement took first priority, the Shanklins also tried to promote pride in the students' cultural heritage as African Americans. Such teaching was vital at a time when hurtful stereotypes of grinning, pop-eyed children and grotesquely distorted mammies appeared in advertising, popular music and other elements of mainstream commercial culture. As a folklore collector, Christensen must have considered the cultural as well as the economic purposes of forming an African American school. The Shanklin School united with Hampton and other African American educational institutions in promoting African American culture through the music of spirituals. The school also joined the Penn School in keeping alive the local folk art of sea-grass basketry.[71]

Compared to later "folk schools" for southern white mountain children, the emphasis on folk culture was minimal. For example, at the Pine Mountain Settlement School in Kentucky, Abbie's daughter Winnie taught English folk dances and sought to reintroduce students to English customs such as May Day festivals. Ballad singing and mountain instruments such as dulcimers were also celebrated. Other white "folk schools" sought to make local crafts such as split-oak basketry and wood carving into sources of income. Still the idea was shared—poor southerners had white and black folk cultures that should be part of schools' curriculums for the benefit of both races.[72]

For black Sea Islanders, sea-grass baskets were part of an old African heritage. The craft of weaving baskets from reeds and grasses was brought to the Sea Islands from the Senegambian region of West Africa. During slavery times the baskets were used as rice fanners and for storage. After Reconstruction rice production nearly ceased, and manufactured containers began to replace the baskets in Sea Islanders' homes. Some of the few remaining practitioners of the art worked with the Penn School to keep it alive. The practice, which had once been largely male, began to be taken over by women as men's jobs took them away from home.[73]

Mr. Browne, a basketry teacher at the Penn School, was hired to spend a few hours each week showing Shanklin students how to make coils of reeds and sew the coils together with pieces of palmetto fronds, making baskets of all sizes and shapes. Browne's son recalled: "My father's grand-uncle who was a slave, taught him how to make the baskets." Shanklin students used Browne's techniques but created their own original style. Because Burton was further inland than Saint Helena Island, more pine needles than sea grasses could be found for making baskets. The students' greater use of these local materials distinguished Shanklin's "pine needle basket making" from the Penn School's sea-grass variety.[74]

In addition to being useful and beautiful items, pine-needle baskets were a source of income at a store set up by the Shanklin School. This store, organized by the Shanklins, sold student-made items such as clothing in addition to goods donated by the students. The Penn School operated a similar shop in addition to marketing its baskets in the North. On at least one occasion Christensen sent sea-grass baskets to be sold in the North. Christensen and other white educators worked with black educators at the turn of the century to keep alive a folk tradition that would later provide an important source of tourist income for African American women in the low country.[75]

The perpetuation of African American culture through baskets and spirituals was an important legacy of the Shanklin and Penn Schools. Leroy Browne characterized their importance: "It's a part of the black heritage; it dramatizes the plight of black people. Some were sung for comfort, hope, joy and for patience. I think that those who composed spirituals also composed poetry. When people were in bondage, they hoped that those chains would be broken. Today, since those chains are broken, some of us feel that there is no need to be singing. But I still say that there are still many chains to be broken. So to me we should cherish the spirituals and not forget them. The spiritual is similar to the baskets which were strictly African. We need to learn more of the spirituals and what they mean to our people." As did churches and families, African American schools such as Shanklin and Penn preserved and modified spirituals and baskets in the hands of each succeeding generation.[76]

African American spirituals were a syncretism between the strong musical tradition of African cultures and the religious songs and hymns blacks learned and re-formed when they were converted to Christianity. These songs were a source of strength and articulations of the black ideology of liberation and transcendence during slavery. Abolitionists such as Lucy McKim and Thomas Higginson had been fascinated with them from their first encounters with freed people in the South. At Hampton Institute, the Penn School, and other black educational institutions African Americans were encouraged to continue this unique tradition because it was seen as a positive and uplifting aspect of black culture.

Abbie Christensen had experienced black religious music in the South and in the North. In Beaufort in the 1860s she had worshiped with black Methodists, and she continued to attend African American religious services even after black and white congregations separated. At Mount Holyoke she had heard the more formalized spirituals sung by the Hampton Singers in 1872. In the 1890s Abbie had described African American "sperrichels" for the World's Columbian Exposition. "The fascination of the music and the swaying motion of the dancers is so great one can hardly refrain from joining the magic circle," she had written. It is no wonder that she and the Shanklins encouraged their students to sing the old songs.[77]

The multiple uses of spirituals illustrate the tensions and conflicts inherent in the different views of African American culture held by students, teachers, and whites such as Christensen and her friends. Spirituals could be inwardly enriching forms of worship and celebration for African American students, but they were also a means of entertaining white visitors and assisting in fund-raising. Christensen urged donors to visit the school and entertained them at her home when they came to Beaufort. Abbie was convinced that once they saw the school and met the Shanklins and the students, they would feel personal obligations as well as satisfaction in seeing how their money was being used. The students were called together on these occasions and asked to sing "plantation songs" for their white guests. Joseph Shanklin Jr. remembered Christensen's visits as important occasions. He wrote: "Mrs. Christensen had a white horse and a black buggy. . . . She would drive that horse six miles from Beaufort to be at the school by midday.

Then [the students] would be singing." According to Shanklin, Abbie's favorite spirituals were "Roll, Jordan, Roll" and "Climbing Jacob's Ladder." Unfortunately, this use of black music could feel forced, reminding African Americans of their dependence on white donors, rather than being merely providing an opportunity for artistic expressions.[78]

Although they originated in slavery, spirituals were still meaningful to Sea Island African Americans in the first decades of the twentieth century because their suffering and the need for transcendence had not disappeared. Even though they now owned land, they were wandering in the wilderness of severely constrained economic opportunity, enforced notions of inferiority, and political powerlessness. They still awaited their savior, a Moses, a Jesus, and the time when all people finally would be equal.

Different stylistic interpretations of spirituals reveal the competing views of African American culture held by students, teachers, and white "purists" such as Christensen. In a humorous anecdote, Wilhelmina Barnwell, the music teacher at the Shanklin School, remembered conflicting opinions about jazz, the popular new musical style of the 1920s. Barnwell had known Abbie Christensen since the days when her mother was a seamstress for the Christensen household. "She kind of persuaded me to go to Shanklin School and teach because she said she needed somebody and I played piano and they would sing. . . . She was very happy to have me there and she insisted that I take care of the programs." Barnwell recalled that Christensen wanted her to stop playing "Hand Me Down the Silver Trumpet, Gabriel": "Mr. Shanklin used to like it jazzy, you know, but she would say, 'If you have any spirituals, you be sure you aren't jazzing them.' . . . They used to put some words to it that weren't appropriate for something as sacred as a spiritual. I wouldn't play it." Thus, Christensen and Barnwell tried to keep the spirituals "authentic" and "uplifting," free from the influence of secular music. In the same way teachers tried to keep white mountain folk away from new forms of popular "country music" that could be heard on the radio in the 1930s.[79]

In addition to promoting spirituals and basketry, Shanklin tried to instill his version of "black pride" in his students through inspirational talks on black leaders during morning chapel. In the absence of any African American history books, he told what he knew of the lives of leaders such as Booker T. Washington, George Washington Carver, Frederick Douglass, and others.

Fighting to counteract negative stereotypes in mainstream white culture, Shanklin printed a card for students that read: "Do not be ashamed of your race, rather be proud to be as the Lord made you. Be thankful for your great gift of song, for the fortunate race characteristics of cheerfulness, patience, optimism and faith, which with proper education should make the best race of farmers in the world." Through these various means Shanklin tried to counteract the negative black stereotypes of his day and gave his students a homemade elixir of their heritage in daily doses.[80]

A Montessori School

While she maintained her support of the Shanklin School for the rest of her life, Abbie Christensen embarked on a new educational adventure in 1917—a Montessori school. Excited by the new ideas of Italian educational reformer Maria Montessori, Abbie set up a classroom in her home, bringing in her grandchildren and several preschoolers from the neighborhood. This school was one of the first of its kind in the United States. Christensen learned and practiced Montessori methods while teaching alongside the Montessori teachers she hired while running the school from 1917 to 1927. All of the Montessori students were white, and it seems that Abbie never envisioned an incorporation of Montessori methods into the Shanklin School. Although Maria Montessori worked primarily with poor children in Italy, in the United States mostly middle-class white children were enrolled in private Montessori schools. Perhaps Christensen did not introduce Montessori methods to the Shanklin School because she trusted African American teachers to use their own methods, but it is likely that she did not view the needs of black children in quite the same way as those of her own grandchildren. Montessori education stressed cooperation, self-control, peacemaking, and creative self-expression, preparing middle-class white children to be leaders and innovators in a relatively safe world where their dominance was taken for granted. Industrial/agricultural education stressed conformity, hard work, and respect for outside control to prepare rural black children for a harsh and uncompromising world of segregation and limited opportunities. African American children might have benefitted from Montessori emphases on preschool preparation, small classes, play, creativity, and cooperation, but these features were not available to them in 1917.[81]

Beaufort County Training School

By 1919 the Shanklin School was well established with an endowment of $11,000 and hundreds of acres of land. Out of 120 students, 70 boarded at the school, and all the students combined paid $370 in fees. Each student contributed his or her labor to the school farm, helping to bring in more than $1,000 in profits in 1919. Yet the school's running expenses were still nearly $1,000 greater than its income. Hoping to move away from the uncertainty of reliance on private gifts, the trustees applied to become a county training school.[82]

The county training school idea was the brainchild of the General Education Board, the Slater Fund, the Anna T. Jeanes Fund, and the Julius Rosenwald Fund. The Jeanes Fund, established in 1909 by Anna Jeanes, a wealthy Philadelphia Quaker woman, and the Rosenwald Fund, established in 1914 by Julius Rosenwald, Chicago philanthropist and president of Sears, Roebuck and Company, both had the goal of building rural black schools. County training schools were to pool private and public resources to promote industrial education and meet the need for black teachers. In practice, these schools operated at about the same level as high schools. The Port Royal Agricultural School became the Beaufort County Training School in 1920, although it continued to be known locally as the Shanklin School.[83]

By signing the school over to the county, the trustees lost a large measure of control, but they gained money from the Slater and Rosenwald Funds as well as five times the public funds that they had originally been allocated by the county. By these means a teacher-training department was added. It was readily admitted that these teachers were to achieve mastery of elementary subjects but only "an introduction to high school subjects." The classroom building, forty acres of land, and teacher salaries were now in the hands of the county. The Shanklin school board retained its hold on the boarding system, Shanklin's salary, and eight hundred acres of farm and woodland.[84]

Lists of graduates of the school in the 1910s and their occupations reveal some of the successes of the school. While a few students went on to higher education, the majority were engaged in farming, housekeeping, or "working in the city." More specific occupations were "factory work, saw milling, seamstress . . . cooking apprentice, laundry apprentice, waitress and trained nurse apprentice." A few graduates were employed as teachers. One or two students on the list were described as "occupation unknown," while the vocations of soldier, tailor, and hotel worker were represented by one graduate each. Discrimination limited the scope of graduates' achievements, but the school gave them the means to earn a better living than they might have earned without it.[85]

Because of the Shanklin, Penn, and Mather Schools, the Sea Island region was stronger in black education than most rural areas of the South were. Despite the missionary paternalism inherent in these institutions and others, such as Avery in Charleston and Tuskegee in Alabama, these schools bolstered black "initiative" and created a small black power base outside of party politics. In 1924 Isabell Mike, a graduate of the Shanklin School and a student at State College in Orangeburg, South Carolina, wrote a letter to Christensen encouraging her to continue to support the Shanklin School because it helped African Americans such as her. "I am here striding hard each day to make my race problem better in the community in which I live, and throughout the world," Mike wrote. Within the limitations of a white supremacist society, Joseph and India Shanklin were able to use the school to impart pride in culture and the ideals of self-help and community solidarity. Forty years after Paul Watson first approached Abbie Christensen with the idea for the school, she was still a "Northern friend" helping to provide "industrial education for our young people." Although the Shanklin School was Christensen's most far-reaching achievement, it was not her only reform effort. Beaufort and the nation's needs were multiple, and Christensen had energy and creativity to pour into both.[86]

Chapter Ten

CLUBWOMAN

It makes me sick at heart to see how much needs doing that we ladies cannot do, and how little interest the men show in [Beaufort]. The place looks so rough and neglected, it is pitiful.[1]

When Abbie Christensen wrote these lines to her youngest son in 1915, she and her allies in the women's club movement had been trying for several years to smooth Beaufort's rough edges by conserving nature, beautifying public spaces, dispensing charity, and educating children. During the 1900s and 1910s Christensen found a public space for herself by creating the Shanklin and Montessori schools and also by following her adult daughters in joining local and statewide women's clubs. After Niels Christensen Sr.'s death in 1909, fifty-seven-year-old Abbie could have moved back to Boston, but she chose to remain in Beaufort, becoming more committed than ever to cultivating a New South in her adopted town. A lifelong student of botany, Christensen planted private and public gardens and wrote about the conservation of the natural environment, even as she tried to improve the social environment of her time.

As she aged into her fifties and sixties during the 1900s and 1910s, Christensen made her large antebellum home a haven for children, grandchildren, and friends, and it was also the base from which she directed her reform activities. As each new grandchild was born or adopted, Christensen pitched in to baby-sit, sometimes keeping her grandchildren for months at a time. In 1917 she started a Montessori school, which she continued through 1927, enrolling her grandchildren and other white youngsters. Christensen was proud of her status as an educator, and she listed her occupation as "teacher, Montessori" in the 1920 census. Contact with the Montessori children's parents as well as her own children Andrea, Winnie, Niels, and Fred drew her into the circle of a younger generation of white middle-class society in Beaufort. This world and the world of her African American friends were separate, but Abbie enjoyed being a part of both. She now adopted the more usual pattern of vacationing in the North during the hottest summer months of July and August. Although Christensen wrote that she met "few kindred spirits," by the end of the 1910s she had rekindled and established friendships with some of Beaufort's "real southerners."[2]

As always, Christensen had to juggle her reform interests with her care for family and household, managing both with the help of at least two African American workers at all times. As she wrote in 1910, "Nothing accomplished today but a few letters. The chickens, horse, cow, cat, dogs, and servants give me so much to look after I can do little else but I did make cake this P.M. as Mona was so busy." In the 1910s John Simmons tended the grounds and stable, including a cow and chickens that gave the family fresh milk and eggs. Musetta Lawrence Simmons, John's wife, also helped in the Christensen home, along with anonymous washerwomen and the respected seamstresses Della Harvey and Annie Blanding. Even during summers, in the 1900s one servant would travel with Christensen to Brookline. Mona Brown and other cooks fed the Christensen family, as well as their guests, their desired "health food" diet of fruits, nuts, vegetables, soups, wholewheat breads, and salads. This diet helped keep Christensen slim and relatively healthy, even though she occasionally suffered from back pains. She worked in her garden and interacted with various clubs and institutions. In addition, her Montessori school brought up to a dozen preschool-age children to her house during the school days from fall to spring. When she went about her errands, Christensen visited the homes and businesses of blacks and whites, moving easily from one to the other.[3]

One example of Christensen's relationship with an African American family mixed employment with benevolent good deeds. In the 1910s Christensen befriended Annie Blanding, an African American seamstress, who was typical of many single black women living in Beaufort. Blanding had lived on Hilton Head Island, where her husband was a lighthouse keeper, until he died around 1900. After she became a widow, Blanding moved to Beaufort to be near her sister and mother. She was an accomplished needlewoman who took charge of intricate projects such as a trousseau for one of Christensen's friends. Wilhelmina Blanding Barnwell, Blanding's daughter, recalled that Christensen would drive her horse and buggy to visit her mother when she was sick with cancer. Christensen took an interest in the Blanding girls' musical talent and gave them her daughters' old music books. Abbie also gave Annie and her daughters homeopathic pills and weekly quarts of milk from her cow, which the girls would sometimes walk to get. Wilhelmina Barnwell recalled an interchange between Abbie Christensen and Mona

Brown when the girls arrived: "Mrs. Mona Brown was a fine woman, kind to everyone, had a smile for everyone. . . . I can still remember Mrs. Christensen saying to her in her high, precise voice, 'Mona, will you see to that dog! Children, you have to get used to that dog. She won't bite.'" Abbie Christensen was always teaching and instructing children, whether in the treatment of pets or the mastery of music. Wilhelmina Blanding learned well, becoming a teacher in the Shanklin School when she finished her education.[4]

Many white South Carolina women tied their club work to the memorializing of the Confederacy, promoting reforms that would strengthen the white South without compromising the old racial hierarchy. Christensen, however, connected women's clubs to "woman's mission," the ideal of service she had learned at Mount Holyoke. Northern and southern white women of Abbie's and her daughters' generations united behind an ideal of "maternalism." These "maternalists," who were also known as "progressives," emphasized state responsibility for improving the lives of women and children. With the physical work of mothering her own children behind her, Abbie became a part of the metaphorical labor of mothering that progressives such as Chicago's Jane Addams called "social housekeeping."[5]

The major limitation that Abbie Christensen faced when uniting with white southern progressives was their advocacy of reforms "for whites only." Progressives of the early 1900s blamed black political participation for white political violence in the 1890s. They argued that they were acting "in the best interests" of blacks by strengthening disfranchising measures, which would "protect" African Americans from politics where they were potential targets of violence and corruption. In 1910 Christensen clipped an article from the *Augusta Herald,* a Georgia paper that expressed outrage that even one black man had been allowed to vote in the "white" Democratic primary. This was the atmosphere in which progressivism operated. From 1900 to about 1920 southern progressives tried to harness the power of the state to remove corruption and inefficiency in government, enact prohibition and health-and-safety legislation, and build better roads. When progressives improved schools or founded hospitals, libraries, playgrounds, or parks, these public spaces were segregated or available to whites only. The politically active Christensen children fit in nicely with white southern progressives, if not with southerners of a more conservative political stripe. They favored reform, but they did not challenge white supremacy.[6]

On the surface Abbie seemed to accept these developments, pushing for woman suffrage with other white women and stressing relatively uncontroversial issues such as town beautification and the conservation of nature in her public writings for the *Beaufort Gazette*. At the same time she continued to aid individual African Americans and the Shanklin School. Christensen's grandson recalled that Abbie worked behind the scenes to ensure that middle-class African Americans who passed the literacy requirements continued to vote in Beaufort. As she moved into the twentieth century, Christensen looked for ways to fit her older politics of morality and benevolence with the new state-oriented progressivism.[7]

Losses and Gains

From 1906 to 1920 Christensen faced losses as well as gains in her family circle. The 1900s brought the death of her father and her husband, while the 1910s brought a son-in-law, daughters-in-law, and grandchildren. In 1906 Christensen's father, R. G. Holmes, died in Providence, Rhode Island, where he had settled a few years after Abbie's marriage to Niels in 1875. Abbie wrote her father's obituary for the *Beaufort Gazette,* stressing the qualities she admired in him and hoped to emulate. Christensen titled her article "One Who Tried to Make the World Better" and highlighted his work during Reconstruction, particularly his role in the authorship of the 1868 constitution. In keeping with the "progressive" view of suffrage restriction in the 1900s, Christensen also praised her father for trying to insert an educational qualification for suffrage. She explained that Holmes's provision would have gone into effect ten years after emancipation to give African Americans a chance to achieve literacy. This obituary gives a fairly clear indication that Christensen believed suffrage could be restricted by education but should not exclude African Americans. In closing, she noted Holmes's efforts to live without prejudice, writing, "He could say . . . 'I know not what record may await me in the next world, but I know I have never despised any man because he was poor, or because he was ignorant, or because he was black.'" Christensen would spend the rest of her days trying to live up to her father's hope that "the world may be better because I have lived in it."[8]

Three years later Abbie Christensen faced the fatal illness of her husband. Niels Christensen Sr. had long suffered from glomerulonephritis, or Bright's disease, which causes inflammation of the structures in the kidney that produce urine. It is likely that at the age of sixty-nine the damage to his kidneys was so severe that they ceased to function. In his last days Abbie walked with Niels in their beloved garden, their pet dog Razzle at his heels. Soon Niels could no longer climb the stairs, and the family set up a bed on the first floor of their Beaufort home. Abbie drew on all her mental strength and curative power to nurse him as he struggled with death. Abbie's younger sister Georgie was now her greatest comforter, writing her to "keep up all the courage you can." Abbie and Georgie both tried to use mental power to heal Niels, but his strength slowly slipped away. As Niels Christensen died, his last words were an expression of concern for his wife. He leaned on his son Fred's arm and begged him to "stay up tonight and help your Mutter, she is so tired." In his last half-hour Niels drew on Danish, the language of his childhood, to describe Abbie, the mother of his children. Abbie did not leave his side, and during the night of 4 February 1909 Abbie's husband of thirty-four years died quietly, "almost in my arms," according to Abbie. Their marriage had not been easy or conventional, but Abbie's and Niels's abiding respect and love for each other had allowed them both to pursue their dreams.[9]

With an American flag and flowers from his garden Niels Christensen was buried as he had chosen to live, among black and white southerners and northerners. He was an immigrant who became an American, "a most valuable citizen." Niels's obituary in the *Beaufort Gazette* bears the unmistakable imprint of Abbie's writing and is a clear statement of her values and beliefs. Its text begins with a meditation on death as "a part of the main design of the Creator, a turning to new paths, as it were, a reaching to a higher altitude in the eternities, where knowledge is increased, and the mysteries of the universe are laid wide." Reviewing his life, Christensen noted her husband's success in business and his commitment to public service in Beaufort. "Unselfishly charitable, hundreds can attest to his generosity," she stressed, noting that his giving was usually "hidden from the world." She continued, "With determination, he set to work and rebuilt waste places in the town. And this same skill as a landscape gardener has made his own gardens perhaps the most attractive of many pretty ones in town." It was this work of charity and botanical improvement that Abbie would carry on after her husband's death, but there was also something more. In closing, Abbie wrote, "Hundreds of colored people, to whom Capt. Christensen had always been a friend, sat in the galleries of the church during the services and were sorrowful spectators at the ceremonies around the grave." Though the advent of segregation had pushed them back into the slave gallery, African Americans were still important to Abbie, and she also wished to be "a friend."[10]

Just as there are no records of Abbie's personal writings immediately after her mother's death, there are no diaries or letters among Abbie's papers from the year after Niels Sr.'s death. In the years thereafter Abbie wrote in her diary on the anniversary of the occasion, proclaiming, "A year since Niels died . . . I am so glad I could nurse him, a most beautiful death it seemed. . . . He seems very near today."[11]

Abbie's loss left her lonely at times, but it also gave her more room to do as she pleased with the rest of her life. It would be unfair to say that Niels had held Abbie back; she had pushed the boundaries of acceptable wifehood more than most women of her time. Perhaps more important, by 1909 Christensen's children were grown and no longer needed her constant care. Arthur, Andrea, and Niels all married and had children in the 1910s, while Fred and Winnie remained single. Even though Abbie was an active and involved grandparent, she was no longer the main caregiver for several young children. Like other southern "public women," Christensen entered public life more fully when her children were mostly out of the house. At the same time, her status as a mother and grandmother aided her as she pushed for progressive reforms to benefit other mothers and children.[12]

Sons

Abbie Christensen's close ties to her two oldest sons were assets as well as liabilities. Even before Abbie settled back into the life of Beaufort, Niels Jr. and Fred had been establishing themselves as business and political leaders in the late 1890s and early 1900s. Along with their father, they ran the Christensens' hardware, lumber, building contracting, and real estate businesses, controlling a large proportion of the area's home building and holding mortgages throughout Beaufort County. In 1902 Niels Jr. purchased the *Beaufort Gazette,* the town's main Democratic paper. This mouthpiece was a powerful asset as Niels Jr. entered politics, winning a seat in the South Carolina Senate in 1904 and holding that office until 1924. Both Niels Jr. and Fred were committed to woman suffrage, but Niels Jr. in particular seems to have been much more inclined to restrict blacks' rights than his mother was. These sons gave Abbie Christensen clout and influence in her reform causes, but they limited their efforts to a strictly segregated format.[13]

The racial and political atmosphere in which Niels Jr. and Fred operated was far different from the Reconstruction era of their grandfather or the fusionist 1880s that had been their father's heyday. After the new state constitution was passed in 1895, fewer and fewer African Americans were able to qualify for registration to vote. During this nadir in American race relations separation became the order of the day, and black voters became associated with ignorance and corruption. In the early 1900s Niels Jr. wrote that his primary motivation in seeking office was the development of Beaufort's resources. He also relished a "lively contest" with what he saw as "a corrupt local ring," which also happened to be a biracial coalition.[14]

In the 1900s and 1910s the town of Beaufort remained a small southern municipality, and its population decreased dramatically from 4,110 in 1900 to 2,286 in 1910. By 1920 the town had recovered somewhat, increasing to a population of 2,831. During these years many black residents left for greater opportunities and freedom in southern and northern cities. Still, African Americans made up about 50 percent of the town's population, with the majority being black women. Many single African American women worked in the homes of whites or ran small businesses. The Christensens were closest to the small but influential minority of the white population, which was composed of Yankees or immigrants and their children, including German Jews, who were also business leaders in the town. Partly as a result of boundary changes, but also because of outmigration, Beaufort County, with its rural mainland and numerous islands, declined from 30,355 residents in 1910 to 22,269 in 1920. In Beaufort County the black population outnumbered whites by nearly seven to one in 1910, but the ratio declined to approximately four to one in 1920.[15]

By 1904 most whites, including Yankees and European immigrants, had affiliated with the Democratic Party. Black men who paid the poll tax and passed the literacy test held the balance of power when they voted as a bloc for the white candidate of their choice in the race for Intendant (mayor). The town council was made up of six wardens, each representing a neighborhood ward. In order to discuss issues, form consensus, and vote as a group, African American men met in Republican Party gatherings or mass meetings of "Colored Citizens." During the period from 1900 to 1920 white Democrats, including Niels Christensen Jr., tried various means to deprive African Americans of their voting power, relying mostly on white-only primaries and later on a commission form of government with a city manager and a council of aldermen elected at large. Without the division of the town into wards with a black majority, African Americans lost the ability to elect one of their own in at-large races. Though debate was often heated, black and white citizens and leaders were able to avoid violent conflicts, in part because of Beaufort's biracial police force. Most of the town's white leaders took pride in their paternalistic attitude toward African Americans, eschewing the violently racist speeches and tactics of South Carolina governors Tillman and Blease. Still, town Democrats maintained that they stood for white supremacy.[16]

As the new editor of the *Beaufort Gazette* in 1903, Niels Christensen Jr. attacked a mass meeting of blacks for issuing a resolution "that the abridgement of the suffrage in most, if not every Southern State is a standing menace to this great Government" and charging that the public had been "kept in ignorance of the unfortunates on the chain gang" who bore evidence of whippings on their backs. Christensen deplored the threat of using federal power to return the county to the "dark days" of "negro rule." He also wrote a series of articles based on his visits to the chain gang, endorsing punishment by whipping as necessary and declaring that although conditions were "not ideal," they were "near to what they ought to be." African American opposition to oppression had not died out, but Niels Christensen's newspaper tried to undermine that opposition as exaggerated rhetoric.[17]

In 1904 Niels Jr. led a court fight against the black town marshal and Beaufort's black policemen, charging them with incompetence. William Whipper and Julius I. Washington, two African American lawyers, and a black-white coalition fended off these attempts for a time, but enforcement of state disfranchising measures soon had their effect. In 1907 there were only twenty-five black registered voters, and more were eliminated by a "rigid examination" in 1908. Though Fred Christensen admitted that Niels Jr. was attempting to install a white marshal, he also recorded his own efforts to rally African American voters to his brother's side. In his diary in 1908 Fred noted the discrepancy in voter registration procedures for blacks as compared to those for whites. He wrote that "negroes crowd about the door of the room where the examination is held. Those that have registration certificates dating back to 1898 . . . are entitled to new certificates. Others are put through a more or less rigid examination that few can stand." Fred wrote that, in contrast, "the white applicant gets his certificate by merely asking for it, unless some negroe may be in the room." In 1913 he again deplored the fraud used to exclude black voters, but he does not seem to have stated his condemnation publicly.[18]

During these years Niels Christensen Jr. repeatedly had to answer charges that his family was too racially liberal. In 1904 his white opponent tried to smear him with the charge that one of his sisters had kissed a Negro girl after a baptismal service. Niels settled this dispute as a matter of southern honor by besting the supposed witness in a fistfight. The man then confessed that he did not really know the identity of the white girl he had seen. The fact that such an innocent show of affection would be an issue at all is indicative of the racial temper of the times.[19]

Time and again charges of racial liberalism distracted the senator from the progressive reforms for which he wanted to be remembered. Nowhere was this more evident than in Christensen's most famous act, his exposure of corruption in the state-run liquor dispensary. Established by Gov. Ben Tillman in 1892 as a compromise between free-market sale of liquor and Prohibition, the dispensary sold alcohol and used the profits as state revenue. Abbie's temperance influence and her low opinion of Tillman must have helped motivate Niels to try to destroy the dispensary. Research by Senator Christensen and another young legislator in 1905 showed that some officials were pocketing much of the cash earned. In retaliation, a Beaufort dispensary official brought up the charge that Niels's father had led Negro troops against southerners in the Civil War. Niels replied that he was proud of his father and added, rather weakly, that the black troops under Christensen's command never saw action. A number of Beaufort's Confederate veterans rallied behind the captain as well. Christensen's fight ended with success when the state dispensary was temporarily closed in 1907. The institution was finally abolished in 1916. This crusade against liquor was a continuation of Niels's training in Abbie Christensen's 1880s Band of Hope. Niels Christensen's Jr. loyalty was squarely with those middle-class southern women and clergymen who sought to cleanse small towns of the rowdy southern "male" culture of drinking.[20]

During his investigation Niels also made an enemy of state senator Cole Blease, who had the firm support of the state's liquor and gambling interests, as well as its mill workers. When Blease became governor of South Carolina in 1910, he tried to block Christensen's legislative efforts at every turn. In 1914 Blease again attacked Niels Christensen by criticizing the Shanklin School, of which Christensen was a trustee, for advocating "social equality."[21]

In town Niels and Fred were on the other side of the racial divide as they tried to defeat the "ring" and change the county to a commission form of government. This "progressive" reform did away with wards, eliminating neighborhood and ethnic loyalties. It was also supposed to make town government more efficient and lower costs. During the debate over the change to a commission in 1915, eighty-three African Americans were able to vote in Beaufort, and they held the balance of power between divided whites. Because most blacks were against the commission, Niels tried to bypass them by moving decisions on all issues to the Democratic primary, which excluded black voters. He charged the other side with "using" the Negro vote and invited in a Democratic speaker who denounced as race traitors those whites who abstained from the primary and voted with blacks in the general election. The commission plan eventually was carried through the votes of whites outside the city limits.[22]

Abbie Christensen saw this struggle as a fight for "clean government" against "the ring." She did not mention any racial dimension, noting only that "the best men" of the town were for the commission plan. Abbie was, however, aware of the racial politics of the day. She probably applauded the few African Americans who were in favor of Beaufort's commission plan, but most voted as a bloc against it. Such bloc voting was anathema to progressives such as Abbie Christensen who believed in individualized, nonpartisan politics. Excluded from these political deliberations because she was a woman, she waited for news from her sons and prayed for their success.[23]

In contrast Abbie seems to have played a large role in helping Niels reform conditions and increase expenditures at the state insane asylum, an institution with a high death rate and a lower rate of recovery than any other state asylum. The issue must have been close to her heart because of her mother's mental illness, and she took an active role in Niels's work. In her diary she recorded: "Asylum bill passed, I wrote most of it." There is no record in her diaries or letters that Christensen ghostwrote for her son at other times, but the possibility exists. When Governor Richard Manning took over from Blease in 1915, Niels won a progressive ally. Abbie thought that the new governor promised "much good" for South Carolina, and Niels agreed, adding that the governor stood for "white rule." During Manning's administration and after, Christensen was able to create state institutions such as a state board of charities and corrections, a boys' reformatory, a home for the feeble-minded, and a girls' reformatory. In fact, Niels was behind nearly every South Carolina reform known as "southern progressive." Niels also found and reformed waste in printing and other government functions, furthering his and his mother's progressive pursuit of a cleaner, more efficient government.[24]

Abbie's role in Niels's political career was chiefly one of support and inspiration, although their letters and conversations on politics undoubtedly influenced him. "Don't imagine I'm not thinking of you all the time," her son wrote her in 1913 as he worked on compulsory education, primary election reform, and school tax bills. Niels wrote, "There is a framed kodak picture of you on the bureau that is a comfort." He invited his mother to visit him in the legislature and regularly informed her about his work. Abbie helped to manage the *Gazette* while Niels was away at the legislature from 1905 to 1908. She checked the proofs, recruited others to write articles, and "furnished most of the copy from cuttings and original bits." Abbie sometimes wrote unsigned articles herself, though it was obvious in only a few nonpolitical stories that she was the author.[25]

Some Beaufort residents suspected, however, that Abbie Christensen was a frequent ghostwriter for her sons. A story illustrating this belief was often repeated in Christensen's later days. The story concerned a speech that Fred Christensen gave at Memorial Day services in 1917. "When Fred recited the Gettysburg Address a southern woman leaned over to her neighbor & said, 'All very fine, but you needn't tell me his mother didn't write it for him!'" This anecdote illustrates the unfamiliarity of southerners with Lincoln's words as well as the power they believed that Abbie held "behind the scenes" of her sons' careers.[26]

In the 1900s and 1910s, while African American activists such as Ida B. Wells and W. E. B. Du Bois exposed the lynchings that continued to mar the United States' claim to "civilization," Abbie Christensen's sons tried to play a part in banning this crime from the Sea Island region. Niels Christensen Jr. did not endorse federal antilynching legislation, but locally he and his brother Fred played a part in preventing a number of lynchings that might have occurred. In 1901 the National Association for the Advancement of Colored People (NAACP) reported the lynching of William Cornish at Port

Royal. Although Frederik Christensen believed that Cornish escaped to Savannah, Georgia, after a beating by the masked men who took him from authorities, this mob violence may have prompted Niels Christensen to speak out against lynching a few months later at a Beaufort memorial service for President William McKinley, who had been assassinated. Niels made a speech praising the justice of trying the assassin according to the law, and he criticized the logic of the lynchings that had taken place across the land that summer: "We assert that at times it is unwise to submit to law . . . and in defiance of law and government slay our fellow man. We have done this thing till the land is sprinkled with the blood of our victims and remotest history will tell of the fiendishness of our tortures. . . . The best tribute to [the president] would be blotting out this sin." The speech was reprinted in the *Beaufort Gazette,* which joined the state's leading papers, the *Charleston News and Courier* and the *Columbia State,* in opposing lynching. More important, Niels and his brother Fred personally intervened on several occasions to reduce tensions and to transport black suspects to safety.[27]

During the summer of 1906, which Abbie and Niels Sr. spent in Vermont, Fred wrote a letter to Abbie retelling the story of his brother Niels's efforts to calm angry whites after a young white man named Hugo Schlegelmilch, the son of a local merchant, was killed by blacks in the area of Hardeeville, about thirty miles southwest of Beaufort. After the incident the man's father visited Fred and told him the details: "He was glad that Niels had gone down there because he had talked with the men and had helped materially in preventing violence. I told him that Niels had said that it was due to Mr. S[chlegelmilch], his son and Mr. Martin that there had been no lynching. . . . [He] said the men only waited for a word from him to string the murderers up and that there were 50 men at Hardeeville, who had been ready to go with him to the plantation and 'massacre' everything there." Such massacres did occur in the Atlanta race riot of 1906 and in race riots in northern cities such as East Saint Louis, Illinois, in 1917, when white residents, angry over real or imagined black crimes, took revenge on whole African American neighborhoods. In Hardeeville, Niels acted in concert with other whites, most significantly Mr. Schlegelmilch, but the power of his position as a political leader was undoubtedly key in preventing a horrific mass lynching.[28]

Frederik Christensen also took part in efforts to avert lynching. In 1913, as Fred told it, a white dispensary official had "just shut down 3 blind tigers, probably with unnecessary harshness, on Saint Helena when he was ambushed with buckshot" and was killed. After two African American bootleggers were arrested as suspects, armed white men began marching from the rural area of Burton to the Beaufort jail, where one of the suspects was held. Fearing a lynching, Fred armed himself and rode through town, catching up with a few white friends who had already taken the prisoner from the custody of the black jailor. Fred and the others then spirited him away in a boat to Charleston and finally to authorities in Columbia. Niels's and Fred's actions took place during a time when the NAACP counted 54 African Americans lynched in South Carolina from 1900 to 1918. According to the same study, a total of 1,502 people of all races were lynched in the entire United States during these nineteen years. Abbie and her sons were probably aware of these statistics. A notation in her 1910 diary that "Fred read to me Stannard Baker's Negro Vote in a Democracy" was undoubtedly not the only instance when mother and son informed themselves about the facts of race relations in America. Baker's muckraking journalism was praised by both Booker T. Washington and W. E. B. Du Bois; it condemned lynching in no uncertain terms. Abbie Holmes Christensen praised the *Charleston News and Courier* when it took a stand against lynching in 1906. In 1931 she joined the Association of Southern Women for the Prevention of Lynching, must have been proud that her sons' actions prevented further additions to "Judge Lynch's" long list of victims.[29]

Niels Christensen III, Abbie's grandson, recalled that his father, Niels Jr., considered his mother fifty years ahead of her time on most issues. Race was probably one of those issues, but as another grandson remembered, Abbie Christensen was also "a realist" who remained inside the boundaries of her community. In one of her few public writings on race, Abbie wrote a letter to the editor of the *Boston Evening Transcript* publicly defending Beaufort African Americans against unfounded charges of rioting in the crisis atmosphere after a huge Beaufort fire. Within her circle of family and friends she spoke out for the valor of black troops in the Spanish-American-Cuban-Filipino War and against police brutality in the Houston, Texas, shooting of black soldiers in 1917. In that year Christensen also used what power she had to try to ostracize socially a white Beaufort man who had gone unpunished by the law, even though he had shot and killed an unarmed black man.[30]

As circumscribed as they were, Abbie's views were a constant danger to Niels Jr. For example, in 1914 Christensen's support for the Shanklin School had provided a target for Niels's enemy Cole Blease. In 1916 a Democratic faction in Beaufort organized a rival newspaper and printed a cartoon that lampooned his parents' racial views. Niels was shown running from a large black mammy whose skirt was labeled "Family Record." The ugly caricature was depicted as saying, "Come back here Niels. You got to stay wid de fambly." In response, the Niels caricature protested, "But I have always voted the Democratic ticket." The mammy character may have represented Abbie, using gender as well as a racial stereotyping to emasculate Niels rhetorically. In response, Niels took the high ground of honor and printed a statement that warned his opponents "to leave reference to my people out of their attacks on me." Niels weathered this tempest and went on to win two more elections to the senate.[31]

"See how useful our sons are in S.C.," Abbie wrote in her diary in 1910. Yet Niels's and Fred's activities, rather than giving a clear indication of her own beliefs, provide only the parameters in which she was able to act. As a woman, different and more limited paths of participation were open to Christensen. First as a writer and later as club woman, Abbie Christensen tried to reform Beaufort.[32]

A Stroller in Beaufort Fields and Gardens

One of the first ways Abbie Christensen sought to beautify Beaufort was through a series of writings in the *Beaufort Gazette* from 1906 to 1910 promoting the conservation of nature and praising public and private gardens. As the "Stroller," Christensen described Beaufort's wildflowers and gardens, giving advice about pests, explaining medicinal uses, and imparting local legends surrounding the blooms. Reflecting her wide range of interests, Christensen also tied nature to literature, philosophy, and religion, meditating on the seasons of life and the "late-blooming" of human beings as well as trees.[33]

How did Christensen come to choose this subject? Botany had been a passion of Abbie's since her days at Ipswich, and throughout her adult life she included descriptions of the blossoms around her and sent pressed flowers in countless letters to friends and relatives. Her marriage to Niels Christensen Sr., an avid gardener who landscaped Beaufort's National Cemetery, also encouraged this interest. Christensen found the deepest motivation for her nature writings in transcendentalism, particularly Ralph Waldo Emerson's "Nature." She asked her readers, "In these strenuous days are we not all prisoners shut in with the daily round of details more or less petty and unsatisfactory? Are we not in sore need of the inspiration kind Nature offers to us all when we do but look and listen? . . . may we Strollers learn to see the soul of things in the daily round, the common task, that furnish all we need to ask." Christensen urged her readers to take the time to stroll past homes, gardens, and vacant lots where they could enjoy the buzzing of bees and hummingbirds among unknown red flowers and easily recognized roses and honeysuckle. Pushing them further, she urged them to visit the Atlantic Ocean beaches of the furthest Sea Islands, where they would find "life-giving air and the tonic of the surf bathing." Here also tall stems topped with waxy white yucca blossoms pierced the flat expanse of "marshy grass that swept from the shore to the woods." Christensen believed that this sensual and meditative experience of nature was inherently good for the soul.[34]

Christensen was not alone in this belief. Early environmentalists included urban reformers who believed that environment affected people's mental and moral outlook. Founders of parks and parklike cemeteries sought to improve urban residents' lives through new public gardens. Civic beautification became a nationwide reform led by middle-class women who brought their domestic skills at beautifying their private homes into the public sphere. These women spearheaded "village improvement" by promoting tree plant-ing, landscaping railroad stations, and establishing public libraries and parks. As the nation industrialized and urbanized at an ever more rapid pace, these women sought to stop the sacrifice of trees and wildlife to new technology such as telegraph and telephone lines and streetcar suburbs.[35]

Even before she published her first Stroller column, Christensen may have influenced Niels Christensen Jr. to give prominence to the new Arbor Day movement in a 1903 editorial in the *Beaufort Gazette*. This editorial high-lighted the efforts of the South Carolina Federation of Women's Clubs to make a program on Arbor Day available to the public schools. It urged Beaufort's public schools to follow the program and provide trees and shrubs for children to plant in public places. In this way children would learn both "appreciation of nature" and good citizenship as they watched trees grow in the years that followed.[36]

Shortly thereafter, in 1904, Beaufort's Civic League, a club dedicated to public landscaping and nature education, was founded by members of Beaufort's literary Clover Club, who asked a few other Beaufort women to join them in beautifying the town's public spaces. Christensen addressed the women of the Civic League as well as male citizens when she urged her readers to become politically active conservationists. "All good citizens should rally to rescue what we have left of wayside trees and shrubs or soon we shall have no coverts left for the birds," she wrote at the end of one column in 1908. Such public exhortation was one way that Christensen tried to cultivate a New South. Another way, which she rediscovered, was the power of women's voluntary associations—most notably the Civic League.[37]

Daughters

Through her daughters, Andrea and Winnie, Christensen began to take note of a growing women's club movement. Abbie's daughters, who had enjoyed the social and intellectual companionship of other young women in art school and college, immediately looked for similar companionship in women's clubs when they returned to the South.

Andrea, who was twenty-five in 1909, returned to Beaufort in that year after studying art in Massachusetts. Along with her brother Fred, she helped her mother through her father's illness and death. An attractive young woman with her mother's delicate features and her father's thick, light brown hair, Andrea played tennis, went dancing, and became an early member of Beaufort's literary Clover Club. By 1910 she was representing the club at the South Carolina Federation of Women's Clubs meeting in Charleston. In that same year, after a brief courtship, Andrea married one of her brother Niels's best friends in the South Carolina legislature, Lawrence Patterson. Abbie took delight in this marriage and in her new son-in-law, describing Lawrence as "an abstainer from liquor, tobacco, tea & coffee, a clean, healthy man who looks his best in a bathing suit." Andrea Christensen Patterson moved to Greenville, South Carolina, and joined another women's club, the Thursday Club, and was an officer in the State Federation of Women's Clubs. Of all the Christensen children, Andrea was the closest to her mother in terms of both looks and thoughts. In their many letters to each other the two agreed on women's rights, education, health foods, and religion. Abbie considered Andrea "sensitive," and she seems to have suffered from depression, which deprived her of the energy of her mother and her other siblings. Nevertheless, Andrea continued to draw and paint; adopted a daughter, Dorothy; and participated actively in the social, cultural, and reform life of Greenville. Like Christensen's other children, Andrea was not as interested in African

Americans as her mother was, turning her attention instead to the large population of poor white women and children whom she encountered in the textile mills of her adopted city.[38]

After attending Radcliffe College, Andrea's sister, Winnie, also returned to Beaufort in 1910 and joined the Clover Club and its offshoot, the Civic League. Blessed with good looks, good health, great intelligence, and good humor, Winnie was a "New Woman" who chose to pursue higher education, a profession, and reform work. Winnie never married, preferring the friendship of other women, and she assumed the task of caring for her mother as she aged. With so many talents and interests, Winnie had trouble settling on a career. In 1914 she followed in the footsteps of her gardening father and her botanist mother, becoming one of the first American women to earn a degree in landscape architecture at the Massachusetts Institute of Technology. In 1918 Winnie was offered a position as a professor at Smith College. However, she declined, engaging instead in various kinds of reform work, from Young Men's Christian Association (YMCA) Relief Corps work in France after World War I to teaching white Appalachian children at the Pine Mountain School in Kentucky in the 1920s. These choices left Winnie time to pursue her passions for folk dancing and art, while occasionally engaging in freelance work as a landscape architect.[39]

White Women's Clubs

Andrea and Winnie were part of a nationwide proliferation of women's clubs, beginning in the 1890s and continuing through the 1910s. These clubs and voluntary associations fueled a revival of women's political participation as a major force in the progressive era. In the 1910s Abbie Christensen joined them in three women's associations: the Beaufort Female Benevolent Society, the Beaufort Civic League, and the South Carolina Equal Suffrage League.[40]

Abbie Christensen remained most comfortable in women's organizations that represented clear moral issues, as the Woman's Christian Temperance Union and the South Carolina Equal Rights Association had done. Christensen did not join the literary Clover Club until the 1920s, uniting instead with an older type of women's association, the Beaufort Female Benevolent Society, which appealed to her morality and concern for the poor. This organization was founded in 1814 to provide employment, lodging, and other aid to the poor white women of the town. It died out during the Civil War but was re-formed in 1892 with the participation of northern white women who settled in the area. At that time the organization changed to a more equalitarian format, aiding any needy individual on a case-by-case basis. The fact that Christensen joined this organization indicated her greater willingness to affiliate with southern white women, although Abbie continued to work with the black community as well. It also demonstrated her continuing concern for the poorest Beaufort residents. In 1903, for example, Christensen had written: "There are frequent applications for clothing from those who are old, feeble or sick. A woman came yesterday on such an errand. I had heard she had been stealing your Pa's fence, but when I heard her tale, of her old husband being sick, unable to work, for four years—which is true—and they with next to nothing to live on, I decided that I w'd steal too were I in her place. How else can they keep from freezing? . . . They ought to be in a home for aged couples—but there isn't any here. I gave her a few pieces, but had not much, there are so many calls." Joining with other women in the Benevolent Society to provide aid was one way that Christensen could alleviate poverty. Christensen represented the organization for two years in a row, in 1913 and 1914, at the State Federation of Women's Clubs.[41]

The women's clubs that the Christensens joined operated at a number of levels. Because they were exclusive, clubs could be used at a class level as markers of social distinction, leisure, and education. At another level they provided a base of female friendship and learning that was free from men's control. In this space radical ideas might be explored. For example, Andrea Christensen Patterson invited feminist social theorist Charlotte Perkins Gilman to speak at the Thursday Club.[42]

Women's clubs were divided by race as well as class. Segregation was the unsisterly side of the women's club movement. Despite their objections to this segregation, African American women were more interested in improving their communities than in trying to affiliate with white women. Their organizations were part of the settlement house and progressive social welfare movements.[43]

As their mothers had done in benevolent societies and temperance organizations, white and black club women gained experience with speaking in public and organizing groups. Many women's literary clubs soon moved from self-improvement to spreading the joys of learning to others. They founded libraries and worked to improve local schools. In the New South women's clubs spread quickly because they seemed less directly threatening to a traditional image of women than did suffrage organizations. Nevertheless, these clubs became the seedbeds for renewed suffrage organizing in 1914 when delegates from various South Carolina women's clubs gathered for the annual meeting of the State Federation of Women's Clubs.[44]

In the 1900s and 1910s the all-male world of Beaufort politics was starting to converse with the female world of women's clubs. Voluntary activity involving public spaces had to be coordinated with the intendant and the town council, a body that had rarely dealt with women. When the Civic League approached the council regarding the transformation of a vacant lot into a park, they were greeted with chivalry rather than shock. The intendant gave charge of the town lot to the league, which planned and paid for the landscaping of the grounds. Winnie Christensen designed the plan, but none of these women actually did the physical work of gardening. Instead, they paid African American men to do the planting, pruning, and mowing that needed to be done.[45]

Other projects of the Civic League included maintaining a public fountain for the town's horses, introducing nature study in the white public schools, supporting public health measures, inviting in out-of-town speakers, and creating a new cemetery. This last project, across from the National Cemetery, was a pet project of Abbie and her daughter. Winnie laid out the grounds, while Abbie chaired the tree-planting committee, spending many days with gardener John Simmons, who did the work of planting.[46]

During the 1900s and 1910s the Civic League exchanged gifts and money with various local government entities. From fountains, shrubs, and trees at the courthouse to street signs and playgrounds, the women of the Civic League beautified. They also led private citizens in an annual town clean-up day. When the town council established a department of parks and playgrounds in 1918, this was to be run "in conjunction with the Civic League."[47]

White women in the Clover Club and the Civic League were successful in influencing the town council because they worked within the system of white supremacy and because they presented themselves as the civilizers of public space in much the same way as middle-class women were the civilizers of the home. Because of Beaufort's unique history as a haven for northerners and even immigrants, the Civic League never played up the idea of the

Lost Cause or portrayed themselves as dependent southern ladies. The public spaces they created, however, were usually segregated. Most of the progressive improvements desired by the league were for whites only—for example, a playground for white children and drinking fountains and nature instruction in the white public schools. Indeed, while white supremacy campaigns over adding white primaries or abolishing the offices of wardens raged in the 1910s, white women's requests for conservation and beautification might have seemed a welcome distraction, and fulfilling them legitimized a local government that might otherwise have accomplished little.[48]

Like many other women's service clubs, the Civic League raised money through events such as teas, baby contests, and flower shows. None of these activities challenged the traditional female roles that these single women, wives, and mothers inhabited. On the other hand, the Civic League entered a more masculine domain when members called for the prosecution of men who cut down trees, killed songbirds, or abused horses. To convey its message, the Civic League used an old tactic of women's groups, the right of petition. Women in the league petitioned county and state authorities to enforce the laws protecting roadside trees and flowers. They also asked the town to join them in a tree planting program. Sixty-six men and women signed the petition, but whether it had an effect is unclear, as Abbie and other league members continued to express outrage over wanton tree cutting.[49]

The town government's responses to these issues ranged from immediate action to avoidance. As Abbie Christensen put it in her diary in 1910, "Civic League meeting. Very interesting. . . . Great unanimity of opinion, & after the meeting ten of us went to interview the Intendant about the protection of grass and trees and still more of horses. He, prudently, was not at home." Undaunted, the women published the minutes of their meeting, including the attempted visit with the intendant, in that week's paper. The intendant and town council responded by publishing ordinances regarding the penalties for cutting down trees without permission or violating hack (horse drawn taxi) regulations. It is not clear, however, that police were vigorous in pursuing violators. One indication that the problems were not resolved is the fact that these themes of protection or conservation came up again in articles on the Civic League until 1931.[50]

Because the women of the Civic League were able to publish well-written and forceful letters in the local paper, members of the town council were sometimes put on the spot and felt obliged to explain themselves to the league. In 1912, in response to a Civic League letter calling for improved sanitary conditions, one warden wrote: "We would . . . ask that they be slow to condemn for there are many circumstances & conditions existing of which they have little knowledge & I feel that we can assure them . . . in due time every particular practicable measure will be carried out." Though they could have been seen as nagging, the white women of the Civic League were treated with respect by the town council and the newspaper. The worst criticism published in the local newspaper came from R. F. Fripps, who wrote, "I wish some of the parties who are forever writing about protecting the birds had all that are at my place eating his fruit." Of course, the good press of the Civic League was aided by the fact that Niels and Fred Christensen, editors of the *Beaufort Gazette,* were supporters of the league.[51]

In 1909 the Civic League set the council onto so many different tasks that they addressed the league's concerns at three successive meetings. At the suggestion of the Civic League, the fire committee was instructed to examine all "old, dilapidated structures" that posed a fire risk. The council passed "an ordinance creating a tree and park commission" as well as an ordinance against spitting on sidewalks. The intendant attended to the fountains, and the marshal was instructed to report all citizens who did not place their trash in receptacles. The only requests the council did not fulfill were objections to billboards and the building of a town cemetery. However, when the Civic League moved to create its own cemetery with private backers, the council supported their efforts.[52]

A Segregated Public Library

Because the work of the Clover Club and the business of the Civic League were tied but not identical, a controversy arose when the Christensen men, in cooperation with the Clover Club, proposed to build a library for whites on the site of a public park created by the Civic League. In 1915 Senator Christensen helped the club get a Carnegie grant to build a library building, and Fred rallied the town to levy a tax to provide matching funds. A few members of the Civic League felt slighted that they had not been consulted about the change. In response, Abbie wrote a letter to the editor, arguing that a library would "beautify" the park. Library proponents prevailed, but not without hard feelings on the part of those who opposed them—a few Civic League members and African Americans, who were taxed but excluded from borrowing privileges. Abbie made no public comment on this racial exclusion, though she must have been aware of it.[53]

For African Americans, access to books and libraries was a continuing struggle. Christensen contributed to the formation of the Julia Watson Library and Reading Room in 1897, and this black institution continued to invite readers in 1904. This was a private effort, however, and could not provide the number and variety of books in the Clover Club's library, particularly after it became the white public library. In 1931 the old Carteret Street church, which Christensen had helped to build, was purchased "with funds from a trust held by the Library Board 'for library purposes for the colored citizens of Beaufort township.'" The church became the J. I. Washington branch library for service to black residents in 1932. Other efforts included the Laura Towne public library and bookmobile on Saint Helena Island and the India Shanklin Library in Port Royal, established after Christensen's death. In 1963 the public library system finally became fully integrated.[54]

Woman Suffrage (Again)

The 1915 controversy over the library led to a renewed interest in votes for women. In that year Fred Christensen wrote a *Beaufort Gazette* editorial that praised the Civic League, pushed the library, and promoted woman suffrage. As a trustee for the proposed library, Fred apologized for the "oversight" of forgetting to consult the Civic League. Such mistakes could be avoided, he argued, if women had the vote. He stated, "The Gazette hopes the time is not far off when women will be given, through the ballot, a greater influence in public affairs, and that then these matters will be accomplished with less friction and more tact." In his public pronouncement Fred was not far behind his sister and mother, who had already joined the new South Carolina Equal Suffrage League at its founding in 1914.[55]

This time there was an even stronger movement in the North and the West, and the southern movement spread much further than it had in the 1890s. Marjorie Wheeler has argued that a group of strong, socially prominent, and well-educated southern women leaders led the movement of the 1910s as effectively as was possible in this conservative region. Increased urbanization and educational opportunities for middle-class southern white women also gave these leaders a larger following than Abbie's cohort had found. The progressive movement and dissatisfaction with the callous policies of New South political leaders, such as South Carolina governors Benjamin Tillman and Cole Blease, pushed southern women to seek more political power for themselves.[56]

In addition to these factors, Abbie and her daughters' experiences suggest that in South Carolina the logistical organization as well as the work of the women's club movement proved essential. By affiliating together in statewide and national Federations of Women's Clubs, South Carolina women had formed a network of women reformers ready to push for suffrage. In 1913 Christensen and her daughters attended the federation convention in Florence, with Abbie representing the Beaufort Female Benevolent Society, Winnie the Civic League, and Andrea the Thursday Club. "Now wasn't that a representation from one family?" Abbie proudly wrote her son Arthur. The meeting brought Christensen into contact with other active South Carolina women. "I was most agreeably surprised to learn how much is being accomplished by the women of this state, and how many of them are waking up to the needs of their children, their homes, and their communities where they live," she wrote. The South Carolina Federation of Women's Clubs stressed civics, philanthropy, horticulture, village improvement, libraries, and improving education. Christensen was able to unite with these goals, ignoring South Carolina club women's embracing of the Confederacy.[57]

Dissatisfied with the limits on what they could do for home and community without the vote, a group of South Carolina club women came together after the convention the next year and formed the South Carolina Equal Suffrage Association. Abbie Christensen and her daughter Andrea were at the convention, and they were among the founders of the new South Carolina suffrage organization.[58]

After the death of South Carolina suffragist Virginia Young, Abbie had kept up with the national suffrage movement through her northern friends and her subscription to Alice Stone Blackwell's *Woman's Journal.* Abbie also sent the magazine to friends whom she hoped to win over to the cause.[59]

Christensen was encouraged by the fact that some western states had passed woman suffrage amendments and frustrated that South Carolina lagged behind. She wrote her son Fred, "I am sorry enough that S.C. is likely to be disgraced with such a scoundrel as Blease for governor. In states where women vote such characters as he haven't a chance even for nomination."

Sometime after 1913 she or Andrea obtained a poster showing the progression of suffrage through the various states. When suffrage was achieved, Abbie was convinced that women would clean up politics and reform the world.[60]

In fact, the aims of the South Carolina Equal Suffrage Association went far beyond the vote. Like many other southern suffrage organizations, the association called for equal guardianship of children, equal pay for equal work, equal educational opportunities for women, raising the age of consent for girls from fourteen to twenty-one, an end to the double standard of sexual morality, compulsory education for South Carolina children, an end to child labor, the promotion of temperance, and international arbitration. Abbie Christensen's contribution was a resolution supporting President Woodrow Wilson in "the Mexican trouble." Her stand is not surprising, given her loyalty to this president, though it could be argued that Wilson's use of troops was hardly in the spirit of international arbitration.[61]

Nowhere was race mentioned, but in South Carolina it was assumed that all suffragists were white and that equal rights for black women were not part of the program. The southern strategy of the NAWSA was to let local chapters decide whether or not to admit blacks. In practice, this meant segregation. Although Christensen worked with middle-class African American women on other issues, for example the Shanklin School and the judging of student work at the annual Exhibit of Negro Schools, she never included them in suffrage organizing. Perhaps one indication of her sympathies was a positive article on an African American woman suffrage organization that she clipped and inserted in her diary in 1911. Abbie's friend Laura Bragg mentioned "the Negro question" in a 1915 letter about suffrage activities, but Abbie's reply is unknown. In this respect Abbie was not unlike most of the major southern white suffrage leaders of the 1910s. They did not challenge the racial order while fighting for suffrage, but some of them joined black women in the interracial movement when suffrage was achieved. Antisuffragists, on the other hand, were explicitly racist in their arguments.[62]

Though the Equal Suffrage Association spread throughout the state, suffrage at that time did not stand a chance in South Carolina. From 1914 to 1917 the league grew from 450 to 3,000 members and encompassed twenty-five city leagues, all affiliated with the National American Woman Suffrage Association. Several South Carolina women were also prominent members of the Congressional Union (later the Woman's Party), which drew attention to the cause with more militant direct action. Racism and gender conservatism proved southern suffragists' undoing. White South Carolina politicians feared that any federal intervention in suffrage would open up the issue of black disfranchisement. Antisuffragists also argued that voting would debase women who were kept pure by their distance from the political process.[63]

For all these reasons local suffrage work was hard for Abbie Christensen. Only ten women attended a 1914 meeting at Christensen's home to discuss the new state league. Abbie's daughter-in-law Nancy Stratton Christensen and two visitors from Colorado were the only convinced suffragists even in this small group. By 1915 Mabel Runette, a young Beaufort milliner and later the town librarian, led Beaufort's small group of about a dozen suffragists. When Abbie invited Hannah Coleman, president of the state's Equal Suffrage League to Beaufort in 1915, she had to squeeze her speech in between a magician and a humorist during the town Chautauqua. Twenty-five women and men out of two hundred in the audience stood as suffrage supporters. Abbie's work was largely symbolic. Though she did not carry her knot of white and yellow ribbon any longer, Christensen deliberately served tea on a yellow tablecloth when she entertained Runette to "talk suffrage."[64]

Even though her Beaufort supporters were few, Christensen received encouragement from suffragist family members and out-of-town friends who shared her views. Fred used his influence locally in the town paper, and Andrea became vice president of the South Carolina Equal Suffrage League in 1915. Andrea hosted suffrage speakers and worked through the Federation of Women's Clubs for the remaining years of the fight. In addition, the memory of Niels Christensen Sr.'s support strengthened Abbie. Two of her children remained unconvinced: Arthur Christensen opposed woman suffrage, and Winnie remained undecided.[65]

Niels Christensen Jr. was undoubtedly Abbie's most important ally in the suffrage fight. Few southern men supported woman suffrage, especially in South Carolina, but Niels Jr. was a public advocate for the cause. He and his wife Nancy, a devoted suffragist, entertained the Charlestonian Congressional Union leader Susan Pringle Frost and her sister and allowed them to display a "silent speech" promoting woman suffrage in a window of their home. In 1918, at the convention of the South Carolina Democratic Party,

Niels Christensen proposed a resolution to allow women to vote in the primary. The resolution was rejected. Undaunted, in 1920 Senator Christensen introduced another resolution to ratify the proposed Federal Suffrage Amendment. Again his committee reported unfavorably. The vote by the entire senate resulted in ninety-three against woman suffrage and twenty for it. After suffrage was granted in 1920, Niels worked closely with Beaufort women, organizing them into local political clubs together with men.[66]

Outside of Beaufort, Abbie Christensen persuaded one of South Carolina's most prominent women to join the suffrage cause. During the 1910s Christensen corresponded with Laura Bragg, director of the Charleston Museum. Though she was the age of Christensen's youngest daughter, Bragg shared with Christensen a common background and similar interests, including suffrage. Bragg's father, a transcendentalist, moved to Charleston in the 1890s to teach at a school for African Americans. Laura headed the natural history portion of the Charleston Museum and belonged to the Society for the Preservation of Negro Spirituals. She visited the Christensens in Beaufort and kept Abbie informed about the news of the suffrage movement in Charleston. The two women also corresponded about native botanical specimens. Northern abolitionist ties continued to draw Abbie to women similar to her.[67]

The entry of the United States into World War I in 1917 temporarily interrupted the suffrage campaign, as American women worked as volunteers and in war industries. Suffragists later used this volunteer work to their advantage, pushing for the vote as a reward for their patriotic service. Although many notable suffragists were pacifists, Christensen joined the majority in supporting the war. Given her devotion to Woodrow Wilson, a Democratic progressive who resembled her son in looks and politics, it is not surprising that Abbie cheered the war. She encouraged her sons to enlist and went to work writing a patriotic song called "Allies All," which could be sung to the tune of "Dixie." Although she did not meet with success in publishing her work, Christensen printed hundreds of copies herself and distributed them to soldiers at the training camp near Beaufort. World War I provided Christensen with an opportunity to erase regional differences and stress the fact that southerners and northerners were all Americans.[68]

As the Stroller and as an anonymous contributor to her sons' newspaper in the 1900s and 1910s, Christensen played a quiet, almost invisible role behind the scenes of the male-dominated politics in her town. Together with other women in women's clubs and the suffrage movement, Christensen raised an audible voice. Together with her children Christensen participated enthusiastically in the white southern progressive movement. After women obtained the right to vote in 1920, Christensen's voice and actions would speak louder than ever before.

Chapter Eleven

HER MIND WAS ALWAYS ADVENTURING

*How can you say you **own** a watch, sewing machine, etc. All that's good & useful was put in our hands by God. . . . This realization leads us to another wonderful law which mystics delight to know. It is that we are all one, each dependent on another, bound together like Brothers and Sisters.*[1]

Every Saturday night during March 1929, Abbie Holmes Christensen sat in her Beaufort house in a room she had transformed into her "sanctum." She was seventy-seven years old; her eyes were weak, her hands were less steady, and her joints ached with rheumatism. Still, she was ready for a new adventure. Focusing intently, Christensen chanted and lit two candles. She spoke the words of a prayer: "God of our hearts, permit thy divine vibrations to fill this holy place, attune me with the Cosmic Soul, and make me receptive to the lessons and inspirations of this hour." As the minutes crept toward midnight, Christensen turned on one electric light and studied the neophyte lectures of the Rosicrucian Order, a mystical sect. On one late night she wrote in her notebook, "Just now I feel such nerve vibrations as I felt in 1900," describing a tingling in her fingers, hands, and arms. Christensen studied and meditated upon the tenets of the Rosicrucians for over a year, connecting ideas about the exchange and movement of atoms and energy throughout the planet to ideas of universal brotherhood and an egoless existence that promoted healing and justice for all. Her Rosicrucian meditations reinforced her interest in socialism and prompted her to make her most radical move for a New South. She entered the male preserve of party politics and went "against the grain" of the region's conservatism as an elector for Socialist Party candidate Norman Thomas in 1932.[2]

Several years after Abbie Holmes Christensen's death in 1938, her daughter-in-law Helen Burr Christensen wrote of her, "She was the most advanced thinker in our rather radical family. Her mind was always adventuring." These words could be applied to most of Abbie's life, but never so much as when she was in her seventies and eighties. Abbie's daughter Andrea attributed her mother's successful aging to her "enthusiasm" for causes and a "tough New England back ground that gave you a healthy body and . . . a happy philosophy of life that helped you to make the most of everything." Old age gave Christensen a prim, grandmotherly appearance, which made her enthusiasm for socialism seem eccentric rather than threatening. In addition, Christensen publically respected the boundaries of Jim Crow, never outwardly challenging segregation. Christensen remained as she had described herself, a "free lance with just a streak of conservatism."[3]

As she aged, taking care of her health occupied Christensen's attention more than ever. Soreness in her eyes, arthritis in her hands and back, and a feeling of being "run down" prompted Christensen to spend time at a Massachusetts sanitarium in 1915. At the sanitarium she ate vegetarian food and received massages and electrical treatments. In the years thereafter she avoided sugar and meat and sought out stone-ground wheat flour for her kitchen. Together with her daughter Andrea, Abbie moved on to embrace the "Nature Cure." In 1919, Andrea and her husband, Lawrence, had discovered Nature Cure at the Lindlahr Health Resort in Elmhurst, Illinois. Afterward they began "depending more and more on fruits and vegetables, and less and less on meats, breads and other starches." The following year, Abbie persuaded Niels Jr. to join her at Lindlahr for a month of deep breathing, cold water bathing, exercise, "balanced" eating, sleep, rest, massage, sunbathing, "right thinking," and daily "confidential talk[s] with a trusted friend or relative." Abbie enjoyed her visit and continued eating vegetarian meals with her son Fred, who also came to practice Nature Cure. Abbie returned to Lindlahr in 1923 with Andrea and her daughter, Dorothy. Abbie particularly enjoyed the Lindlahr sunbaths, especially when sunshine turned to showers and the women had "a great frolic . . . dancing, laughing, playing in the rain." Nature Cure's diet and exercise helped give Christensen greater health and energy to make the most of her waning years.[4]

In the 1920s and 1930s Christensen's typical day found her discussing housework with the servants, assisting with her Montessori school, pruning rosebushes in the garden, calling on friends and family, attending political and organization meetings in the evenings, and enjoying her view of the sunset or the moonlight on the river behind her home. As her daughter Winnie put it, "Housekeeping shore isn't enough for the likes of you & me, you know." White women's organizations continued to draw Christensen's interest, and she joined the new League of Women Voters (LWV), the Parent

Teacher Association (PTA), and the Association of Southern Women for the Prevention of Lynching (ASWPL).[5]

Increasingly, however, Christensen looked to younger women friends and her children and grandchildren to carry on her legacy. Her son Arthur and his second wife, Lillian, moved to Beaufort, soon adding two granddaughters, Cornelia and Carroll, to her growing family. By the 1920s Niels and Nancy had four children: Niels III, Anne, Andrea, and Stratton. Winnie Christensen remained single, spending most of the 1920s in Harlan, Kentucky, as a teacher at the Pine Mountain Settlement School. Frederik Christensen married in 1929, drawing Helen Burr, Abbie's longtime neighbor and friend, into the family as his wife. In the 1930s they had a child, Frederik Burr Christensen. As she aged, Christensen slowed her "flitting hither & thither pro bono publico," but her granddaughter Carroll Christensen Eve still remembered her as "four foot ten [inches] and ninety pounds of dynamite." In the area of reform, friends such as India Shanklin and Catherine DeVeaux, a nurse who founded a Beaufort clinic, were forces for the advancement of the African American community, while Clare Macdonald and Fred Christensen forged ahead as white participants in the South's new movement for interracial cooperation.[6]

During the 1920s and 1930s South Carolina went through an economic and political transition. Poor, worn-out land; overproduction; the loss of overseas markets; drought; and the boll weevil caused a rural depression beginning in the 1920s. The black exodus that had been so dramatic in the 1900s slowed in the town of Beaufort but continued in the rural areas of Beaufort County during the 1920s. Because the Christensen family business depended on the mortgage payments and purchasing power of rural South Carolinians, the family's fortune dwindled considerably during this time. As rural poverty increased in the 1930s, many whites threw off some of their fears of federal interference and welcomed the assistance of the New Deal. Unfortunately, the agricultural programs of Franklin Roosevelt mostly benefitted large landowners at the expense of yeomen and tenant farmers. Some landowners shared government payments with their tenants, but most did not. The socialist movement that Christensen joined managed to organize a number of white and black sharecroppers, coal miners, and other oppressed people of the South, but it had little impact on federal programs.[7]

The nation's second Ku Klux Klan (KKK) and the southern Commission for Interracial Cooperation (CIC) represented opposite poles of race relations in the 1920s and 1930s. By far the more popular organization, the KKK was refounded in 1915 at Stone Mountain, Georgia, but did not really expand until it hired a marketing team that successfully promoted the organization. The new Klan mixed white protestant Christianity and fears of foreigners, Catholics, Jews, and African Americans, as well as the "new morality" of young people who enjoyed jazz music, socialized "promiscuously," and violated Prohibition. From 1921 to 1924 the KKK spread like wildfire, capitalizing on the anxieties of the white middle class, particularly in towns and smaller cities throughout the nation. In 1922 and 1923 Beaufort was targeted by KKK propagandists, including revival preacher Bob Jones, and over seventy of the protestant white men of the town joined the white-sheeted organization. The Christensens were prominent in their opposition.[8]

The resurgence of racist violence and intolerance of leftists and foreigners after World War I benefitted the KKK, but it horrified southern liberals. In 1919 race riots by whites wreaked havoc in black neighborhoods in twenty-five U.S. cities, and lynchings of African Americans increased. In response, southerner Will Alexander, a young Methodist minister and YMCA activist, formed the Commission on Interracial Cooperation (CIC). Like Abbie Christensen, the movement did not question segregation but sought to build bridges between the two races. In 1922 Niels Christensen Jr. joined the CIC and was followed by his brother Frederik.[9]

Frederik Christensen recorded evidence of both the KKK and the CIC in his 1923 diary. First he noted his attendance at a meeting of the Interracial Relations Committee, a local branch of the CIC led by Clare Macdonald. The sixteen black and white members gave "general talks" at this early stage of the committee's work. Fred's description of the KKK contrasts the bland conversation of the CIC with the pageantry and pressure tactics of the Klan:

Wednesday evening the Ku Klux Klan had a meeting at the Community Club to which all the white protestant men of Beaufort and vicinity were invited with the only exceptions of the Christensens. I learn they had a good speaker who gave the principals of the Klan and asked all who could endorse those principals to stand. One man who did not was invited to leave the hall. Then all who would like to join were asked to stand and those who did not were shown the door. R. V., Bert Kinghorn, Hal Pollitzer, Rev. Burns, McGee and a few more left. It is reported they netted 75 new members at $10.00 per.

R. V. told me last night that he learns that the Klan now proposes a boycott against Kinghorn and ourselves.[10]

Community opinion did not turn against the Christensen business, but the KKK became more and more important in local politics, while the CIC remained a friendly but largely ineffective organization.

Woman Citizen

In 1920 Abbie Christensen joined her sister suffragists and became a "woman citizen." Christensen immediately registered to vote in 1920, but at age sixty-eight she stood behind the scenes as younger white women made their political debut. These women's political activities coalesced around the Community Club, a mixed-gender organization open to the white public and run by a board of six women and six men. Their primary purpose was the operation of a community club building for recreational and political activities. In 1921 a group of twenty-five white women "invaded" the hall during a citizen's meeting on a road improvement bond and stated that they "wanted to understand these matters and . . . help with them." The persistent women helped push through the bond, which probably never would have passed without their support. On 4 July 1922 Abbie lent her large American flag for a meeting "to welcome *new voters*—men and women." Her action was symbolic, and she stayed away from local politics, perhaps because her son Niels was still a state senator in 1922. Christensen was more comfortable putting her energies into supporting women's groups, especially the new incarnation of the NAWSA, the League of Women Voters.[11]

The NAWSA had hoped that suffrage would create a unified progressive voting bloc of "woman citizens." This dream, however, soon dissolved in the atmosphere of apathy and conservatism that dominated politics in the 1920s. The LWV was much smaller than the NAWSA. Its members were primarily "social feminists," such as Jane Addams, who promoted social welfare legislation and international peacemaking. A smaller band of younger, "hard-core feminists" campaigned for the Equal Rights Amendment, while the great majority of women dropped out of political organizations. For the rest of her life Christensen remained a social feminist who channeled much of her political energy into the LWV and other women's interest groups.[12]

The League of Women Voters

In 1921 Christensen wrote to her daughter-in-law Nancy Stratton Christensen: "I was so interested to read of . . . the L. of W.V. I'll enclose my $1 for my membership fee. I can't wait to get home. I wish so much to join an organization to *end wars*. Please get my name on the list as soon as you can." Christensen also subscribed to the LWV's magazine, *Woman Citizen,* and sent it to Helen Burr, who put it in the library of the Boston home for working women where she served as a matron.[13]

After the horrors of World War I, peacemaking became a major theme for women activists in the 1920s. Christensen's impetus for peacemaking may have come from her growing international awareness, as well as her "religious ardor" for Wilson's League of Nations. In 1919, a year after the war, Christensen's daughter Winnie began YMCA work with American soldiers still stationed in France. The youngest Christensen wrote positively of the French people and their culture. About a year later mother and daughter traveled to Europe together, visiting Norway and England. Christensen's international peacemaking, however, never went further than supporting the LWV.[14]

In Beaufort, Christensen served on the LWV's Nominating Committee and developed a friendship with Helen Kinney, an LWV officer. In 1922 Kinney was one of the first women to attend a Democratic campaign meeting. She asked each of the candidates to tell whether or not they would enforce jail sentences for violators of Prohibition. The LWV made its wishes known by sending a position paper to the city council urging Sunday observance, liquor-selling suppression, and a garbage ordinance. Several of the members were women of Abbie's age, and the older women's issue of Prohibition was combined with the social housekeeping of garbage collection. Younger women such as Winnie Christensen were not as serious about Prohibition, but they went along with their elders. In her diary Abbie noted that Winnie was "much amused" when one of the ladies "discourzed on the Band of Hope work I did here in the 1880s." Though her leadership role had diminished, Abbie's earlier work served as an inspiration for the younger generation. Through the LWV and her other volunteer work, Abbie supported the issues she had promoted years earlier in the WCTU, the Female Benevolent Society, and the Civic League, including temperance, tree preservation, clean politics, and social welfare legislation. Through her friend Clare

MacDonald, she also supported the beginnings of white interracial work in the 1920s and 1930s.[15]

Clare MacDonald

In the 1910s Christensen befriended a younger woman, the wife of one of the owners of the Macdonald-Wilkins cotton firm on Saint Helena Island and the mother of a son and two daughters. After Macdonald's husband died in 1917, Christensen's and Macdonald's common interests and shared experiences drew them closer together. The two women were northern outsiders who fit into southern society well enough to work with white southerners, but not so well as to refrain from being its occasional critics. Macdonald often stayed with Christensen when she traveled to Beaufort on the ferry because the journey took up to six hours. Abbie, in turn, usually spent the night when she visited the Macdonalds on Saint Helena. As she did with other friends, Abbie sent positive thoughts to Clare in her times of need. Clare responded in kind, writing in 1925, "I've been carrying you in my heart" and "I am needing your thoughts right now. My youngest brother . . . is critically ill. . . . God Grant Our Hopes may work into this Plan for us."[16]

Like Abbie, Clare cultivated a keen interest in Sea Island African Americans. Macdonald was one of only a few whites living on Saint Helena Island. She often ventured over to the Penn School as well as the Saint Helena Island public schools, serving as trustee and financial benefactor to both. The two women attended Penn School functions and black Memorial Day services together. Like Christensen, Macdonald was intrigued by the Sea Island dialect and employed it in a small book she wrote about "Juliana," her cook. MacDonald did not use this African American woman's last name in the title, but she acknowledged the complexities of Juliana's personality, her own occasional lack of understanding, and Juliana's tragic accidental death by fire. In another parallel to Abbie, Clare used the proceeds of this book to aid African American schools on Saint Helena Island.[17]

In 1924, when the KKK seemed to be taking over the town, Macdonald and Christensen joined forces to fight this racist organization through their women's weapons of social ostracism and community organizing. As Niels Christensen III recalled, "When the Episcopal Minister down here announced he was Secretary of the Ku Klux Klan, she and Mrs. MacDonald had a real stiff talk with him about it and they quit the church." In addition, Macdonald formed a countergroup, the "Interracial Relations Committee" of black and white residents, including Fred Christensen, to discuss and improve the race relations of Beaufort County.[18]

Clare Macdonald organized the Interracial Relations Committee, a local branch of the CIC, in Beaufort County in 1923 as an effort to bring blacks and whites together to talk about the needs and concerns of African Americans in the community. Macdonald had attended a conference on the issue in Columbia and brought Will Alexander's CIC ideas back to Beaufort. Four representatives of each race and gender formed the local organization of sixteen members. Abbie, however, remained outside this local CIC, perhaps because her son Frederik was already a member and because the committee wished to reach out to other representatives of the white community.[19]

MacDonald was one of the group of southern white women who were working more closely with black women in educational work, settlement houses, the YWCA, and the Methodist Church. Urban African American women had organized settlement houses and called for more equitable distribution of city services since the 1900s. Progressive white southern Methodist women began to do home mission work in African American communities around the same time. When these white and black women activists obtained the vote in 1920, they also joined the South's new interracial movement.[20]

In 1920 a group of African American women invited white Methodist women to a meeting of the National Association of Colored Women. One white attender spoke for others when she wrote that she was struck by the recognition that African American women had "all the aspirations for their homes and their children that I have for mine." At subsequent meetings African American leaders stressed the injustice of segregation and the need for respect, including courtesy titles such as "Mrs." for black women, protection from rape by white men, and fair working conditions for African American servants. A shared religion bound the women together, although respect from white women was never total. Nevertheless, the women's CIC organized throughout the South.[21]

Despite MacDonald's good intentions, Beaufort's CIC was not particularly successful. Not only was the group ignored by the Beaufort press, but, as member Fred Christensen explained in his dry way, two of the white men in the group were members of the KKK and "out of tune with the key note." Moreover, no one had "a clear idea of what is to be done." Fred concluded,

"So far the colored women are the only ones to bring forward any constructive suggestions. The women of that race ask for cooperation in getting a Community House." The African American women could see that the Community Club had aided white women in politics. They were excluded and wanted such an institution for themselves. Overall, such efforts moved the South slightly closer to the era of the civil rights movement, but the efforts of the CIC were timid when compared to the more radical efforts at integration in the 1950s.[22]

In the 1920s, through Clare Macdonald, Christensen became friends with another important woman member of the CIC, Clelia P. McGowan, who resided in nearby Charleston. An impeccably dressed "aristocrat" and a former head of the United Daughters of the Confederacy, McGowan was an unlikely radical. Like Christensen, she exhibited evidence of paternalism in her attitude toward African Americans, calling them a "race still in its childhood." Nevertheless, McGowan *was* considered a radical in the racial climate of South Carolina in the 1920s because she regularly met with black women's clubs and spoke out against ill-treatment of African Americans in the educational and judicial systems. McGowan faced almost total opposition from former friends and family because of her interracial work, so friendships with white women such as Macdonald, Bragg, and Christensen were important to her. McGowan headed the Charleston CIC in the 1920s and the South Carolina branch of the Association of Southern Women for the Prevention of Lynching (ASWPL), a movement that grew out of the CIC in the 1930s.[23]

Christensen's name is on the 1931 list of members of this organization next to Clare Macdonald's. The ASWPL mobilized white women in small town church groups to pressure men not to engage in lynchings. When lynchings did occur, the group tried to prosecute those responsible. Most important, the white women stated publicly that they did not want black men to be lynched for their "protection." It is difficult to gauge the group's effectiveness, but the number of lynchings declined during the ASWPL's period of activity from 1930 to 1940.[24]

Christensen and her northern and southern-born friends confronted racism in a number of other ways. When the KKK mounted a takeover of the Community Club in 1923, Abbie urged her friends Mary Waterhouse and Mary Stuart Fuller Hull to take a stand along with Fred Christensen. Waterhouse delivered "a severe arraignment of the Klan" at a meeting of the club's board of directors. She and four others voted against the KKK, but they were in the minority. Christensen corresponded with other young white and black women outside of Beaufort who were involved in activities bene-fitting African Americans. Their causes included a utopian community of African Americans in Arkansas and Young Women's Christian Association (YWCA) work for African American women. After living through the nadir of American race relations, Abbie had reason to be encouraged. By support-ing antiracist white friends in her region and throughout the nation, Chris-tensen indirectly furthered the ideals her abolitionist forebears had championed. Her most effective younger friends in this work, however, were black women—India Shanklin and a new friend, Catherine DeVeaux.[25]

Catherine DeVeaux

A native of Beaufort and a graduate of Hampton Institute's School of Nurs-ing, Catherine DeVeaux was a brown-skinned African American woman with great physical and spiritual presence. When her duties took her on walks through Beaufort's sleepy streets, she wore an immaculate white nurse's uniform, a cap, and a billowing pale blue cape. This mode of dress high-lighted her professional status so that whites would not confuse her with a domestic servant and so that her education and credentials were readily apparent. DeVeaux was a large woman, but her cap and cape made her an even more imposing figure. The crisp whiteness of the uniform also showed her neatness and certified her adherence to the medical standards of cleanliness.[26]

In 1910 DeVeaux financed what ultimately became a "Colored Hospital" out of her income from black and white patients and private nursing serv-ices she provided to wealthy tourists. DeVeaux's niece Katherine Doctor recalled her aunt's enterprising spirit: "When she finished Hampton School of Nursing, she came here to Beaufort and bought a little piece of property. I have the deed. That was the beginning of the hospital." DeVeaux's entre-preneurial parents were former slaves who could not read or write. Benjamin and Flora DeVeaux had moved to Beaufort from Hilton Head Island and operated a horse-and-buggy taxi service and an "eat shop," or restaurant. The DeVeaux parents saved and sacrificed in order to give their daughters a higher education. Catherine DeVeaux and her sisters were the first generation of teachers and nurses in their family. While her sisters married, Catherine remained single and lived with her parents in an antebellum home next to the house that served as her hospital.[27]

Black professional women such as DeVeaux were important leaders in African American communities during the Jim Crow era. Because black men were the targets of so much hostility and fear among whites, black women were sometimes better able to serve as ambassadors when negotiating with whites for needed community services. While this was less true in Beaufort, where a black men's Citizen's Committee of Colored People negotiated with the white town council, African American women still had a leadership role there. Black professional women such as DeVeaux were the products of families and schools, such as Hampton Institute, that instilled in them a confident sense of their possibilities and their duty to serve their race. This was a slightly different calling than the "Woman's Mission" Abbie had learned at Mount Holyoke, but it invoked similar strains of self-discipline and Christian service.[28]

The exclusion and segregation of the Jim Crow era created a need for professional medical care and facilities specifically for African Americans. When health services were established for African Americans in southern towns and cities, black nurses and laywomen frequently took the lead. While some white doctors treated black patients, Beaufort had no hospital for blacks or whites.[29]

DeVeaux's "Colored Sanitorium" provided such services as an adenoid and tonsil clinic, treatment for broken bones, and maternity care. Patients paid what they could, and sometimes the town paid for indigent patients. DeVeaux treated white and black, rich and poor. She also ventured out into the wider community, visiting isolated islands and preaching preventive health care and the value of greens and turnips for better nutrition. Once a week she put on her cape and walked to the Gold Eagle Inn to give massages to tourists. A wealthy patron gave her one thousand dollars to add a men's wing to her sanitorium, which had previously only boarded women. In the 1930s DeVeaux was joined by an African American physician, Dr. M. P. Kennedy, who set up an office, making the sanitorium an official hospital.[30]

An intangible element of DeVeaux's path to leadership and entrepreneurial success was her persona as a clairvoyant. "[DeVeaux] wasn't only a masseur and a nurse, but she was clairvoyant, like a fortune teller. She was always reading the tea leaves for somebody. They were really crazy about her," recalled her niece. DeVeaux's clairvoyant charisma cemented her friendship with Abbie Christensen, who believed that the spirits were also at work in her own life. These shared beliefs gave the two women a greater sense of mission and "chosenness" within the community.[31]

Abbie Christensen's ties with Catherine DeVeaux were both professional and personal. Abbie was a regular financial contributor to the clinic, which also received funding from the town. According to Abbie's grandson, Abbie "created [the hospital for blacks] and she had an R.N. down there and finally got a black doctor, Dr. Kennedy." While DeVeaux deserves the main credit for starting and expanding her practice, Christensen may have used her ties to local politicians such as her sons as well as links to Mabel Runette, her suffragist friend and now a Red Cross worker, to assist DeVeaux's work.[32]

Christensen also hired DeVeaux to give her massage treatments in her home. For Abbie, an elderly Victorian woman, DeVeaux's massages were probably the closest physical contact she had with any of her friends. During her 1923 stay at the Lindlahr "Nature Cure" resort, which encouraged nude sunbathing, her roommate had jokingly called her "the lady of the petticoat" because of her modesty. In Abbie's home, the two women had plenty of time to talk while DeVeaux was assuaging Christensen's aches and pains, and sometimes DeVeaux stayed overnight. A degree of mutuality in their relationship is evidenced by the fact that Christensen worried about DeVeaux's pain as much as she did her own. In her diary she wrote that Catherine was "broken down with long strain," and for weeks thereafter she closely monitored DeVeaux's progress in getting better. When Abbie was away, she asked her daughter-in-law Helen Burr Christensen to check on Catherine and report on her well-being.[33]

Christensen and DeVeaux shared an interest in improving community life for Beaufort African Americans. DeVeaux was part of a network of women leaders that included India Shanklin and Della Harvey. Abbie enjoyed looking in on the clinic and seeing Catherine work with her patients. In addition, DeVeaux may have been one of the black women whom Fred referred to as most constructive members of the 1924 Interracial Relations Committee. In an effort to secure a public playground for black children, DeVeaux used the methods pioneered by the progressive women reformers at Hull House, researching social conditions and bringing them before the public and those in power. She wrote, "I made myself busy and made all of the investigations and took them before the men's committee (colored). . . . But they refuse to co-orporate with our plans." Christensen had sent a contribution for the playground, and DeVeaux returned her check. Despite this setback, both women continued their efforts at reform.[34]

During the 1920s, when the KKK gained in strength in Beaufort, DeVeaux praised Christensen and her children for their stand against the organization. In 1923 Abbie wrote in her diary that Catherine had told her "how blacks and whites esteem the Christensens." Nearly seventy years later another African American community leader, Wilhelmina Blanding Barnwell, agreed with that assessment. After Wilhelmina Blanding had served as a teacher at the Shanklin School and the Penn School on Saint Helena Island, she married Benjamin Barnwell, the first black county extension agent in South Carolina. Wilhelmina Barnwell went on to start the county's first bookmobile, the first step toward integrating the Beaufort County Library. When her daughter-in-law asked her how blacks and whites got along in Beaufort in the 1920s, Abbie Christensen was the first person she thought of as an example of the "finer white people" who were "alright."[35]

By the 1930s, when both Christensen and DeVeaux were older, they wrote often of their health, DeVeaux's work, the passing of loved ones, and the life of the spirit. DeVeaux "was a very open, compassionate person, with listening," DeVeaux's niece recalled. Jesus' words and "New Thought" phrases such as "Divine love and peace" are woven throughout DeVeaux's everyday correspondence with Christensen. These shared ideas were part of Abbie's bond with Catherine. They were also part of Christensen's lifelong quest for spiritual knowledge and growth.[36]

In her 1929 notebook of Rosicrucian meditations Abbie wrote, "We are all one, each dependent on another, bound together like Brothers and Sisters." Though she never totally escaped the prejudices of her time, such thinking was a part of her racial politics and her espousal of socialism. Abbie's nontraditional, mystical beliefs led her to see women, including herself, as spiritual leaders. Inside and outside of churches her beliefs united her with others, white and black, with whom she shared a spiritual connection.[37]

Rosicrucianism

In the late 1920s, when her family and community were in financial crisis, Abbie turned to various harmonial sects to help her influence the events around her. After a brief investigation of the Self-Improvement League and the Order of Christian Mystics, Christensen moved on to Rosicrucianism.[38]

Because Rosicrucians went further than, for example, mind curists or New Thought leaders in incorporating the magic and mystery of the occult, it is interesting to speculate whether Christensen's knowledge of African American occult religious practices may have made her more receptive to this group. With her early interest in African American folklore, Abbie must have been aware of Sea Island voodoo practices in addition to Catherine DeVeaux's fortune-telling. Christensen was probably aware that Beaufort's sheriff J. E. McTeer, the son of one of her white friends, practiced voodoo as a means of psychological help and social control in the black community. The magic in the African American folk community, which surrounded the dull, middle-class world of the Christensens, may have made Abbie curious about how she too could have some of this power. On a subconscious level, perhaps, knowing the magical beliefs of African Americans on the Sea Islands prepared her to explore these mysteries on her own.[39]

In 1929 Abbie chose to enlist in the program of the Ancient and Mystical Order of Rosae Crucis, an American manifestation of the Rosicrucians that originated in Europe in the seventeenth century. This group reinforced her earlier transcendentalist beliefs and led Christensen to more radical conclusions about the sisterhood and brotherhood of humankind.[40]

The word *Rosicrucian* is derived from the name Christian Rosencreutz, or Rose Cross. The Rosicrucian Manifestos were written under this pseudonym in Kassel (in what is now Germany) in 1614 and 1615. Their author was probably Johann Andreae, a Lutheran pastor. In 1616 he published *The Chemical Wedding of Christian Rosencreutz* under his own name. Together these works tell the story of a philosopher and alchemist born in 1378, Christian Rosencreutz, who started the Fraternity of the Rosy Cross. The purpose of this fraternity was the "Universal and General Reformation of the whole wide world" through a Protestant organization meant to rival the Jesuits. Its brothers sought to bring science, religion, and social ethics together.[41]

The story of Christian Rosencreutz was probably meant to be allegorical, but Andreae's writings inspired the founding of actual Rosicrucian societies in the 1600s. Rosicrucianism became a religious movement that engaged in a program of research and reform in the sciences. Historian Frances Yates sees the Rosicrucians and their interest in science and morality, free from the organized church, as a transitional link between the Renaissance and the Enlightenment. The parts of this ancient secret society that probably appealed to Christensen were their aims to reform the world, learn the secrets of the universe, and heal the sick gratis. She had always offered free healing to those friends and family who accepted it.[42]

Rosicrucians in America were a heterogeneous group. The first American Rosicrucians were German colonists. The next and larger wave in the nineteenth century was headed by Paschal Beverly Randolph, an African American, whose mother was from Madagascar. Randolph studied the occult in Europe and the Middle East, returned to the United States, and recruited for the Union army during the Civil War. He founded several lodges and wrote many books, teaching sexual magic to married couples. European, African, and Eastern spirituality were all combined in Rosicrucianism.[43]

Abbie's group, the Ancient and Mystical Order of Rosae Crucis (AMORC), was a mostly American group held together by pamphlets and mail-order lectures. The AMORC was begun in 1915 by H. Spencer Lewis, an occultist who had been associated with various British orders before arriving in America. Lewis emphasized the Egyptian origins of the Rosicrucian philosophy and set up a museum of Egyptian artifacts at his headquarters in San Jose, California. The order grew rapidly in the 1920s through the use of "Public Inquiry Leaflets." Christensen possessed such a pamphlet with the leading title "Why Are We Here? and Why Are Our Lives Unequal?" The booklet explained the group's belief in reincarnation as an explanation for inequality.[44]

Although the Rosicrucians called themselves a fraternity, the AMORC shared many traits with the woman-led Theosophists and praised their founder, Helena Blavatsky. Like the Theosophists, the Rosicrucians believed in a genderless God, the "Cosmic Soul." Both masculine and feminine qualities, respectively represented in meditative chants by the r and m sounds, were essential to a Rosicrucian's balance and well-being. In fact, the first incantatory sound a neophyte learned was "OOM," which called upon the "infinite and maternal," the "timeless and protective," to guide the seeker in her sanctum.[45]

Beginning in March 1929 Christensen received a series of lectures and instructions from AMORC headquarters in San Jose, California. Abbie kept a notebook in which she recorded her understanding of the "neophyte lectures" she was sent. She set aside one evening a week to study and meditate in a room that was designated her "sanctum." The weakness of her eyes eventually led Abbie to abandon her efforts to learn the Rosicrucian mysteries, but not before she had completed several months of intensive study.[46]

Like earlier forms of harmonial spirituality Abbie had encountered, Rosicrucianism centered much of its thinking on the idea that the soul had to direct the brain. This teaching echoed Emerson's "Oversoul." In her 1929 notes she quoted Emerson: "What we commonly call man, the eating, drinking counting man does not represent, but misrepresents himself. Him we do not respect, but the soul, whose organ he is, would he let it appear tho' his action would make our knees bend. . . . All reform aims, in some one particular, to let the soul have its way thro' us; in other words, to engage us to obey."[47]

Abbie's Rosicrucian notes on conscience and intuition recalled her 1895 address to other Unitarian women, "The Importance of Being Well," wherein she had argued that women's intuition was trying to tell them to raise their servants' wages. Like other Unitarians and social gospel followers in her day, Abbie focused on the life of Christ and the brotherhood of humanity. In her Rosicrucian notes she wrote: "The great trouble for centuries has been that man in his egotism does not listen to his conscience and finds no time for silent concentration and attunement. The duty of the church should be to give all its members an opportunity to come together and sit in silence attuning themselves to the Divine Mind and Conscience." Rosicrucian meditation offered Abbie the time and space she needed to be in tune with the "Divine Mind."[48]

Rosicrucian teaching emphasized unselfishness and the value of losing one's individuality for the common good. In her notes Abbie underlined the notion that "the *soul* is *always* a part of the Great Soul of God, never Individualized. It belongs not to us but to God; it is not separated but united." Abbie was instructed to avoid using the pronoun "I" and to stop thinking that she "owned" anything in her everyday life. This last concept was readily translatable into socialism.[49]

In her studies Abbie traced the history of her gold watch. Though she legally "owned" it, she wrote that it was made by men who had "seized" the land and the gold that was its material. Christensen concluded that the only man who had been rightfully paid was the man who gave his labor to make the watch. Renouncing ownership, Abbie wrote, "All that's good & useful was put in our hands by God. . . . we are all one, each dependent on another, bound together like Brothers and Sisters." Such thinking reinforced her socialist beliefs and may have helped reignite ideas of racial equality.[50]

Because of her earlier interest in mind cure, Christensen must have been especially intrigued by the later lessons that showed her how to use her mental powers and spiritual energy to heal others. Although Abbie eventually abandoned systematic study of Rosicrucianism, she added its insights to her eclectic mixture of beliefs in the healing of body and spirit through homeopathy, mind cure, and nature cure and the healing of society through socialism.[51]

Abbie's leap from Rosicrucianism to radical politics was one that had been made before by inquisitive and reform-minded men and women in the centuries preceding the twentieth. The original Rosicrucians in seventeenth-century Palatine were considered too radical in their anticlerical, universalist views and were nearly destroyed in the German Thirty Years War. Their ideas, however, were carried on to the early Masons in Scotland, who incorporated Rosicrucian symbols and ideas into their rituals. Holding on to that link, historian Margaret Jacob argues that Masonic lodges (which incorporated Rosicrucianism) were important agencies for spreading the ideas of the Enlightenment and democracy in eighteenth-century Europe.[52]

Twentieth-century American Rosicrucians were universalists. They rejected exclusive Christianity and sought instead the elements that united all world religions. Music, love, and goodness were the best concepts of a true universal language that the Rosicrucians offered. "No matter what country we're in nor how ignorant we are of the language, if we see a person happy, living a life of Goodness & love we understand," Abbie noted. They also held out the promise that through learning how to "vibrate in unison" with other Rosicrucians around the world, a greater harmony and worldwide sense of understanding could be developed. Taking these teachings to heart, Abbie committed herself of socialism.[53]

Socialism

Abbie Christensen's Christian and Rosicrucian beliefs in the kinship of all humanity and the injustice of private property were part of the influences that led her to espouse socialism in the 1930s. As she had done in so many other aspects of her life, Christensen stepped into socialism in the company of one of her children. Abbie looked more and more to her last unmarried child, Winnie, as her companion in advanced old age. Winnie Christensen was influenced by the radical politics she found at the Pine Mountain School in Harlan, Kentucky, where she taught during spring seasons from 1924 to 1938. Like many other educated elites who were fascinated by the folk tradition, Winnie was drawn to socialism. Mother and daughter joined the Socialist Party in 1932, with Abbie taking her beliefs one step further to become a presidential elector for Socialist candidate Norman Thomas in the same year.[54]

Abbie was a latecomer to American socialism, which had experienced its heyday in the 1910s. Though Christensen expressed interest in socialist ideas as early as 1911 and rubbed elbows with Socialist Party presidential candidate Eugene Debs at a sanitorium in 1922, she was a loyal supporter of Woodrow Wilson during the 1910s.[55]

Christensen saw herself as nonpartisan. She does not seem to have registered in time to vote in the presidential election of 1920, but in 1924 Christensen voted for Calvin Coolidge because she respected his New England heritage. In 1928 she chose Herbert Hoover because of his stands for Prohibition and peace. As she expressed it in a 1932 interview, "I have never belonged to any one political party . . . I vote for the man and not the party."[56]

Christensen's political values were built around the philosophy of women's voluntary associations such as the League of Women Voters. Most politically active women were not interested in the kind of friendship and steadfast club and party loyalty that were part of men's political culture in the nineteenth century. For example, Abbie's former schoolmate Anna Eddy was reading all the candidates' speeches in 1924 because, she said, "I'm no partisan, I like to see all sides." Intelligence and Christian values mattered most to these women. Without these principles, Abbie's friend Frances Willard had said, political parties were "of no more value than so many tin cans."[57]

As a consequence, Christensen expressed repugnance for the southern Democratic practice of pledging to support the whole party ticket no matter who won the primary. In 1930 she explained her position to Fred: "On the whole Winnie and I think we were wise not to register on the Beaufort Club roll. I object to the idea that I can not vote independently of the party nomination. If a ballot cannot represent free choice it seems to me it is a mere farce, and worse."[58]

In 1932 Christensen was searching for a promising candidate of character, but she was also concerned about the Great Depression. As she put it, the country was "seething with dissatisfaction," and Norman Thomas's "cooperative commonwealth" seemed to be the remedy.[59]

Even though her sons were businessmen and leaders of the board of trade and chamber of commerce, Christensen could easily have seen capitalism as failing both them and their community. Like most rural areas, Beaufort County had already begun to experience the Depression by the mid-1920s as crop prices fell and cotton farmers struggled to overcome the boll weevil. Although truck farming of vegetables diversified the region's crops, agricultural income kept dropping. The Christensens, who depended on Beaufort's farmers for their income, were also hard hit. Over the years Fred Christensen had tried various enterprises, including a corncob-pipe factory and a tenant farm, but the family's mainstays were N. Christensen and Sons Hardware and their vast real estate investments. In the 1920s Fred and Niels also experimented with a Ford dealership, a packing company, a petroleum business, and a real estate company, which built a whites-only subdivision called Beaufort Shores. All of these efforts were to no avail, however, and the Christensen business went into receivership in November 1925. It seemed that only a miracle could save the Christensens.[60]

A small miracle did occur. In a show of support much like that expressed in Frank Capra's 1946 film *It's a Wonderful Life,* the citizens of Beaufort came to the Christensens' rescue a few days before Christmas in 1925. They held a citizens' meeting and promised to pay fifty thousand dollars over the next two years to the firm's creditors, all without looking at the Christensens' books or asking them to repay the loan. "They kept on coming," Fred wrote in his diary; "Jew and gentile, merchant and farmer, Baptist minister, business competitors and political opponents along with the rest crowded the room." The state's largest newspapers all featured front-page stories of the event, and Abbie wept at this amazing act of faith. It was a sign of the Christensens' acceptance by white southerners and northerners in the town.[61]

Abbie and Georgie also gave some of their money to keep the business afloat, but even this huge cooperative effort was not enough. Along with the rest of the country, the Christensens experienced serious reverses when a local bank failure and the stock market crash of 1929 worsened a bad situation. Many of those who had promised aid simply could not pay. The Christensens, who had been among the town's largest landowners, barely hung onto their hardware store after a complex reorganization backed by Abbie's money. In the end it was the investments of Abbie and Nancy Stratton Christensen that kept the family solvent.[62]

From 1926 to 1932 the town's and the Christensens' financial situations only worsened. The family saved money by eating homegrown food as much as possible and reducing the distances they traveled. Their lifestyle began to bear some resemblance to the subsistence agriculture practiced by many African American and poor white farmers in the area. At the same time, those farmers were even worse off. Abbie's daughter-in-law Nancy reported anemia and hunger among her children's white classmates, and black patients died of malnutrition at Catherine DeVeaux's hospital. Cotton factors closed their doors, and the military laid off civilians on the nearby Parris Island marine base. In this crisis atmosphere Abbie resolved to give 10 percent of her reduced income to charity. She saw, however, that charity was not enough.[63]

Even hard times and a longtime sympathy with socialism would not have been enough to push Christensen to support Norman Thomas in 1932 if he had not also embodied the Christian values, intelligence, and cooperative ethic that Christensen respected. Biographers have described Thomas as a "respectable rebel," "selfless," and "an idealist." Abbie simply said that he was "the only man capable of bringing . . . much needed change about."[64]

Thomas was a Presbyterian minister and a graduate of Princeton who conducted a ministry to the urban poor before taking the message of the social gospel to its logical conclusion in embracing socialism. He joined the American Socialist Party around 1920 and stuck with it through the lean times of the 1920s. Norman emerged as a promising candidate for president in 1932 when capitalism was laid low by the Great Depression.[65]

Thomas excelled as an orator, debater, and writer. Christensen may have come across his ideas for the first time through his articles in liberal publications that she often read. Abbie also might have read Thomas's 1931 book, *America's Way Out: A Program for Democracy.* This accessible volume exploded myths about the universal benefits and opportunities of American capitalism and argued that socialism would create a truer democracy by removing excesses of wealth and power.[66]

As socialist historian Irving Howe describes it, a "radiant and selfless" Norman Thomas "brought a new luster to the movement." His character and skillful oratory combined with the timeliness of his message to draw twenty-five thousand members into the Socialist Party. Forty full-time unpaid organizers worked for the party in the field, and twenty-two thousand people came to hear him speak at Madison Square Garden in New York City.[67]

For all these reasons, in August 1932 Christensen wrote to leaders of the Socialist Party, stating that she and her daughter wanted to become members. She and Winnie also signed up to receive the party publication, the *New Leader,* and purchased a Socialist plate for their automobile. When party officials asked if she could do more, Christensen stated that at the age of eighty she was no longer able to take an active part in campaigning. This answer, however, was not her final word. Soon Mrs. Niels Christensen Sr. was heading the list of South Carolina electors for Norman Thomas.[68]

The key person who moved Christensen from private to public socialist was a young woman Abbie hardly knew. In one brief visit to Abbie's home, volunteer socialist organizer Nelle Gentry of Charleston was able to convince Christensen to serve as elector. Christensen was receptive to the ideas of younger women such as Gentry, counting Clare MacDonald, Helen Burr, and even Alice Stone Blackwell among her friends in the 1920s and 1930s.[69]

In the 1920s and 1930s Abbie Christensen watched her family's political influence and fortunes wane, but this decline brought greater freedom as well as hardship. The KKK's entry into politics in 1924 marked the end of Niels Christensen Jr.'s career as a state senator. This change made it easier for Abbie to become a public socialist. With Niels no longer campaigning for elected office, no one seems to have opposed Abbie's action. When Niels mentioned Abbie's affiliation, he expressed only pride. Because of her age, her gender, her race, and the large store of goodwill the Christensen family had built up, Abbie Christensen's socialism seems to have been more of a curiosity than a threat to Beaufort whites. A few years later, for example, her son Fred noted that Christensen received the "heartiest applause" of any woman honored at the Beaufort Rotary Club's "Lady's Night."[70]

At her age and in the place she lived, Abbie was not able to accomplish much for the Socialist Party. She could take pride in the seven Beaufort County votes for Thomas in 1932, for she was able to sway a few friends. As her grandson recalled, "My grandmother offered to take Mrs. Bristol to the polls. Well it takes a few minutes to get to the polls in a horse and buggy. When they counted the votes that year there were two socialist votes." It was a good example of Christensen's power of persuasion at work.[71]

Third parties have always had a difficult time in the United States, and 1932 proved no exception. Thomas polled only 903,286 votes in the presidential election, fewer than Debs at his height. Part of the reason was the charisma and popularity of Democrat Franklin Roosevelt, but an even bigger cause was the enormous public dislike of Hoover. Even those who agreed with Thomas at his rallies told him that they were voting for Roosevelt because they wanted to make sure Hoover was thrown out of office. After taking office Roosevelt implemented many planks of the socialist platform, such as a shorter work week, public relief, and the abolition of child labor. In this way he lured even more left-leaning voters to his side in the presidential election of 1936. Abbie continued to support Thomas, but she was not able to serve as an elector again because the party ran no South Carolina slate in the next national election.[72]

During those years Christensen must have noted Thomas's special interest in the South and the fate of tenant farmers, black and white. Thomas had been critical of discrimination and disfranchisement before 1934, but in that year his support for the biracial Southern Tenant Farmer's Union (STFU) challenged many of the South's most taboo subjects, including integration and labor organizing. Thomas criticized the New Deal for blatant abuses in the implementation of the Agricultural Adjustment Act. Large-scale white landowners were refusing to share government payments with their primarily black tenants and were conducting widespread evictions. Although Beaufort County was mostly free from the blight of sharecropping, Abbie would have been aware of its problems in the wider South through her connections with agricultural issues at the Shanklin School.[73]

Despite her socialist allegiance, Abbie seems to have approved of much in Franklin Roosevelt's New Deal, especially after Thomas and other leftists pushed Roosevelt to implement more sweeping social welfare legislation before the 1936 election. Christensen was proud when her son Niels was appointed as a state official in the New Deal's Social Security Administration. Niels Christensen's connections with Abbie's female friends turned out to be his best assets in that administration. Clare Macdonald and Penn School principal Rossa Cooley had the ear of southern liberals in the administration and helped Niels obtain a minor but respectable post. As he told his mother while he waited for his appointment in Washington, D.C., "I keep in touch with the leftists in the city." Abbie's influence was clear.[74]

Reality

Christensen kept up with politics and issues of race and gender after 1932, but she gradually grew less active. Abbie's last year was filled with concerns about her failing feet, eyes, and ears. Yet she still cultivated a healthy interest in the lives of others, writing letters to friends and family as regularly as she could with her shaky but clear schoolteacher's script.

As she neared the end of her life, Abbie did not fear death. She was more concerned about those still on earth. Christensen maintained her contributions to Catherine DeVeaux's hospital and the Shanklin School, despite the fact that her finances were low. Her friend Clare Macdonald expressed the women's shared vision in the last year of Christensen's life: "I am . . . feeling so strongly that we must strive to make Heaven on Earth," echoing the notions of Abbie's father. Upon the death of R. G. Holmes in 1906, a friend had written Abbie, "I never knew a man so willing to give himself to promote his ideals of the kingdom of heaven." The abolitionist legacies of their fathers lived on in these two women.[75]

Abbie had always considered her work as a mother and grandmother her most important mission. Part of her desires for her family were based on her feelings of the moral superiority of the North over the South, a legacy of abolition and the Civil War. She had worked hard to mold her Beaufort-born children into good New Englanders despite their residence in the South. With her grandchildren she was less successful, but she continued to try. Carroll Eve remembered her grandmother's elocution lessons, given in an effort to reduce the children's southern, Gullah-influenced dialect: "She would tell us girls. Say 'How now brown cow.'" In subversive defiance, the granddaughters would dutifully repeat the words, drawling them out in the most "southern-fried" voices they could affect. More important, however, was Christensen's desire to see her grandchildren develop social consciences and senses of civic responsibility. One of the last things she wrote to Niels Christensen III, her eldest grandson, was the reminder that she and her husband "helped prepare our children to be workers in the world which they are helping to make better." Niels III did feel that his grandmother had a tremendous influence on him, helping him to see the importance of social work, New Deal programs for the poor, and the justice of the civil rights movement. Abbie thought of her father as "One Who Tried to Make the World Better." It was a goal she had aspired to and one she wished to pass on.[76]

In 1933 Abbie wrote down her vision of heaven in fictional form. Underscoring her belief that spiritual existence outweighed the life of the body, she entitled her vision "Reality." Abbie wrote, "At early dawn the Grandmother awoke, hearing a clear voice that said 'Those were but dreams, here is a Reality.'" Christensen described this reality as "a far reaching plain covered with living green, bordered by lofty woods, where she recognized all her favorite trees, shrubs and vines." Such a natural/spiritual world was particularly congenial to the former botany student and Stroller.[77]

Christensen described the humans in her vision as "arrayed in festal robes." They beckoned to the Grandmother to join them, but she was stopped by "masses of blue pansies and violets" that fell before her like waves. Three times the scene was repeated. Abbie wrote that the Voice finally said, "'Louis is *there*.' So [the Grandmother] knew it was not true that he was *dead* for he had entered Eternal Life." Perhaps Abbie intended Louis to mean Jamie or some other loved one. Like her folklore character Alice, the Grandmother could easily have been herself, since by 1933 she was a grandmother many times over.[78]

For Abbie, death was not the end. Christensen believed that the afterlife was a "higher and more important place in the divine economy." When she remembered Niels Sr. and Jamie, she imagined them growing spiritually and helping others in this higher place. Her fondest hope was to be reunited with her husband and do the same. Christensen believed that after death her spirit would still be "adventuring." In her final hour Abbie was content knowing that she was leaving the confines of the material world—leaving region, race, class, and gender—and moving to the higher spiritual plane that she had sought for so long.[79]

On 21 September 1938 Abbie Christensen died and entered into the mystery she had long contemplated. Christensen had been staying at Andrea's home in Greenville, South Carolina, awaiting the return of Andrea and her husband from Europe. The cause of death listed on her death certificate was lobar pneumonia, a common ailment for a person of eighty-six years.[80]

In death as in life, Abbie put her resources and hopes into the generations that followed her. Her will, written in 1930, expressed the priorities of other nineteenth-century women by providing a livelihood for her unmarried daughter in an economic world dominated by men. Abbie left her most valuable property, her home, to Winnie and her beloved daughter-in-law

Helen Burr Christensen. Thus she kept power in the hands of the women of her family. Christensen gave her personal effects to Andrea and Winnie, to be divided equally. In addition, Abbie left over thirty thousand dollars in trust for all of her children and grandchildren, to be divided equally among them.[81]

Christensen's wishes were also evident in the final drama of her life, her funeral. Fred wrote that her closed casket was placed in the parlor and covered with flowers, the natural beauty she had always loved. "Colored friends" were the first to pay their respects, and they stayed for the simple service performed in her home. Psalms were read, and friends sang "Heaven Desired," the song Christensen had selected. As she was buried next to her husband in the old Baptist churchyard, a quartet from the Shanklin School sang one of her favorite spirituals, "Swing Low, Sweet Chariot," connecting her memory with the folk heritage she had so prized.[82]

Epilogue

When Abbie Christensen died in 1938, Margaret Mitchell's novel *Gone with the Wind* was sweeping the nation. In 1939 David Selznick's film version of the novel did even more to reinvigorate the plantation myth of the South, a myth that villainized women such as Abbie Holmes Christensen, an abolitionist and suffragist, as the antithesis of the southern belle. Wilbur Cash summarized this negative view when he wrote in 1941 that "[the Yankee schoolmarm] was no proper intellectual, but at best a comic character, at worst a dangerous fool." In 1939 novelist Francis Griswold misrepresented the schoolmarm in a different way. In *A Sea Island Lady* he made his white northern heroine a critic of black equality and married her to a white southerner, a participant in the Red Shirt rebellion of 1876, which he portrayed as a heroic action against dangerous and ignorant African Americans. This biography of Abbie Holmes Christensen, a real Sea Island woman and Yankee schoolmarm, is offered as a counter to Cash's caricature and the myth perpetuated in Griswold's novel. Christensen's nonfictional story of loyalty to the abolitionist cause on the Sea Islands is no less a southern story than *Gone with the Wind* or *A Sea Island Lady*. Christensen and other northern and southern women played their part in shaping the New South that developed after the Civil War.[1]

Although she never articulated it formally, Christensen's actions as an educator, a suffragist, and a socialist indicate her vision for a New South where equal opportunities were accorded to women and men, blacks and whites, privileged and poor. Christensen was limited by the restrictions of segregation in her time and place, the New South. Yet she saw this place as open to change through her influence. At times she was unable to remove the paternalistic blinders of her times when it came to portraying and treating African Americans as equals. In this way she was similar to the northern and southern white women reformers of the South Carolina coast with whom she worked in cooperation: Clare Macdonald and Rossa Cooley of Saint Helena Island, Laura Bragg and Clelia McGowan of Charleston. Nevertheless, these women, along with India Shanklin, Catherine DeVeaux, and others, worked for better opportunities for African Americans in an extremely racist time. Through her writing, her family, her women's organizations, and her own political action, Christensen cultivated a New South that held more educational opportunities, a greater number of social services, and closer contact between the races than it might have had without her. What she could not achieve Christensen left to future generations, especially those she had raised as a mother and grandmother.

Christensen's main contribution to African American history, *Afro-American Folk Lore*, bore results in unforeseen ways. Her collected stories form a part of the store of black history and culture to which scholars have access today. In addition, publishing her book led her to the Shanklin School. Christensen's collection of African American folklore and the Shanklin School were her greatest legacies—taking from and giving back to the black community, always trying to influence it, but at the same time preserving and cultivating its creative energy.

After her death Christensen still inspired fund-raising efforts for the Shanklin School. In a printed announcement in 1938 her friends requested that mourners make donations to the school "to perpetuate the memory of her life and spirit." The donations were pooled into an Abbie Christensen Memorial Fund, which helped Joseph and India Shanklin continue to lead the school into the 1940s, when it was replaced by Robert Smalls High School. A Beaufort middle school now bears the name of Joseph S. Shanklin, in tribute to his memory.[2]

Yet Abbie had wanted more for the black community around the school. "I'm just sorry her dream didn't come true," Joseph Shanklin Jr. said of Christensen. "She wanted [the eight hundred acres of school land] to be parceled out into acreages for the people to own and farm." He recalled that after Christensen died, the Christensen children shared membership on the board of trustees of the Abbie Christensen Memorial Fund with Joseph Shanklin. The family had control, however, and the Christensens sold the land and used the money for a purpose they thought was more advantageous to local African Americans—scholarships that enabled black students to obtain higher education, in areas such as medicine and law, outside the segregated South.[3]

And then history repeated itself. In 1973 Abbie Christensen's great-grand-daughter Anne Christensen Pollitzer returned from the Peace Corps and decided to start a Montessori school in Beaufort. To her surprise, her father, Niels Christensen III, knew all about the Montessori method because he had been one of his grandmother's first pupils. The Christensen family decided to use the memorial fund to start an integrated Montessori school in Beaufort. Scholarships were provided to needy children. The Eleanor Christensen Montessori School, named for Anne's mother, continued under Anne Pollitzer's leadership until the 1990s.[4]

Anne Christensen Pollitzer was not the only family member who took a stand against racism and for positive change. Abbie's daughter-in-law Helen Burr Christensen wrote a courageous article in support of integration in the book *South Carolinians Speak: A Moderate Approach to Race Relations*, published in 1957 after the *Brown v. Board of Education* decision. After *South Carolinians Speak* became public, Christensen received threatening phone calls, while the home of another contributor was bombed by the Ku Klux Klan. Christensen's ideas, rather than the KKK's, however, endure to point the way toward the future. Helen cited statistics on African American contributions to the nation and praised the integration of the armed forces. She criticized inferior educational opportunities for blacks and called on white Christians to "harmonize our actions with our beliefs . . . that all men are created in the image of God, and all races are equal in his sight."[5]

Like her daughter-in-law, Abbie Holmes Christensen lived her life as "an ardent supporter of causes" and "one who tried to make the world better." The best parts of Christensen's abolitionist vision and her sense of "woman's mission" survived to be revived in the era of the civil rights and women's movements of the 1950s, 1960s, and 1970s. Their fulfillment awaits the ardent women and men of our time.[6]

Notes

Notes to Introduction

1. Abbie Holmes Christensen, *Afro-American Folk Lore as Told 'Round Cabin Fires on the Sea Islands of South Carolina* (1892; repr., New York: Negro Universities Press, 1969). For references to Christensen, see Lawrence Levine, *Black Culture and Black Consciousness: Afro-American Folk Thought from Slavery to Freedom* (New York: Oxford University Press, 1977), 87–101; William Wiggins, "Afro-Americans as Folk: From Savage to Civilized," in *One Hundred Years of American Folklore Studies: A Conceptual History,* ed. William Clements (Washington, D.C.: American Folklore Society, 1988), 29; Florence Baer, *Sources and Analogues of the Uncle Remus Tales,* Folklore Fellows Communications no. 228 (Helsinki: Finnish Scientific Academy, 1981), 30; Monica Maria Tetzlaff, "Abigail Mandana Holmes Christensen," in *American Folklore: An Encyclopedia,* ed. Jan Brunvand (New York: Garland Publishing, 1996), 142.

2. *A Guide to Historic Beaufort* (Beaufort, S.C.: Historic Beaufort Foundation, 1970), 93; "Ledbetter Home on Beaufort Tour," *Beaufort Gazette,* 6 Mar. 1978, clipping, collection of Wyatt and Sally Pringle, Beaufort, S.C. (hereafter Pringle); Niels Christensen Sr. (hereafter NC) to Abbie Holmes Christensen (hereafter AHC), 28 Aug. 1893, repr. in *Boston Transcript,* 9 Sept. 1893. See John Simmons to AHC, 15 Sept. 1915; Frederik Holmes Christensen (hereafter FHC) to AHC, 8 Apr. 1916; AHC diaries, 1910–13 and 1915–18, all in Christensen Family Papers (hereafter CFP), South Caroliniana Library, University of South Carolina, Columbia (hereafter SCL). See also FHC diary, vol. 11, 12 May 1910, SCL.

3. AHC diary, 20, 28 Feb. 1910; Abby Winch Christensen (hereafter AWC) to AHC, 9 July 1913; John Simmons to AHC, 23 Aug. 1915; AHC diary, 7, 11, 13–15, 27 Jan., 4 Feb., 5 Mar., 7 Apr. 1917, all in CFP, SC; U.S. Census manuscript, Beaufort County, S.C. 1910 (T624), reel 1450, p. 54.

4. Wilbur J. Cash, *The Mind of the South* (1941; repr., New York: Random House, 1991), 29–58; Lawrence Powell, *New Masters: Northern Planters during the Civil War and Reconstruction* (New Haven, Conn.: Yale University Press, 1980); James McPherson, *Abolitionist Legacy: From Reconstruction to the NAACP* (Princeton, N.J.: Princeton University Press, 1975); Paul Escott, "Clinton A. Cilley, Yankee War Hero in the Postwar South: A Study in the Compatibility of Regional Values," *North Carolina Historical Review* 68, no. 4 (1991): 404–26; Jacqueline Jones, *Soldiers of Light and Love: Northern Teachers and Georgia Blacks, 1865–1873* (Chapel Hill:

University of North Carolina Press, 1980); Elizabeth Jacoway, *Yankee Missionaries in the South: The Penn School Experiment* (Baton Rouge: Louisiana State University Press, 1980); David Whisnant, *All That Is Native and Fine: The Politics of Culture in an American Region* (Chapel Hill: University of North Carolina Press, 1983).

5. C. Vann Woodward, *Origins of the New South, 1877–1913* (Baton Rouge: Louisiana State University Press, 1951); George B. Tindall, *The Emergence of the New South, 1913–1945* (Baton Rouge: Louisiana State University Press, 1967); Paul Gaston, *The New South Creed: A Study in Southern Mythmaking* (New York: Knopf, 1970); Edward Ayers, *The Promise of the New South: Life after Reconstruction* (New York: Oxford University Press, 1992); Abbie Holmes Christensen, *Afro-American Folk Lore,* xii.

6. On the need to put folklore or ethnological writing in its political context, see James Clifford, "Introduction," in *Writing Culture: The Poetics and Politics of Ethnography,* ed. James Clifford and George Marcus (Berkeley: University of California Press, 1986), 1–26. For the history of American folklorists, see Rosemary Zumwalt, *American Folklore Scholarship: A Dialogue of Dissent* (Bloomington: Indiana University Press, 1988), 13–21; William Clements, ed., *100 Years of American Folklore Studies: A Conceptual History* (Washington, D.C.: American Folklore Society, 1988), xi–63; and John Roberts, "African American Diversity and the Study of Folklore," *Western Folklore* 52 (Apr., July, Oct. 1993): 157–70. On Frances Ellen Watkins Harper and "Woman's Era," see Hazel Carby, *Reconstructing Womanhood: The Emergence of the Afro-American Woman Novelist* (New York: Oxford University Press, 1987), 69.

7. George Fredrickson, *The Black Image in the White Mind: The Debate on Afro-American Character and Destiny, 1817–1914* (New York: Harper & Row, 1972), 204–5; Joel Williamson, *The Crucible of Race: Black-White Relations in the American South Since Emancipation* (New York: Oxford University Press, 1984), 88–93.

8. Michael Montgomery, ed., *The Crucible of Carolina: Essays in the Development of Gullah Language and Culture* (Athens: University of Georgia Press, 1994); Daniel Littlefield, *Rice and Slaves: Ethnicity and the Slave Trade in Colonial South Carolina* (Baton Rouge: Louisiana State University Press, 1981); Peter Wood, *Black Majority: Negroes in Colonial South Carolina from 1670 through the Stono Rebellion* (New York: Knopf, 1974); Theodore Rosengarten, *Tombee: Portrait of a Cotton Planter with the Journal of Thomas B. Chaplin (1822–1890)* (New York: William Morrow, 1986); Lawrence Rowland, Alexander Moore, and George Rogers Jr., *The History of Beaufort County, South Carolina, vol. 1, 1514–1861* (Columbia: University of South Carolina Press, 1996); Margaret Washington Creel, *"A Peculiar People": Slave Religion and Community Culture among the Gullahs* (New York: New York University

Press, 1988); Charles Joyner, *Down by the Riverside: A South Carolina Slave Community* (Urbana: University of Illinois Press, 1984); Lorenzo Dow Turner, *Africanisms in the Gullah Dialect* (1949; repr., New York: Arno Press, 1969); and Dale Rosengarten, *Row upon Row: Sea Grass Baskets* (Columbia: McKissick Museum, University of South Carolina, 1986). Not all African Americans in Beaufort County spoke Gullah, especially in the town of Beaufort. I will be using the adjective "Gullah" only when I refer to black sea islanders in a folkloristic context.

9. Kurt Wolf, "Laura M. Towne and the Freed People of South Carolina, 1862–1901," *South Carolina Historical Magazine* 98 (Oct. 1997): 349–74; Jacoway, *Yankee Missionaries;* Louise Anderson Allen, *A Bluestocking in Charleston: The Life and Career of Laura Bragg* (Columbia: University of South Carolina Press, 2001); Sidney Bland, *Preserving Charleston's Past, Shaping Its Future: The Life and Times of Susan Pringle Frost* (Columbia: University of South Carolina Press, 1999); Katherine Smedley, *Martha Schofield and the Re-Education of the South, 1839–1915* (Lewiston, N.Y.: Edwin Mellen Press, 1987); Elsa Barkley Brown, "What Has Happened Here?," in *"We Specialize in the Wholly Impossible": A Reader in Black Women's History,* ed. Darlene Clark Hine, Wilma King, and Linda Reed (Brooklyn, N.Y.: Carlson, 1995), 41.

10. Orville Vernon Burton, "'The Black Squint of the Law': Racism in South Carolina," in *The Meaning of South Carolina History: Essays in Honor of George C. Rogers,* ed. David Chesnutt and Clyde Wilson (Columbia: University of South Carolina Press, 1991), 171; W. Fitzhugh Brundage, *Lynching in the New South: Georgia and Virginia, 1880–1930* (Urbana: University of Illinois Press, 1993), 130–33; Walter Fraser, *Charleston! Charleston! The History of a Southern City* (Columbia: University of South Carolina Press, 1989), 336; George B. Tindall, *South Carolina Negroes, 1877–1900* (Columbia: University of South Carolina Press, 1952), 54–56, 61–62; Mary Jennie McGuire, "Getting Their Hands on the Land: The Revolution in St. Helena Parish, 1861–1900" (Ph.D. diss., University of South Carolina, 1985).

11. Evelyn Wells to AWC, 22 Oct. 1938, CFP, SCL.

12. Mary Rhiel and David Suchoff, eds., *The Seductions of Biography* (New York: Routledge, 1996), ix–11.

Chapter One

1. AHC, handwritten manuscript, n.d., CFP, SCL.

2. Abbie Holmes was not given the proper first name Abigail, even at birth. See listing for "Abbie Mandana Holmes," 28 Jan. 1852, Westborough Book of Births,

Town Hall, Westborough, Mass.; and Rachel Reed Dearing, "Westborough Commemorative Booklet, 1717–1967" (North Conway, N.H.: Reporter Press, 1967), 47.

3. Account books, deeds, receipts, and tax collection books of James Winch, 1806–48; Clarissa Kilburn to Mr & Mrs Calvin Kilburn, 13 Nov. 1817; Harriet Winch to Sally Winch, 4 Jan. 1837?; Inventory of the Estate of James Winch, 6 June 1848, all in CFP, SCL. See also Abbie Holmes (hereafter AH) diary, 17 Aug. 1872; and Arthur Christensen, "Genealogy of Niels Christensen, Jr., Apr. 21, 1902," collection of Carroll Eve and Arthur Sommerville, Beaufort, S.C. (hereafter CE).

4. James Winch, manuscript, 3 Nov. 1837, CFP, SCL; AHC, handwritten manuscript on life of Abbie Winch Coes, n.d., CFP, SCL; Emory Washburn, *A Brief Sketch of the History of Leicester Academy* (Boston: Phillips, Sampson & Co., 1855), 131.

5. Rebekah [*sic*] Winch to Jos. L. Partridge, receipt for room and board, 15 Feb. 1843; promissory note: Alden Winch, John D. Lowell, Reuben G. Holmes of Westboro, Lucinda K. Winch, and Abigail Winch of Holden to Sally Winch, 15–16 Nov. 1848, all in CFP, SCL.

6. Clarence H. Danhof, "The Tools and Implements of Agriculture," *Agricultural History* 46 (1972): 84. See Reuben Graves Holmes (hereafter RGH), "reminiscences," 1905?, 2–18, 96; and RGH to "My Dear Children," Aug. 1905, both in CFP, SCL. In order to avoid interrupting the flow of their writing, I have chosen not to note misspellings or punctuation errors in texts quoted from Reuben Holmes or others with the designation [*sic*]. See also Sarah Elizabeth Holmes, "Olive Graves (Holmes) Harrington (1810–1883)," 1, New England Historic Genealogical Society, Boston, Mass. On her father's education, see AHC to Arthur Olaf Christensen (hereafter AOC), 14 Feb. 1906, CFP, SCL.

7. Adult photograph of RGH in Illustrations; RGH, "Reminiscences," 1905?, 2–8, 103, all in CFP, SCL.

8. RGH, "reminiscences," 1905?, 20–21, CFP, SCL.

9. Ibid., 22–35; Sarah Holmes?, "A COPY OF THE SKETCH OF THE LIFE OF COL. PETER HOLMES. (Written about 1875 for the 'Mack Book' which was never published)"; RGH to Children, Aug. 1905, all in CFP, SCL.

10. RGH, "reminiscences," 1905?, 34–38, CFP, SCL; *Valuation and Taxes of the Town of Westborough* (Worcester, Mass.: Howland, 1856), 12.

11. Kristina Allen, *On the Beaten Path: Westborough, Massachusetts* (Westborough, Mass.: Westborough Civic Club and Historical Society, 1984); Dearing, "Westborough Commemorative Booklet," 58–59; Herman De Forest and Edward Bates, *The History of Westborough, Massachusetts* (1891; repr., Boston New England Genealogical Society, 1998), 344–49.

12. AHC, typed manuscript, 1934?, 8–10; photograph, "Grandmother, very young" in Illustrations, both in CFP, SCL.

13. AHC, manuscript, 1934?, 8–9, CFP, SCL; RGH, "reminiscences," 1905?, 54–59, CFP, SCL; Rachel Dearing?, "Reuben Holmes," handwritten note in local history files, Westborough Public Library, Westborough, Mass.

14. Rachel Dearing?, "Reuben Holmes," handwritten note in local history files, Westborough Public Library, Westborough, Mass.

15. Ibid. On the Lyman School, see "School of Reform, Westborough, Massachusetts," *The National Magazine* (Apr. 1854): 165–76; and Alfred Roe, "Creating Character at the Lyman School for Boys, Westborough, Massachusetts," *New England Magazine* 26 (June 1902): 399–412, both in Westborough Public Library, Westborough, Mass. See also RGH, "reminiscences," 1905?, 36, 63–66, CFP, SCL.

16. RGH, "reminiscences," 1905?, 40, 112, CFP, SCL.

17. *Valuation and Taxes of the Town of Westborough* (Worcester, Mass.: Howland, 1858), 16; RGH, "reminiscences," 1905?, 126, CFP, SCL. One of Holmes's frequent literary errors was his use of "collard" for "colored."

18. RGH, "reminiscences," 1905?, 61, 80–81; RGH to Children, Aug. 1905, both in CFP, SCL.

19. Abbie Winch to Rebecca Winch, ca. 1859?; AHC, manuscript, 1934?, 9–10, both in CFP, SCL. On Higginson's church, see Franklin Rice, *Dictionary of Worcester, Massachusetts and Its Vicinity,* 2d ed. (Worcester, Mass.: F. S. Blanchard, 1893). On abolitionism and women's rights movements in Worcester, see Franklin Rice, *The Worcester Book: A Diary of Noteworthy Events in Worcester, Massachusetts from 1857–1883* (Worcester, Mass.: Putnam, Davis and Co., 1884).

20. AHC, manuscript, 1934?, 9–10, CFP, SCL.

21. RGH, "reminiscences," 1905?, 61, CFP, SCL. Abbie corrected her father's reminiscences about her mother's insanity on p. 126, writing in "Bellevue Asylum." Her son Frederik Christensen recorded that Abbie read her father's reminiscences to the family shortly after he died. See Frederik Christensen diary, vol. 9, 25 Mar. 1906, SCL. See also Lizzie [Elizabeth Harrington] Bonham to Rebecca Holmes, 22 Sept. 1860; RGH to Rebecca Holmes, 7 Oct. 1860; and AHC to AOC, 27 Feb. 1898, all in CFP, SCL. See also Gerhard Spieler, "Remembrances of Beaufort: Mrs. Andrea Rebecca Christensen Patterson," *Beaufort Gazette,* 24 Feb. 1977, clipping, Pringle.

22. AHC, manuscript, 1934?, 9–10, CFP, SCL.

23. *The Mother's Assistant and Young Lady's Friend* 7 (Jan. 1854); Rebecca Holmes?, "Abbie & her kittens," n.d.; AHC to AOC, 27 Feb. 1898, all in CFP, SCL.

24. AHC, typed manuscript, 1934?, 10, CFP, SCL.

25. Ibid., 11; Abbie Winch Coes to AH, 5 Jan. 1862; Sarah Pickett to RGH, 27 Oct. 1862; Olive Holmes to RGH, 31 Dec. 1862; T. B. Lamb to AH, 6 Nov. 1863, all in CFP, SCL.

26. In a 24 Dec. 1861 legal document RGH bought out his partner, Jonathan Luther, for one thousand dollars in order to have exclusive rights to sell his patented Improved Clothes Washer & Wringer. On 27 Jan. 1862, Holmes sold these rights for one dollar to a firm that agreed to market the machine and give Holmes and his heirs twenty-five cents for every machine sold. There is no evidence that Holmes ever earned a significant amount from this arrangement, or even recovered his one thousand dollars. See above dated documents and AHC, typed manuscript, 14 Jan. 1934, CFP, SCL.

27. Rebecca [Holmes] to Husband, 2 Dec. 1862, CFP, SCL; AHC, typed manuscript, 14 Jan. 1934, 12–13, CFP, SCL; John S. C. Abbott, *The History of the Civil War in America*, vol. 1 (New York: L. Bill, 1863).

28. AHC, typed manuscript, 14 Jan. 1934, 13; H. W. Beach to [Rebecca Holmes], 5 May 1865; T. B. Lamb to AH, 6 Nov. 1863, all in CFP, SCL.

29. AHC, typed manuscript, 14 Jan. 1934, 14, CFP, SCL.

Chapter 2

1. AH diary, 31 Dec. 1865, CFP, SCL.

2. AHC, typed manuscript, 1934?, 17; RGH, "reminiscences," 1905?, 61, both in CFP, SCL.

3. Edward Miller Jr., *Gullah Statesman: Robert Smalls from Slavery to Congress, 1839–1915* (Columbia: University of South Carolina Press, 1995), 1–8.

4. For an overview of the "Experiment," see Willie Lee Rose, *Rehearsal for Reconstruction: The Port Royal Experiment* (New York: Vintage Books, 1964). AHC, typed manuscript, 14 Jan. 1934, 13, CFP, SCL.

5. Fredrickson, *Black Image*, 97–129; McPherson, *Abolitionist Legacy*; Robert F. Engs, *Educating the Disfranchised and Disinherited: Samuel Chapman Armstrong and Hampton Institute, 1839–1893* (Knoxville: University of Tennessee Press, 1999).

6. Rose, *Rehearsal for Reconstruction*, 63–103, 196, 273–319; James Anderson, *The Education of Blacks in the South, 1860–1935* (Chapel Hill: University of North Carolina Press, 1988), 5–6; Rupert S. Holland, ed., *Letters and Diary of Laura M. Towne* (1912; repr., New York: Negro Universities Press, 1969), 98, 103, 140–41; Brenda Stevenson, ed., *The Journals of Charlotte Forten Grimke* (New York: Oxford

University Press, 1988), 400, 428–35. Thomas Wentworth Higginson marveled at the former slaves in his troop, writing that "their love of the spelling book is perfectly inexhaustible" (Thomas Wentworth Higginson, *Army Life in a Black Regiment* [1869; repr., New York: W. W. Norton, 1984], 48). On school farms, see Powell, *New Masters,* 4.

7. RGH, "reminiscences," 1905?, 42, CFP, SCL

8. Ibid., 45, 118; Frank Holmes to RGH, 2 Apr. 1864; P[atterson] P. Holmes to Lydia Holmes, 15, 31 Mar. 1864, all in CFP, SCL.

9. RGH, "reminiscences," 1905?, 45, 61, 118, CFP, SCL; AHC typed manuscript, 14 Jan. 1934, 13–14, CFP, SCL; Frank Holmes to RGH, 2 Apr. 1864, CFP, SCL; P[atterson] P. Holmes to Lydia Holmes, 15, 31 Mar. 1864, CFP, SCL; Helen M. Philbrick to AHC, 22 Dec. 1906, CFP, SCL; Rose, *Rehearsal for Reconstruction,* 32–62. Perfectionism was a branch of Methodism that held that perfect emulation of God was the achievable goal of all Christians through constant devotional communion in worship and daily life. See Richard Rabinowitz, *The Spiritual Self in Everyday Life: The Transformation of Personal Religious Experience in Nineteenth-Century New England* (Boston: Northeastern University Press, 1989). On education and the distrust and resistance of freed people who worked for northern planters, see Powell, *New Masters,* 93–122.

10. AHC, typed manuscript, 14 Jan. 1934, 14; RGH, "reminiscences," 1905?, 118–23, both in CFP, SCL.

11. AHC, typed manuscript, 14 Jan. 1934, 14; RGH, "reminiscences," 1905?, 128; AH diary, 5 Nov. 1865?, all in CFP, SCL.

12. AHC, typed manuscript, 14 Jan. 1934, 15, CFP, SCL.

13. Ibid., 14.

14. Ibid., 16–17; Elizabeth Ware Pearson, ed., *Letters from Port Royal, 1862–1868* (1906; repr., New York: Arno Press, 1969), 144; Rose, *Rehearsal for Reconstruction,* 227. For an examination of black and white southern food ways, see Sam Hilliard, "Hogmeat and Cornpone: Foodways in the Antebellum South," in *Material Life in America, 1600–1860,* ed. Robert Blair St. George (Boston: Northeastern University Press, 1988), 311–32.

15. AHC, typed manuscript, 14 Jan. 1934, 16–17, CFP, SCL.

16. Ibid., 14 Jan. 1934, 17; Frank Holmes to RGH, 20 Feb. 1865, CFP, SCL; Powell, *New Masters,* 21.

17. AH diary, 8, 22 Sept., 6–9, 21 Oct., 10 Nov. 1865, all in CFP, SCL. See also chap. 8, "The Original Uncle Remus," in this book; Miss A[bbie] M[andana] Holmes, "The Story Aunt 'Tilda Told," *New York Independent* 26 (5 Nov. 1874): 14;

and Mrs. A[bbie] M[andana] Christensen, "Negro Folklore: The Elephant and the Rabbit," *New York Independent* 27 [2 Sept. 1875]: 25, for a more complete version of the stories of Alice.

18. AHC, typed manuscript, 1930?, 6, CFP, SCL.

19. Ibid., 4; Martha Holmes to Rebecca Holmes, 5 Dec. 1865, CFP, SCL; Rose, *Rehearsal for Reconstruction,* 320–21; William T. Sherman, *Memoirs of General William T. Sherman,* vol. 2 (New York: Appleton, 1875), 231.

20. RGH, "reminiscences," 1905?, 45–70, CFP, SCL. For another description of the hardships endured by the mainland refugees, see Elizabeth Hyde Botume, *First Days amongst the Contrabands* (Boston: Lee and Shepard, 1893), 78–81.

21. RGH, "reminiscences," 1905?, 45–70, CFP, SCL; Frederik Christensen diary, 23 Oct. 1906, SCL.

22. RGH, "reminiscences, 1905?, 46–73, 123–25, CFP, SCL.

23. RGH to Frank Holmes, 20 Feb. 1865, CFP, SCL; Powell, *New Masters,* 73.

24. RGH, "reminiscences," 1905?, 126, Frank Holmes to RGH, 21 Mar. 1865, both in CFP, SCL. On the emergence of the plantation store, merchant-planters in general, and Holmes in particular, see Powell, *New Masters,* 87–93; Joel Williamson, "New Patterns in Economics," in Joel Williamson, *After Slavery: The Negro in South Carolina during Reconstruction, 1861–1877* (Chapel Hill: University of North Carolina Press, 1965), 27–163, 173; and Woodward, *Origins of the New South.* For a work that argues the dominance of southern planter persistence as merchant-landlords, see Jonathan Wiener, *Social Origins of the New South: Alabama, 1860–1885* (Baton Rouge: Louisiana State University Press, 1978).

25. RGH to Frank Holmes, 20 Feb. 1865, CFP, SCL; Rose, *Rehearsal for Reconstruction,* 73–75, 80.

26. AHC, typed manuscript, 1930?, 6–7, CFP, SCL.

27. Rose, *Rehearsal for Reconstruction,* 286–89; Theodore Rosengarten, *Tombee,* 260.

28. Rose, *Rehearsal for Reconstruction,* 327–28, 350–51.

29. Williamson, *After Slavery,* 64–95, 126–63; Powell, *New Masters,* 103–5, 114–15. See also Leslie Schwalm, *A Hard Fight for We: Women's Transition from Slavery to Freedom in South Carolina* (Urbana: University of Illinois Press, 1997); Philip Morgan, "Work and Culture: The Task System and the World of Lowcountry Blacks, 1700–1880," in *Material Life in America, 1600–1860,* ed. Robert Blair St. George (Boston: Northeastern University Press, 1988), 203–23; and John Strickland, "Traditional Culture and the Moral Economy: Social and Economic Change in the South Carolina Low Country, 1865–1910," in *The Countryside in the Age*

of Capitalist Transformation, ed. Steven Hahn and Jonathan Prude (Chapel Hill: University of North Carolina Press, 1985), 141–78. On landownership, see McGuire, "Getting Their Hands on the Land."

30. AH diary, 1–2, 11–12, 14, 29 Sept., 2, 12, 21 Oct. 1865, CFP, SCL.

31. AHC, typed manuscript, 1930?, 4; AHC, "Miss Ellen Murray," 30 Oct. 1933, p. 1, both in CFP, SCL; Tilden Edelstein, *Strange Enthusiasm: A Life of Thomas Wentworth Higginson* (New Haven: Yale University Press, 1968).

32. AH diary, 1–2, 10, 12, 14, 27 Sept., 23 Oct. 1865; P[atterson] P. Holmes to Lizzie Holmes, 29 Oct. 1865, copied by AHC, all in CFP, SCL.

33. AH diary, 8 Sept., 24 Oct. 1865; Patterson P. Holmes to Lizzie Holmes, 29 Oct. 1865, all in CFP, SCL.

34. Olive Holmes Harrington to Rebecca Holmes, 26 Mar. 1867, CFP, SCL. On relations between Yankees and southerners, see Powell, *New Masters,* 123–50, esp. 140–41.

35. Olive Holmes Harrington to Rebecca Holmes, 26 Mar. 1867, CFP, SCL.

36. Botume, *First Days,* 55.

37. AH diary, 31 Dec. 1865, in CFP, SCL.

Chapter 3

1. Olive Harrington to Rebecca Holmes, 26 Mar. 1867, CFP, SCL.

2. Elizabeth Harrington to Reuben and Rebecca Holmes, 22 Apr. 1854, in CFP, SCL; AH diary, 6–22, 25–26 Mar. 1867, CE; Carroll Smith-Rosenberg, "The Female World of Love and Ritual: Relations between Women in Nineteenth Century America," in Carroll Smith-Rosenberg, *Disorderly Conduct: Visions of Gender in Victorian America* (New York: Oxford University Press, 1985), 53–76.

3. *Catalogue of the Officers and Members of the Ipswich Female Seminary* (Boston: Rand, Avery & Cornhill, 1864), CFP, SCL; Helen Lefkowitz Horowitz, *Alma Mater: Design and Experience in the Women's Colleges from Their Nineteenth Century Beginnings to the 1930s* (New York: Knopf, 1984), 11.

4. Thomas Franklin Waters, *Ipswich in the Massachusetts Bay Colony,* vol. 2 of *A History of the Town from 1700–1917* (Ipswich: Ipswich Historical Society, 1917), 571, 538–75; AH diary, 2, 4 Jan. 1867, CE.

5. Jane Hunter argues that although Victorian girls were encouraged to write in diaries in order to develop orderly habits and moral introspection, young women also used them to develop a sense of self that transcended what others wanted them to be; see Jane Hunter, "Inscribing the Self in the Heart of the Family: Diaries and

Girlhood in Late-Victorian America," *American Quarterly* 44, no. 1 (Mar. 1992): 51–81. See also AH diary, 2 Feb., 5 Mar., 28 May 1867, CE.

6. In her 1867 diary (CE), Abbie listed correspondence with her mother on the following dates: 7, 10, 25 Feb., 17, 20 Mar., 3 Apr., 2 May, 1 June 1867. AHC, note appended to letter by Patterson P. Holmes to Lizzie Holmes, 29 Oct. 1865, copied by AHC, CFP, SCL.

7. AH diary, 1 May 1867, CE.

8. AH diary, 2 Jan., 26 Feb. 1867, CE; Horowitz, *Alma Mater,* 18. A "series" seems to have been a class period, although Holmes also may be referring to the lesson of that class period.

9. AH diary, 13 July, 13 June 1867, CE; AHC, "A Stroller in Beaufort Fields and Gardens," ca. 1910, CFP, SCL. On women and botany, see Annette Kolodny, *The Land Before Her: Fantasy and Experience of the American Frontier, 1630–1860* (Chapel Hill: University of North Carolina Press, 1984), 48; and Anne T. Shteir, "Linneaus's Daughters: Women and British Botany," in *Women and the Structure of Society: Papers from the Fifth Berkshire Conference on the History of Women,* ed. Barbara J. Harris and Jo Ann McNamara (Durham, N.C.: Duke University Press, 1984), 67–73.

10. AH diary, 26 Feb. 1867, CE.

11. AH diary, 9 Jan. 1867, CE.

12. AH diary, 23 Mar., 12 April, 18 May, 25 June 1867, CE. Jane Hunter mentions the importance of novels in addition to journal writing in forming Victorian girls' identity; see Hunter, "Inscribing the Self," 52. See also Mary Poovey, *Uneven Developments: The Ideological Work of Gender in Mid-Victorian England* (London: Virago Press, 1989), 126–63.

13. AH diary, 28 Jan., 3 Feb., 13 May, 1 June 1867, CE. Abbie was probably influenced by the personal turn that evangelicalism took in the second half of the nineteenth century, emphasizing devotional stillness and emotional connection with aspects of the liturgy such as communion. See Richard Rabinowitz, *Spiritual Self,* 201–2.

14. AH diary, 17 Feb. 1867, CE.

15. AH diary, 13 Feb., 6 Mar., 19 Apr., 9, 18 June, 1867, CE; Smith-Rosenberg, *Disorderly Conduct,* 67–68.

16. AH diary, 25 Jan., 8, 28 Feb., 6 Mar., 8 Apr. 18, June, 11, 12, 13 July 1867, CE; Helen Woods Roberts to AHC, 10 Nov. 1907, CFP, SCL.

17. RGH, "reminiscences," 1905?, 129, CFP, SCL.

18. "English Course of Study," in *Catalogue of the Officers and Members of the Ipswich Female Seminary,* 15; Abbie M. Holmes, "Teacher's Monthly School Report, State of South Carolina," 3 Nov. 1870, both in CFP, SCL.

Chapter 4

1. AH diary, 12 Mar. 1871, CE.

2. AH diary, 1 Sept. 1867, CE.

3. AH diary, 10 Jan. 1868, CE.

4. AH diary, 1, 25, 5 Sept., 19, 21, 23–24, 26 Oct. 1867, CE.

5. AH diary, 1 Sept. 1867, CE. On relations between mistresses and servants, see Faye Dudden, *Serving Women: Household Service in Nineteenth-Century America* (Middletown, Conn.: Wesleyan University Press, 1983); and David Katzman, *Seven Days a Week: Women and Domestic Service in Industrializing America* (Urbana: University of Illinois Press, 1981).

6. Lizzie Bonham to Rebecca Holmes, 22 Sept. 1860; Olive Holmes to RGH, 31 Dec. 1862, both in CFP, SCL; Katzman, *Seven Days a Week,* 153–54.

7. These elisions appear in the diary whenever Abbie seems about to express excessive anger or despair. See AH diary, 3 Sept., and after 12 January, 1867, CE; Katzman, *Seven Days a Week,* 153, 166, 200–201; and Dudden, *Serving Women,* 176.

8. AH diary, 1, 3 Sept. 1867, CE.

9. AH diary, 2, 6, 7, 25, 27 Sept., 17–18, 20 Oct., 7, 18 Nov. 1867, CE.

10. AH diary, 2 Sept., 21 Oct., 6 Nov. 1867, CE. On the slow economy and northern planters' interests in politics, see Powell, *New Masters,* 146, 152.

11. AH diary, 8, 20, 22 Nov. 1867; 11 Jan. 1868, CE; RGH, "reminiscences," 1905?, 180, CFP, SCL; Gerhard Spieler, "Remembrances of Beaufort: Mrs. Andrea Rebecca Christensen," *Beaufort Gazette,* 24 Feb. 1977, clipping, Pringle.

12. J. G. Holland, "God Is Almighty . . . ," 21 Mar. 1868; "Led through Sorrow," 1868, both in "Selection Book," CFP, SCL.

13. AHC to AOC, 27 Feb. 1898, CFP, SCL.

14. RGH, "reminiscences," 1905?, 78–79, CFP, SCL.

15. Ibid., 73–77; "One Who Tried to Make the World Better," *Beaufort Gazette,* 15 Feb. 1906; Williamson, *After Slavery,* 367–68, 377; Thomas Holt, *Black over White: Negro Political Leadership in South Carolina during Reconstruction* (Urbana: University of Illinois Press, 1979), 36–38. Perhaps the best-known critique of Reconstruction had been in circulation for many years; see James Pike, *The Prostrate State: South Carolina under Negro Government* (New York: Appleton and Company, 1874).

16. RGH, "reminiscences," 1905?, 85–89, 131, CFP, SCL. On the land commission, see Carol Bleser, *The Promised Land: The History of the South Carolina Land Commission, 1869–90* (Columbia: University of South Carolina Press, 1969); and Williamson, *After Slavery,* 146–48.

17. RGH, "reminiscences," 1905?, 85–89, 131, CFP, SCL.

18. AH diary, 26 Sept. 1870; "One Who Tried to Make the World Better," *Beaufort Gazette,* 15 Feb. 1906; RGH, "reminiscences," 1905?, 132, all in CFP, SCL. See also receipts, 4 Nov. 1868 and undated 1868, from State Commission on Elections and Completed Electoral Ballot, 3 Nov. 1868, in RGH Papers, SCL; Rose, *Rehearsal for Reconstruction,* 389–94; Williamson, *After Slavery,* 389; Walter Edgar, *South Carolina: A History* (Columbia: University of South Carolina Press, 1998), 394–95; and Miller, *Gullah Statesman,* 57–66.

19. "One Who Tried to Make the World Better," *Beaufort Gazette,* 15 Feb. 1906; RGH, "reminiscences," 1905?, 132, both in CFP, SCL.

20. U.S. Census manuscript, Beaufort County, S.C., 1870 (M593), reel 1485, p. 1.

21. AH diary, 25 Dec. 1870, CFP, SCL; AH diary, 28 Jan., 25 Feb., 25 Mar., 10, 26, 30 Apr., 30 June 1871, CE. See AH diaries, 1870, 1871, passim, CE, for references to "mother."

22. AH diary, 8 Dec. 1870, CFP, SCL; AH diary, 28 Jan. 1871, CE.

23. AH diary, 14 Sept. 1870; "Teacher's Second Grade Certificate Beaufort, SC No. 11 Abby M. Holmes, Sept. 22, 1870"; Abbie M. Holmes, Teacher's Monthly School Report, State of South Carolina, 3 Nov. 1870, all in CFP, SCL. See also Jacqueline Jones, *Soldiers of Light,* 112.

24. AH diary, 14 Sept., 30 Dec. 1870; 5 Jan. 1871, CFP, SCL. On Langley, see Holt, *Black over White,* 76, 125, App. A; and Williamson, *After Slavery,* 220, 224, 365–66.

25. Abbie M. Holmes, Teacher's Monthly School Reports, State of South Carolina, 3, 29 Nov., 22 Dec. 1870; 27 Jan., 24 Feb., 24 Mar. 1871, CFP, SCL. For a profile of Hastings Gantt, who became a state representative for Beaufort, see Holt, *Black over White,* 47.

26. AH diary, 31 Jan. 1871, CE.

27. Holland, *Letters and Diary of Laura M. Towne,* 41; Stevenson, *Journals of Charlotte Forten Grimke,* 396–97, 399.

28. AH diary, 21 Oct., 9 Nov. 1870, CFP, SCL; Sarah Chisholm to AH, 16 Nov. 1871, CE.

29. AH diary, 7, 14 Oct., 21 Nov. 1870; 12 Jan. 1871, CFP, SCL. For biographical information on Langley, see Holt, *Black over White,* 125. See also AH diary, 15 Mar., 28 Apr., 3 May 1871, CE; Holland, *Letters and Diary of Laura M. Towne,* 140; and Jacqueline Jones, *Soldiers of Light,* 125.

30. AH diary, 2, 6 June 1871, CE.

31. AH to L.S. Langley, 3 Apr. 1871, CFP, SCL; AH diary, 3–5 Apr. 1871, CE.

32. AH diary, 27–28, 31 Oct., 3 Nov. 1871, CE.

33. AH diary, 6 Nov. 1871, CE; Daniel Bythewood to AH, 13 June 1873, CFP, SCL; "Beaufort County Library History," Beaufort County Library, Beaufort, S.C.

34. AH diary, 8 Jan., 7, 22, 29 Feb., 18, 21, 26 Mar., 2, 8–9, 27, 30 Apr. 1872, CE.

35. AH diary, 11, 17 Feb., 10 Mar., 19 May 1871, CE; Botume, *First Days.*

36. AH diary, 25, 30 Apr., 2 May 1872, CE; Monica M. Tetzlaff, "Shout," in *American Folklore: An Encyclopedia,* ed. Jan Brunvand (New York: Garland Publishing, 1996), 667–68. The American Folklore Society styled its name with the hyphenated term in the nineteenth century, as did its journal, *American Folklore.*

37. Andrea Kerr, *Lucy Stone: Speaking Out for Equality* (New Brunswick, N.J.: Rutgers University Press, 1992), 22–49.

38. Eric Foner, *Reconstruction: America's Unfinished Revolution, 1863–1877* (New York: Harper & Row, 1988), 228–80; McGuire, "Getting Their Hands on the Land," 176.

39. On social events involving northern whites, see AH diary, 2 June 1871, passim, CE. On churches, see AH diary, 9, 11, 27 Nov. 1870; 8 Jan. 1871, CFP, SCL; AH diary, 29 Jan., 12 Feb., 7 May, 31 Dec. 1871, CE; and History Committee, St. Helena Episcopal Church, Beaufort, S.C., *The History of The Parish Church of St. Helena* (Columbia, S.C.: R. L. Bryan Co., 1990), 79.

40. AH diary, 9, 16, 18, 27 Nov. 1871, CE.

41. AH diary, 31 Dec. 1870, CFP, SCL; AH diary, 26 Apr. 1871, CE.

42. AH diary, 8–9, 21 May 1871, CE. On the Ku Klux Klan Act see Foner, *Reconstruction,* 454–55.

43. AH diary, 28–30 May 1871, CE; undated typed manuscript on NC, CFP, SCL. For Judd's poem and a further description of the Emancipation Day festivities, see Botume, *First Days,* 76–78. On Judd, see U.S. Census manuscript, Beaufort County, S.C., 1870 (M593), reel 1485, p. 18.

44. AH diary, 1 Jan. 1872, CE.

45. AH diary, 15–17 July, 11–17 Sept. 1871, CE. On women performing the rituals of burial for one another, see Smith-Rosenberg, *Disorderly Conduct,* 70–72.

46. AH diary, 13 Oct. 1871, CE.

47. AH diary, 27 Mar., 22 Apr., 21 June, 27 Oct. 1871; AH diary 2 Jan. 1872, both CE. Riding was popular with northerners and southerners of both genders at this time. Its seductive pleasures kept at least one young northern plantation owner from tending to the duties of his business; see Powell, *New Masters,* 134.

48. AHC, undated manuscript, CFP, SCL; AH diary, 29, 30 Jan., 4, 5, 11 Feb., 22, 25, 26, 31 Mar., 6 Apr., 1, 5–12 May, 2–3, 6–8, 12–13, 17–20, 30 June 1871, CE; AH diary, 17, 24 Nov., 1, 2 Dec. 1867, CE.

49. AH diary, 17 Feb., 5, 14 Sept., 15, 22, 26 Dec. 1867; 1 Jan. 1868; 24 Oct., 11, 23 Dec. 1870; 19, 24 Feb., 11 Mar., 4 Apr. 1871; 20–21 Mar., 5, 18, 29–30 Apr., 4, 12 May 1871, CE; "so long," undated, handwritten manuscript, CFP, SCL; Mrs. A. D. T. Whitney, *Hitherto: A Story of Yesterdays* (Boston: Loring, 1869).

50. AH diary, 5, 24, 26 Feb., 20, 30 Nov. 1871, CE.

51. AH diary, 6, 11–13 Mar. 1871, CE.

52. AH diary, 14 May 1871, CE.

53. AH diary, 1, 8, 10, 17, 23–26, 29, 31 Dec. 1871; 1–4, 7–9, 11, 13–17, 19–22, 24–26, 28 Jan., 3–6, 8, 10, 15–16, 18–19, 22, 25–29 Feb., 3–5, 9–11, 21–22, 25–30 Mar., 5–6, 15, 19–22, 26–27, 29–30 Apr., 1–2, 4 May 1872; 18 Apr. 1873, CE.

54. On the evolution of romantic love in the nineteenth century, see Karen Lystra, *Searching the Heart: Women, Men and Romantic Love in Nineteenth Century America* (New York: Oxford University Press, 1989), esp. "Not for God Only," 227–58.

55. AH diary, 22 Apr. 1871; 26 Mar., 10 Apr. 1872, CE. For profiles of black Beaufort politicians, see Holt, *Black over White,* 48, 54, 70, 185.

Chapter 5

1. AH diary, 23 Sept. 1872, CE.

2. AH diary, 12 July, 13 Aug. 1872, CE.

3. AH diary, 29–30 July 1872, CE; Frank[lin] Holmes to RGH, 13 Sept. 1872, CFP, SCL.

4. AH diary, 9–16 Aug. 1872, CE.

5. AH diary, 15 Aug. 1873; 17 Aug. 1872, CE.

6. AH diary, 21, 22 Aug. 1872; AH, manuscript, n.d., all in CE. Although a record of Abbie granting Carrie forgiveness is not in the diary that survives, it may have been on pp. 57–62, which have been torn out. For a discussion of middle-class women's benevolent redemption of prostitutes and victims of "seduction," see Carroll Smith-Rosenberg, "Beauty, the Beast, and the Militant Woman: A Case Study of Sex Roles and Social Stress in Jacksonian America," *American Quarterly* 23 (Oct. 1971): 562–84; and Lori Ginzberg, *Women and the Work of Benevolence: Morality,*

Politics and Class in the Nineteenth Century United States (New Haven, Conn.: Yale University Press, 1990).

7. Olive Holmes Harrington to RGH, 11 Feb. 1872, CFP, SCL; AH diary, 23–27 Aug. 1872, CE.

8. AH to RGH, 28 Oct. 1872, CFP, SCL; AH diary, 2 Sept. 1872, CE. Abbie tried to pay for the pictures of Rebecca Holmes from her own savings but needed help from her father when he was late in sending her money, 10 Aug. 1872. She recorded that she finally paid the balance due on "pictures of mother" as two dollars on 8 Nov. 1872 (AH account book, 1872–74, CFP, SCL).

9. AH diary, 23, 30 July, 30 Aug.–2 Sept. 1872; 19 Feb., 4, 10 Mar., 21 May, 16, 26 June 1873, CE.

10. AH diary, 4 Sept. 1872, CE; Horowitz, *Alma Mater,* 11, 14–25; AH to RGH, 20 Aug. 1872; AH account book, 2 Dec. 1872, CFP, SCL.

11. From 1837 to 1887, 10,500 out of 12,500 students did not graduate. See *Historical Sketch of Mount Holyoke Seminary* (Springfield, Mass.: Clark W. Bryan & Co., 1878), 9; and Thomas Woody, *A History of Women's Education in the United States* (New York: Octagon Books, 1966), 361.

12. Horowitz, *Alma Mater,* 4.

13. AH diary, 10 Sept., 5, 12 Oct., 16 Nov. 1872; 11 Mar. 1873, CE.

14. AH account book, Sept. 1872–Feb. 1874, CFP, SCL.

15. *American Journal of Education* 30 (September 1880), 620, quoted in Woody, *History of Women's Education,* 351. See also AH diary, 31 May 1873, CE.

16. AH diary, 31 Jan., 15–16 Apr., 19 May 1873, CE.

17. AH diary, 6, 10 Sept. 1872, CE.

18. Joanne Braxton, *Black Women Writing Autobiography: A Tradition within a Tradition* (Philadelphia: Temple University Press, 1989), 85; AH diary, 12 Sept. 1872, CE.

19. AH diary, 29 Dec. 1872; 12 Jan. 1873, CE; "Extract from 'Stepping Heavenward' Advice to a Young Christian," in AH diary, 14 Jan. 1873; Hunter, "Inscribing the Self," 62.

20. AH diary, 17 Sept., 3 Dec. 1872; 24, 31 Dec. 1873; 1, 5–6 Jan. 1874, CE. References to sermons occur on: 15 Sept., 6, 13 Oct. 1872; 31 Jan., 2 Mar., 6 Apr., 25 May, 8, 22 June 1873.

21. AH diary, 26 Oct., 3, 18 Nov. 1872; 1, 6, 28 Jan., 16–17 Feb., 18, 24 May 1873, CE; AH, "Miss Spooner's Section, '72 & '73," handwritten manuscript, n.d., CE.

22. AH diary, 23 Sept. 1872; 15 June 1873; 22 Oct. 1872; 20 Jan., 1, 20–21 Feb., 10, 29 June 1873, CE.

23. AH diary, 29 Nov. 1872; 17 Jan., 2, 4, 21, 24 Feb., 5 Mar., 13 Apr., 19 June 1873, CE; AH to Miss D., handwritten manuscript, n.d., CE.

24. See AH diary, 11 Dec. 1872; 23 Feb., 14, 16 Apr., 3–4 June 1873, CE, for walks and visits with friends. See AH diary, 3 Feb., 3 Apr., 1 June 1873, CE, for passages on Emma Holmes. See also AHC to Emma Holmes, 20 Aug. 1875, CFP, SCL.

25. AH diary, 18 Mar. 1873, CE.

26. AH diary, 25 Mar. 1873, CE.

27. On Table conversations, see handwritten manuscript, n.d., in AH diary, 7 Jan. 1873, CE. On elections, see AH diary, 5 Nov. 1872, CE.

28. AH diary, 16 Mar. 1873, CE.

29. AH diary, 23 Apr., 5 May 1873, CE.

30. AH diary, 10 May 1873, CE.

31. AH diary, 12, 14 May 1873, CE.

32. AH diary, 1–2 July 1873, CE.

33. AH diary, 31 Dec. 1872; 2, 5 July 1873, CE.

34. Abbie Holmes Christensen, "Folklore on Sea Islands," *Mount Holyoke Alumnae Quarterly* 16 (Feb. 1933): 203; A. J. Wakefield to AHC, 22 May 1892, CFP, SCL.

35. AHC to Alumnae Association of Mount Holyoke College, Dec. 1937, CFP, SCL; AHC, "Folklore on Sea Islands," 204; AH diary, 31 Dec. 1872, 30 June 1873, 4 July 1873, CE.

36. AHC, *Afro-American Folk Lore,* ix. On "romantic racialism," see Fredrickson, *Black Image,* 97–129. For a more recent analysis of postwar northern views of blacks, see Nina Silber, *The Romance of Reunion: Northerners and the South, 1865–1900* (Chapel Hill: University of North Carolina Press, 1993), 75–79, 124–58. See also Harriet Beecher Stowe, *Uncle Tom's Cabin* (Boston: J. P. Jewett, 1851); and Mark Twain, *The Adventures of Huckleberry Finn* (1884; repr., Berkeley: University of California Press, 1988).

37. Eric Lott, *Love and Theft: Blackface Minstrelsy and the American Working Class* (New York: Oxford University Press, 1993); AHC, "Folklore on Sea Islands," 204.

38. AH diary, 11–23 Aug. 1873, CE.

39. AH diary, 24 Aug. 1873; 1 Jan. 1874, CE; Harriet Beecher Stowe, *Uncle Tom's Cabin* (1852; repr., New York: Penguin, 1981), 412–38; Ann Douglas, *The Feminization of American Culture* (New York: Knopf, 1977), 3–4, 202, 207.

40. AH account book, Nov.–Dec. 1873, CFP, SCL; AH diary, 18 Aug., 13 Dec. 1872; 9, 25, 27 Feb., 8 Mar. 1873, CE. Kathryn Kish Sklar, *Catharine Beecher: A Study in American Domesticity* (New Haven, Conn.: Yale University Press, 1973), esp. 37–42, 184–87, provides an example of an intelligent, ambitious, and religious

nineteenth-century woman who worried over the state of her soul and retreated into illness and restful treatment when she encountered setbacks in her life.

41. AH diary, 3–6, 20–21 Nov. 1873, CE.

42. AH diary, 22 Nov., 4 Dec. 1873, CE.

43. AH diary, 13 Dec. 1873, CE; E. H. Clarke, *Sex in Education, or A Fair Chance for Girls* (Boston: J. R. Osgood & Co., 1873); Julia Ward Howe, *Sex and Education: A Reply to Dr. E. H. Clarke's Sex in Education* (1874; repr., New York: Arno Press, 1972).

44. AH diary, 13 Dec. 1873, CE; FHC diary, vol. 14, 26 Sept. 1922, SCL. On homeopathic treatment of consumption and "neuralgia" or "insanity," see J. H. Carmichael, "Homeopathy: Remedies and Treatment," in *Best Physicians and Surgeons of Modern Practice, The Cottage Physician* (Springfield, Mass.: King, Richardson, 1895); and Rollin Gregg, *Consumption: Its Cause and Nature* (Ann Arbor, Mich.: Ann Arbor Register, 1889). On tuberculosis, see Sheila Rothman, *Living in the Shadow of Death: Tuberculosis and the Social Experience of Illness in American History* (Baltimore, Md.: Johns Hopkins University Press, 1995). The infectious nature of tuberculosis had not yet been recognized in the United States in the 1870s. Homeopathic medicine advocated the use of drugs made from infinitesimal doses of substances that in larger doses would cause the symptoms of the disease the patient had contracted. Because homeopathy did not involve such practices as bleeding or large doses of mercury, it was usually less harmful than conventional "heroic medicine" in the nineteenth century. On the history of homeopathy, see Martin Kaufman, *Homeopathy in America: The Rise and Fall of a Medical Heresy* (Baltimore, Md.: Johns Hopkins University Press, 1971). On the openness and appeal of this alternative practice for women, see Naomi Rogers, "Women and Sectarian Medicine," in *Women, Health and Medicine: A Historical Handbook*, ed. Rima Apple (New Brunswick, N.J.: Rutgers University Press, 1990), 273–302.

45. AH diary, 24, 31 Dec. 1873, CE. See Ann Douglas Wood, "'The Fashionable Diseases': Women's Complaints and Their Treatment in Nineteenth Century America," in Judith Leavitt, *Women and Health in America* (Madison: University of Wisconsin Press, 1984), 222–38.

46. AH diary, 28–30 Jan. 1874, CE.

47. A[bbie] M[andana] H[olmes], "De Wolf, De Rabbit and De Tar Baby," *Springfield Daily Republican,* 2 June 1874. That day the paper also contained "Civil Rights at Suffield: The Experience of Two Colored Boys at the Connecticut Literary Institute," written by two black students who left the Connecticut Literary Institute

because they had been treated unfairly. See also "Abby Smith, Again: Her Appeal for Equal Rights before the Connecticut Legislative Committee on Woman Suffrage," *Springfield Daily Republican,* 5 June 1874; and "The News from South Carolina," *Springfield Daily Republican,* 8 June 1874.

48. Abbie Mandana Holmes, "De Wolf, De Rabbit and De Tar Baby."

49. Ibid.; AHC, "Folklore on Sea Islands," 204.

50. AH diary, 30 Jan., 17 Feb. 1874, CE.

51. AH diary, 26–28 Feb. 1874, CE. On women doctors in the late nineteenth century, see Ruth Abram, ed., *"Send Us a Lady Physician": Women Doctors in America, 1835–1920* (New York: W. W. Norton, 1985); Regina Markell Morantz-Sanchez, *Sympathy and Science: Women Physicians in American Medicine* (New York: Oxford University Press, 1985); Gloria Moldow, *Women Doctors in Gilded-Age Washington: Race, Gender and Professionalization* (Urbana: University of Illinois Press, 1987); and Mary Roth Walsh, *Doctors Wanted. No Women Need Apply: Sexual Barriers in the Medical Profession, 1835–1975* (New Haven, Conn.: Yale University Press, 1977).

52. AH diary, 21 Sept. 1872; 30 Jan. 1874, CE.

Chapter 6

1. "Holmes, Abbie Mandana, Association of Collegiate Alumnae—Census of College Women, 1915," in Mount Holyoke College Archives, South Hadley, Mass.

2. AH diary, 3 Mar. 1874, CE.

3. On the end of Reconstruction, 1876–77, see Foner, *Reconstruction,* 564–601; and Woodward, *Origins of the New South,* 1–107. For South Carolina and the Red Shirts in particular, see Holt, *Black over White,* 173–207, 212; Williamson, *After Slavery,* 266–73, 404–17 (quotation by Wade Hampton on 408); William Cooper, *The Conservative Regime, South Carolina, 1877–1890* (Baltimore, Md.: Johns Hopkins University Press, 1968); Tindall, *South Carolina Negroes;* and Stephen Kantrowitz, *Ben Tillman and the Reconstruction of White Supremacy* (Chapel Hill: University of North Carolina Press, 2000), 110–46. On northern ideologies and practices regarding race see, for example, Silber, *Romance of Reunion,* 66–158; Gail Biderman, *Manliness and Civilization: A Cultural History of Gender and Race in the United States, 1880–1917* (Chicago: University of Chicago Press, 1995), 16–44; and Fredrickson, *Black Image,* 228–55.

4. Rayford Logan, *The Negro in American Life and Thought: The Nadir, 1877–1901* (New York: Dial Press, 1954); Nell Painter, *Standing at Armageddon: The United States, 1877–1919* (New York: W. W. Norton, 1987), esp. 164.

5. On the different meanings of historical periods for women, see Joan Kelly, "Did Women Have a Renaissance?," in *Becoming Visible: Women in European History*, 2d ed., ed. Renate Bridenthal and Claudia Koonz (Boston: Houghton Mifflin, 1987), 175–202. For an analysis of the different patterns of nineteenth-century women's lives, see Carroll Smith-Rosenberg, "The Female World of Love and Ritual," *Signs* 1 (Autumn 1975): 1–29; and Carroll Smith-Rosenberg, "From Puberty to Menopause: Sex Roles and Role Conflict in Nineteenth Century America," in Smith-Rosenberg, *Disorderly Conduct,* 182–96. On the application of women's life cycles to biography, see Carolyn Heilbrun, *Writing a Woman's Life* (New York: Ballantine, 1988); and Sara Alpern, Joyce Antler, Elisabeth Perry, and Ingrid Scobie, "Introduction," in *The Challenge of Feminist Biography,* ed. Sara Alpern, Joyce Antler, Elisabeth Perry, and Ingrid Scobie (Urbana: University of Illinois Press, 1992), 1–15. See AHC diary, 25 Jan., 4 Mar. 1881, CFP, SCL. On "separate spheres," see Barbara Welter, "The Cult of True Womanhood, 1820–1860," *American Quarterly* 18 (1966): 131–75; and Nancy Cott, *The Bonds of Womanhood: "Women's Sphere" in New England, 1780–1835* (New Haven, Conn.: Yale University Press, 1977); and Linda Kerber, "Separate Spheres, Female Worlds, Women's Place: The Rhetoric of Women's History," *Journal of American History* 75 (June 1988): 8–37. For definitions of "public" and "private" and a new interpretation of their intersection, see Mary Ryan, "Introduction," in Mary Ryan, *Women in Public: Between Banners and Ballots, 1825–1880* (Baltimore, Md.: Johns Hopkins University Press, 1990), 3–18. See AHC diary, 10 July 1912, CFP, SCL.

6. AHC to Niels Christensen III, undated manuscript, CFP, SCL.

7. NC, "Descriptive List," 22 Aug. 1870; Georgie Holmes French to AHC, ca. 1919, both in CFP, SCL. See Silber, *Romance of Reunion,* 19–21, on northern standards of masculinity immediately following the Civil War. On southern standards, see Bertram Wyatt-Brown, *Southern Honor: Ethics and Behavior in the Old South* (New York: Oxford University Press, 1982), 117–272; and Ted Ownby, *Subduing Satan: Religion, Recreation and Manhood in the Rural South, 1865–1920* (Chapel Hill: University of North Carolina Press, 1990).

8. AOC, "Ancestors of Niels Christensen, Jr.," 21 Apr. 1902, CE; NC to Chief Signal Corps Officer, 4 Sept. 1870; Niels Christensen Jr. (hereafter NC Jr.) to AHC, 29 July 1935; "In Appreciation," *Beaufort Gazette,* 5 Feb. 1909, clipping; Andrea Christensen Patterson (hereafter ACP) to AHC, 11 Aug. 1938, all in CFP, SCL.

9. Philander Wakin to NC, 14 Jan. 1865; "Til Min Moders Minde," n.d., both in CFP, SCL.

10. Geo. Andrews to NC Jr, 9 Feb. 1914, CFP, SCL. See Joseph Glatthaar, *Forged in Battle: The Civil War Alliance of Black Soldiers and White Officers* (New York: Free Press, 1990).

11. Philander Wakin? to NC, 14 Jan. 1865, CFP, SCL; Glatthaar, *Forged In Battle,* 103, 43.

12. A. W. Mussey, Col. 100th U.S.C.I., and Com'r Org'n U.S.C.T. to NC, 23 Aug. 1864, CFP, SCL; Andrew N. Bowns to NC, 25 Mar. 1865, CFP, SCL; F. W. Root to NC, 1 Apr. 1865, CFP, SCL; "Address of Col. Johnson to the 44th U.S. Colored Infantry," 29 Apr. 1866, clipping, CFP, SCL; Glatthaar, *Forged in Battle,* 87, 98.

13. Powell, *New Masters,* 10; manuscript contract, 10 Mar. 1866; H. W.. Meeker to NC, 14 Mar. 1866; manuscript "Article of Agreement," 24 Mar. 1866; manuscript contract, 15 May 1866; manuscript contract, June 1866; manuscript lien agreement, 1 Aug. 1866; manuscript bill of sale, 20 Aug., 26 Dec. 1866, all in CFP, SCL. On share wage contracts, see Roger Ransom and Richard Sutch, *One Kind of Freedom: The Economic Consequences of Emancipation* (New York: Cambridge University Press, 1977).

14. H. W. Meeker to NC, 8 Feb. 1866; Jo. H. Peck to NC, 18 Aug. 1866; manuscript Letter of Attorney, 27 Oct. 1866; NC to R. W. Johnson, 1 Nov. 1866; R. W. Johnson to NC, 9 Nov. 1866, all in CFP, SCL.

15. Charles A. Saville to NC, 19 Dec. 1868, "Address of Col. Johnson to the 44th U.S. Colored Infantry," 29 Apr. 1866, clipping, both in CFP, SCL; Geo. Andrews to NC Jr, 9 Feb. 1914, CFP, SCL; Powell, *New Masters,* 10, 17; Glatthaar, *Forged in Battle,* 244–45.

16. C. Saville to NC, 13 Jan. 1869; receipt, E. T. Barnum, 16 Jan. 1869; Hugh Higgins to NC, 4 Apr. 1870; AHC, manuscript, ca. June 1918; *Report of the Inspector of National Cemeteries, 1870–1871,* all in CFP, SCL.

17. AHC, typed, undated manuscript, 1–2; NC, manuscript report on cemetery, ca. 1870; *Report of the Inspector of National Cemeteries, 1870–1871;* John Davis to NC, 13 Jan. 1872; John Davis to NC, Dec.? 1872, all in CFP, SCL; Thomas Bender, "The 'Rural' Cemetery Movement: Urban Travail and the Appeal of Nature," in *Material Life in America, 1600–1860,* ed. Robert Blair St. George (Boston: Northeastern University Press, 1988), 505–18; Douglas, *Feminization of American Culture,* 201, 209–13.

18. AH diary, 4, 22 Apr. 1872, CE; Department of Agriculture to NC, 1 Mar. 1872, CFP, SCL.

19. AH diary, 26, 28, 31 Jan., 10, 18, 20–21, 23 Feb., 3, 8, 10 Mar., 4 Apr. 1875, CFP, SCL; AHC, typed manuscript, n.d., 2, CFP, SCL; Abbie Mandana Holmes, "The Story Aunt 'Tilda Told," 14.

20. AH diary, 17 Feb. 1875, CE; AHC to Kathryn Dallas, 4 Jan. 1934, CFP, SCL; AHC, "Folklore on Sea Islands," 204.

21. *New York Independent,* 1874–79; Luther Mott, *A History of American Magazines* (New York: D. Appleton & Co., 1938), 2:367–79; 3:63–65.

22. Thomas Wentworth Higginson, "The Boston Radical Club," *New York Independents,* vol. 26 (5 Nov. 1874); Abbie Mandana Holmes, "The Story Aunt 'Tilda Told," 14.

23. AHC to Niels Christensen III, undated manuscript; manuscript receipts for lumber, from RGH to NC, ? Aug., 12, 15 Sept. 1874; NC to AHC, 14 Sept. 1879, all in CFP, SCL.

24. AH diary, 28, 31 Jan., 2, 7 Feb. 1875, CE; undated typed manuscript on NC; NC to Miss Holmes, ca. Sept. 1874; NC to Miss Holmes, ca. 1874; NC to "Darling," 12 Apr. 1875, all in CFP, SCL.

25. AH diary, 20 Mar. 1875, CE; AH to Olive Holmes Harrington, 15 Mar. 1875; AHC to Niels Christensen III, undated manuscript, both in CFP, SCL.

26. On the new expectations of love and companionship in marriage and the contours of courtship in which these were played out, see Ellen Rothman, *Hands and Hearts: A History of Courtship in America* (New York: Basic Books, 1984).

27. AH diary, 22 Feb., 11–12, 20 Mar. 1875, CE.

28. Heilbrun, *Writing a Woman's Life,* 87–93.

29. AH diary, 28–29 Jan., 19–20, 25 Feb., 29 Mar., 8, 10 Apr. 1875, CE; AH to Olive Holmes Harrington, 15 Mar. 1875, CFP, SCL.

30. AH diary, 28, 31 Jan., 2, 24 Feb., 11 Apr. 1875, CE; AH to Olive Holmes Harrington, CFP, SCL.

31. Silber, *Romance of Reunion,* 21.

32. Sklar, *Catharine Beecher;* Carl Degler, *At Odds: Women and Family in America from the Revolution to the Present* (New York: Oxford University Press, 1980), v–51; Stephen Mintz and Susan Kellogg, *Domestic Revolutions: A Social History of American Family Life* (New York: Macmillan, 1988), 43–66; Daniel Scott Smith, "Family Limitation, Sexual Control and Domestic Feminism in Victorian America," *Feminist Studies* 1 (winter–spring 1973): 40–57; Douglas, *Feminization of American Culture.* On the law and limits of companionate marriage, see Susan Lebsock, *The Free Women of Petersburg: Status and Culture in a Southern Town, 1784–1860* (New York: W. W. Norton, 1984), 17–33.

33. AHC to Emma, 1 July, 20 Aug. 1875, CFP, SCL.

34. Ibid.; Virginia Burr, ed., *The Secret Eye: The Journal of Ella Gertrude Clanton Thomas, 1848–1889* (Chapel Hill: University of North Carolina Press, 1990), 122, 280; Nell Painter, "Introduction," in Burr, *The Secret Eye,* 1–67.

35. AHC to Emma Holmes, 1 July, 20 Aug. 1875; Niels to "Goosie Dear," 10 July 1875; Niels to Abbie, n.d.; Niels to "Goosie Dear," n.d. all in CFP, SCL. The Danish phrases are translated as "your loving husband" and "your little wife."

36. AHC to Emma Holmes, 1 July, 20 Aug. 1875; AHC, typed undated manuscript, 7, CFP, SCL. On women and the material culture of middle-class homes, see Harvey Green, *The Light of the Home: An Intimate View of the Lives of Women in Victorian America* (New York: Pantheon, 1983).

37. "The motherless" was a term Christensen adopted from sea island African Americans. See AHC diary, 21 Jan. 1881, CFP, SCL, and Laura Towne's references to the "mudderless" in Holland, *Letters and Diary of Laura M. Towne*, 190. AHC diary, 17, 18, 20–21, 26, 27 Jan., 10, 15, 22, 24–26, 28 Feb., 3–4, 5, 7, 14 Mar. 1881; "Program Round-About Club," 1881, all in CFP, SCL. Mrs. A[bbie] M[andana] Christensen, "Negro Folklore: The Elephant and the Rabbit," *New York Independent* 27 (28 Oct. 1875): 25; Mrs. A[bbie] [andana] H[olmes] Christensen, "A Story-Teller," *New York Independent* 27 (28 Oct. 1875): 26; Mrs. A[bbie] M[andana] Christensen, "The Rabbit, the Wolf, and the Keg of Butter: A Negro Legend," *New York Independent* 27 (18 Nov. 1875): 27; Mrs. A[bbie] H[olmes] M[andana] Christensen, "Negro Folk Lore: The Rabbit Desires a Long Tail," *New York Independent* (9 Mar. 1876): 26; Mrs. A[bbie] M[andana] Christensen, "The Reason Why Brother Rabbit Wears a Short Tail: A Negro Legend," *New York Independent* 28 (1 June 1876): 25–26; and Mrs. Abbie M[andana] Christensen, "The Rabbit and the Wolf Plant Potatoes and Hunt Honey," *New York Independent* 29 (1 Nov. 1877): 26.

38. AHC to Emma Holmes, 1 July, 20 Aug. 1875; AHC diary, 25 Jan., 4 Mar. 1881; 10 July 1912, all in CFP, SCL. On public and private spheres, see Barbara Welter, "The Cult of True Womanhood, 1820–1860," *American Quarterly* 18 (1966): 131–75; and Nancy Cott, *The Bonds of Womanhood: "Woman's Sphere" in New England, 1780–1835* (New Haven, Conn.: Yale University Press, 1977); and Linda Kerber, "Separate Spheres, Female Worlds, Women's Place: The Rhetoric of Women's History," *Journal of American History* 75 (June 1988): 8–37. For definitions of "public" and "private" and a new interpretation of their intersection, see Mary Ryan, "Introduction," in Mary Ryan, ed., *Women in Public: Between Banners and Ballots, 1825–1880* (Baltimore, Md.: Johns Hopkins University Press, 1990), 3–18.

39. Geo W. McCrasy? to Alfred Williams, 1 Jan. 1878; NC to AHC, 7 Sept. 1879; AHC to NC Jr., 2 Dec. 1888, all in CFP, SCL. On Niels Christensen's business, see "N. Christensen," *Palmetto Post*, 12 Jan. 1882; "Palmetto Leaves," *Palmetto Post*, 18 May 1882; and "Beaufort Happenings," *Palmetto Post*, 24 Apr. 1884, 29 Nov. 1888.

For NC's real estate dealings see, for example, Deeds: Richard Simmons to NC (ten acres of land) and "NC to Richard Simmons" (one bay horse and colt); rental agreement, NC to Richard Simmons, 14 Aug. 1875, all in CFP, SCL. See also "Sheriff's Sale. State of South Carolina, Beaufort County. N. Christensen vs. J. E. Hayne," *Palmetto Post,* 22 Mar. 1888; "Sheriff's Sale. State of South Carolina, Beaufort County. N. Christensen vs. John Barnwell," *Palmetto Post,* 19 July 1888; "In Appreciation," *Beaufort Gazette,* 5 Feb. 1909; "Beaufort Comes Out All Right," *Charleston News and Courier,* 1 Jan. 1889; and McGuire, "Getting Their Hands on the Land," 152–53.

40. ? to Maj. R. N. Batchelder, 17 Oct. 1885, copy, CFP, SCL; "Gentle Spring. The Beautiful Flower Gardens of Beaufort," *Palmetto Post,* 5 Apr. 1888.

41. *1880 U.S. Census,* vol. 1: *Population* (Washington, D.C.: Government Printing Office, 1882), 407; Edward King, *The Great South* (Hartford, Conn.: American Publishing, 1875), 427; "The Sea Islands," *Harper's* 57 (Nov. 1878): 856.

42. Miller, *Gullah Statesman,* 70–73, 113–39; William Harrison Shirley Jr, "A Black Republican Congressman during the Democratic Resurgence in South Carolina: Robert Smalls, 1876–1882" (Master's thesis, University of South Carolina, 1970), 32–47; Holland, *Letters and Diary of Laura M. Towne,* 252–55, 269–74, 279, 283–84, 289–93. On the racial and political climate of the 1880s, see Eric Anderson, *Race and Politics in North Carolina, 1872–1901: The Black Second* (Baton Rouge: Louisiana State University Press, 1981); Holt, *Black over White,* 208–24; and C. Vann Woodward, *The Strange Career of Jim Crow,* 3d ed. (New York: Oxford University Press, 1974), 31–66.

43. Certificate from the governor of South Carolina appointing N. Christensen commissioner of elections for Beaufort County, 5 Sept. 1878; NC Jr to AHC, 9 July 1934, both in CFP, SCL; Holland, *Letters and Diary of Laura M. Towne,* 291–92; William Cooper, *Conservative Regime,* 94–97; Tindall, *South Carolina Negroes,* 33–36; Holt, *Black over White,* 215; Shirley, "A Black Republican Congressman," 33–40. Arthur Gelston, "Radical Versus Straight-out in Post-Reconstruction Beaufort County," *South Carolina Historical Magazine* 75 (October 1974), 231.

44. Tindall, *South Carolina Negroes,* 55–56, 61–64.

45. NC to AHC, 24 July 1886; 21 May 1893; NC, "The Sea Islands and Negro Supremacy," 1888?; NC, manuscript attached to clipping, ca. 1884; NC, manuscript, ca. 1890; NC and Cole Townsend to the Intendant and Wardens of the Town of Beaufort, 7 Sept. 1891; S. Wheeler to "Esteemed Friend," 1 Nov. 1891; NC to AHC, 29 Oct. 1894, all in CFP, SCL; "Who Signed against Smalls," *Palmetto Post,* 1 Aug. 888. On "Intendant" as "head of city government" see Fraser, *Charleston! Charleston!,* 443.

46. Miller, *Gullah Statesman,* 142, 182–244, 249; NC to AHC, 28 Sept. 1879, CFP, SCL; AHC diary, 15 Mar. 1881, CFP, SCL. Gelston, "Radical Versus Straight-out," 231.

47. NC to AHC, 21 Sept. 1879; 24 July 1886, CFP, SCL.

48. NC to AHC, 21 May 1893, CFP, SCL.

49. NC, "The Sea Islands and Negro Supremacy," manuscript 1888?, CFP, SCL; Wade Hampton, "What Negro Supremacy Means," *Forum* 5 (June 1888): 383–95. On the first Charles Cotesworth Pinckney, see Fraser, *Charleston! Charleston!,* 176; and Marvin Zahniser, *Charles Cotesworth Pinckney, Founding Father* (Chapel Hill: University of North Carolina Press, 1967). Rev. Charles Cotesworth Pinckney was also the author of *The Life of General Thomas Pinckney* (Boston: Houghton Mifflin, 1895).

50. AHC to NC Jr., ca. 1888; NC to AHC, 21 May 1893, both in CFP, SCL; *Charleston News and Courier,* 8 July 1892, 20–22 Apr. 1893; Kantrowitz, *Ben Tillman,* 174–81; Tindall, *South Carolina Negroes,* 253; Williamson, *Crucible of Race,* 133.

51. AHC diary, 21 Apr. 1876, 2 Jan. 1881, CFP, SCL.

52. Degler, *At Odds,* 52–85; AHC diary, 22–23 Apr., 5 May, 12–14 June 1876, passim, CFP, SCL; *Homeopathic Medical Primer* (Baltimore, Md.: Waverly Press, n.d.), CFP, SCL. AHC to AOC & Helen Eddy Christensen, 18–19 Aug. 1913 (in the possession of Paul Sommerville, Beaufort, S.C.) On homeopathic publications, see Ronald Numbers, "Do-It-Yourself the Sectarian Way," in *Medicine without Doctors: Home Health Care in American History,* ed. Guenter Risse, Ronald Numbers, and Judith Walzer Leavitt (New York: Science History Publications, 1977), 59.

53. "Holmes, Abbie Mandana, Association of Collegiate Alumnae—Census of College Women, 1915," in Mount Holyoke College Archives, South Hadley, Mass.; AHC diary, 3 Jan. 1881, CFP, SCL.

54. AHC diary, 22 Jan. 1881, CFP, SCL; Frances Willard, "The Doll Question," *Union Signal,* 5 July 1888, 9.

55. AHC diary, 21 Apr. 1876, CFP, SCL; AHC diary, 15–16, 18, 23, 30 Jan., 6, 13, 20, 27 Feb., 5 Mar. 1881, CFP, SCL; AHC to AOC, 25 Mar. 1913 (in the possession of Paul Sommerville, Beaufort, S.C.).

56. NC to "Nielie boy," 20 Aug. 1879; AHC to NC Jr., 2 Dec. 1888; NC to WC, Dec. 1892; NC to AOC, Dec. 1892; NC to NC Jr., 1 Jan. 1893; AHC to NC, 2 Sept. 1890, all in CFP, SCL.

57. AHC to NC Jr., 9, 21 Oct., 12, 22 Nov., 2, 5, 23, 26 Dec. 1888, CFP, SCL.

58. "National School Diary," Frederik Christensen, 14 May–24 Dec. 1886; AHC to FHC, 23 May 1903, both in CFP, SCL.

59. "Beaufort Happenings," *Palmetto Post,* 15 Oct. 1885. ? to Major R. N. Batchelder, 17 Oct. 1885, copied by NC; "Copy of Jamie Winch's first letter," 17 Sept. 1885; NC to AHC, 10 July 1887; undated clipping, "Obituaries"; NC to AHC, 25 July 1886; 10 July, 11 Sept. 1887, all in CFP, SCL.

60. See Gail Thain Parker, *Mind Cure in New England from the Civil War to World War I* (Hanover, N.H.: University Press of New England, 1973); and Charles M. Barrows, *Bread-Pills: A Study of Mind-Cure* (Boston: Deland and Barta, 1885). See also AHC to AOC, ca. 1915 (in the possession of Paul Sommerville, Beaufort, S.C.). AOC, typed manuscript, 1918?; Addie Barrows to AHC, 16, 17 Oct. 1885; 26, 31 Mar. 1892; AHC to NC, 23 Oct., 25 July 1886; 26 June, 20 July, 1 Nov. 1888; NC to AHC, 24, 31 July, 27 Oct. 1886; C. M. Barrows to FHC, 22 Dec. 1889; Addie Barrows to FHC, 10 Dec. 1888; AHC to NC Jr., 20 Oct., 12, 22 Nov. 1888; NC to AHC, 17, 19, 20, 31 Aug., 7, 14, 21, 28 Sept. 1879, all in CFP, SCL. It is not clear how Christensen and Barrows met. The meaning of "cranky" in this context is "overzealous."

61. "Obituary," unidentified clipping, probably *Worcester (Mass.) Daily Spy,* 1882, Herbert Greenwood (American News Company) to AHC, 6 May 1927, both in CFP, SCL; AOC, "Alden Winch," in "Genealogy of Niels Christensen, Jr., Apr. 21, 1902, CE," List of land sales of Ledbetter home (Pringle).

62. Suzanne Lebsock, "Radical Reconstruction and the Property Rights of Southern Women," *Journal of Southern History* 2 (May 1977): 195–216, esp. 198–202.

63. AHC to NC, 17 June, 7, 19, 20 July, 13, 17, 21, 23 Aug., 20, 30 Sept., 12, 19, 24, 25 Oct. 1888; AHC diary, 8 Mar. 1911; AHC diary, 13 Jan. 1912, all in CFP, SCL. See also "Beaufort Happenings," *Palmetto Post,* 5 July 1888; *Brookline Directory,* 1891–95; *Blue Book,* 1891–95; *Spencer's Brookline Directory,* 1894–97; and *Yearbook of the Brookline Education Society,* 1896–1900 (Brookline, Mass.: Riverdale), all in Brookline Room, Brookline Public Library, Brookline, Mass.

64. Heilbrun, *Writing a Woman's Life,* 94–95. See NC to AHC, 2 Oct. 1887; AHC to NC, 7 July 1888; and other correspondence between AHC and NC, all in CFP, SCL.

65. On the changing view of children in Victorian America, see Viviana Zelizer, *Pricing the Priceless Child: The Changing Social Value of Children* (New York: Basic Books, 1985).

66. AHC to NC, 16 Oct. 1887, CFP, SCL; AOC to Lillian Dutton (in possession of Paul Sommerville, Beaufort, S.C.), n.d., ca. 1919. Carroll Eve, interview by author, Pleasantview, Va., 30 Sept. 1991.

67. AHC to NC, 20 July, 23 Sept., 2 Dec. 1888; FC to NC, 11 Oct. 1891; NC to FC, Jan. 1893, all in CFP, SCL.

68. Addie Barrows to AHC, 15 Apr. 1892, CFP, SCL.

69. Georgie to AHC, 5 Sept 1890; NC to AWC, 14 Feb. 1892, both in CFP, SCL.

70. Joyce Antler, "Was She a Good Mother: Some Thoughts on a New Issue for Feminist Biography," in *Women and the Structure of Society: Papers from the Fifth Berkshire Conference on the History of Women,* ed. Barbara Harris and Jo Ann McNamara (Durham, N.C.: Duke University Press, 1984), 53–66; "Having It All, Almost: Confronting the Legacy of Lucy Sprague Mitchell," in *The Challenge of Feminist Biography,* ed. Sara Alpern et al., 95–115; *Lucy Sprague Mitchell: The Making of a Modern Woman* (New Haven: Yale University Press, 1987), 360–62.

71. On child-rearing in the nineteenth century, see Philippe Aries, *Centuries of Childhood: A Social History of Family Life,* translated by Robert Baldick (New York: Random House, 1962); Mintz and Kellogg, *Domestic Revolutions,* 43–66; Degler, *At Odds,* 66–110.

72. "Holmes, Abbie Mandana, Association of Collegiate Alumnae—Census of College Women, 1915," in Mount Holyoke College Archives, South Hadley, Mass.; FHC diary, vol. 12, 7 Feb. 1915, SCL; "Why We Are Suffragists," *Beaufort Gazette,* 9 July 1915; Ida Harper, ed., *The History of Woman Suffrage* (New York: National American Woman Suffrage Association, 1922), 6:583–84; FHC diary, vol. 14, 30 Aug. 1922, SCL; AHC to AOC, 23 Apr. 1918; AOC to Lillian Dutton, 27 Dec. 1919, 3 Jan. 1920 (both in the possession of Paul Sommerville, Beaufort, S.C.).

73. NC to AHC, 17, 20 Aug., 7, 21, 28 Sept. 1879; AHC to NC, 15 Oct. 1887, all in CFP, SCL.

74. AHC to Sylvia, 7 July 1888, CFP, SCL.

75. AHC diary, 30 May, 31 Oct. 1876, CFP, SCL; NC to AHC, 20 Aug., 7, 21, 28 Sept. 1879, CFP, SCL; AHC diary, 23 Jan. 1881, CFP, SCL; unidentified photographs, CFP, SCL; AHC to NC, 1 Sept. 1910, CFP, SCL; Mona Brown to AHC, 30 June 1912; 19 July 1914, CFP, SCL; John Simmons to AHC, 4 Oct. 1915, CFP, SCL; Essie to AHC, 15 Aug. 1922, CFP, SCL; Katzman, *Seven Days a Week.* On servant invisibility see Judith Rollins, *Between Women: Domestics and Their Employers* (Philadelphia, Pa.: Temple University Press, 1985), 207–32. On race and servants in the South, see Susan Tucker, *Telling Memories among Southern Women: Domestic Workers and Their Employers in the Segregated South* (Baton Rouge: Louisiana State University Press, 1988).

76. AHC diary, 23–24 Jan. 1881, CFP, SCL. See Tucker, *Telling Memories,* 270, 279; Jacqueline Jones, *Labor of Love,* 79–110; and Elizabeth Clark-Lewis, *Living In, Living Out: African American Domestics in Washington, D.C., 1910–1940* (Washington D.C.:

Smithsonian Institution Press, 1994); and Victoria Austin, interview by author, Port Royal, S.C., 21 Nov. 1991.

77. AHC diary, 14, 16 Jan. 1881, CFP, SCL.

78. AHC to Kathryn Dallas, 4 Jan. 1934, CFP, SCL.

79. D. Lothrop & Co. to AHC, 26 July 1883, CFP, SCL.

80. AHC, "Folklore on Sea Islands," 204; AHC to Kathryn Dallas, 4 Jan. 1934, CFP, SCL.

Chapter 7

1. AHC to "Boys," 4 July 1892, CFP, SCL.

2. Barbara Bellows, *Benevolence among Slaveholders: Assisting the Poor in Charleston, 1670–1860* (Baton Rouge: Louisiana State University Press, 1993), 43–51; Elizabeth Fox-Genovese, *Within the Plantation Household: Black and White Women of the Old South* (Chapel Hill: University of North Carolina Press, 1988), 58–82; Jean Friedman, *The Enclosed Garden: Women and Community in the Evangelical South, 1830–1900* (Chapel Hill: University of North Carolina Press, 1985), xi–xvi, 110–27; Lebsock, *Free Women of Petersburg,* 195–249. For works that examine the changes wrought during and after the Civil War, see Painter, "Introduction," 1–71; John McDowell, *The Social Gospel in the South: The Woman's Home Mission Movement of the Methodist Episcopal Church, South, 1886–1939* (Baton Rouge: Louisiana State University Press, 1982), 1–35; Anne Scott, *The Southern Lady: From Pedestal to Politics, 1830–1930* (Chicago: University of Chicago Press, 1970); and Silber, *Romance of Reunion.*

3. Kantrowitz, *Ben Tillman,* 158–97, lynching statistics on 165; Ida B. Wells, *Southern Horrors and Other Writings: The Anti-Lynching Campaign of Ida B. Wells* (Boston: Bedford, 1997), 152; Logan, *Negro in American Life;* Woodward, *Strange Career of Jim Crow;* John Cell, *The Highest Stage of White Supremacy: The Origins of Segregation in South Africa and the American South* (New York: Cambridge University Press, 1982); Williamson, *Crucible of Race;* William Cooper, *Conservative Regime;* Tindall, *South Carolina Negroes;* Rose, *Rehearsal for Reconstruction,* 378–408; Rosalyn Terborg-Penn, *African American Women in the Struggle for the Vote, 1850–1920* (Bloomington: Indiana University Press, 1998); Paula Baker, "The Domestication of Politics: Women and American Political Society, 1780–1920," *American Historical Review* 89 (June 1984): 620–47; Aileen Kraditor, *The Ideas of the Woman Suffrage Movement, 1890–1920* (1965; rev. ed., New York: W. W. Norton, 1981), 163–218. On prejudice in the North, see "Sarcastic: The

Negro North of the Mason Dixon Line" (extract from the *New York Sun*), *Palmetto Post,* 11 Oct. 1894.

4. AHC, notes "For the Moral Education Association," 18 Apr. 1895, CFP, SCL; Anne Scott, *Southern Lady,* 141; Dorothy Bass, "'Their Prodigious Influence': Women, Religion, and Reform in Antebellum America," in *Women of Spirit: Female Leadership in the Jewish and Christian Traditions,* ed. Rosemary Ruether and Eleanor McLaughlin (New York: Simon and Schuster, 1979), 279–300.

5. AHC, "The Beginning of the Carteret St. Church," undated manuscript, CFP, SCL; AHC, undated typed manuscript, CFP, SCL; E. H. Botume to AHC, 9 Oct. 1883, CFP, SCL; AHC, undated typed manuscript, CFP, SCL; "Rules for the temporal government of the Corporation of the Carteret Street Union Church Society," 22 May 1884, papers donated by Carroll Eve to Carteret Street Methodist Church, Beaufort, S.C.

6. Holland, *Letters and Diary of Laura M. Towne,* 129, 177–78; Williamson, *After Slavery,* 275–99; Howard Rabinowitz, *Race Relations in the Urban South, 1865–1890* (1978; rev. ed., Urbana: University of Illinois Press, 1980), 198–225; C. Eric Lincoln and Lawrence Mamiya, *The Black Church in the African American Experience* (Durham, N.C.: Duke University Press, 1990); James Melvin Washington, *Frustrated Fellowship: The Black Baptist Quest for Social Power* (Macon, Ga.: Mercer University Press, 1985). On Beaufort's Episcopal church, see History Committee, St. Helena Episcopal Church, Beaufort, S.C., *History of the Parish Church of St. Helena.*

7. Cuta Wallace to AHC, 21 May 1884; F. E. Stuart, Chairs and Settees to AHC, 22, 31 Mar., 7 June 1884; Jas. G. Bailie Carpets to AHC, 28 Mar. 1884; Harwood Manufacturing to AHC, 16 July, 22 Aug., 10 Sept. 1884, all in CFP, SCL; AHC, "The Beginning of the Carteret St. Church," undated manuscript; AHC, undated typed manuscript, both in Carteret Street Methodist Church, Beaufort, S.C. On the church as public space for women, see Ruth Bordin, *Frances Willard: A Biography* (Chapel Hill: University of North Carolina Press, 1986), 8–9; Evelyn Brooks Higginbotham, *Righteous Discontent: The Women's Movement in the Black Baptist Church, 1880–1920* (Cambridge: Harvard University Press, 1993), 10–11; and Anne Firor Scott, *Southern Lady,* 141. See also Barbara Epstein, *The Politics of Domesticity: Women, Evangelism and Temperance in Nineteenth-Century America* (Middletown, Conn.: Wesleyan University Press, 1981); and Bass, "'Their Prodigious Influence,'" 279–300.

8. "The Beginning of the Carteret St. Church," undated manuscript; AHC, undated typed manuscript, "Rules for the temporal government of the Corporation of the Carteret Street Union Church Society," 22 May 1884, both in Carteret Street

Methodist Church, Beaufort, S.C.; "Carteret Street Methodist Church," *The Sea Islander,* 22 Mar. 1965.

9. "Carteret Union Church in a/c with N. Christensen," n.d.; NC to AHC, 29 Oct. 1894, both in CFP, SCL; *A Guide to Historic Beaufort* (Beaufort, S.C.: Historic Beaufort Foundation, 1970), 102. In later years Abbie Christensen and the Ladies Aid Society of the Carteret Street Church raised funds for a parsonage and a Sunday school library. See "A Leap-Year Sociable," *Palmetto Post,* 19 Apr. 1888.

10. There are many references to New Thought ideas in the Christensen Papers. See, for example, Dr. Neal Aradyne, "Why I believe in the more abundant Life," n.d.; and *Unity Scientific Christianity Church Bulletin,* 17 Oct. 1926, both in CFP, SCL. See also Charles Braden, *Spirits in Rebellion: The Rise and Development of New Thought* (Dallas, Tex.: Southern Methodist University Press, 1963), 153; Sidney Ahlstrom, *A Religious History of the American People* (New Haven, Conn.: Yale University Press, 1972), 1019, 1026–27. See AHC to Miss Hunn, 27 July 1883; AHC to AOC, 30 Aug. 1915; New England Sanitarium Dinner Menu, 4 Sept. 1915; and ACP to AHC, 13 Mar. 1920, all in CFP, SCL. On women's interest in alternative medicine, see Rogers, "Women and Sectarian Medicine," 273–302; and Susan Cayleff, "Gender, Ideology and the Water Cure Movement," in *Other Healers: Unorthodox Medicine in America,* ed. Norman Gevitz (Baltimore, Md.: Johns Hopkins University Press, 1988), 82–98.

11. See Regina Markell Morantz, "Nineteenth Century Health Reform and Women: A Program of Self-Help," in *Medicine without Doctors: Home Health Care in American History,* ed. Guenter Risse, Ronald Numbers, and Judith Leavitt (New York: Science History Publications, 1977), 73–93. On such homeopathic publications, see Numbers, "Do-It-Yourself the Sectarian Way," 59.

12. Addie Barrows to AHC, 17 Oct. 1885; AHC to NC, 24, 28 June 1888; AHC to NC Jr., 20 Oct., 12 Nov., 23, 25 Dec. 1888, all in CFP, SCL.

13. Eunice Hale Cobb and Sylvanus Cobb, *The Memoir of James Arthur Cobb,* 2d ed. (Boston: S. Cobb, 1852); Douglas, *Feminization of American Culture,* 204–13; Zelizer, *Pricing the Priceless Child,* 26; AHC to NC, 25 July 1886; 24 June 1888, CFP, SCL.

14. AOC on C. M. Barrows, typed manuscripts, 1918?; Addie Barrows to AHC, 17 Oct. 1885; Charles M. Barrows, *Bread-Pills,* 42, 75, 85, all in CFP, SCL; Parker, *Mind Cure,* ix, passim; Donald Meyer, *The Positive Thinkers: A Study of the American Quest for Health, Wealth and Personal Power from Mary Baker Eddy to Norman Vincent Peale* (New York: Doubleday, 1965); Richard M. Huber, *The American Idea of Success* (New York: McGraw-Hill, 1971). Charles Braden writes that Barrows was

one of the first to connect Emerson with mind cure or New Thought; see Braden, *Spirits in Rebellion*, 161, 153.

15. Douglas, *Feminization of American Culture*, 138; AHC, notes "For the Moral Education Association," 18 April 1895, 4, 6–7, CFP, SCL. Parker, *Mind Cure*, 18–21.

16. AHC to AOC, 5 Feb. 1906; AHC to NC, March 1894; AHC to AOC, 19 May 1903, 21 Jan. 1906; AHC, "From Emerson's Journal," ms., n.d., all in CFP, SCL. Ralph Waldo Emerson, "The Oversoul," in *Essays First Series* (1841); repr. in *Ralph Waldo Emerson: Selected Essays, Lectures, and Poems*, ed. Robert Richardson (New York: Bantam Books, 1990), 172–88. William Hutchison, *The Transcendentalist Ministers: Church Reform in the New England Renaissance* (Boston: Beacon Press, 1959), 142–52; Edelstein, *Strange Enthusiasm*, 42. For insight into another nineteenth-century reforming woman liberated by Unitarianism, see Mary Livermore, *The Story of My Life* (1897; repr., New York: Arno Press, 1974), 40–41, 53–64, 135–42, 379–80, 384–97. See also "Abbie M. Holmes Christensen, Beaufort, SC and Brookline, MA; Niels Christensen, Frederik Holmes Christensen," 6 Jan. 1895, names of members, Church of the Disciples, Boston, Mass.

17. AHC, notes "For the Moral Education Association," 18 Apr. 1895, CFP, SCL; 1894–95 Notebook, "Disciples Br[anch] of Women's Alliance," 12 March 1895, Church of the Disciples, Boston, Mass. On the nineteenth-century idea of "vital force," or energy of the body, see Charles Rosenberg, "The Therapeutic Revolution," in *Explaining Epidemics and Other Studies in the History of Medicine* (Cambridge: Cambridge University Press, 1992), 9–31.

18. AHC, notes "For the Moral Education Association," 18 Apr. 1895, CFP, SCL.

19. Ruth Bordin, *Woman and Temperance: The Quest for Power and Liberty, 1873–1900* (1981; repr., New Brunswick, N.J.: Rutgers University Press, 1990), 3, 95, passim; Epstein, *Politics of Domesticity*, 89–151; AHC, typed manuscript, n.d., 14; RGH, "reminiscences," 1905?, 104–9; AHC to NC, 25 July 1886, all in CFP, SCL; AH diary, 3 Feb., 6 Mar., 26 May 1871, CE.

20. Holland, *Letters and Diary of Laura M. Towne*, 216–17, 220, 284, 296; *Annual Report of the Penn School*, 1898, York Bailey Library, Penn Center, St. Helena Island, S.C.

21. "Port Royal the Nightmare of Savannah," *Palmetto Post*, 12 July 1888; "The Cause of Temperance," *Palmetto Post*, 18 Mar. 1886; "Mr. Hay's Sermon," *Palmetto Post*, 8 Apr. 1886; S. F. Chapin, "Southern Correspondence," *Union Signal*, 4 Jan. 1888, 4; Frances Willard, "Tidings from the South," *Union Signal*, 23 Feb. 1888; "Beaufort Happenings," *Palmetto Post*, 19 Jan., 26 Apr. 1888; Bordin, *Frances Willard*, 114; AHC to NC Jr., 23 Dec. 1888, CFP, SCL. On Mary Hamilton, see

AHC diary, 29 Jan., 20 Feb. 2, 23, Mar., 9 Apr. 1920; AHC diary, 20 June 1922, CFP, SCL.

22. AHC to NC Jr., 2 Dec. 1888, CFP, SCL; "Anti-treating pledge," 1888, CFP, SCL; AHC, "Band of Hope," manuscript, 23 June 1890, CFP, SCL; "B. of H." manuscript, 12 May, 24 June, n.d., CFP, SCL; "Band of Hope Anniversary," *Palmetto Post,* 17 May 1888.

23. AHC to NC, 17 June, 16, 17, 21 Aug. 1888; AHC to NC Jr., 1, 12 Nov., 5 Dec. 1888; 13 Feb. 1889; abstention pledge cards signed by NC Jr., FC, and ARC, all in CFP, SCL.

24. "Annual Meeting of the Stockholders of W.T.P.A.," *Union Signal,* 19 Jan. 1888, 8; "A Good Investment for Women," *Union Signal,* 16 Feb. 1888, 8; "From the Watch Tower," *Union Signal,* 4 Oct. 1888, 9; Kathryn Kish Sklar, *Florence Kelley and the Nation's Work: The Rise of Women's Political Culture, 1830–1900* (New Haven, Conn.: Yale University Press, 1995), 151.

25. Bordin, *Frances Willard,* xi–13; Robert Wiebe, *The Search for Order: 1877–1920* (New York: Hill and Wang, 1967), 63; AHC to NC Jr., 7 Apr. 1889, CFP, SCL. Whittier was a beloved abolitionist poet, and Brooks was considered the abolitionist movement's most eloquent speaker.

26. Frances Willard, "Correspondence," *Union Signal,* 25 Apr. 1889, 4.

27. Bordin, *Frances Willard,* 113–16; Frances Willard, "Correspondence," *Union Signal,* 25 Apr. 1889, 4; Fredrickson, *Black Image,* 198–227.

28. Frances Willard, "Correspondence," *Union Signal,* 25 Apr. 1889, 4; AHC to NC Jr., 7 Apr. 1889, CFP, SCL.

29. "From the Watch Tower," *Union Signal,* 4 Oct. 1888; Frances Willard, "Correspondence," *Union Signal,* 25 Apr. 1889; "Annual Meeting of the Stockholders of W.T.P.A.," *Union Signal,* 23 Jan. 1890.

30. "Programme of the Massachusetts Woman's Christian Temperance Union 16th Annual Convention," 8–10 Oct., 1889, CFP, SCL; F[rances] E[llen] W[atkins] [Harper] to AHC, n.d., CFP, SCL; AHC to "Miss W.," n.d., CFP, SCL; E. H. C. Cutter to AHC, Jan. 1896, CFP, SCL; Mary S. Hamilton to AHC, 21 Feb. 1901, CFP, SCL; FC to AHC, 24 Feb. 1901, CFP, SCL; Niels Christensen, typed manuscript for David Duncan Wallace, *History of South Carolina,* bio. vol. (New York: American Historical Society, Inc., 1934), 3–4, CFP, SCL; Francis Butler Simkins, *Pitchfork Ben Tillman: South Carolinian* (Gloucester, Mass.: Peter Smith, 1964), 234–61, 458; David Duncan Wallace, *South Carolina: A Short History, 1520–1948* (1951; repr. Columbia: University of South Carolina Press, 1966), 653–59.

31. Paula Baker, "Domestication of Politics," 620–47; Ellen DuBois, "The Radicalism of the Woman Suffrage Movement: Notes toward the Reconstruction of Nineteenth-Century Feminism," *Feminist Studies* 3 (fall 1975): 63–71.

32. Judith Wellman, "The Seneca Falls Women's Rights Convention: A Study of Social Networks," *Journal of Women's History* 3 (spring 1991): 9–37; Barbara Berg, *The Remembered Gate: Origins of American Feminism* (New York: Oxford University Press, 1978); Kerr, *Lucy Stone*, 59–60; Rice, *The Worcester Book.*

33. Ellen DuBois, *Feminism and Suffrage: The Emergence of an Independent Women's Movement in America, 1848–1869* (Ithaca, N.Y.: Cornell University Press, 1978); Eleanor Flexner, *Century of Struggle: The Women's Rights Movement in the United States* (1959; rev. ed., Cambridge: Harvard University Press, 1975); Kraditor, *Ideas of the Woman Suffrage Movement;* William O'Neill, *Everyone Was Brave: The History of Feminism in America* (Chicago: Quadrangle, 1969); Anne Firor Scott and Andrew MacKay Scott, *One Half the People: The Fight for Woman Suffrage* (Urbana: University of Illinois Press, 1982).

34. Kerr, *Lucy Stone*, 4; Edelstein, *Strange Enthusiasm*, 147–50.

35. Kerr, *Lucy Stone*, 206–37; DuBois, *Feminism and Suffrage*, 27–29, 163, 188–200; Alice Stone Blackwell, *Lucy Stone: Pioneer of Woman's Rights* (Norwood, Mass.: Plimpton Press, 1930).

36. Lucy Stone to AHC, 28 July 1889, 30 Jan. 1892; n.d. 1892? Myra D. Gage to AHC, 16 Dec. 1890; AHC to NC Jr., 31 Mar. 1892; Olive Schreiner, "Three Dreams in a Desert," *Woman Suffrage Leaflet* 27 (Sept. 1889), all in CFP, SCL; AHC to Alice Stone Blackwell, 30 Jan. 1923, 14 Dec. 1931, Blackwell Family Papers, Library of Congress, Washington, D.C.; Marjorie Spruill Wheeler, *New Women of the New South: The Leaders of the Woman Suffrage Movement in the Southern States* (New York: Oxford University Press, 1993), 47–48, 63.

37. Bordin, *Frances Willard*, 100–108; Bordin, *Woman and Temperance*, 56–61, 147.

38. Barbara Bellows Ulmer, "Virginia Durant Young: New South Suffragist" (M.A. thesis, University of South Carolina, 1979), 3–4, 9–12.

39. Ibid., 13–33. See also Antoinette Elizabeth Taylor, "South Carolina and the Enfranchisement of Women: The Early Years," *South Carolina Historical Magazine* (Apr. 1976), 115–126.

40. Ulmer, "Virginia Durant Young," 15–18; Virginia Young to Editors, *Woman's Journal*, 19 Apr. 1892, clipping, CFP, SCL.

41. Wheeler, *New Women*, 17, 20–23; Susan B. Anthony and Ida Harper et al., eds., *The History of Woman Suffrage* (Rochester, N.Y.: Susan B. Anthony, 1902), 4:923.

42. Virginia Durant Young (hereafter VDY), "Names of E.R.A."; Miss A. E. Scammon to AHC, 12 June 1892; Marian Gage to AHC, n.d.; AHC to AOC, 26 Dec. 1902, all in CFP, SCL.

43. Blanche Wiesen Cooke, "Female Support Networks and Political Activism: Lillian Wald, Crystal Eastman, Emma Goldman," in *A Heritage of Her Own: Toward a New Social History of American Women,* ed. Nancy Cott and Elizabeth Pleck (New York: Simon and Schuster, 1979), 412–44; Silber, *Romance of Reunion.*

44. VDY to AHC, 21 Mar., 8–9, 16 May, 12–13 June, 20 Nov. 1892; 27 Apr. 1905, CFP, SCL; VDY, "Names of E.R.A.," n.d., CFP, SCL; AHC to NC Jr., 31 Mar. 1892, CFP, SCL; Ulmer, "Virginia Durant Young," 96–98.

45. Kerr, *Lucy Stone,* 230; Kraditor, *Ideas of the Woman Suffrage Movement,* 163–218; Flexner, *Century of Struggle,* 316–18; Suzanne Lebsock, "Women and American Politics, 1880–1920," in *Women, Politics and Change,* ed. Louise Tilly and Patricia Gurin (New York: Russell Sage Foundation, 1990), 35–62; Wheeler, *New Women,* 101, 113–20.

46. Mrs. Virginia D. Young, "The Star in the West," *Woman Suffrage Leaflet* 6 (Jan. 1893); NC to AHC, 16 Apr. 1895, both in CFP, SCL.

47. NC to AHC, 20 Apr. 1893, CFP, SCL; "Programme of the Massachusetts Woman's Christian Temperance Union 16th Annual Convention," 8–10 Oct. 1889, CFP, SCL; "Programme," Anti-Slavery Memorial Meeting, People's Church, Boston, Mass., 7 Apr. 1897, CFP, SCL; William Still, *The Underground Railroad* (1872; repr. New York: Arno Press, 1968). On Harper, see Frances Harper, *Iola Leroy* (1893; repr., New York: Oxford University Press, 1988); Carby, *Reconstructing Womanhood,* 62–95; Frances Smith Foster, ed., *A Brighter Coming Day: A Frances Ellen Watkins Harper Reader* (New York: Feminist Press, 1990), 3–43, 122–409; and Bert Loewenberg and Ruth Bogin, *Black Women in Nineteenth-Century American Life: Their Words, Their Thoughts, Their Feelings* (University Park: Pennsylvania State University Press, 1976), 243–52.

48. Anna Julia Cooper, *A Voice from the South* (1892; repr., New York: Oxford University Press, 1988), 80, 122–23, 231; "Frances Ellen Watkins Harper," in Loewenberg and Bogin, *Black Women,* 247; Wells, *Southern Horrors.*

49. F[rances] E[llen] W[atkins] [Harper] to AHC, n.d., CFP, SCL; AHC diary, 23 June 1917, CFP, SCL; *"NOTICE,"* 1931, CFP, SCL; FHC diary, vol. 1, 28 Sept. 1893, SCL; FHC diary, vol. 2, 29 Aug. 1894, SCL.

50. See O'Neill, *Everyone Was Brave,* 71–75.

51. Frances Willard to AHC, 28 Feb. 1892; Lucy Stone to AHC, 30 Jan. 1892, both in CFP, SCL.

52. Addie Barrows to AHC, 26, 31 Mar. 1892; "Program of Southern Assembly and School of Methods of the WCTU," July 1892; Martha Lowe, "Anna Ella Carroll" and "Relief for Anna Ella Carroll," *Woman's Journal* (23 Apr. 1892), all in CFP, SCL.

Chapter 8

1. AHC, "Folklore on Sea Islands," 204.

2. A portrait of Abbie Holmes Christensen was viewed at an interview with Carroll Eve by the author, Beaufort, S.C., 20 Nov. 1991. A photograph of the portrait is in the author's collection; the portrait artist was Margaret Walker and the painting is now in the possession of Paul Sommerville. See Gerhard Spieler, "Continuing the Christensen Saga," *Beaufort Gazette,* 3 Mar. 1977, clipping, Pringle.

3. William Francis Allen, Charles P. Ware, and Lucy McKim Garrison, eds., *Slave Songs of the United States* (1867; repr. Baltimore, Md.: Clearfield Co., 1997); James Miller McKim, "Songs of the Port Royal 'Contrabands,'" *Dwight's Journal of Music* 22 (Nov. 1862), 254–55; W. F. Allen, "The Negro Dialect," *The Nation* 1 (14 Dec. 1865), 427; Stevenson, *The Journals of Charlotte Forten Grimke;* Charlotte Forten, "Life on the Sea Islands," *Atlantic Monthly,* 13 May 1864, 587–96; (June 1864): 666–76.

4. Botume, *First Days;* Higginson, *Army Life.* Botume's book was considered significant enough to the study of folklore to be reviewed in the *Journal of American Folklore.* See W. W. Newell, review of *First Days amongst the Contrabands, Journal of American Folklore* 6 (Oct.–Dec. 1893): 325–26. For a discussion of abolitionists' "romantic racialism," see Fredrickson, *Black Image,* 97–129. It could be argued that Christensen was part of the generation of racial liberals McPherson identifies in *Abolitionist Legacy.*

5. Fredrickson, *Black Image,* 204–5; Williamson, *Crucible of Race,* 88–93; Joel Chandler Harris, *Uncle Remus: His Songs and Sayings* (New York: Appleton, 1880); Joel Chandler Harris, *Nights with Uncle Remus: Myths and Legends of the Old Plantation* (Boston: Houghton Mifflin, 1883); McPherson, *Abolitionist Legacy;* Engs, *Educating the Disfranchised;* Whisnant, *All That Is Native.*

6. AHC, "Negro Folklore: The Elephant and the Rabbit," 25.

7. Ibid.

8. AHC, "A Story-Teller," 26.

9. Fredrickson, *Black Image,* 198–227; Robert Bannister, *Social Darwinism: Science and Myth in Anglo-American Social Thought* (Philadelphia: Temple University Press, 1979), 184–88. See also George Stocking, *Race, Culture and Evolution: Essays in the History of Anthropology* (New York: Free Press, 1968), 121; and Sklar, *Florence Kelley,* 259–60. Years later Christensen taught a Sunday school lesson on evolution

and had a pamphlet on Herbert Spencer's "Social Darwinism" in her possession. See NC to AHC, 20 Apr. 1893; and Daniel Greenleaf Thompson, *Herbert Spencer. His Life, Writing, and Philosophy,* vol. 1 (Boston: George H. Ellis, 15 Jan. 1889), both in CFP, SCL. The Thompson pamphlet disagrees with Spencer's stand against education and charity. On Dixon, see Williamson, *Crucible of Race,* 140–79. *The Clansman: An Historical Romance of the Ku Klux Klan* (1905; repr. Ridgewood, N.J.: Gregg Press, 1967), which retells the story of Reconstruction to make heroes of the Ku Klux Klan, was later remade as the motion picture *Birth of a Nation.*

10. AHC, "A Story-Teller"; John Roberts, *From Trickster to Badman: The Black Folk Hero in Slavery and Freedom* (Philadelphia: University of Pennsylvania Press, 1989), 22–44; "Folktales," in *The Norton Anthology of African American Literature,* ed. Henry Louis Gates Jr. and Nellie McKay (New York: W. W. Norton, 1997), 102–3.

11. AHC, "The Rabbit, the Wolf, and the Keg of Butter"; AHC, "Negro Folk Lore: The Rabbit Desires a Long Tail"; AHC, "The Reason Why Brother Rabbit Wears a Short Tail"; AHC, "The Rabbit and the Wolf Plant Potatoes and Hunt Honey."

12. AHC, "Folklore on Sea Islands," 204.

13. AHC, *Afro-American Folk Lore;* folklore notes in undated manuscript in CFP, SCL.

14. AHC, *Afro-American Folk Lore,* ii–iii, xiii.

15. Ibid., x.

16. Fredrickson, *Black Image,* 204–5, 256–82; Williamson, *Crucible of Race,* 88–93, 11–139.

17. For biographies of Harris, see William Brasch, *Brer Rabbit, Uncle Remus, and the "Cornfield Journalist"* (Macon, Ga.: Mercer University Press, 2000); Bruce Bickley Jr. *Joel Chandler Harris* (Boston: Twayne, 1978); Paul Cousins, *Joel Chandler Harris* (Baton Rouge: Louisiana State University Press, 1968); and Julia Collier Harris, *The Life and Letters of Joel Chandler Harris* (New York: Houghton & Mifflin, 1918).

18. See Eric Montenyohl, "The Origins of Uncle Remus," *Folklore Forum* 18 (spring 1986): 136–67.

19. Montenyohl, "The Origins of Uncle Remus," 136–67. On northerners and Harris, see Silber, *Romance of Reunion,* 139–41.

20. Joel Chandler Harris, *Uncle Remus;* Joel Chandler Harris, *Nights with Uncle Remus;* AHC, "Folklore on Sea Islands," 204.

21. Joel Chandler Harris, *Uncle Remus,* vii.

22. On critics, see Alice Walker, "The Dummy in the Window: Joel Chandler Harris and the Invention of Uncle Remus," in *Living by the Word: Selected Writings, 1973–1987* (New York: Harcourt, Brace, Jovanovich, 1988), 25–32; Darwin Turner,

"Daddy Joel Harris and his Old-Time Darkies," in *Critical Essays on Joel Chandler Harris,* ed. Bruce Bickley (Boston: G. K. Hall, 1981), 113–29; and Robert Bone, "The Oral Tradition," in *Critical Essays on Joel Chandler Harris,* ed. Bruce Bickley (Boston: G. K. Hall, 1981), 130–45. On defenders of Harris, see Wayne Mixon, "The Ultimate Irrelevance of Race: Joel Chandler Harris and Uncle Remus in Their Time," *Journal of Southern History* 3 (Aug. 1990): 457–80, esp. 459–61; "Joel Chandler Harris and the Yeoman Tradition," in *Southern Writers and the New South Movement, 1865–1913* (Chapel Hill: University of North Carolina Press, 1980), 73–84; and Brasch, *Brer Rabbit,* 102, 289–322. On Henry Grady, see Thomas Gossett, *Race: The History of an Idea in America* (Dallas, Tex.: Southern Methodist University Press, 1963), 264; and Don Doyle, *New Men, New Cities, New South: Atlanta, Nashville, Charleston, Mobile, 1860–1910* (Chapel Hill: University of North Carolina Press, 1990), 260.

23. John G[reenleaf] Whittier, "Song of the Negro Boatmen at Port Royal," in AHC, *Afro-American Folk Lore,* v.

24. AHC, *Afro-American Folk Lore,* 1–3, xii; AHC to Kathryn Dallas, 4 Jan. 1934, CFP, SCL. Friedrich Froebel (1782–1852) was the founder of the kindergarten movement. Vernon Williams, *Rethinking Race: Franz Boas and His Contemporaries* (Lexington, Ky.: University Press of Kentucky, 1996), 4–53; George Stocking, "Anthology as *Kulturkampf:* Science and Politics in the Career of Franz Boas," in *The Ethnographer's Magic and Other Essays in the History of Anthropology* (Madison: University of Wisconsin Press, 1992), 92–113; Stocking, *Race, Culture, and Evolution: Essays in the History of Anthropology* (New York: Free Press, 1968); Marshal Hyatt, *Franz Boas, Social Activist: The Dynamics of Ethnicity* (New York: Greenwood Press, 1990).

25. AHC, *Afro-American Folk Lore,* xii.

26. For an analysis of the New South ideology, see Gaston, *New South Creed;* Roberts, *From Trickster to Badman,* 20; and *The New South,* 15 Mar. 1862–5 Aug. 1865, SCL.

27. AHC, *Afro-American Folk Lore,* 10–14, xiii.

28. I am thinking of language in the way that M. M. Bakhtin discusses it in "Discourse in the Novel," in M. M. Bakhtin, *The Dialogic Imagination,* ed. Michael Holquist, trans. Caryl Emerson (Austin: University of Texas Press, 1981). The words the storytellers use have meaning and power in their own vernacular usage and in the understanding of each different reader. By "vernacular," I mean forms of expression used by everyday African American people, such as animal tales during slavery and blues in a later period. Both Henry Louis Gates Jr., *The Signifying Monkey: A Theory of African-American Literary Criticism* (New York: Oxford University Press, 1988); and Houston Baker, *Blues, Ideology and Afro-American Literature: A Vernacular Theory*

(Chicago: University of Chicago Press, 1984), inform my usage of this term. See also John Roberts, "African American Diversity and the Study of Folklore," *Western Folklore* 52 (Apr., July, Oct. 1993), 157–71.

29. AHC, *Afro-American Folk Lore,* 15–18.

30. Ibid., 10–14, xiii.

31. Gates, *Signifying Monkey,* 1–88. See also Robert Faris Thompson, *Flash of the Spirit: African and Afro-American Art and Philosophy* (New York: Vintage Books, 1983), 18–33.

32. AH diary, 17 Feb. 1875, CE; AHC, "Folklore on Sea Islands," 204; Levine, *Black Culture,* 190–297; Alaine Locke, *The New Negro: An Interpretation* (New York: A. and C. Boni, 1925).

33. AHC, *Afro-American Folk Lore,* xii; AHC to Kathryn Dallas, 4 Jan. 1934, CFP, SCL; AHC, "Folklore on Sea Islands," 204. Thomas Wentworth Higginson also belonged to the Author's Club. See Edelstein, *Strange Enthusiasm,* 395.

34. Zumwalt, *American Folklore Scholarship,* 14, 22.

35. Helen Bassett to AHC, 10 Jan., 3 Aug., 8, 19 Sept. 1892; NC to AHC, 2 Jan., 30 Apr., 14 May 1893, all in CFP, SCL.

36. W. W. Newell to AHC, 6 Oct. 1892, CFP, SCL. "Members of the American Folklore Society (for the year 1893)," *Journal of American Folklore* 6 (Oct.–Dec. 1893), 329–30.

37. W. W. Newell, review of AHC, *Afro-American Folk Lore, Journal of American Folklore* 5 (July–Sept. 1892): 258–60. There were actually eighteen tales in the book, but only seventeen were listed in the table of contents.

38. Joel Chandler Harris, preface to *Nights with Uncle Remus;* Joel Chandler Harris, *Wally Wanderoon and His Story-Telling Machine* (New York: McClure, Philips, 1903), cover illus., 32. See Eric Montenyohl, "Joel Chandler Harris and the Ethnologists: The Folk's View of Early American Folkloristics," *Southern Folklore* 47, no. 3 (1990): 227–37; and Eric Montenyohl, "Joel Chandler Harris and American Folklore," *Atlanta Historical Review* 30 (fall–winter 1986–87): 79–88.

39. AHC to George Wauchope (rough draft), ? Mar. 1924, CFP, SCL; AHC, *Afro-American Folk Lore,* xiii, 4; Adolf Gerber, "The Relation of the Tales of Uncle Remus to the Animal Stories of Other Countries," preliminary program for the annual meeting of the American Folklore Society, Boston, Mass., Dec. 28–29, 1892, in CFP, SCL; Gerber, "Uncle Remus Traced to the Old World," *Journal of American Folklore* 6 (Oct.–Dec. 1893): 245–57.

40. AHC, *Afro-American Folk Lore,* xii; Joel Chandler Harris, *Uncle Remus,* vi–vii. For an analysis of the John and the Old Master tales see Roberts, *From Trickster to Badman,* 44–61.

41. W. W. Newell to AHC, 24 Nov. 1892, CFP, SCL; W. W. Newell, review of Elizabeth Hyde Botume, *First Days amongst the Contrabands, Journal of American Folklore* 6 (Oct.–Dec. 1893): 326.

42. John Roberts, "African American Diversity and the Study of Folklore," *Western Folklore* 52 (Apr., July, Oct. 1993): 161; W. W. Newell to AHC, 24 Nov. 1892, CFP, SCL; "Local Meetings and Other Notices," *Journal of American Folklore* 5 (Oct.–Dec. 1892): 338.

43. W. W. Newell, "Folklore at the Columbian Exposition," *Journal of American Folklore* 5 (July–Sept. 1892): 239–40; Frederick P. Noble to AHC, 25 Dec. 1892, CFP, SCL; Zumwalt, *American Folklore Scholarship,* 22–44.

44. Frederic P. Noble, "Suggestions for a Program for the African Congress, Aug. 1893"; handwritten manuscript in CFP, SCL; Mrs. Abigail M. Holmes Christensen, "Spirituals and 'Shouts' of Southern Negroes," *Journal of American Folklore* 7 (Apr.–June 1894): 154–55. Neither Christensen's paper nor any other literature section papers were published in C. S. Wake, ed., *Memoirs of the International Congress of Anthropology* (Chicago: Schulte Publishing Co., 1894).

45. AHC, "Spirituals and 'Shouts' of Southern Negroes"; John Roberts, "African American Diversity and the Study of Folklore," *Western Folklore* 52 (Apr., July, Oct. 1993): 162. On the shout, see Albert Raboteau, *Slave Religion: "The Invisible Institution" in the Antebellum South* (New York: Oxford University Press, 1978), 66–73, 339–40; Sterling Stuckey, *Slave Culture: Nationalist Theory and the Foundations of Black America* (New York: Oxford University Press, 1987), 3–97; and Tetzlaff, "Shout," 667–68. For a recent account of a shout, see Guy and Candie Carawan, eds., *"Ain't You Got a Right to the Tree of Life?,"* rev. ed. (Athens: University of Georgia Press, 1989), 64–74. On praise houses, see Creel, "A Peculiar People,: 277; and Patricia Guthrie, "'Catching Sense': The Meaning of Plantation Membership among Blacks on St. Helena Island, South Carolina" (Ph.D. diss., University of Rochester, 1977), passim.

46. J. G. Cupples to AHC, 28 Mar. 1892, CFP, SCL; H[enry] B. B[lackwell], review of AHC, *Afro-American Folk Lore, Woman's Journal* 23 (23 Apr. 1892): 132. "Members of the American Folklore Society (for the year 1894)," *Journal of American Folklore* 7 (Oct.–Dec. 1894), 339–46.

47. William Lloyd Garrison to AHC, 1 June 1893; Lucy Stone to AHC, n.d., both in CFP, SCL.

48. Virginia Durant Young to AHC, 21 Mar., 20 Nov. 1892; A. J. Wakefield to AHC, 28 Nov. 1892; NC to AHC, 16 Apr. 1895, all in CFP, SCL.

49. F[rances] E[llen] W[atkins] Harper to AHC, ca. 1892, CFP, SCL.

50. F[rances] E[llen] W[atkins] Harper to AHC, ca. 1892; J. G. Cupples to AHC, 28 Mar. 1892, both in CFP, SCL.

51. Charles Colcock Jones, *Negro Myths of the Georgia Coast* (1888; repr., Columbia, S.C.: The State Printing Co., 1925). On Jones, see Susan Millar Williams, foreword to Charles Colcock Jones Jr., *Gullah Folktales from the Georgia Coast* (Athens: University of Georgia Press, 2000), xi–xxxv.

52. AHC, undated manuscript detailing terms of Lee and Shepard's publication of AHC, *Afro-American Folk Lore,* ca. 1898; NC to AHC, 16 Apr. 1895, both in CFP, SCL. AHC to Niels Christensen, in blank pages in front of AHC, *Afro-American Folk Lore* (repr., Boston: Lee and Shepard, 1898) (courtesy of Frederik Burr Christensen, Aiken, S.C.).

53. NC to AHC, 24 Sept. 1893; 22 Jan., 11 Feb. 1894, CFP, SCL; E[llen] Murray to AHC, 3 Jan. 1894, CFP, SCL; AHC, "Help for Port Royal's Survivors," *Boston Evening Transcript,* 2 Sept. 1893; AHC, "Sea Island Survivors," *Boston Evening Transcript,* 9 Sept. 1893.

54. Elizabeth Lyman to AHC, 10 Apr. 1902, CFP, SCL; Mary Schlesinger to AHC, 20 Apr. 1902, CFP, SCL; Gerhard Spieler, "Remembrances of Beaufort: Mrs. Andrea Rebecca Christensen," *Beaufort Gazette,* 24 Feb. 1977, clipping, Pringle.

55. "The Listener," *Boston Evening Transcript,* 6 May 1903. AHC to "Editor," "Glimpses of Bay Point," Apr. ? 1903, CFP, SCL.

56. AHC to "Editor," "Glimpses of Bay Point," Apr.? 1903; AHC to "Listener," 25 Apr. 1903, both in CFP, SCL. Cupid and Chloe sang "Mary and Martha," "Oh Believer," "Swing Low Sweet Chariot," "Roll Jordan," and others.

57. AHC to AOC, 20 Jan. 1903 (in the possession of Paul Sommerville, Beaufort, S.C.); Kantrowitz, *Ben Tillman,* 257–58.

58. AHC to "Editor," "Glimpses of Bay Point," Apr.? 1903; AHC to "Listener," 25 Apr. 1903, both in CFP, SCL.

59. The Port Royal Agricultural School later became the Beaufort County Training School, but it was known from 1902 on as the Shanklin School because that was the name of the school's black principal. See Charles V. Singleton, interview by author, 3 Mar. 1992; Ambrose Gonzales, *The Black Border* (Columbia, S.C.: The State Printing Co., 1922); John G. Williams, *De Ole Plantation* (Charleston, S.C.: Walker, Evans & Cogswell, 1895), autographed copy (Frederik Burr Christensen, Aiken, S.C.).

60. On creolization as a metaphor for African-American cultural creation, see Joyner, *Down by the Riverside.* For another recent study of Gullah in historical context, see Creel, *Peculiar People.* See also Turner, *Africanisms.*

61. George Philip Krapp to AHC, 21 Mar., 14 Apr. 1923; George Armstrong Wauchope to AHC, 29 Feb. 1924; AHC to George Wauchope (rough draft), Mar.? 1924; Reed Smith to AHC, 27 June, 31 July 1926, all in CFP, SCL.

62. Elsie Clews Parsons, *Folklore of the Sea Islands, South Carolina* (Cambridge, Mass.: American Folklore Society, 1923), 1 n, xxii, xxv. On Parsons, see Rosemary Zumwalt, *Wealth and Rebellion: Elsie Clews Parsons, Anthropologist and Folklorist* (Urbana: University of Illinois Press, 1992).

63. Elsie Clews Parsons, "Joel Chandler Harris and Negro Folklore," *The Dial* 66 (17 May 1919): 491–93.

64. Elsie Clews Parsons, *Folk-Tales of Andros Island, Bahamas* (Cambridge, Mass.: American Folklore Society, 1918); AHC to Elsie Clews Parsons, n.d. 1919?, Elsie Clews Parsons Papers, American Philosophical Society, Philadelphia, Pa. (hereafter APS).

65. Parsons, *Folklore of the Sea Islands,* xxiii (note 1); Elsie Clews Parsons, "The Provenience of Certain Negro Folk-Tales: The Chosen Suitor or the Rescued Sister," undated manuscript, 8n. 2a, Elsie Clews Parsons Papers, APS.

66. Elsie Clews Parsons to AHC, 20 May 1920, CFP, SCL; Parsons, preface, *Folklore of the Sea Islands,* xx; Zumwalt, *Wealth and Rebellion,* illustration following p. 122 and 162–83; Robert Hemenway, *Zora Neale Hurston: A Literary Biography* (Urbana: University of Illinois Press, 1977). AHC to Kathryn Dallas, 4 Jan. 1934 (rough draft), CFP, SCL.

67. Reed Smith to AHC, 31 July 1926, CFP, SCL.

68. FHC, undated notebook of dialect and clippings, CFP, SCL; FHC diary, vol. 10, 24 Feb., 14 July 1908, SCL; "Rev. Obadiah on Defeated Candidates," *Beaufort Gazette,* 24 Sept. 1908; "Kumbee Brown on Election Matters," *Beaufort Gazette,* 19 Nov. 1908; "At Miss Othank's," *Beaufort Gazette,* 13 Mar. 1924.

69. AWC to AHC, 5, 7–8, 11, 23, 27, 31 Oct., 4, 10, 17 Nov., 8? Dec. 1924; 8 Feb., 26 Aug., 6, 12, 14, 24, 30 Sept., 4, 9,16, 19, 28 Oct., 9, 20 Nov., 2 Dec. 1925; 15, 26, 28 Jan., 8 Feb., 10, 22 Apr., 11, 17 May, 18, 28 Oct., 15, 24 Nov., 9, 12 Dec. 1926; 5, 17–18, 22 Jan., 7, 17, 23 Feb., 4, 10, 18, 27, 30 Mar., 3, 8, 12, 22 Apr., 2, 8 May 1927; Ethel Zande to AHC, 16 June 1927; *Notes from the Pine Mountain Settlement School,* Mar. 1927, all in CFP, SCL. For more on the folkloristic and "uplift" efforts of missionary women among Appalachian whites, see Whisnant, *All That Is Native.*

70. AHC to Kathryn Dallas, 4 Jan. 1934 (rough draft); Kathryn Dallas to AHC, 12 Jan. 1934, both in CFP, SCL.

71. AHC, "Folklore on Sea Islands," 205.

72. AHC, *Afro-American Folk Lore,* ix.

Chapter 9

1. Paul Watson to AHC, 21 Aug. 1897, CFP, SCL.

2. The phrase "One Who Tried to Make the World Better" is taken from the title of the obituary Abbie Christensen wrote for her father in the *Beaufort Gazette,* 15 Feb. 1906. In Boston, Christensen's children first boarded with her suffragist friend Matilde Allen. Later they lived in dormitories or with other families. See Matilde C. Allen to AHC, 2, 16, 31 Jan., 12, 25 Feb., 25 Mar., 13, 27 Apr. 1899. On letters between AHC and children see, for example, AHC to AOC, 4 Feb., 1, 3 May, 4, 15, 22 June 1903; 1 Jan. 1906; ARC to AHC, 1, 5, 7, 15, 22, 25, 27 Jan., 2, 8, 12, 18–19, 26 Feb., 8–19 Mar. 1899; AOC to AHC, 1, 7–8, 18, 21–22 Jan. 1899, all in CFP, SCL.

3. FHC diary, vol. 2, 29 Aug. 1894, SCL; FHC diary, vol. 3, 24 Dec. 1895, SCL; "CONDITIONS IN BEAUFORT COUNTY, SOUTH CAROLINA," 1902, CFP, SCL; "Programme," Anti-Slavery Memorial Meeting, People's Church, Boston, Mass., 7 Apr. 1897, CFP, SCL; Williamson, *Crucible of Race,* 111–39.

4. Mrs. A. H. Christensen, "Help for Port Royal's Survivors," *Boston Evening Transcript,* 2 Sept. 1893; Mrs. A. H. Christensen, "The Sea Island Survivors," *Boston Evening Transcript,* 9 Sept. 1893; Mrs. A. H. Christensen, "An Appeal from Brookline," *Boston Evening Transcript,* 15 Sept. 1893; "CONDITIONS IN BEAU-FORT COUNTY, SOUTH CAROLINA," 1902, CFP, SCL; FHC diary, vol. 1, 17 Sept. 1893, SCL; Clara Barton, *The Red Cross* (1898; repr. New York: Classics of Medicine Library, 1992), 197–274; Fraser, *Charleston! Charleston!,* 326–27. In later years Abbie's daughter recalled, "There is a story that when Clara Barton, the founder of the American Red Cross, came to Beaufort after the storm of 1893, that she at Mother's invitation, stayed at the Christensen home." This is possible, since Niels was one of the leaders of relief work, but no other confirmation exists. See Gerhard Spieler, "Continuing the Christensen's [*sic*] Saga," *Beaufort Gazette,* 3 Mar. 1977, clipping, Pringle.

5. AHC, "Folklore on Sea Islands," 204–5; AHC to AOC, 31 Jan., 7, 9, 15 Feb. 1898, CFP, SCL.

6. AHC to AOC, 31 Jan., 7, 9, 15 Feb. 1898, CFP, SCL; NC to AHC, 24 Oct. 1898, CFP, SCL; NC Jr. to AHC, 1 Nov. 1898, CFP, SCL; Katherine Doctor, interview by author, Beaufort, S.C., 25 July 1996.

7. AHC to Miss M., ca. 1903, CFP, SCL.

8. AHC, typed manuscript draft of "Folk Lore on Sea Islands," ca. 1933, CFP, SCL.

9. Wolf, "Laura M. Towne," 349–74; Edmund Drago, *Initiative, Paternalism, and Race Relations: Charleston's Avery Normal Institute* (Athens: University of Georgia Press, 1990), 62–128; Smedley, *Martha Schofield,* 123–278; McPherson, *Abolitionist Legacy.*

10. Louis Harlan, *Separate and Unequal: Public School Campaigns and Racism in the Southern Seaboard States* (1958; New York: Atheneum, 1968), 75–88; "Manual Training Needed," *Charleston News and Courier,* 30 Jan. 1898; Joan Marie Johnson, "'This Wonderful Dream Nation!': Black and White South Carolina Women and the Creation of the New South, 1898–1930" (Ph.D. diss., University of California, Los Angeles, 1997), 365–66.

11. Engs, *Educating the Disfranchised,* xiv; Robert Engs, *Freedom's First Generation: Black Hampton, Virginia, 1861–1890* (Philadelphia: University of Pennsylvania Press, 1979), 139–60. On industrial education, see also James Anderson, *Education of Blacks,* 33–78; and Donald Spivey, *Schooling for the New Slavery* (Westport, Conn.: Greenwood Press, 1978), 71–76. Washington has historically been viewed in opposition to W. E. B. Du Bois, the Harvard-trained African American intellectual who advocated protest, in contrast to Washington's accommodation. Both, however, were in favor of industrial training for *some* black students. Du Bois emphasized that such training should not be the *only* education available to blacks. See W. E. B. Du Bois, "Of Booker T. Washington and Others," in W. E. B. Du Bois, *The Souls of Black Folk* (1903; repr., New York: Vintage Books, 1990), 36–48; August Meier, *Negro Thought in America, 1880–1915: Racial Ideologies in the Age of Booker T. Washington* (Ann Arbor: University of Michigan Press, 1963); Elliott Rudwick, *W. E. B. Du Bois: Voice of the Black Protest Movement* (Urbana: University of Illinois Press, 1982); Louis Harlan, *Booker T. Washington: The Making of a Black Leader, 1856–1901,* vol. 1 (New York: Oxford University Press, 1972); and Louis Harlan, *Booker T. Washington: The Wizard of Tuskegee, 1901–1915,* vol. 2 (New York: Oxford University Press, 1983).

12. Some historians have seen this board as a direct tool of men such as Rockefeller in their quest for a docile black labor force in the South and later in the North. While their motives were probably more complex, involving religious feeling and a desire to improve society, there is no doubt that industrialists were in favor of docile laborers, be they black or white. See James Anderson, *Education of Blacks,* 79–109; Harlan, *Booker T. Washington: The Wizard of Tuskegee* 2: 186–87; Harlan, *Separate and Unequal,* 75–101; Spivey, *Schooling,* 83–101; and Jacoway, *Yankee Missionaries,* 52–53.

13. AH diary, 26 Oct. 1873, CE; FHC diary, vol. 2, 17 Apr., 8 May, 10 Dec. 1894, SCL; FHC diary, vol. 5, 25 June 1897, SCL; Carey Gray to AHC, 1 June 1901, CFP, SCL.

14. FHC diary, vol. 5, 18 Apr.–3 May 1897, SCL; AHC to AOC, 2 Apr. 1903, CFP, SCL; AHC to AOC, 23 Feb. 1906, CFP, SCL. See also Wolf, "Laura M. Towne," 400–405.

15. FHC to AHC, 5 May 1901, CFP, SCL; Carline Robinson and William Dortch, *The Blacks in These Sea Islands Then and Now* (New York: Vantage Press, 1985), 278; "A Story Without a Finis," typed manuscript, n.d., and Margaret Wenger, "Mather Made History," typed manuscript, 13 Feb. 1966, courtesy of Benedict College, Columbia, S.C.; Gerhard Spieler, "The Mather School," *Beaufort Gazette,* 28 Apr. 1981.

16. AHC to AOC, 10 Mar. 1898, CFP, SCL; "Daniel W. Bythewood," in *History of the American Negro,* ed. A. B. Caldwell, South Carolina ed. (Atlanta, Ga.: A. B. Caldwell, 1919), 729.

17. P. P. Watson, "General Missionary Speaks to Brotherhood," Columbia, S.C., 15 Mar. 1924, CFP, SCL; "Beaufort Happenings," *Palmetto Post,* 6 Aug. 1885; Caldwell, "Paul Philemon Watson" and "Daniel Webster Bythewood," in *History of the American Negro,* ed. A. B. Caldwell, South Carolina ed. (Atlanta, Ga.: A. B. Caldwell, 1919), 253–57; 729.

18. FHC to AHC, 24 Mar. 1901, CFP, SCL; FHC diary, vol. 4, 19 Apr. 1896, SCL.

19. Matilde Allen to AHC, 2, 16 Jan., 11 May 1899, CFP, SCL; AHC, "Folklore on Sea Islands," 205.

20. NC Jr. to AHC, 15 Feb. 1900, CFP, SCL; Ellen Murray to AHC, 21 Aug. 1900, CFP, SCL; *Annual Report of the Penn School,* 1898, York Bailey Library, Penn Center, St. Helena Island, S.C.

21. FHC to AHC, 24 Mar. 1901, CFP, SCL; AHC diary, 22 Mar. 1910, CFP, SCL; Jacoway, *Yankee Missionaries,* 32–61.

22. Kantrowitz, *Ben Tillman,* 225, 258–61, 268–86; Benjamin Ryan Tillman Papers, pt. 1., Special Collections, Robert Muldrow Cooper Library, Clemson University, Clemson, S.C.; Benjamin Tillman to Rev. J. L. Dart, 26 Aug. 1899, quoted in Kantrowitz, *Ben Tillman,* 258.

23. NC Jr. to AHC, 11 Nov. 1900, CFP, SCL.

24. Ibid.

25. AHC to FHC, 7 Aug. 1898, CFP, SCL.

26. AHC to "Sons," 28 Aug. 1903; AHC to FHC, 26 July 1907, both in CFP, SCL; AOC to AHC, 1, 7–8 Jan., undated 1899 (in the possession of Paul Sommerville, Beaufort, S.C.); W. E. B. Du Bois, *Souls of Black Folk.* In 1903 Christensen was probably referring not only to the extremely violent and racist rhetoric of Tillman, but also to his nephew, James or "Jim," the lieutenant governor of South Carolina, who had murdered Narciso Gonzales, editor of the *Columbia State.* See Kantrowitz, *Ben Tillman,* 255–56, passim.

27. NC Jr. to AHC, 25 May 1901; FHC to AHC, 9 June 1901, both in CFP, SCL.

28. Minutes of first meeting of PRAS, 7 Nov. 1902, untitled ledger book, 1902–1903; "Port Royal Agricultural School, Beaufort, South Carolina," ca. 1902; Joseph Shanklin Sr. to AHC, 2 Sept. 1911, all in CFP, SCL.

29. For rural/urban population statistics, see Mary Beth Norton et al., *A People and a Nation: A History of the United States,* 2d ed., vol. I (Boston: Houghton Mifflin, 1994), 22A. On the southern economy after the Civil War, see Gavin Wright, *Old South, New South: Revolutions in the Southern Economy Since the Civil War* (New York: Basic Books, 1986), 3–123; Jay Mandle, *The Roots of Black Poverty: The Southern Plantation Economy after the Civil War* (Durham, N.C.: Duke University Press, 1978). On the local region, see McGuire, "Getting Their Hands on the Land."

30. Mrs. Booker T. Washington to AHC, 6 Nov. 1900; AHC to Miss M., ca. 1902, both in CFP, SCL.

31. Edinburgh Mahone to AHC, 14 Nov. 1900; AHC to Miss M., ca. 1902, both in CFP, SCL.

32. NC Jr. to AHC, 4 Apr. 1901; FHC to AHC, 18, 25 Nov. 1900; 31 Mar. 1901; "Port Royal Agricultural School, Beaufort, South Carolina," ca. 1903, all in CFP, SCL.

33. Edinburgh Mahone to AHC, 7 Nov. 1901; FHC to AHC, 6 Jan. 1902, both in CFP, SCL. See James Anderson, *Education of Blacks,* 149.

34. FHC to AHC, 5 Jan. 1902; AHC to Miss M., 1902; Elisabeth R. Lyman to AHC, 10 Apr. 1902; Mary Schlesinger to AHC, 20 Apr. 1902; AHC to AOC, 27 Oct. 1902; E. C. Higginson to AHC, all in CFP, SCL.

35. ARC to AOC, May 1903?; AHC to AOC, 23 Apr., 3 Dec. 1904; AHC to AOC, 8 Feb., 21 Mar. 1906; AHC to FHC, 26 July 1907; AWC to AHC, 26 Nov. 1907, all in CFP, SCL.

36. NC to AHC, 27 Sept. 1902, CFP, SCL; Joseph Shanklin Jr., interview by author, Burton, S.C., 25 Sept. 1991.

37. FHC to AHC, 20 July 1902; Minutes of PRAS Board of Trustees meetings, 3 Feb., 31 Mar. 1903, all in CFP, SCL.

38. FHC to AHC, 20 July 1902; untitled ledger book, 1902–4, both in CFP, SCL.

39. FHC to AHC, 20 July 1902, 9 Sept. 1906, CFP, SCL.

40. AHC to AOC, 10 Mar. 1898; Wallace Buttrick to NC Jr., 30 June, 14, 30 July, 29 Oct. 1902; NC Jr. to Wallace Buttrick, 24 Oct. 1902, copy; AHC, manuscript, n.d.; "CONDITIONS IN BEAUFORT COUNTY, SOUTH CAROLINA," 1902, all in CFP, SCL. On the General Education Board, see James Anderson, *Education of Blacks,* 83–86; Harlan, *Booker T. Washington: The Wizard of Tuskegee,* 2:130, 186–89, 193–95; and Harlan, *Separate and Unequal,* 82, 94.

41. E. Mahone to Board of Trustees, 1902?; Board of Trustees to E. Mahone, 1902?; AHC to "Boys," 2 Oct. 1902; Mary Schlesinger to AHC, 20 Apr. 1902, all in CFP, SCL. Schlesinger was the president of the Brookline Equal Suffrage Association. See Brookline Equal Suffrage Association, 1901 booklet, CFP, SCL; Isabella Haynes [secretary to Edith Carow Roosevelt] to AHC, 29 Sept. 1902; Thomas Wentworth Higginson, reference, 12 May 1904; list of names on manuscript with "Expenditures," 1906; and AHC, "Contributors," 1907, all in CFP, SCL.

42. AHC to AOC, 6, 13, 20 Nov., 17–18 Dec. 1902; 26 Mar. 1903; "Port Royal Agricultural School, Beaufort, South Carolina," ca. 1903, all in CFP, SCL.

43. AHC to AOC, 14 Feb. 1903, CFP, SCL; "Port Royal Agricultural School, Beaufort, South Carolina," ca. 1903, CFP, SCL; Harlan, *Booker T. Washington: The Wizard of Tuskegee,* 2:212–13.

44. AHC to AOC, 14 May 1903; AHC to FHC, 14 June, 19, 25 Aug. 1903; AHC to Sons, 28 Aug. 1903; "Port Royal Agricultural School, Beaufort, South Carolina," ca. 1903; Edinburgh Mahone to Trustees, 1904; *Annual Report of the Port Royal Agricultural School, Beaufort, South Carolina, 1903–1904* (Savannah, Ga.: Morning News, 1904), all in CFP, SCL. For comparison, see the similar pamphlet of the Penn School, Henry Wilder Foote, *The Penn School on St. Helena Island* (Hampton, Va.: Hampton Institute Press, 1904).

45. J. S. Shanklin to AHC, 24 June 1904; AHC, minutes of meeting, board of trustees, Port Royal Agricultural School, 11 Nov. 1904; "To the Patrons of the Port Royal Agricultural School," 15 Nov. 1904, all in CFP, SCL.

46. "Minutes of the Meeting of the Board of Trustees of the Port Royal Agricultural School," 13 Jan. 1904; AHC to E. B. Haskell, 22 Jan. 1906; FHC to AHC, 1 July 1906; AHC to NC, 7 July 1906; Chas. I. Travelli to NC, 22 Sept. 1906, all in CFP, SCL.

47. "Joseph S. Shanklin," in *History of the American Negro,* ed. A. B. Caldwell, South Carolina ed. (Atlanta, Ga.: A. B. Caldwell, 1919), 3:605–7.

48. Thelma Shanklin West, interview by author, Beaufort, S.C., 26 July 1996; Joseph Shanklin Jr., interview by author, Beaufort, S.C., 25 Sept. 1991; Stephanie Shaw, *What a Woman Ought to Be and Do: Black Professional Women Workers during the Jim Crow Era* (Chicago: University of Chicago Press, 1996), 216.

49. Shaw, *What a Woman Ought to Be and Do,* 78, 83–87; Mrs. Booker T. Washington, "What Girls Are Taught and How," in *Tuskegee and Its People: Their Ideals and Achievements,* ed. Booker T. Washington (New York: D. Appleton, 1905), 72.

50. In 1924 Christensen wrote a fund-raising letter ("Concerning the Port Royal Agricultural School") describing "Mr. and Mrs. Joseph S. Shanklin" as "*superintendents* of

this school for the children of negro farmers, since 1905" (emphasis mine). See AHC to AOC, 25–26 Nov. 1905, CFP, SCL; AHC to Miss Lulu, 14 Jan. 1906, CFP, SCL; AHC to E. B. Haskell, 22 Jan. 1906, CFP, SCL; India Shanklin to AHC, 1907, CFP, SCL; "Joseph S. Shanklin," in *History of the American Negro,* ed. A. B. Caldwell, South Carolina ed. (Atlanta, Ga.: A. B. Caldwell, 1919), 3: 605–7 (in the possession of Charles Singleton, Burton, S.C.), courtesy of Shanklin School Alumni Club; Thelma Shanklin West, interview by author, Beaufort, S.C., 26 July 1996; Charles Single-ton, interview by author, Burton, S.C., Nov. 1991; Joseph S. Shanklin Jr., interview by author, Burton, S.C., 25 Sept. 1991; Fred Washington, telephone Interview by author, 26 July 1996. See also Kibibi Voloria Mack, *Parlor Ladies and Ebony Drudges: African American Women, Class, and Work in a South Carolina Community* (Knoxville: University of Tennessee Press, 1999), 41–42; and Jacqueline Rouse, *Lugenia Burns Hope: Black Southern Reformer* (Athens: University of Georgia Press, 1989).

51. AHC to E. B. Haskell, 22 Jan. 1906, CFP, SCL; AHC, "Concerning the Port Royal Agricultural School," ca. 1924, CFP, SCL; Joseph Shanklin Jr., interview by author, Burton, S.C., 25 Sept. 1991, 25 July 1996; Thelma Shanklin West, inter-view by author, Beaufort, S.C., 26 July 1996.

52. NC Jr. to AHC, ca. 1904, CFP, SCL; India Shanklin to AHC, 1907, CFP, SCL; Joseph Shanklin Jr., interview by author, Burton, S.C., 25 Sept. 1991; Har-lan, *Booker T. Washington: The Wizard of Tuskegee,* 2:108. On wives of black col-lege presidents, see Johnson, "'This Wonderful Dream Nation!,'" 108–67; Mack, *Parlor Ladies,* 41–42, 54–60; and Rouse, *Lugenia Burns Hope.* On self-help activ-ities of African American women, see Glenda Gilmore, *Gender and Jim Crow: Women and the Politics of White Supremacy in North Carolina, 1896–1920* (Chapel Hill: University of North Carolina Press, 1996); Higginbotham, *Righteous Dis-content,* 185–229; and Cynthia Neverdon-Morton, *Afro-American Women of the South and the Advancement of the Race, 1895–1925* (Knoxville: University of Ten-nessee Press, 1989).

53. AHC diary, 22 Mar., 28 Oct., 8, 11, 12, 17, 19 Nov., 3, 15 Dec. 1910; AHC diary, 29 July, 2 Aug., 10, 11, 16, 30 Nov., 1 Dec. 1911; AHC diary, 18 Apr., 14, 29 May, 14 June, 24 July 1912; J. S. Shanklin, 15, 29 June, 9 Nov., 21 Dec. 1912; AHC diary, 2 Nov. 1915; AHC diary, 7 Feb., 11–12 May, 19, 25, 27 Nov., 4 Dec. 1916; AHC diary, 3 Jan., 11 June 1917; AHC diary, 15, 24 Mar., 6, 8, 28 Apr. 1920; AHC diary, 19, 26 1921; 21 Jan. 1922; AHC diary, 1 Jan., 20 Apr., 3–4, 11, 25 May, 16 June 1923, all in CFP, SCL. See also AHC to India Shanklin, 9 Aug. 1936, courtesy of Thelma Shanklin West, Beaufort, S.C.; Septima Clark, *Echo in My Soul* (New York: Dutton, 1962), 25; and Johnson, "'This Wonderful Dream Nation,'" 251–53.

54. AHC diary, 20–22 Mar., 19, 29 Apr., 31 May, 28 Oct., 12, 19, 22, 24 Nov., 3 Dec. 1910; AHC diary, 13 Jan. 1917, all in CFP, SCL.

55. India Shanklin to AHC, 27 Aug. 1907; 3 Sept. 1911; 10 Oct. 1913; 27 Aug. 1916; ca. 1920; 4 Oct. 1921; Aug. 1922; 20 Aug., 4, 13 Sept. 1923; ca. 1924; 11 Sept. 1925; 12 Aug. 1926; 1 Sept. 1932, all in CFP, SCL. See also AHC to India Shanklin, 9 Aug. 1936 (in the possession of Thelma Shanklin West, Beaufort, S.C.); and Thelma Shanklin West, interview by author, Beaufort, S.C., 26 July 1996.

56. India Shanklin to AHC, 27 Aug. 1907, 3 Sept. 1911, 10 Oct. 1913, 27 Aug. 1916, CFP, SCL; AHC to India Shanklin, 9 Aug. 1936 (in the possession of Thelma Shanklin West, Beaufort, S.C.).

57. AHC, notes on speech at Petersham, Mass., ca. Aug. 1922; Nancy Stratton Christensen to AHC, 10 Aug. 1922, ca. Aug. 1922; FHC to AHC, 13 Aug. 1922; NC Jr. to AHC, ca. 1922; 31 Aug. 1925, all in CFP, SCL.

58. Bryant Simon, "The Appeal of Cole Blease in South Carolina: Race, Class and Sex in the New South," *Journal of Southern History* 1 (Feb. 1996): 57–86; Kantrowitz, *Benjamin Tillman*, 296–99; Cash, *Mind of the South*, 247–52; Ownby, *Subduing Satan*, 1–18. On Blease and his relationship to mill workers, see also David Carlton, *Mill and Town in South Carolina, 1880–1920* (Baton Rouge: Louisiana State University Press, 1982).

59. *Pages from the Senate Journal* (28 Jan. 1914), 14–15, 19–20, CFP, SCL; *Pages from the Senate Journal* (4 Feb. 1914), 3–13, CFP, SCL; "Governor Attacks Senator Christensen" and "Mr. N. Christensen, Sr. and His War Record," clippings in Frederik Holmes Christensen diary, vol. 12, 62–63, SCL; "Passed the House," *Beaufort Gazette,* 5 Feb. 1914; "Senator Christensen's Statement as to the Port Royal Agricultural School," *Beaufort Gazette,* 12 Feb. 1914; "Clears His Name," *Beaufort Gazette,* 26 Feb. 1914. In South Carolina in 1914 many schools for black pupils still had white teachers. As late as 1916 the Charleston public schools did not hire black teachers for black students. See Clark, *Echo in My Soul,* 22.

60. Niels Christensen III, interview by author, Beaufort, S.C., 24 Sept. 1991; Thelma Shanklin West, interview by author, Beaufort, S.C., 26 July 1996.

61. "To the Patrons of the Port Royal Agricultural School," 13 Jan. 1905, CFP, SCL.

62. W. E. B. Du Bois, "Of Booker T. Washington and Others," in Du Bois, *Souls of Black Folk,* 36–48; "To the Patrons of the Port Royal Agricultural School," 13 Jan. 1905, CFP, SCL; manuscript list of PRAS graduates and their occupations, ca. 1912, CFP, SCL.

63. AHC to Miss Lulu, 14 Jan. 1906; FHC to AHC, n.d.; FHC to AHC, 1 Sept. 1907; AHC to E. B. Haskell, 22 Jan. 1906; AWC to AHC, 24 Jan. 1909; AHC to

FHC, 28 Sept. 1910; J. S. Shanklin to "Dear Sir," ca. 1918, all in CFP, SCL; Joseph S. Shanklin Jr., interview by author, Burton, S.C., 25 Sept. 1991.

64. FHC, "Receipts," 1906, CFP, SCL.

65. Lottye Wright to AHC, 11, 24 Feb. 1905; AHC to Miss Lulu, 14 Jan. 1906; Wilhelmina Kaintuck to AHC, 20 July 1907; Martha Gregory to AHC, 21 July 1907; Jannie Young to AHC, 13 Aug. 1907; Julia Fripp to AHC, 27 Aug. 1916; AHC, "Concerning the Port Royal Agricultural School," ca. 1924, all in CFP, SCL.

66. Julia Fripp to AHC, 27 Aug. 1916, CFP, SCL.

67. Lottye Wright to AHC, 11, 24 Feb. 1905, CFP, SCL; Joseph Shanklin Jr., interview by author, Burton, S.C., 25 Sept. 1991; Wilhelmina Barnwell, interview by author, Port Royal, S.C., 21 Nov. 1991.

68. Wilhelmina Kaintuck to AHC, 20 July 1907; Martha Gregory to AHC, 21 July 1907; Jannie Young to AHC, 13 Aug. 1907; Celia to Mr. Shanklin, 3 Nov. 1907, all in CFP, SCL.

69. Mary Clayton to AHC, 14 Aug. 1907, CFP, SCL; Victoria Frazier to AHC, 14 Aug. 1907, CFP, SCL; Inez Singleton, interview by author, Lady's Island, S.C., Mar. 1992.

70. AHC diary, 5 Nov. 1910; AHC, "Concerning the Port Royal Agricultural School," ca. 1924, both in CFP, SCL. For the logic that propelled black families to protect their daughters from the sexual vulnerability of domestic work, see Shaw, *What a Woman Ought to Be and Do*, 24–25.

71. Grace Elizabeth Hale, *Making Whiteness: The Culture of Segregation in the South, 1890–1940* (New York: Vintage Books, 1998), 151–170; Kenneth Goings, *Mammy and Uncle Mose: Black Collectibles and American Stereotyping* (Bloomington: Indiana University Press, 1994).

72. AWC to AHC, 11, 23, 27 Oct., 4 Nov. 1924; 8 Feb., 24 Sept., 9, 16, 28 Oct., 2 Dec. 1925; 23 Feb., 15 Oct., n.d. 1927; 4 May 1928; 7 Apr., ca. 1 May, 26 June, 6 Oct. 1933; 10 Oct. 1934; 29 Mar.–1 Apr., 5 Apr. 1936; 18 Apr. 1937; 2 Apr. 1938; *Notes from the Pine Mountain Settlement School* 2, no. 7 (Mar. 1927), all in CFP, SCL. On mountain schools, see Whisnant, *All That Is Native*.

73. Dale Rosengarten, *Row upon Row;* Gerald Davis, "Afro-American Coil Basketry in Charleston County, South Carolina," in *American Folklife,* ed. Don Yoder (Austin: University of Texas Press, 1976), 151–81; John Michael Vlach, *The Afro-American Tradition in Decorative Arts* (Cleveland, Ohio: University of Cleveland Museum, 1978), 8–11.

74. India Shanklin to AHC, 1907, CFP, SCL; J. S. Shanklin to J. B. Felton, 10 Sept. 1920, in "Statements by the State and Local School Authorities as to the Beaufort County Training School" (1 Oct. 1920), 5, CFP, SCL; Leroy Browne Sr.,

edited excerpt of interview by Cece Byers, 23 Sept. 1980, manuscript, SCL; Joseph S. Shanklin Jr., interview by author, Burton, S.C., 25 Sept. 1991; sea-grass and pine-needle baskets (in the possession of Paul Sommerville, Beaufort, S.C.).

75. Matilde C. Allen to AHC, 27 Apr. 1899, CFP, SCL; India Shanklin to AHC, 1907, CFP, SCL; Dale Rosengarten, *Row upon Row*, 26–30; Leroy Browne Sr., edited excerpt of interview by Cece Byers, 23 Sept. 1980, manuscript, SCL.

76. Leroy Browne Jr, edited excerpt of interview by Cece Byers, 23 Sept. 1980, Manuscript, SCL.

77. AHC, "Spirituals and 'Shouts' of Southern Negroes." The tradition of spirituals was also kept alive by special concerts given by Beaufort's First African Baptist Church. See AHC diary, 19 May 1920, and undated program, "Old Folk's Concert," First African Baptist Church, CFP, SCL.

78. AHC to E. B. Haskell, 22 Jan. 1906, CFP, SCL; AHC to AOC, 23 Feb., 3–4 Apr. 1906, CFP, SCL; AHC diary, 8 Nov. 1910, CFP, SCL; Joseph Shanklin Jr., interview by author, Burton, S.C., 25 Sept. 1991.

79. Wilhelmina Barnwell, interview by author, Port Royal, S.C., 21 Nov. 1991; Whisnant, *All That Is Native*, 17–102.

80. Charles Singleton, interview by author, Burton, S.C., 3 Mar. 1992; clipping, FHC diary, vol. 12, p. 62, SCL.

81. AHC to AOC, 8 Aug. 1913, CFP, SCL; Irma Page to AHC, 17 Oct. 1913, CFP, SCL; Anne Howe to AHC, 30 Mar. 1917, CFP, SCL; Mrs. S. McDaniel to AHC, 11 Nov. 1918, CFP, SCL; ACP to AHC, 19 Feb. 1919, CFP, SCL; "Class Record," 1917–24, CFP, SCL; FHC to AHC, 14 Aug. 1921, CFP, SCL; 22 Oct. 1922, 4 Sept. 1927, CFP, SCL; Florence Cook to AHC, n.d., CFP, SCL; AHC to AOC, 3, 27 Nov., 6 Dec. 1916; 22 Jan., 24 Feb., 24 Apr., n.d. 1917; 3 Jan., 4 Feb. 1918 (in the possession of Paul Sommerville, Beaufort, S.C.). Only one reference to a Montessori book appears in Christensen's records: Dorothy Canfield Fisher's *A Montessori Mother* (New York: Holt, 1912). Other books Christensen may have consulted include Maria Montessori, *The Montessori Method*, trans. Anne George (1912; repr., New York: Schocken, 1964); and Maria Montessori, *Dr. Montessori's Own Handbook* (Cambridge, Mass.: R. Bentley, 1914). See also, Luella Cole, *A History of Education: Socrates to Montessori* (New York: Rinehart, 1950); Martin Dworkin, ed., *Dewey on Education* (New York: Bureau of Publications, Teacher's College, Columbia University, 1959); Lawrence Cremin, *The Transformation of the School: Progressivism in American Education* (New York: Vintage Books, 1961); and Maurice Berube, *American School Reform: Progressive, Equity, and Excellence Movements, 1883–1993* (Westport, Conn.: Praeger, 1994).

82. "A Statement by the Trustees of the Port Royal Agricultural School, Beaufort, SC," 1 Aug. 1919, CFP, SCL. Abbie had also unsuccessfully applied for public funds in earlier years; see AHC to B. B. Hare, 6 Dec. 1911, CFP, SCL.

83. Harlan, *Booker T. Washington: The Wizard of Tuskegee*, 2: 194–95; James Anderson, *Education of Blacks*, 110, 137–47, 152–53.

84. "A Statement by the Trustees of the Port Royal Agricultural School, Beaufort, SC," 1 Aug. 1919, CFP, SCL; "Statements by the Local and State Authorities as to the Beaufort County Training School," 1 Oct. 1920, CFP, SCL; James Anderson, *Education of Blacks*, 110, 137–47.

85. AHC to Miss Lulu, 14 Jan. 1906; India Shanklin to AHC, 27 Aug. 1914; J. S. Shanklin to "Dear Sir," ca. 1918; AHC, "Concerning the Port Royal Agricultural School," ca. 1924; Lists of students, ca. 1911, ca. 1915, all in CFP, SCL.

86. Drago, *Initiative*, 44–88; Isabelle Mike to AHC, 19 Feb. 1924, CFP, SCL.

Chapter 10

1. AHC to AOC, 23 Feb. 1915 (in the possession of Paul Sommerville, Beaufort, S.C.).

2. Mary Hamilton to AHC, 21 Feb. 1901, CFP, SCL; AHC Diaries, 1910–13, 1915–18, CFP, SCL; Mona Brown to AHC, 1 Sept. 1913, CFP, SCL; John Simmons to AHC, 4 Oct. 1915, CFP, SCL; Andrea Christensen Patterson (hereafter ACP), to AHC, 31 Jan. 1919, CFP, SCL; AWC to AHC, 21 Apr. 1919, CFP, SCL; Nancy Stratton Christensen to AHC, 1919?, CFP, SCL; AHC to Lillian Dutton, 27 Dec. 1919, CFP, SCL; U.S. Census manuscript, Beaufort County, S.C., 1920 (T625), reel 1686, p. 35; AHC to Elsie Clews Parsons, n.d. 1919?, Elsie Clews Parsons Papers, APS.

3. AHC diary, 11, 28, 30 Nov., 5–6, 8, 11,17 Dec. 1910; AHC diary, 30 June, 6 Aug., 23 Nov., 7 Dec. 1911; AHC diary, 2–4 June, 30, 31 Aug. 1–8 Sept. 1915; AHC diaries, 1917–18; FHC to AHC, 6 Oct. 1913; Mona Brown to AHC, 2 Sept. 1913; John Simmons to AHC, 4 Oct. 1915; New England Sanitarium Dinner Menu, Melrose, Mass., 4 Sept. 1915; ACP to AHC, 29 Jan. 1919, all in CFP, SCL; AHC to AOC, 30 Aug. 1915, 8 Mar. 1917 (in the possession of Paul Sommerville, Beaufort, S.C.). See also Clyde Kiser, *Sea Island to City: A Study of St. Helena Islanders in Harlem and Other Urban Centers* (New York: Columbia University Press, 1932), 99.

4. AHC diary, 6 Nov., 8 Dec. 1911, CFP, SCL; AHC diary, 13 July 1913, CFP, SCL; Wilhelmina Barnwell, interview by author, Port Royal, S.C., 21 Nov. 1991.

5. On maternalism, see Seth Koven and Sonya Michel, eds., *Mothers of a New World: Maternalist Politics and the Origins of Welfare States* (New York: Routledge,

1993), 2; Molly Ladd-Taylor, *Mother-Work: Women, Child Welfare, and the State, 1890–1930* (Urbana: University of Illinois Press, 1994), 3. On women's political culture during this time, see Sklar, *Florence Kelley*, xi–xvi; Paula Baker, "The Domestication of Politics," 620–47; and Lebsock, "Women and American Politics," 3–32. For information on "social housekeeping," see Anastatia Sims, *The Power of Femininity in the New South: Women's Organizations in North Carolina, 1880–1930* (Columbia: University of South Carolina Press, 1997), 51, 128–54; and Johnson, "'This Wonderful Dream Nation,'" 1–21, 168–229.

    6. "Negro Voting in the Primary," *Augusta Herald*, 30 Aug. 1910, clipping in AHC diary, 1910, CFP, SCL; Woodward, *Strange Career of Jim Crow*; Cell, *Highest Stage of White Supremacy*, 82–183; Williamson, *Crucible of Race*; Jack Kirby, *Darkness at the Dawning: Race and Reform in the Progressive South* (Philadelphia: Lippincott, 1972); Morgan Kousser, *The Shaping of Southern Politics: Suffrage Restriction and the Establishment of the One-Party South, 1880–1910* (New Haven, Conn.: Yale University Press, 1974); Dewey Grantham, *Southern Progressivism: The Reconciliation of Progress and Tradition* (Knoxville: University of Tennessee Press, 1983), xv–xxii.

    7. Niels Christensen III, interview by author, Beaufort, S.C., 24 Sept. 1991; Grantham, *Southern Progressivism*, 178–245; Johnson, "'This Wonderful Dream Nation,'" 338–442; Lori Ginzburg, *Women and the Work of Benevolence: Morality, Politics and Class in the Nineteenth Century United States* (New Haven, Conn.: Yale University Press, 1990). Carroll Smith-Rosenberg defines the "New Woman" as a college-educated American woman, born between the late 1850s and 1900, who rejected a conventional female role and asserted her right to a career and a public voice; see Smith-Rosenberg, *Disorderly Conduct*, 176–77. Christensen's daughters would fit in with Marjorie Wheeler's second-generation suffragists. See Wheeler, *New Women*, xiii–xxi, 55–71, 74–99.

    8. "One Who Tried to Make the World Better," *Beaufort Gazette*, 15 Feb. 1906.

    9. Georgie Holmes French to AHC, ?, 13 Jan., ? Feb. 1909; AWC to AHC, 5 Jan. 1909; AHC diary, 3 Feb. 1910; AHC diary, 14 Nov. 1911; AHC diary, 17 Feb. 1912, all in CFP, SCL.

    10. "An Appreciation," *Beaufort Gazette*, 7? Feb. 1909, clipping, CFP, SCL.

    11. AHC diary, 4, 6 Feb. 1910; AHC diary, 4 Feb. 1913; AHC diary, 4 Feb. 1916, all in CFP, SCL.

    12. For an example of another southern club woman who entered public life after her children were older, see Anastatia Sims, "Sallie Southall Cotten and the North Carolina Federation of Women's Clubs" (M.A. thesis, University of North Carolina,

1976), 14–52. Arthur Christensen married in 1911 but became divorced in 1916. In 1920 he remarried. See AOC to AHC, 13 May 1916; Nov. 1919, CFP, SCL.

13. FHC diary, vol. 8, 30 June, 4, 27 July, 7–8, 10 Nov., 22 Dec. 1901; 8 Nov. 1902; FHC diary, vol. 11, 2, 7, 23, 27 Dec. 1909, SCL; "Christensen, Niels," in *Biographical Directory of the Senate of South Carolina, 1776–1964,* ed. Emily Reynolds and Joan Faunt (Columbia: South Carolina Archives, 1964), 197.

14. AHC to AOC, 27, 31 Jan. 1898, CFP, SCL; Mr. James G. Thomas, "The Point," Papers of the Beaufort Historical Society, Beaufort County Library, Beaufort, S.C.; NC Jr. to AHC, 18 Jan. 1901, CFP, SCL; NC Jr. manuscript, 8 Jan. 1905, CFP, SCL.

15. Numbers based on U.S. Bureau of the Census, *Thirteenth Census of the U.S.: 1910,* vol. 3: *Population* (Washington, D.C.: Government Printing Office, 1913), 658; and U.S. Bureau of the Census, *Fourteenth Census of the U.S.: 1920,* vol. 3: *Population* (Washington, D.C.: Government Printing Office, 1922), 929. The main reason for the out-migration of Beaufort residents was better economic opportunities in the larger cities of the South and the North. See FHC diary, vol. 11, 3 Oct., 23 Apr. 1910, SCL. See also Kiser, *Sea Island to City.*

16. FHC diary, vol. 11, 3 Nov. 1909; 7 May, 1 Aug. 1910, SCL.

17. "An Answer," *Beaufort Gazette,* 16 July 1903; "Chain Gang Investigated," *Beaufort Gazette,* 3 Sept. 1903; "Investigation of the Chain Gang," *Beaufort Gazette,* 3 Sept. 1903. Little did Niels Christensen Jr. know that in 1935 his own son would be arrested without trial and put to work on a chain gang in an obvious abuse of this system. See NC Jr. to Georgie French, 14 Aug. 1935, CFP, SCL.

18. FHC diary, vol. 8, 4–21 Mar. 1904; 9–12 Jan. 1907; 7 July 1908; FHC diary, vol. 12, 23 Oct. 1913, all in SCL.

19. FHC diary, vol. 8, 2–4 Aug. 1904, SCL. On southern honor, its origins and its persistence, see Wyatt-Brown, *Southern Honor;* and Steven Stowe, *Intimacy and Power in the Old South: Ritual in the Lives of the Planters* (Baltimore, Md.: Johns Hopkins University Press, 1987).

20. Simkins, *Pitchfork Ben Tillman,* 234–61, 458; Wallace, *South Carolina,* 653–59; "Niels Christensen," typed manuscript for David Duncan Wallace, *History of South Carolina,* vol. 4, biographical (New York: American Historical Society, Inc., 1934), 3–4, CFP, SCL; "Mr. N. Christensen, Sr. and His War Record," *The (Columbia, S.C.) State,* Aug. 1906, clipping attached to FHC diary, vol. 8, 22 Aug. 1906, SCL; Ownby, *Subduing Satan.*

21. NC Jr. manuscript; NC Jr. to AHC, 8, 10, 12, 13, 16, 18, 22, 24 Jan., 5, 9 Feb., 27 Dec. 1905; 10 Apr., 10, 17 June, 29 July 1906, CFP, SCL; AHC to NC Jr., 7 Jan. 1906, CFP, SCL; AHC to AOC, 25 Jan. 1906, CFP, SCL; *Pages from the*

Senate Journal (28 Jan. 1914), 14–15, 19–20, CFP, SCL; *Pages from the Senate Journal* (4 Feb. 1914), 3–13, CFP, SCL; FHC diary, vol. 12, 1 Jan. 1916, SCL; "Governor Attacks Senator Christensen" and "Mr. N. Christensen, Sr. and his War Record," clippings in FHC diary, vol. 12, 62–63, SCL; "Passed the House," *Beaufort Gazette,* 5 Feb. 1914; "Senator Christensen's Statement as to the Port Royal Agricultural School," *Beaufort Gazette,* 12 Feb. 1914; "Clears His Name," *Beaufort Gazette,* 26 Feb. 1914; Wallace, *South Carolina,* 653–59; Grantham, *Southern Progressivism,* 57–58; Walter Edgar, *South Carolina in the Modern Age* (Columbia: University of South Carolina Press, 1992), 32–39; Carlton, *Mill and Town in South Carolina,* 215–72, esp. 231; see also chap. 9, "The Shanklin School."

22. FHC diary, vol. 12, 4, 19 Feb., 14 Mar.–19 Apr., 17–24 May, 16 Aug.–1 Oct. 1915, SCL; "Enthusiastic Meeting of Colored Voters" and "Danner and Marscher Win in Election," *Beaufort Gazette,* 1 Oct. 1915.

23. AHC diary, 28 Oct. 1910; "Negro Votes in the Primary," *Augusta Herald,* ca. 1910, clipping; AHC diary, 1–2 Feb. 1915, all in CFP, SCL.

24. "Niels Christensen," typed manuscript for *History of South Carolina,* 3–4, CFP, SCL; AHC diary, 20 Feb. 1910, CFP, SCL; NC Jr. to AHC, 29 Jan. 1915, CFP, SCL; FHC diary, vol. 11, 17 Feb. 1910, SCL; AHC to AOC, 14–15 Jan. 1915 (in the possession of Paul Sommerville, Beaufort, S.C.); Grantham, *Southern Progressivism,* 60; Wallace, *South Carolina,* 666–67; "Manning for White Rule," *Beaufort Gazette,* 1 Oct. 1915.

25. AHC to FHC, 19 Aug. 1903; Anna Eddy to AHC, ca. 1905; AHC to AOC, 27 Apr. 1906; 3 May ca. 1906; AHC to NC Jr., 7 Jan. 1906, 15 Feb. 1907; NC Jr. to AHC, 2 Sept. 1908; NC Jr. to AHC, 24 Jan. 1913, 29 Jan. 1915, all in CFP, SCL.

26. AHC diary, 29 Mar., 30 May 1917, CFP, SCL; "Lincoln's Gettysburg Address," F. H. Christensen, program of National Memorial Day, 30 May 1917, CFP, SCL; Nancy Stratton Christensen to AHC, 28 Jan. 1930, CFP, SCL; Herbert Keyserling, interview by author, Beaufort, S.C., Nov. 1991.

27. Wells, *Southern Horrors;* National Association for the Advancement of Colored People, *Thirty Years of Lynching in the United States, 1889–1918* (1919; repr., New York: Negro Universities Press, 1969), 89; *Beaufort Gazette,* 26 Sept. 1901; Edgar, *South Carolina in the Modern Age,* 39; Biderman, *Manliness and Civilization,* 45–76; Patricia Schechter, "Unsettled Business: Ida B. Wells against Lynching, or, How Antilynching Got Its Gender," in *Under Sentence of Death: Lynching in the South,* ed. W. Fitzhugh Brundage (Chapel Hill: University of North Carolina Press, 1997), 292–310; David Levering Lewis, *W. E. B. Du Bois: Biography of a Race* (New York: Henry Holt, 1993), 411–14.

28. AHC to AOC, 25 Jan. 1906; NC Jr. to AHC, 8, 13 July 1906; FHC to AHC, 29 July 1906, 2 Sept. 1906, all in CFP, SCL.

29. AHC to AOC, 25 Jan. 1906, CFP, SCL; FHC to AHC, 8, 29 July, 2 Sept. 1906, CFP, SCL; AHC diary, 30 Oct. 1910, CFP, SCL; AHC diary, 3 Apr. 1913, CFP, SCL; FHC diary, vol. 11, 29–30 Mar., 3–5 Apr. 1913, SCL; "New Primary System Needed," *Beaufort Gazette,* 14 May 1914; National Association for the Advancement of Colored People, *Thirty Years of Lynching,* 29, 89–91; Ray Stannard Baker, *Following the Color Line: American Negro Citizenship in the Progressive Era* (New York: Harper and Row, 1964), 175; Dewey Grantham, "Introduction to the Torchbook Edition," in Ray Stannard Baker, *Following the Color Line,* viii.

30. Niels Christensen III, interview by author, Beaufort, S.C., 24 Sept. 1991; Frederik Burr Christensen, interview by author, Aiken, S.C., 7 Nov. 1991; AHC to AOC, 25 Jan. 1906, CFP, SCL; AHC, "The Truth about Beaufort," manuscript, ca. 1907, CFP, SCL; AHC diary, 30–31 Oct. 1910, CFP, SCL; AHC diary, 27 May 1917, CFP, SCL; FHC diary, vol. 9, 21 Jan. 1907; vol. 13, 8 May 1917, SCL; AHC to AOC, 3 Sept. 1917 (in the possession of Paul Sommerville, Beaufort, S.C.); "Beaufort in Flames," "The Shooting of Bennett," and "Mass Meeting," *Beaufort Gazette,* 24 Jan. 1907.

31. *Beaufort County Ledger,* 30 June 1916, cartoon on front page, CFP, SCL; Niels Christensen, "Reduced to an Absurdity," *Beaufort Gazette,* 7 July 1916.

32. AHC diary, 13 Apr. 1910, CFP, SCL.

33. AHC, "An April Stroller," *Beaufort Gazette,* 19 Apr. 1906; AHC, "The Stroller in May," *Beaufort Gazette,* 24 May 1906; AHC, "The Stroller in March," *Beaufort Gazette,* 28 Mar. 1907; AHC, "The April Stroller," *Beaufort Gazette,* 25 Apr. 1907; AHC, "The Stroller in June," *Beaufort Gazette,* 4 July 1907; AHC, "The December Stroller," *Beaufort Gazette,* 26 Dec. 1907; AHC to AOC, 2 Mar. 1906, CFP, SCL; AHC, *A Stroller in Beaufort Fields and Gardens,* ca. 1910, CFP, SCL.

34. India Shanklin to AHC, 4 Oct. 1921, CFP, SCL. AHC, "Stroller's Foreword" and "The Stroller in March," in AHC, "A Stroller," CFP, SCL; AHC, "An April Stroller," *Beaufort Gazette,* 19 Apr. 1906; AHC, "The Stroller in May," *Beaufort Gazette,* 24 May 1906. Ralph Waldo Emerson, *Nature* (1836; repr. in *Ralph Waldo Emerson: Selected Essays, Lectures, and Poems,* ed. Robert Richardson [New York: Bantam Books, 1990], 13–56).

35. William Wilson, *The City Beautiful Movement* (Baltimore, Md.: Johns Hopkins University Press, 1989), 43; "Good Work of Civic League," *Beaufort Gazette,* 30 Apr. 1908; Paul Boyer, *Urban Masses and Moral Order in America, 1820–1920* (Cambridge: Harvard University Press, 1978), 220–77; Thomas Bender, "The

'Rural' Cemetery Movement: Urban Travail and the Appeal of Nature," in *Material Life in America, 1600–1860,* ed. Robert Blair St. George (Boston: Northeastern University Press, 1988), 505–18.

36. "Arbor Day," *Beaufort Gazette,* 5 Nov. 1903.

37. AHC, "The Stroller in February," in AHC, *A Stroller;* AHC diary, 16 Nov., 14 Dec. 1910, all in CFP, SCL.

38. "Clover Club Members," papers of the Clover Club, collection of the Beaufort County Library, Beaufort, S.C.; AHC diary, 5 Apr., 2, 5, 6, 11, 15, 16 May, 7 June, 16 Nov. 1910; AHC diary, 21 July 1911; AHC diary, 25 Apr. 1912; ACP to AHC, 19, 21 Feb., 28 May, 27 Sept. 1913; 19 Jan. 1917; 10, 17 Mar. 1918; n.d., 17 Feb. 1919; Lawrence Patterson to AHC, 30 Apr. 1919, all in CFP, SCL.

39. ACP to AHC, 20 Jan. 1913, CFP, SCL; AWC to AHC, 8, 15, 24 Jan., 13 Mar., 23 May 1914; 11 Mar., 30 Apr. 1916; 20 Nov. 1918; 9, 15, 27 Jan., 1, 24 Feb., 1, 3, 10, 14 Mar., 5, 21 Apr., 2 May, ? Oct. 1919, CFP, SCL; "Miss Christensen, Landscape Architect," card, n.d., CFP, SCL; FHC diary, vol. 13, 27 Jan. 1917, SCL.

40. Karen Blair, *The Clubwoman as Feminist: True Womanhood Redefined, 1868–1914* (New York: Holmes and Meier, 1980), 1–5, 34–35; Anne Firor Scott, *Natural Allies: Women's Associations in American History* (Urbana: University of Illinois Press, 1991), 111–74; AHC diary, 11 Jan. 1911, CFP, SCL.

41. AHC to AOC, 20 Jan. 1903 (in the possession of Paul Sommerville, Beaufort, S.C.); AHC diary, 10 Apr. 1913, CFP, SCL; AHC diary, 16 Dec. 1915, CFP, SCL; Female Benevolent Society Papers, Collection at the Beaufort County Library, Beaufort, S.C.; "The Women's Benevolent Society," *Palmetto Post,* 18 Oct. 1894; "100th Anniversary Benevolent Society," *Beaufort Gazette,* 10 Dec. 1915; "History of the Beaufort Female Benevolent Society," *Beaufort Gazette,* 24 Dec. 1915. For a work on a similar organization, see Bellows, *Benevolence among Slaveholders.*

42. Andrea to AHC, 26 Jan. 1913, CFP, SCL; AHC diary, 26 Apr. 1920, CFP, SCL; Ann Lane, *To Herland and Beyond: The Life and Work of Charlotte Perkins Gilman* (New York: Penguin, 1990).

43. See Johnson, "'This Wonderful Dream Nation'"; and Sims, *Power of Femininity* for the relationship between white and black women's clubs. On black club women, see Elsa Barkley Brown, "Womanist Consciousness: Maggie Lena Walker and the Independent Order of Saint Luke," *Signs* 14 (spring 1989): 610–33; Kathleen Berkeley, "'Colored Ladies Also Contributed': Black Women's Activities from Benevolence to Social Welfare, 1866–1896," in *The Web of Southern Social Relations: Women, Family and Education,* ed. Walter J. Fraser, R. Frank Saunders, and Jon Wakelyn

(Athens: University of Georgia Press, 1985), 181–203; Anne Firor Scott, "Most Invisible of All: Black Women's Voluntary Associations," *Journal of Southern History* 56 (Feb.1990): 3–22; Stephanie Shaw, "Black Club Women and the Creation of the National Association of Colored Women," in *"We Specialize in the Wholly Impossible": A Reader in Black Women's History,* ed. Darlene Clark Hine, Wilma King, and Linda Reed (Brooklyn, N.Y.: Carlson, 1995), 433–47; Linda Gordon, "Black and White Visions of Social Welfare: Women's Welfare Activism, 1890–1945," in *"We Specialize in the Wholly Impossible": A Reader in Black Women's History,* ed. Darlene Clark Hine, Wilma King, and Linda Reed (Brooklyn, N.Y.: Carlson, 1995), 449–85.

44. Anne Firor Scott, *The Southern Lady,* 158–63. See also Elizabeth Enstam, "They Called it 'Motherhood': Dallas Women and Public Life, 1895–1918," in *Hidden Histories of Women in the New South,* ed. Virginia Bernhard, Betty Brandon, Elizabeth Fox-Genovese, Theda Purdue, and Elizabeth Turner (Columbia: University of Missouri Press, 1994), 71–95.

45. "Good Work of the Civic League," *Beaufort Gazette,* 30 Apr. 1908. AHC diary, 19 Feb. 1915, CFP, SCL.

46. AHC diary, 14 Apr., 12 June 1912, CFP, SCL; AWC to AHC, 8 Jan. 1914, CFP, SCL; AHC diary, 19 Feb., 11 Nov. 1915, CFP, SCL; "Your committee appointed last year . . . ," manuscript, n.d., CFP, SCL; "A Little Housecleaning," *Beaufort Gazette,* 13 Sept. 1906; "The Work of Beaufort's Civic League," *Beaufort Gazette,* 21 Feb. 1907; "The Court House Fountain," *Beaufort Gazette,* 20 June 1907; "A Lawn Party," *Beaufort Gazette,* 30 Apr. 1914; "Trees Wanted," *Beaufort Gazette,* 28 Jan. 1915; "Regular Meeting of the Civic League," *Beaufort Gazette,* 11 Feb. 1915; "Cemetery Work Progressing," *Beaufort Gazette,* 11 Feb. 1915; AHC to AOC, 23 Feb. 1915 (in the possession of Paul Sommerville, Beaufort, S.C.).

47. "Good Work of the Civic League," *Beaufort Gazette,* 30 Apr. 1908; "Court House Fountain," *Beaufort Gazette,* 20 June 1907; "Civic League Granite Fountain for Animals," *Beaufort Gazette,* 23 July 1914; "Regular Meeting of Town Council Held," *Beaufort Gazette,* 25 Feb. 1916; City of Beaufort Minute Books, 11 Mar. 1918, Beaufort County Library, Beaufort, S.C. (hereafter cited as City of Beaufort Minute Books).

48. "Amount Nearly Secured for Drinking Fountains," *Beaufort Gazette,* 25 Nov. 1909; "A Lawn Party," *Beaufort Gazette,* 30 Apr. 1914; "Successful Lyceum Course Closes Here," *Beaufort Gazette,* 14 May 1920; "Community Club Dots," *Beaufort Gazette,* 3 Dec. 1920; "Annual Report of Civic League of Beaufort 1930–31," *Beaufort Gazette,* 18 June 1931; "What It All Means," *Beaufort Gazette,* 25 Aug. 1915; "Mr. Legare Writes of Past and Present," *Beaufort Gazette,* 16 Dec. 1910; "Republican Convention Endorsement," *Beaufort Gazette,* 6 Jan. 1911; "Commission

Government Wins Fourth Time," *Beaufort Gazette,* 16 Apr. 1915; "Special Session of Town Council," *Beaufort Gazette,* 30 Apr. 1915; "The New Issue," *Beaufort Gazette,* 10 Sept. 1915.

49. FHC diary, vol. 12, Jan. 1915, SCL; "Lawn Party and Baby Show to Be Held," *Beaufort Gazette,* 6 May 1915; "Civic League Asks for Prosecutions," *Beaufort Gazette,* 2 Nov. 1905; "Civic League Urges Tree Preservation," manuscript, n.d., CFP, SCL; Mary Cutler to AHC, 15 Mar. 1912, CFP, SCL; AHC diary, 1 Mar. 1912, CFP, SCL.

50. "The Trees Must Be Protected," *Beaufort Gazette,* 5 Mar. 1908; AHC diary, 14 Dec. 1910, CFP, SCL; "Notice: Trees Standing Near Public Road Not to Be Cut," *Beaufort Gazette,* 12 Mar. 1908; "Annual Report of Civic League of Beaufort 1930–31," *Beaufort Gazette,* 18 June 1931.

51. City of Beaufort Minute Books, 20 May 1912; "Does Not Like the Birds," *Beaufort Gazette,* 12 Aug. 1909.

52. City of Beaufort Minute Books, 20 May, 10, 24 June 1909.

53. "Letter from a Civic League Member," *Beaufort Gazette,* 16 July 1915; AHC, "To the Editor of the Beaufort Gazette," 27 July 1915, CFP, SCL; AHC diary, 11 Nov. 1915, CFP, SCL; Nancy Stratton Christensen to AHC, n.d., CFP, SCL; FHC to AHC, 5 Sept. 1915, CFP, SCL; "Public Library Building Proposed," *Beaufort Gazette,* 28 Jan. 1915; "Clover Club Library," 1914, clipping in Clover Club Papers, Beaufort County Library, Beaufort, S.C.

54. Paul Watson to AHC, 21 Aug. 1897, CFP, SCL; "Of Interest to Our Colored Readers," *Beaufort Gazette,* 11 Feb. 1904; "Beaufort County Library History," typed manuscript; Courtney Siceloff to Ethelyn Walker, 13 Sept. 1958; Hillary Barnwell, "'Book Outposts' Became Bookmobile," *Beaufort Gazette,* 19 Apr. 1985 clipping, all in Beaufort County Library, Beaufort, S.C.

55. "Why We Are Suffragists," *Beaufort Gazette,* 9 July 1915.

56. Wheeler, *New Women,* 38–71.

57. Johnson, "'This Wonderful Dream Nation,'" 355–56; "South Carolina Federation of Women's Clubs," *The Keystone,* 1915, clipping in Clover Club Papers, Beaufort County Library, Beaufort, S.C.; AHC diary, 5 Apr. 1910; South Carolina Federation of Women's Clubs, registration card, 1913, both in CFP, SCL; AHC to AOC, 19 May 1913 (in the possession of Paul Sommerville, Beaufort, S.C.).

58. On the link between southern women's clubs and suffrage see Jacquelyn Dowd Hall, *Revolt against Chivalry: Jessie Daniel Ames and the Women's Campaign against Lynching* (New York: Columbia University Press, 1974), 24–25.

59. AWC to AHC, 16 Oct. 1911; Elizabeth N. Richards to AHC, 22 Dec. 1911; AHC diary, 10 Mar. 1910; AHC diary, 17 Jan., 17 Feb. 1912; Ferdinanda

Wesselhoeft, *Jonathan's Night Shirt* (Boston: The Woman's Journal, 1916); AHC check to *Woman's Journal,* 12 Feb. 1916; AHC diary, 10 Mar. 1910; AHC diary, 16 Oct. 1915; Mary Beecher to AHC, ca. 1934; Marian Gage to AHC, n.d., all in CFP, SCL.

60. AHC to FHC, 28 Sept. 1910; "Votes for Women a Success," poster, both in CFP, SCL; J. Stanley Lemons, *The Woman Citizen: Social Feminism in the 1920s* (Urbana: University of Chicago Press, 1973), vii–x; Nancy Cott, "Across the Great Divide: Women in Politics before and after 1920," in *Women, Politics, and Change,* ed. Louise Tilly and Patricia Gurin (New York: Russell Sage Foundation, 1990), 155–59.

61. "Women Form Suffrage League Today Here" and "Women Will Meet in Bennettsville Next Year," *Spartanburg Journal and Carolina Spartan,* 15 May 1914, CFP, SCL; Josephina Vazquez and Lorenzo Meyer, *The United States and Mexico* (Chicago: University of Chicago Press, 1985); Karl Schmitt, *Mexico and the United States, 1821–1973* (New York: Wiley, 1974); Arthur Link, ed., *Woodrow Wilson and a Revolutionary World, 1913–1921* (Chapel Hill: University of North Carolina Press, 1982); Wheeler, *New Women,* 79–91.

62. "Welcome Negro Suffrage Club," *New York Herald,* 10 Oct. 1911, clipping in AHC diary, 10 Oct. 1911; Laura Bragg to AHC, 31 Aug. 1915; AHC diary, 24–25, 27 Feb., 2–3 Mar. 1917, all in CFP, SCL. On southern suffragists and race, see Sims, *Power of Femininity,* 155–88; Gilmore, *Gender and Jim Crow,* 203–4; Terborg-Penn, *African American Women;* Roslyn Terborg-Penn, "African American Women and the Woman Suffrage Movement," in *One Woman, One Vote: Rediscovering the Woman Suffrage Movement,* ed. Marjorie Spruill Wheeler (Troutdale, Oreg.: NewSage Press, 1995), 135–56; Adele Logan Alexander, "How I Discovered My Grandmother . . . and the Truth about Black Women and the Suffrage Movement," *Ms.* (12 Nov. 1983), 29–37; Kraditor, *Ideas of the Woman Suffrage Movement,* 163–218; Anne Firor Scott, *Southern Lady,* 164–83; Wheeler, *New Women,* 100–132; and Suzanne Lebsock, "Woman Suffrage and White Supremacy: A Virginia Case Study," in *Visible Women: New Essays in American Activism,* ed. Nancy Hewitt and Suzanne Lebsock (Urbana: University of Illinois Press, 1993), 62–100.

63. Ida Harper, *History of Woman Suffrage* (New York: National American Woman Suffrage Association, 1922), 6:580. Antoinette Elizabeth Taylor, "South Carolina and the Enfranchisement of Women: The Later Years," *South Carolina Historical Magazine* 80, no. 4 (1979): 298–310; Sidney Bland, "Fighting the Odds: Militant Suffragists in South Carolina," *South Carolina Historical Magazine* 82, no. 1 (1981): 32–43; Anne Firor Scott, *Southern Lady,* 165–84; Hall, *Revolt against Chivalry,* 17–45; and Wheeler, *New Women.* For the southern antisuffrage ideologies,

see Elna Green, "'Ideals of Government, Home and of Women': The Ideology of Southern White Antisuffragism," in *Hidden Histories of Women in the New South,* ed. Virginia Bernhard, Betty Brandon, Elizabeth Fox-Genovese, Theda Purdue, and Elizabeth Turner (Columbia: University of Missouri Press, 1994), 96–113; and Elna Green, *Southern Strategies: Southern Women and the Woman Suffrage Question* (Chapel Hill: University of North Carolina Press, 1997). See also Anastatia Sims, "Beyond the Ballot: The Radical Vision of the Antisuffragists," in *Votes for Women!: The Woman Suffrage Movement in Tennessee, the South, and the Nation,* ed. Marjorie Spruill Wheeler (Knoxville: University of Tennessee Press, 1995), 105–28.

64. FHC diary, vol. 12, 9 June 1914, 23 Apr. 1915, SCL; AHC diary, 23 Apr., 16 Nov., 8 Dec. 1915, CFP, SCL; AHC diary, 12 June 1916, CFP, SCL; AHC diary, 25 Feb. 1917, CFP, SCL; Bland, "Fighting the Odds," 32–33; Antoinette Elizabeth Taylor, "South Carolina and the Enfranchisement of Women: The Early Years," *South Carolina Historical Magazine* 80 (Apr. 1976): 126.

65. "Holmes, Abbie Mandana, Association of Collegiate Alumnae—Census of College Women, 1915," in Mount Holyoke College Archives, South Hadley, Mass.; FHC diary, vol. 12, 7 Feb. 1915, SCL; "Why We Are Suffragists," *Beaufort Gazette,* 9 July 1915; AHC to AOC, 23 Apr., 1918; AOC to Lillian Dutton, 27 Dec. 1919, 3 Jan. 1920 (both in the possession of Paul Sommerville, S.C.).

66. NC to AHC, Dec. 1914; FHC to AHC, 4 July 1915; AHC diary, 16 Oct. 1915; Nancy Stratton Christensen to AHC, n.d.; ACP to AHC, 17 Feb., 2 May 1919; 27 Oct. 1920; Lawrence Patterson to AHC, 30 Apr. 1919; AWC to AHC, 23, 29 May 1914, all in CFP, SCL; FHC diary, vol. 14, 30 Aug. 1922, SCL; Harper, *History of Woman Suffrage,* 6:583–84; Bland, *Preserving Charleston's Past,* esp. 27–45.

67. Laura Bragg to AHC, 23 June, 31 Aug. 1915; AHC diary, 23, 26 May 1920, all in CFP, SCL; "A Lawn Party," *Beaufort Gazette,* 30 Apr. 1914. Laura Bragg to Lyman Bragg, ca. 1917; "Miss Bragg Holds Talk in Beaufort," *Charleston News and Courier,* 11 Dec. 1929, clipping, all in Laura May Bragg Collection, Laura Bragg Biographical and Genealogical File, South Carolina Historical Society, Charleston, S.C.; Louise Anderson Allen, *Bluestocking in Charleston,* 52.

68. AHC diary, 5 June 1915; Mary C. Beecher to AHC, 18 June 1916; AHC diary, 26 Mar., 19 June, 21 June 1917; Mrs. A. H. Christensen, "Allies All," 1917; Everett J. Harrington to AHC, 28 June 1917; Soloman Stratton to AHC, 1 July 1917; W. Forbes Robertson to AHC, 21 July 1917, all in CFP, SCL; AHC to AOC, 29 Mar., 13 Apr. 1917; AHC to AOC, 3 May 1918 (in the possession of Paul Sommerville, Beaufort, S.C.).

Chapter 11

1. AHC, "Notes on Lesson 1st–Grade 2nd," "Notes on A[ncient and] M[ystical] O[rder of] R[osae] C[rucis] (hereafter cited as AMORC lectures), 1929, CFP, SCL.

2. Anthony Dunbar, *Against the Grain: Southern Radicals and Prophets, 1929–1959* (Charlottesville: University of Virginia Press, 1981). AHC, "3rd Lesson–March 23rd," AMORC notebook, CFP, SCL.

3. Helen Burr Christensen to Mount Holyoke College, 1 Feb. 1943, in Mount Holyoke College Library Archives, Mount Holyoke, Mass.; Heilbrun, *Writing a Woman's Life,* 124–31; ACP to AHC, n.d., CFP, SCL; AHC to Elsie Clews Parsons, n.d. 1919?, Elsie Clews Parsons Papers, APS.

4. New England Sanitarium Laboratory, "Examination of Blood," 30 Aug. 1915, and "Examination of Urine," 29 Aug. 1915; New England Sanitarium Dinner Menu, 4 Sept. 1915, Melrose, Mass., all in CFP, SCL. AHC to AOC, 30 Aug. 1915, 8 mar. 1917 (in possession of Paul Sommerville, Beaufort, S.C.); AHC to Old Fashioned Millers, 9 Feb. 1917; Lawrence Patterson to AHC, 18 May 1920; H. Lindlahr to AHC, 2 July 1920; "Suggestions from Nature Cure," pamphlet, n.d.; NC Jr. to AHC, ca. Aug. 1920; ACP to AHC, 13 Mar., 5 July, 3, 6, Aug.; 28 Sept; n.d. 1920; Lillian Dutton Christensen to AHC, 7 Aug. 1920; 5 May 1921; FHC to AHC, 11 July, 10 Oct. 1920, all in CFP, SCL. FHC diary, vol. 13, 11 July 1920; SCL. AHC diary, 3 Aug.–4 Oct. 1923, CFP, SCL.

5. AHC diary, 8 Jan. 1920; AWC to AHC, 7 Feb. 1927, both in CFP, SCL.

6. Helen Burr to AHC, 28 Jan. 1918; 26 Jan. 1926; 12, 14 July, 4 Aug. 1928; Adelaide Keith to AHC, 20 Oct. 1925; AWC to AHC, 24 Nov. 1926, all in CFP, SCL; Carroll Eve, interview by author, Pleasantview, Va., 30 Sept. 1991.

7. U.S. Bureau of the Census, *Fourteenth Census of the United States: 1920: Population* (Washington, D.C.: Government Printing Office, 1922), 929, 935; *Fifteenth Census of the United States: 1930: Population* (Washington, D.C.: Government Printing Office, 1933), 784, 796; Wright, *Old South, New South,* 198–238; Jack Temple Kirby, *Rural Worlds Lost: The American South, 1920–1960* (Baton Rouge: Louisiana State University Press, 1987), 25–79, 115–54; Edgar, *South Carolina in the Modern Age,* 46–50; Edgar, *South Carolina: A History,* 481–511; Dunbar, *Against the Grain,* 48–135.

8. Nancy MacLean, *Behind the Mask of Chivalry: The Making of the Second Ku Klux Klan* (New York: Oxford University Press, 1994), 4–14; Kathleen Blee, *Women of the Klan: Racism and Gender in the 1920s* (Berkeley: University of California Press, 1991); David Chalmers, *Hooded Americanism: The History of the Ku Klux Klan,* 2d. ed. (New York: New Viewpoints, 1981).

9. Morton Sosna, *In Search of the Silent South: Southern Liberals and the Race Issue* (New York: Columbia University Press, 1977), 20–22; NC Jr. to AHC, 1922, CFP, SCL.

10. FHC diary, vol. 14, 30 Mar. 1923, SCL.

11. FHC diary, vol. 13, 6, 22 June, 12, 17, 22 Sept. 1921, SCL; AHC diary, 20 Jan., 10, 25 Feb., 18 May 1920, CFP, SCL; AHC diary, 20 Jan. 1922, CFP, SCL; AHC to Nancy Stratton Christensen, 31 Aug. 1921, CFP, SCL; AHC diary, 20 Jan., 4 July 1922, CFP, SCL; AHC to AWC, 29 Oct. 1926, CFP, SCL.

12. See William Chafe, *The American Woman: Her Changing Social, Economic and Political Roles, 1920–1970* (New York: Oxford University Press, 1972), 25–134; Lemons, *Woman Citizen,* 51–57, 63–65, 123–25, 181–84; Lebsock, "Women and American Politics," 46–59; and Cott, "Across the Great Divide," 153–76.

13. AHC to Nancy Stratton Christensen, 31 Aug. 1921, CFP, SCL; AHC diary, 25 Feb. 1920, CFP, SCL; FHC to AHC, 2 Oct. 1920, CFP, SCL; Helen Burr to AHC, 19 Mar. 1922, CFP, SCL; AHC to AWC, 29 Oct. 1926, CFP, SCL; Mary C. Beecher to AHC, 8 Feb. 1928, CFP, SCL; AHC to AOC, 15 Oct. 1917 (in the possession of Paul Sommerville, Beaufort, S.C.); Cott, "Across the Great Divide," 165.

14. Helen Burr to AHC, ca. 1921; AWC to AHC, 9, 15, 27 Jan., 1, 24 Feb., 1, 3, 10, 14 Mar., 5, 21 Apr., 2 May 1919; United States State Department to AHC, 29 June 1921; AHC to NC Jr., 20 July, 31 Aug. 1921; AHC to Family, 4 Aug., 24 Sept., 6 Oct. 1921; AHC diary, 21–23 July 1921, all in CFP, SCL.

15. AHC diary, 8, 12, 14, 15 May, 2, 4 June 1923, CFP, SCL; Helen Kinney to AHC, ca. 1923, CFP, SCL; FHC diary, vol. 14, 2 Aug. 1922, SCL; AHC diary, 25 Feb. 1920, CFP, SCL; M. L. Davey to AHC, 14 Dec. 1921, CFP, SCL; NC Jr. to AHC, 16 Jan. 1922, CFP, SCL; AHC diary, 24 Jan. 1922, CFP, SCL; AHC to AWC, 29 Oct. 1926, CFP, SCL; Hall, *Revolt against Chivalry;* Lebsock, "Woman Suffrage and White Supremacy," 62–100.

16. AHC diary, 30 Oct., 2 Nov. 1911; Clare MacDonald to AHC, ? 1919; 21 Jan., 1 Feb., 14 June, 8 Sept. 1920; 6, 26 Apr., 30 Aug., 10 Oct. 1922; 9 Sept. 1924; 17 Dec. 1925; 29 July 1938, n.d. (2); AWC to AHC, 1 Apr. 1920; AHC diary, 4 Feb. 1921; AHC diary, 3 July 1923, all in CFP, SCL; FHC diary, vol. 13, 20 Nov. 1917, SCL; FHC diary, vol. 14, 20 Oct. 1927, AHC to AOC, Dec. 1918 (in the possession of Paul Sommerville, Beaufort, S.C.); Niels Christensen III, interview by author, Beaufort, S.C., 24 Sept. 1991.

17. Jacoway, *Yankee Missionaries,* 42, 88; Clare Macdonald, *Recollections of Juliana* (Columbia, S.C.: The State Printing Co., 1924); Clare Macdonald to AHC, 9 Sept. 1924, CFP, SCL.

18. FHC diary, vol. 14, 3 Feb., 30 Mar., 25 Nov. 1923; 4 May 1924; 1 Feb. 1925; 18 Nov. 1928, SCL; Clare Macdonald to AHC, 9 Sept. 1924, CFP, SCL; Niels Christensen III, interview by author, Beaufort, S.C., 24 Sept. 1991. Although Christensen had been a Unitarian in Boston, she attended several different Protestant churches in Beaufort.

19. FHC diary, vol. 14, 3 Feb., 30 Mar. 1924, SCL.

20. Hall, *Revolt against Chivalry*, 80–87; Rouse, *Lugenia Burns Hope;* Neverdon-Morton, *Afro-American Women;* McDowell, *Social Gospel in the South,* 84–115; Anne Firor Scott, *Southern Lady,* 194–99.

21. Hall, *Revolt against Chivalry,* 87–95; Anne Firor Scott, *Southern Lady,* 194–99; Sosna, *In Search of the Silent South,* 29–30.

22. FHC diary, vol. 14, 30 Mar., 4 May 1924, SCL; "The Other Side," *Beaufort Gazette,* 27 Mar. 1924.

23. FHC diary, vol. 14, 1 Feb. 1925, 8 Apr. 1928, 1 June 1930, 7 Feb. 1932, 22 May 1932, 15 Oct. 1933, SCL; AHC diary, 23 May 1920, CFP, SCL; AHC diary, 16 June 1922, CFP, SCL; Helen Burr to AHC, 4 Aug. 1928, CFP, SCL; Clelia McGowan to AHC, 31 Aug. 1931, CFP, SCL; Mamie Garvin Fields, *Lemon Swamp and Other Places: A Carolina Memoir* (New York: Macmillan, 1983), 192; Fraser, *Charleston! Charleston!,* 364, 380; Johnson, "'This Wonderful Dream Nation,'" 319–29.

24. Association of Southern Women for the Prevention of Lynching, "Notice" and "Resolutions deploring lynching and looking to its prevention," Jan.–30 Apr. 1931, CFP, SCL; name list, South Carolina, n.d., ser. 7, Association of Southern Women for the Prevention of Lynching Papers, Trevor Arnett Library, Atlanta University, Atlanta, Ga. (microfilm, reel 7, Indiana University Purdue University Indianapolis, Indianapolis, Ind.); Hall, *Revolt against Chivalry,* 129–253.

25. FHC diary, vol. 14, 13 Apr. 1924, 24 June 1928, SCL; Mary Beecher to AHC, ca. 1920; AHC diary, 7–8 June 1923; FHC to AHC, 7 Sept. 1924; Helen Burr to AHC, ca. 1921, 19 Mar. 1922; 20 Nov., 20 June 1925; AHC to Family, 18 July 1928; Hardina B. Howie to AHC, 28 July 1928, 24 Nov. 1932; J[ohn] A. Patterson to H[ardina] B. Howie, 24 Nov. 1932; Hazel Attaway to AHC, ca. 1938, all in CFP, SCL; Niels Christensen III, interview by author, Beaufort, S.C., 24 Sept. 1991. "Community House," *Beaufort Gazette,* 20 Mar. 1924; "Clover Club Member," Clover Club Papers, Beaufort County Library, Beaufort, S.C.

26. Katherine Doctor, interview by author, Beaufort, S.C., 25 July 1996.

27. Ibid.; Beaufort County, S.C., United States Census, 1910, vol. 10, manuscript census (T624), reel 1451, p. 69, and Beaufort County, S.C., United States Census of

Population, 1920, vol. 9, manuscript census (T625), reel 1686, p. 43, both in Beaufort County Library, Beaufort, S.C.; deed, J. H. L. Waterhouse to Catherine DeVeaux, 9 Apr. 1910, Deed Book 29, Beaufort County Administration Building, Beaufort, S.C.; "Death Claims Well-Known Negroes," *Beaufort Gazette,* 23 July 1903; Mrs. C. G. Bascomb, "Of Interest to Colored Readers," *Beaufort Gazette,* 18 June 1904.

28. Gilmore, *Gender and Jim Crow,* 31–202; Shaw, *What a Woman Ought to Be and Do;* Katherine Doctor, interview by author, Beaufort, S.C., 25 July 1996; City of Beaufort Minute Books, 26 May 1930, 17 May 1934, 9 Oct. 1934, 14 May 1935, 12 May 1936, 8 Jan. 1937, 10 May 1938.

29. Edward Beardsley, *A History of Neglect: Health Care for Blacks and Mill Workers in the Twentieth Century South* (Knoxville: University of Tennessee Press, 1987); Susan Smith, *Sick and Tired of Being Sick and Tired: Black Women's Health Activism in America, 1890–1950* (Philadelphia: University of Pennsylvania Press, 1995); Darlene Clark Hine, *Black Women in White: Racial Conflict and Cooperation in the Nursing Profession, 1890–1950* (Bloomington: Indiana University Press, 1989); Nancy Hewitt, "Politicizing Domesticity: Anglo, Black and Latin Women in Tampa's Progressive Movements," in *Gender, Class, Race and Reform in the Progressive Era,* ed. Noralee Frankel and Nancy Schrom Dye (Lexington: University of Kentucky Press, 1991), 33–34; Darlene Clark Hine, "'We Specialize in the Wholly Impossible': The Philanthropic Work of Black Women," in *Lady Bountiful Revisited: Women, Philanthropy and Power,* ed. Kathleen McCarthy (New Brunswick, N.J.: Rutgers University Press, 1990), 70–93.

30. AHC diary, 2 July 1923, CFP, SCL; Catherine DeVeaux to AHC, 26 July 1925, 24 July 1938, CFP, SCL; Katherine Doctor, interview by author, Beaufort, S.C., 25 July 1996; Robinson and Dortch, *Blacks in These Sea Islands,* 72. On visits to the islands, see "Septima Clark Interview," Septima Poinsette Clark Collection, Avery Institute of Afro-American History and Culture, Charleston, S.C.

31. Katherine Doctor, interview by author, Beaufort, S.C., 25 July 1996; Abbie H. Christensen, Notes on AMORC Lectures, 1929, CFP, SCL.

32. Niels Christensen III, interview by author, Beaufort, S.C., 24 Sept. 1991; "Public Health Nurse for Beaufort County," *Beaufort Gazette,* 21 Nov. 1919; "Beaufort County Now Has Public Health Nurse," *Beaufort Gazette,* 18 Feb. 1921.

33. AHC diary, 2 Feb. 1920; AHC diary, 10 Jan., 6 July 1922; AHC diary, 8, 10, 21, 26 May, 15 June, 2, 7 July, 14 Aug. 1923; Catherine DeVeaux to AHC, 26 July 1925; Helen Burr Christensen to AHC, 8 Aug. 1933; AHC to Helen Burr Christensen, ca. 1934, 24 July 1938, all in CFP, SCL.

34. AHC diary, 2 July 1923; Catherine DeVeaux to AHC, 22 Sept. 1924, 26 July 1925, all in CFP, SCL. On playground appropriation, see City of Beaufort Minute Books, 9 Oct. 1934; and Kathryn Kish Sklar, "Hull House Maps and Papers: Social Science as Women's Work in the 1890s," in *The Social Survey in Historical Perspective, 1880–1940,* ed. Martin Bulmer, Kevin Bales, and Kathryn Kish Sklar (Cambridge: Cambridge University Press, 1991), 111–47.

35. AHC diary, 15 June 1923, CFP, SCL; Wilhelmina Barnwell, interview by Hillary Barnwell, Port Royal, S.C., ca. 1991, courtesy of Hillary Barnwell. See also "Shanklin School" chap., above.

36. Katherine Doctor, interview by author, Beaufort, S.C., 25 July 1996; Catherine DeVeaux to AHC, 16 Aug. 1934; 27 July 1936; 24 July, 12 Aug. 1938, CFP, SCL.

37. AHC to AOC, 28 Jan. 1903, 12 Dec. 1905, CFP, SCL; AHC to AOC, Aug. 1915 (in the possession of Paul Sommerville, Beaufort, S.C.); AHC, "Lesson 1st–Grade 2nd," Notes on AMORC Lectures, 1929, CFP, SCL.

38. L. W. Pollack to AHC, 15 Jan., 3 Mar. 1927; Order of Christian Mystics to AHC, 31 Jan. 1928, all in CFP, SCL.

39. AHC diary, 3 Apr. 1920, CFP, SCL; AHC diary, 27 July 1922, CFP, SCL; Parsons, *Folklore of the Sea Islands;* Georgia Writer's Project, *Drums and Shadows: Survival Studies among the Georgia Coastal Negroes* (Athens: University of Georgia Press, 1940); J. E. McTeer, *Fifty Years as a Low Country Witch Doctor* (Beaufort, S.C.: Beaufort Book Co, 1976); Kathryn Heyer, "Rootwork: Psychosocial Aspects of Malign Magical and Illness Beliefs in a South Carolina Sea Island Community" (Ph.D. diss., University of Connecticut, 1981); Juanita Jackson, Sabra Slaughter, and J. Herman Blake, "The Sea Islands as a Cultural Resource," *Black Scholar* 5 (Mar. 1974): 32–39; Patricia Jones-Jackson, *When Roots Die: Endangered Traditions on the Sea Islands* (Athens: University of Georgia Press, 1987); S. S. Walker, "African Gods in the Americas—The Black Religious Continuum," *Black Scholar* 11, no. 8 (1980): 25–36.

40. ACP to AHC, n.d., CFP, SCL.

41. Frances Yates, *The Rosicrucian Enlightenment* (London: Routledge & Kegan Paul, 1972), 30–31.

42. Ibid., 42, 44; J. Gordon Melton, *The Encyclopedia of American Religions* (Wilmington, N.C.: McGrath, 1978), 2:178; Niels Christensen III, interview by author, Beaufort, S.C., 24 Sept. 1991; Carroll Eve, interview by author, Pleasantview, Va., 30 Sept. 1991; Wilhelmina Barnwell, interview by author, Port Royal, S.C., 21 Nov. 1991.

43. J. Gordon Melton, "Introduction," in his *Rosicrucianism in America* (New York: Garland, 1990), 2–5; AHC, "Grade Two, Lesson Three," Notes in AMORC Lectures, 1929, CFP, SCL.

44. Ahlstrom, *Religious History,* 1044–45; Melton, *Encyclopedia,* 180, 182; AMORC, "Why Are We Here? and Why Are Our Lives Unequal," CFP, SCL.

45. AMORC, "For Meditation"; AHC, "2nd Grade, Lecture 4"; AHC, "Grade Two, Lesson Three," all in Notes on AMORC Lectures, 1919, CFP, SCL. For comparison to theosophy, see Mary Bednarowski, "Women in Occult America," in *The Occult in America: New Historical Perspectives,* ed. Howard Kerr and Charles Crow (Urbana: University of Illinois Press, 1983), 178–79, 183–88.

46. AMORC, Neophyte Lectures, Grade 1, 1–6 and Grade 2, 7; "The Book of Suggestions"; "For Meditation," all in AMORC Lectures; R. M. Lewis to AHC, 21, 25 Mar., 9, 24 May, 30, 31 Aug. 1929; AHC to R. M. Lewis, n.d., all in CFP, SCL.

47. AHC, "First Lesson—Mar. 9th" and "Third Lesson—Mar. 23rd"; Notes on AMORC Lectures, 1929; AHC to AOC, 19 May 1903, all in CFP, SCL. On Emerson's influence on Christensen's beliefs, see ch. 7, section on Unitarianism. Emerson, "The Oversoul," in *Ralph Waldo Emerson: Selected Essays, Lectures, and Poems,* 174–75.

48. A. H. Christensen, "For the Moral Education Association," 18 Apr. 1895; AHC, "First Lesson—Mar. 9th," Notes on AMORC Lectures, both in CFP, SCL; Niels Christensen III, interview by author, Beaufort, S.C., 24 Sept. 1991; Walter Hilton, "The Brotherhood of Man," in *The Open Door* (Boston: Unitarian Laymen's League, 1922); AHC, untitled poem, n.d.; Rev. Charles Ames, *The Judgement Day of the Church* (Boston: American Unitarian Association, n.d.); Charles Park, "The Greater Demand," n.d., CFP, SCL; AHC, "Lesson 12—Subject Concentration," Notes on AMORC Lectures, 1929, CFP, SCL.

49. AHC, "Lesson 12—Subject Concentration," Notes on AMORC Lectures, 1929, CFP, SCL.

50. AHC, "Lesson 1st—Grade 2nd," AMORC Notebook, 1929, CFP, SCL.

51. Nature cure involved vegetarianism and health foods such as bran bread. ACP to AHC, 28 Sept. 1920; AWC to AHC, 24 Nov. 1926; AHC, "Grade 2—Lecture 6," Notes on AMORC Lectures, 1929, CFP, SCL.

52. Margaret Jacob, *Living the Enlightenment: Freemasonry and Politics in Eighteenth-Century Europe* (New York: Oxford University Press, 1991), 23, 36.

53. AHC, "Lesson Eleven," Notes on AMORC Lectures, 1929, CFP, SCL.

54. AWC to AHC, 11, 23, 27 Oct., 4 Nov. 1924; 8 Feb., 24 Sept., 9, 16, 28 Oct., 2 Dec. 1925; 23 Feb., 15 Oct., n.d., 1927; 4 May 1928; 7 Apr., ca. 1 May, 26 June, 6 Oct. 1933; 10 Oct. 1934; Mar. 1935; 29 Mar.–1, 5 Apr. 1936; 18 Apr. 1937; 2 Apr. 1938; Evelyn K. Wells to AWC, 20 Jan., 15 Sept. 1934; Dr. Walter Mendelson to Sally Putnam and AWC, 8 Jan. 1937, all in CFP, SCL; Dunbar, *Against the Grain,*

50–82; T. J. Jackson Lears, *No Place of Grace: Antimodernism and the Transformation of American Culture, 1880–1920* (New York: Pantheon Books, 1981), 63–65, 88–89, 204, 209–14.

55. AHC diary, 8 Jan. 1911, CFP, SCL; AHC diary, 3 Sept. 1923, CFP, SCL; AOC to Lillian Dutton, 3 Jan. 1920 (in the possession of Paul Sommerville, Beaufort, S.C.).

56. FHC to AHC, 2 Oct. 1920; AHC, voter registration card, 7 July 1924; NC to AHC, 2 Sept. 1924; AHC to Family, 18 July 1928; Georgie French to AHC, 27 July 1929; Helen Burr Christensen to AHC, ca. 1931; AHC to Georgie French, 21 July 1931; Anna Eddy to AHC, 12 Aug. 1932; "Beaufort Woman of Eighty to Support Norman Thomas," ca. 1932, clipping, all in CFP, SCL.

57. Anna Eddy to AHC, 7 Sept. 1924, CFP, SCL; Willard quoted in Lebsock, "Women and American Politics," 55.

58. AHC to FHC, 31 Aug. 1930, CFP, SCL; Paula Baker, "The Domestication of Politics," 643–47; Lebsock, "Women and American Politics," 54–59.

59. AHC diary, 26 Mar. 1917; "Beaufort Woman of Eighty," ca. 1932, clipping, both in CFP, SCL.

60. "Truck News This Week," *Beaufort Gazette,* 17 April 1924; "Truck Market—Prices, Etc." *Beaufort Gazette,* 15 May 1924; FHC to Ladies, 19 July 1925, CFP, SCL; FHC to AHC, 6 Sept. 1925, CFP, SCL; AWC to AHC, 14 Sept. 1925, CFP, SCL; AWC to AHC, 8, 15 Dec. 1925, CFP, SCL; FHC diary, vol. 14, 15, 22 Feb., 16 Aug., 4 Oct., 13 Sept. 1925, SCL.

61. FHC diary, vol. 14, 20 Dec. 1925, SCL; Helen Burr to AHC, ca. 1925, CFP, SCL; "Beaufort Spirit Demonstrated in Notable Proffer" and "Right Sort of Spirit," *Beaufort Gazette,* 24 Dec. 1925; Niels Christensen and Frederik H. Christensen, "Word of Appreciation for Community Action," *Beaufort Gazette,* 31 Dec. 1925.

62. James G. Thomas, "Bay Street and Beaufort in the 1920's As I Remember It: A Speech to the Beaufort Historical Society," 25 July 1985, Beaufort County Library, Beaufort, S.C.; Sohier Welch to AHC, 13 June 1927, CFP, SCL; Herbert Greenwood to AHC, 6 May 1927, CFP, SCL; FHC to AHC, 8 July 1927, CFP, SCL; FHC diary, vol. 14, 31 Jan., 28 Feb., 7 Mar., 11 July 1926; 26 June 1927; 1 Apr. 1928, SCL.

63. AHC to AWC, 29 Oct. 1926, CFP, SCL; Helen Burr Christensen to AHC, 4 Aug. 1928, CFP, SCL; NC to AHC, 2 Sept. 1929, CFP, SCL; AHC to FHC, 28 Sept. 1929, CFP, SCL; AHC to Helen Burr Christensen, 9 Aug. 1930, CFP, SCL; AOC to AHC, 17 Aug. 1932, CFP, SCL; "Mrs. Martin Gives Her Side of the Starvation

Story in Beaufort," *Beaufort Gazette,* 13 Oct. 1932; A Friend, "Sketch of the Life of Mrs. Niels Christensen," *Beaufort Gazette,* 29 Sept. 1938.

64. Murray Seidler, *Norman Thomas: Respectable Rebel* (Binghamton, N.Y.: Syracuse University Press, 1961); W. A. Swanberg, *Norman Thomas: The Last Idealist* (New York: Charles Scribner, 1976); Irving Howe, *Socialism and America* (San Diego, Calif.: Harcourt, Brace, Jovanovich, 1985), 49; "Stores Cooperate in Buying," 18 July 1928, clipping, CFP, SCL; "Beaufort Woman of Eighty," ca. 1932, clipping, CFP, SCL.

65. Seidler, *Norman Thomas,* 1–124; Swanberg, *Norman Thomas,* 1–139; Howe, *Socialism and America,* 15, 42.

66. Seidler, *Respectable Rebel,* 73, 88–89; Norman Thomas, *America's Way Out: A Program for Democracy* (New York: Macmillan, 1931).

67. Howe, *Socialism and America,* 49, 51–52; Swanberg, *Norman Thomas,* 136; Dunbar, *Against the Grain,* 38–39.

68. AHC, "Letters," manuscript, 11 Aug. 1932, CFP, SCL; Julius Gerber to AHC, 13 Aug. 1932, CFP, SCL; FHC diary, vol. 14, 7 Nov. 1932, SCL.

69. FHC diary, vol. 14, 7 Nov. 1932, SCL; Nelle Gentry to AHC, 19 May 1933, CFP, SCL; Alice Stone Blackwell to AHC, Christmas 1922, ca. 1931, CFP, SCL; AHC to Alice Stone Blackwell, 30 Jan. 1923, 14 Dec. 1931, Blackwell Family Papers, Library of Congress, Washington, D.C.

70. FHC diary, vol. 14, 7 Nov. 1932, SCL; FHC diary, vol. 14, 24 Feb. 1935, SCL; NC Jr. to AHC, 13 Feb. 1935, 4 Nov. 1936, CFP, SCL.

71. Grace Imogene to AHC, 3–5 Sept., ca. 1932, CFP, SCL; Richard Britton to AHC, 18 Sept. 1932, CFP, SCL; Alma Holmes to AHC, ca. 1936, CFP, SCL; "Four Boxes Out of Eight Reported," *Beaufort Gazette,* 10 Nov. 1932; Niels Christensen III, interview by author, Beaufort, S.C., 24 Sept. 1991. The discrepancy between seven and two may stem from Christensen's grandson's referral to a different year or his unawareness of the other five votes.

72. AHC to FHC, 26 July 1934, CFP, SCL; AOC to AHC, 4 Sept. 1934, CFP, SCL; Norman Thomas to AHC, 23 Nov. 1934, CFP, SCL; Irving Howe, *Socialism and America,* 52–53; Dunbar, *Against the Grain,* 38–39; Bernard Johnpoll, *Pacifist's Progress: Norman Thomas and the Decline of American Socialism* (Chicago: Quadrangle, 1970), 102–3.

73. Thomas, *America's Way Out,* 223–25; Norman Thomas, *The Plight of the Sharecropper* (New York: League for Industrial Democracy, 1934); Irving Howe, *Socialism and America,* 75; Dunbar, *Against the Grain,* 8, 85–87; Swanberg, *Norman Thomas,* 158–63, 180–84; Seidler, *Respectable Rebel,* 2.

74. NC Jr. to AHC, 26 July, 4 Nov. 1936, CFP, SCL; "Christensen to Get a Good Job," 25 Jan. 1936, clipping, CFP, SCL; William Leuchtenburg, *Franklin Roosevelt and the New Deal, 1932–1940* (New York: Harper and Row, 1963), 95–166; Alan Brinkley, *Voices of Protest: Huey Long and Father Coughlin and the Great Depression* (New York: Random House, 1983), 238–41.

75. Clare Macdonald to AHC, 29 July 1928, CFP, SCL.

76. AHC to NC III, undated manuscript, CFP, SCL; "One Who Tried to Make the World Better," *Beaufort Gazette,* 15 Feb. 1906; Niels Christensen III, interview by author, Beaufort, S.C., 24 Sept. 1991.

77. AHC, "Reality," typed manuscript, n.d., and handwritten manuscript, June 1933, CFP, SCL; AHC, "Stroller," *Beaufort Gazette,* 15 Dec. 1908.

78. AHC, "Reality," typed manuscript, n.d., and handwritten manuscript, June 1933, CFP, SCL.

79. "In Appreciation," *Beaufort Gazette,* 11 Feb. 1909, clipping; AHC diary, 4 Feb.,10 June 1913; AHC diary, 4 Feb. 1916; AHC diary, 31 Jan. 1917; AHC diary, 5 Sept. 1918; AHC to AOC, "From the Song Celestial," 4 Feb. 1918; AHC diary, 28 Sept. 1918, on the afterlife of another friend, all in CFP, SCL.

80. Abbie M. Holmes Christensen, Death Certificate, 21 Sept. 1938, State of South Carolina, Bureau of Vital Statistics, Department of Health and Environmental Control, Columbia, S.C.

81. Abbie M. H. Christensen, "Last Will and Testament," 1 July 1930, and Niels Christensen and Frederik Christensen, "Petition for Executorship," 17 Oct. 1938, Beaufort County Court House, Beaufort, S.C.; Lebsock, *Free Women of Petersburg,* 54–86, 112–45.

82. FHC diary, vol. 15, 23 Sept. 1938, SCL.

Epilogue

1. Margaret Mitchell, *Gone with the Wind* (New York: Macmillan, 1936); Cash, *Mind of the South,* 137; Francis Griswold, *A Sea Island Lady* (New York: William Morrow, 1939), esp. 237–39. On the tremendous power of *Gone with the Wind* to shape popular American attitudes toward southern women's history, see "Front Porch," 1–5; Drew Faust, "Clutching the Chains That Bind: Margaret Mitchell and *Gone with the Wind,*" 6–20; Patricia Yaeger, "Race and the Cloud of Unknowing in *Gone with the Wind,*" 21–28; Anne Goodwyn Jones, "'I Was Telling It': Gender and the Puzzle of the Storyteller," 29–43; and Jacquelyn Dowd Hall, "'The Prong of Love,'" 44–48, all in *Southern Cultures* 5 (spring 1999).

2. Rev. S. M. Atkinson, Mrs. James Ross Macdonald, and Miss Sarah A. Putnam, "In Memoriam," ca. 1938, CFP, SCL.

3. Joseph Shanklin Jr., interview by author, Burton, S.C., 25 Sept. 1991.

4. Niels Christensen III, interview by author, Beaufort, S.C., 24 Sept. 1991.

5. Pete Daniel, *Lost Revolutions: The South in the 1950s* (Chapel Hill: University of North Carolina Press, 2000), 239–42; "Helen Burr Christensen," in Ralph E. Cousins, Joseph R. Horn III, Larry A. Jackson, John S. Lyles, and John B. Morris, comps., *South Carolinians Speak: A Moderate Approach to Race Relations* (N.p., 1957), 22–26; Frederik Burr Christensen, interview by author, Aiken, S.C., 7 Nov. 1991.

6. Evelyn Wells to AWC, 22 Oct. 1938, CFP, SCL.

Bibliography

Primary Sources

Manuscript Collections

Association of Collegiate Alumnae Census of College Women. Mount Holyoke College Archives, Mount Holyoke, Mass.

Beaufort Local History Vertical Files. South Carolina Room, Beaufort County Library, Beaufort, S.C.

Blackwell Family Papers. Library of Congress, Washington, D.C.

Bragg, Laura. Files. Biographical and Genealogical File, South Carolina Historical Society, Charleston, S.C.

Carteret Street Methodist Church. History Files. Beaufort, S.C.

Christensen family. Clippings and photocopies, "House album." Personal collection of Wyatt and Sally Pringle, Beaufort, S.C.

Christensen Family Papers. Personal collection of Carroll Eve and Paul Sommerville, Beaufort, S.C.

Christensen Family Papers. South Caroliniana Library, University of South Carolina, Columbia.

Christensen, Frederik Holmes. Diaries. South Caroliniana Library, University of South Carolina, Columbia.

Church of the Disciples. Notebooks. Boston, Massachusetts.

Clark, Septima Poinsette. Collection. Avery Institute of Afro-American History and Culture, Charleston, S.C.

Commission on Inter-racial Cooperation Collection. Trevor Arnett Library, Atlanta University, Atlanta, Ga. (microfilm).

Holmes Family Papers. New England Historic Genealogical Society, Boston, Mass.

Parsons, Elsie Clews. Papers. American Philosophical Society, Philadelphia, Pa.

Westborough Genealogy and Local History Files. Heritage Room, Westborough Public Library, Westborough, Mass.

Government Documents

Beaufort, City of. Minute Books, 1911–38. Beaufort, S.C. (microfilm).

United States Census of Population: 1880. Washington, D.C.: Government Printing Office.

United States Census of Population: 1910. Washington, D.C.: Government Printing Office.

United States Census of Population: 1920. Washington, D.C.: Government Printing Office.

United States Census of Population: 1930. Washington, D.C.: Government Printing Office.

U.S. Census: 1870, 1880, 1900, 1910, 1920. Population Schedules for Beaufort County. South Carolina State Archives, Columbia (microfilm).

Interviews

Austin, Victoria. Interview by author. Port Royal, S.C., 21 November 1991.

Barnwell, Wilhelmina. Interview by author. Port Royal, S.C., 21 November 1991.

Browne, Leroy, Sr. Edited excerpt of interview by Cece Byers, 23 Sept. 1980. Manuscript, South Caroliniana Library, Columbia, S.C.

Christensen, Frederik Burr. Interview by author. Aiken, S.C., 7 November 1991.

Christensen, Niels III. Interview by author. Beaufort, S.C., 24 September 1991.

Doctor, Katherine. Interview by author. Beaufort, S.C. 25 July 1996.

Eve, Carroll. Interview by author. Pleasantview, Va., 30 September 1991; Beaufort, S.C., 20 November 1991.

Keyserling, Herbert. Interview by author. Beaufort, S.C., November 1991.

Shanklin, Joseph Jr. Interview by author. Burton, S.C., 25 September 1991, 25 July 1996.

Singleton, Charles. Interview by author. Burton, S.C., November 1991, 3 March 1992.

Singleton, Inez. Interview by author. Ladies Island, S.C., March 1992.

Washington, Fred. Telephone Interview by author. 26 July 1996.

West, Thelma Shanklin. Interview by author. Beaufort, S.C., 26–27 July 1996.

Newspapers and Periodicals

Beaufort Gazette
Beaufort New South
Boston Evening Transcript

Charleston News and Courier
Journal of American Folklore
Mother's Assistant and Young Lady's Friend
New York Independent
Palmetto Post (Beaufort, S.C.)
Sea Islander (Beaufort, S.C.)
Springfield Daily Republican
The State
Union Signal
Woman's Journal

Published Works

Allen, W[illiam] F[rancis]. "The Negro Dialect." *The Nation* 1 (14 December 1865).

Allen, William Francis, Charles P. Ware, and Lucy McKim Garrison, eds. *Slave Songs of the United States*. 1867. Reprint, Baltimore, Md.: Clearfield Co., 1977.

Annual Report of the Port Royal Agricultural School, Beaufort, South Carolina, 1903–1904. Savannah, Ga.: Savannah Morning News, 1904.

Anthony, Susan B., and Ida Harper, eds. *History of Woman Suffrage*. Vol. 4. Rochester, N.Y.: Susan B. Anthony, 1902.

Barrows, C[harles] M. *Bread Pills: A Study of Mind-Cure*. Boston: Deland and Barta, 1885.

Blackwell, Alice Stone. *Lucy Stone: Pioneer of Woman's Rights*. Norwood, Mass.: Plimpton Press, 1930.

Bland, Sidney. "Fighting the Odds! Militant Suffragists in South Carolina." *South Carolina Historical Magazine* 82, no. 1 (1981): 32–43.

Botume, Elizabeth Hyde. *First Days amongst the Contrabands*. Boston: Lee and Shepard, 1893.

Caldwell, A. B., ed. *History of the American Negro*. Vol. 3. South Carolina edition. Atlanta, Ga.: Author, 1919.

Catalogue of the Officers and Members of the Ipswich Female Seminary. Boston: Rand, Avery and Cornhill, 1864.

Christensen, Abbie Holmes. *Afro-American Folk Lore as Told 'Round Cabin Fires on the Sea Islands of South Carolina*. 1892. Reprint, New York: Negro Universities Press, 1969.

———. "Folklore on Sea Islands." *Mount Holyoke Alumnae Quarterly* 16 (February 1933): 202–4.

———. "Negro Folklore: The Elephant and the Rabbit." *New York Independent* 27 (2 September 1875): 25.

———. "Negro Folk Lore: The Rabbit Desires a Long Tail." *New York Independent* 28 (9 March 1876): 26.

———. "The Rabbit and the Wolf Plant Potatoes and Hunt Honey." *New York Independent* 29 (1 November 1877): 26.

———. "The Rabbit, the Wolf, and the Keg of Butter: A Negro Legend." *New York Independent* 27 (18 November 1875): 27.

———. "The Reason Why Brother Rabbit Wears a Short Tail: A Negro Legend." *New York Independent* 28 (1 June 1876): 25–26.

———. "Spirituals and 'Shouts' of Southern Negroes." *Journal of American Folklore* 7 (April–June 1894): 154–55.

———. "A Story-Teller." *New York Independent* 27 (28 October 1875): 26.

Christensen, Helen Burr. "Helen Burr Christensen, Beaufort, S.C." In *South Carolinians Speak: A Moderate Approach to Race Relations,* compiled by Ralph E. Cousins, Joseph R. Horn III, Larry A. Jackson, John S. Lyles, and John B. Morris, 22–26. N.p., 1957.

Christensen, Niels. "Fifty Years of Freedom: Conditions in the Sea Coast Regions." In *Annals of the American Academy.* Philadelphia: American Academy of Political and Social Science, 1913.

Clark, Septima Poinsette. *Echo in my Soul.* New York: Dutton, 1962.

———. *Ready from Within: Septima Clark and the Civil Rights Movement.* Navarro, Calif.: Wild Trees Press, 1986.

Cobb, Eunice Hale, and Sylvanus Cobb. *The Memoir of James Arthur Cobb.* 2d ed. Boston: S. Cobb. 1852.

Cooper, Anna Julia. *A Voice from the South.* 1892. Reprint, New York: Oxford University Press, 1988.

Dearing, Rachel Reed. "Westborough Commemorative Booklet, 1717–1967." North Conway, N.H.: Reporter Press, 1967.

De Forest, Heman, and Edward Bates. *The History of Westborough, Massachusetts.* 1891. Reprint, Boston: New England Genealogical Society, 1998.

Dixon, Thomas. *The Clansman: An Historical Romance of the Ku Klux Klan.* 1905. Reprint, Ridgewood, N.J.: Gregg Press, 1967.

Du Bois, W. E. B. *The Souls of Black Folk.* 1903. Reprint, New York: Vintage Books, 1990.

Edgar, Walter. *South Carolina: A History.* Columbia: University of South Carolina Press, 1998.

Emerson, Ralph Waldo. *Nature.* 1836. Reprinted in *Ralph Waldo Emerson: Selected Essays, Lectures, and Poems,* ed. Robert Richardson. New York: Bantam Books, 1990.

———. "The Oversoul." In *Essays, First Series.* 1841. Reprinted in *Ralph Waldo Emerson: Selected Essays, Lectures, and Poems,* ed. Robert Richardson. New York: Bantam Books, 1990.

Fields, Mamie Garvin, with Karen Fields. *Lemon Swamp and Other Places: A Carolina Memoir.* New York: Macmillan, 1983.

Fisher, Dorothy Canfield. *A Montessori Mother.* New York: Holt, 1912.

Foote, Henry Wilder. *The Penn School on St. Helena Island.* Hampton, Va.: Hampton Institute Press, 1904.

Forten, Charlotte. "Life on the Sea Islands." *Atlantic Monthly* 13 (May 1864): 587–96; (June 1864): 666–76.

Gerber, Adolph. "Uncle Remus Traced to the Old World." *Journal of American Folklore* 6 (October–December 1893): 245–57.

Gonzales, Ambrose. *The Black Border.* Columbia S.C.: The State, 1922.

Gordon, Asa. *Sketches of Negro Life and History in South Carolina.* 1929. Reprint, Columbia: University of South Carolina Press, 1971.

Griswold, Francis. *A Sea Island Lady.* New York: William Morrow, 1939.

Hampton, Wade. "What Negro Supremacy Means." *Forum* 5 (June 1888): 383–95.

Harper, Frances. *Iola Leroy.* 1893. Reprint, New York: Oxford University Press, 1988.

Harper, Ida, ed. *The History of Woman Suffrage.* Vol. 6. New York: National American Woman Suffrage Association, 1922.

Harris, Joel Chandler. *Nights with Uncle Remus: Myths and Legends of the Old Plantation.* Boston: Houghton Mifflin, 1883.

———. *Uncle Remus: His Songs and Sayings.* New York: Appleton, 1880.

———. *Wally Wanderoon and His Story-Telling Machine.* New York: McClure, Philips, 1903.

Harris, Julia Collier. *The Life and Letters of Joel Chandler Harris.* New York: Houghton Mifflin, 1918.

Higginson, Thomas Wentworth. *Army Life in a Black Regiment.* 1869. Reprint, New York: W. W. Norton, 1984.

Historical Sketch of Mount Holyoke Seminary. Springfield, Mass.: Clark W. Bryan & Co., 1878.

Homeopathic Medical Primer. Baltimore, Md.: Waverly Press, n.d.

Holland, Rupert S., ed. *Letters and Diary of Laura M. Towne.* 1912. Reprint, New York: Negro Universities Press, 1969.

H[olmes], A[bbie] M[andana]. "De Wolf, De Rabbit an' De Tar Baby." *Springfield Daily Republican,* 2 June 1874, p. 8.

———. "The Story Aunt 'Tilda Told," *New York Independent* (5 November 1874): 14.

Howe, Julia Ward. *Sex and Education: A Reply to Dr. E. H. Clarke's Sex in Education.* 1874. Reprint, New York: Arno Press, 1972.

Ipswich in the Massachusetts Bay Colony. Vol. 2. Ipswich, Mass.: Ipswich Historical Society, 1917.

Jones, Charles Colcock. *Negro Myths of the Georgia Coast.* 1888. Reprint, Columbia, S.C.: The State, 1925.

Keyserling, Harriet. *Against the Tide: One Woman's Political Struggle.* Columbia: University of South Carolina Press, 1998.

King, Edward. *The Great South.* Hartford, Conn.: American Publishing, 1875.

Larcom, Lucy. *A New England Girlhood.* 1889. Reprint, Boston: Northeastern University Press, 1986.

Livermore, Mary. *The Story of My Life.* 1897. Reprint, New York: Arno Press, 1974.

Macdonald, Clare. *Recollections of Juliana.* Columbia, S.C.: The State, 1924.

McKim, James Miller. "Songs of the Port Royal 'Contrabands.'" *Dwight's Journal of Music* 22 (1862), 254–55.

McTeer, J. E. *Fifty Years as a Low Country Witch Doctor.* Beaufort, S.C.: Beaufort Book Co., 1976.

Mitchell, Margaret. *Gone with the Wind.* New York: Macmillan, 1936.

Montessori, Maria. *The Montessori Method.* Translated by Anne George. 1912. Reprint, New York: Schocken, 1964.

Parsons, Elsie Clews. *Folklore of the Sea Islands, South Carolina.* Cambridge, Mass.: American Folklore Society, 1923.

———. *Folk-Tales of Andros Island, Bahamas.* Cambridge, Mass.: American Folklore Society, 1918.

———. "Joel Chandler Harris and Negro Folklore." *The Dial* 66 (17 May 1919): 491–93.

Pearson, Elizabeth Ware, ed. *Letters from Port Royal, 1862–1868.* 1906. Reprint, New York: Arno Press, 1969.

Peterkin, Genevieve. *Heaven Is a Beautiful Place: A Memoir of the South Carolina Coast.* Columbia: University of South Carolina Press, 2000.

Pike, James. *The Prostrate State: South Carolina under Negro Government.* New York: Appleton, 1874.

Pinckney, Rev. Charles Cotesworth. *The Life of General Thomas Pinckney.* Boston: Houghton Mifflin, 1895.

Pringle, Elizabeth Allston. *A Woman Rice Planter.* 1913. Reprint, Columbia: University of South Carolina Press, 1992.

Rice, Franklin. *The Worcester Book: A Diary of Noteworthy Events in Worcester, Massachusetts from 1857–1883.* Worcester, Mass.: Putnam, Davis and Co., 1884.

———. *Dictionary of Worcester (Massachusetts) and Its Vicinity.* 2d ed. Worcester, Mass.: F. S. Blanchard, 1893.

"The Sea Islands." *Harper's* 57 (November 1878): 839–61.

Still, William. *The Underground Railroad.* 1872. Reprint, New York: Arno Press, 1968.

Thomas, Norman. *America's Way Out: A Program for Democracy.* New York: Macmillan, 1931.

———. *The Plight of the Share-Cropper.* New York: League for Industrial Democracy, 1934.

Troward, Thomas. *The Edinburgh Lectures in Mental Science.* 1909. Reprint, New York: McBride, Nast, 1915.

Valuation and Taxes of the Town of Westborough. Worcester, Mass.: Howland, 1856.

Wake, C. S., ed. *Memoirs of the International Congress of Anthropology.* Chicago: Schulte, 1894.

Washburn, Emory. *A Brief Sketch of the History of Leicester Academy.* Boston: Phillips, Sampson and Co., 1855.

Washington, Mrs. Booker T. "What Girls Are Taught and How." In *Tuskegee and Its People: Their Ideals and Achievements,* ed. Booker T. Washington. New York: D. Appleton, 1905.

Wells, Ida B. *Southern Horrors and Other Writings: The Anti-Lynching Campaign of Ida B. Wells.* Boston: Bedford, 1997.

Whitney, A. D. T. *Hitherto: A Story of Yesterdays.* Boston: Loring, 1869.

Williams, John. *De Ole Plantation.* Charleston, S.C.: Walker, Evans and Cogswell, 1895.

Woofter, Thomas Jackson. *Black Yeomanry: Life on St. Helena Island.* New York: Henry Holt, 1930.

Secondary Sources

Abram, Ruth, ed. *"Send Us a Lady Physician": Women Doctors in America, 1835–1920.* New York: W. W. Norton, 1985.

Ahlstrom, Sidney W. W. *A Religious History of the American People.* New Haven, Conn.: Yale University Press, 1972.

Alexander, Adele Logan. "How I Discovered My Grandmother . . . and the Truth about Black Women and the Suffrage Movement." *Ms.* 12 (November 1983): 29–37.

Allen, Kristina. *On the Beaten Path: Westborough Massachusetts.* Westborough, Mass.: Westborough Civic Club and Historical Society, 1984.

Allen, Louise Anderson. *A Bluestocking in Charleston: The Life and Career of Laura Bragg.* Columbia: University of South Carolina Press, 2001.

Alpern, Sara, Joyce Antler, Elisabeth Perry, and Ingrid Scobie, eds. *The Challenge of Feminist Biography.* Urbana: University of Illinois Press, 1992.

Anderson, Eric. *Race and Politics in North Carolina, 1872–1901: The Black Second.* Baton Rouge: Louisiana State University Press, 1981.

Anderson, James. *The Education of Blacks in the South, 1860–1935.* Chapel Hill: University of North Carolina Press, 1988.

Apple, Rima, ed. *Women, Health and Medicine: A Historical Handbook.* New Brunswick: Rutgers University Press, 1990.

Aries, Philippe. *Centuries of Childhood: A Social History of Family Life.* Translated by Robert Baldick. New York: Random House, 1962.

Ayers, Edward. *The Promise of the New South: Life after Reconstruction.* New York: Oxford, 1992.

Bacon, Margaret Hope. "Lucy McKim Garrison: Pioneer in Folk Music." *Pennsylvania History* 54, no. 1 (1987): 1–16.

Baer, Florence. *Sources and Analogues of the Uncle Remus Tales.* Folklore Fellows Communications no. 228. Helsinki: Finnish Scientific Academy, 1981.

Baker, Houston. *Blues, Ideology and Afro-American Literature: A Vernacular Theory.* Chicago: University of Chicago Press, 1984.

Baker, Paula. "The Domestication of Politics: Women and American Political Society, 1780–1920." *American Historical Review* 89 (June 1984): 620–47.

Baker, Ray Stannard. *Following the Color Line: American Negro Citizenship in the Progressive Era.* New York: Harper and Row, 1964.

Bakhtin, M. M. *The Dialogic Imagination.* Edited by Michael Holquist and translated by Caryl Emerson. Austin: University of Texas Press, 1981.

Bannister, Robert. *Social Darwinism: Science and Myth in Anglo-American Social Thought.* Philadelphia: Temple University Press, 1979.

Bardaglio, Peter. *Reconstructing the Household: Families, Sex, and the Law in the Nineteenth Century South.* Chapel Hill: University of North Carolina Press, 1995.

Bass, Dorothy. "'Their Prodigious Influence': Women, Religion, and Reform in Antebellum America." In *Women of Spirit: Female Leadership in the Jewish and Christian Traditions,* ed. Rosemary Ruether and Eleanor McLaughlin. New York: Simon & Schuster, 1979.

Beardsley, Edward. *A History of Neglect: Health Care for Blacks and Mill Workers in the Twentieth Century South.* Knoxville: University of Tennessee Press, 1987.

Bednarowski, Mary. "Women in Occult America." In *The Occult in America: New Historical Perspectives,* ed. Howard Kerr and Charles Crow, 177–95. Urbana: University of Illinois Press, 1983.

Bellows, Barbara. *Benevolence among Slaveholders: Assisting the Poor in Charleston, 1670–1860.* Baton Rouge: Louisiana State University Press, 1993.

Berg, Barbara. *The Remembered Gate: Origins of American Feminism.* New York: Oxford University Press, 1978.

Berkeley, Kathleen. "'Colored Ladies Also Contributed': Black Women's Activities from Benevolence to Social Welfare, 1866–1896." In *The Web of Southern Social Relations: Women, Family and Education,* ed. Walter J. Fraser, R. Frank Saunders, and Jon Wakelyn, 181–203. Athens: University of Georgia Press, 1985.

Berlin, Ira, Steven Miller, and Leslie Rowland. "Afro-American Families in the Transition from Slavery to Freedom," *Radical History Review* 42 (fall 1988): 89–121.

Bernhard, Virginia, Betty Brandon, Elizabeth Fox-Genovese, Theda Perdue, and Elizabeth Hayes Turner, eds. *Hidden Histories of Women in the New South.* Columbia: University of Missouri Press, 1994.

Bickley, Bruce Jr. *Joel Chandler Harris.* Boston: Twayne, 1978.

————, ed. *Critical Essays on Joel Chandler Harris.* Boston: G. K. Hall, 1981.

Biderman, Gail. *Manliness and Civilization: A Cultural History of Gender and Race in the United States, 1880–1917.* Chicago: University of Chicago Press, 1995.

Blair, Karen. *The Clubwoman as Feminist: True Womanhood Redefined, 1868–1914.* New York: Holmes and Meier, 1980.

Bland, Sidney. "Fighting the Odds: Militant Suffragists in South Carolina." *South Carolina Historical Magazine* 82 (January 1981), 32–43.

————. *Preserving Charleston's Past, Shaping Its Future: The Life and Times of Susan Pringle Frost.* Columbia: University of South Carolina Press, 1999.

Blee, Kathleen. *Women of the Klan: Racism and Gender in the 1920s.* Berkeley: University of California Press, 1991.

Bleser, Carol, ed. *In Joy and Sorrow: Women, Family and Marriage in the Victorian South, 1830–1900.* New York: Oxford University Press, 1991.

————. *The Promised Land: The History of the South Carolina Land Commission, 1869–90.* Columbia: University of South Carolina Press, 1969.

Bordin, Ruth. *Frances Willard: A Biography.* Chapel Hill: University of North Carolina Press, 1986.

————. *Woman and Temperance: The Quest for Power and Liberty, 1873–1900.* Philadelphia: Temple University Press, 1981.

Bowie, Fiona, Deborah Kirkwood, and Shirley Ardener, eds. *Women and Missions: Past and Present: Anthropological and Historical Perceptions.* Providence, R.I.: Berg, 1993.

Boyer, Paul. *Urban Masses and Moral Order in America, 1820–1920.* Cambridge: Harvard University Press, 1978.

Braden, Charles. *Spirits in Rebellion: The Rise and Development of New Thought.* Dallas: Southern Methodist University Press, 1963.

Brasch, William. *Brer Rabbit, Uncle Remus, and the "Cornfield Journalist."* Macon, Ga.: Mercer University Press, 2000.

Braude, Ann. *Radical Spirits: Spiritualism and Women's Rights in Nineteenth Century America.* Boston: Beacon Press, 1989.

Braxton, Joanne. *Black Women Writing Autobiography: A Tradition within a Tradition.* Philadelphia: Temple University Press, 1989.

Brinkley, Alan. *Voices of Protest: Huey Long and Father Coughlin and the Great Depression.* New York: Random House, 1983.

Brown, Elsa Barkley. "African-American Women's Quilting: A Framework for Conceptualizing and Teaching African-American Women's History." *Signs* 14 (summer 1984): 921–29.

———. "'What Has Happened Here?': The Politics of Difference in Women's History and Feminist Politics." In *"We Specialize in the Wholly Impossible": A Reader in Black Women's History,* ed. Darlene Clark Hine, Wilma King, and Linda Reed, 449–88. Brooklyn: Carlson, 1995.

———. "Womanist Consciousness: Maggie Lena Walker and the Independent Order of St. Luke," *Signs* 14 (spring 1989): 610–33.

Brundage, W. Fitzhugh. *Lynching in the New South: Georgia and Virginia, 1880–1930.* Urbana: University of Illinois Press, 1993.

Buhle, Mari Jo. *Women and American Socialism, 1870–1920.* Urbana: University of Illinois Press, 1981.

Burr, Virginia, ed. *The Secret Eye: The Journal of Ella Gertrude Clanton Thomas, 1848–1889.* Introduction by Nell Painter. Chapel Hill: University of North Carolina Press, 1990.

Burton, Orville Vernon. "'The Black Squint of the Law': Racism in South Carolina." In *The Meaning of South Carolina History: Essays in Honor of George C. Rogers, Jr.,* ed. David Chesnutt and Clyde Wilson, 161–85. Columbia: University of South Carolina Press, 1991.

———, and Robert McMath Jr. *Toward a New South? Studies in Post–Civil War Communities.* Westport, Conn.: Greenwood Press, 1982.

Carawan, Guy, and Candie Carawan, eds. *"Ain't You Got a Right to the Tree of Life?"* Rev. ed. Athens: University of Georgia Press, 1989.

Carby, Hazel. *Reconstructing Womanhood: The Emergence of the Afro-American Woman Novelist.* New York: Oxford University Press, 1987.

Carlton, David. *Mill and Town in South Carolina, 1880–1920.* Baton Rouge: Louisiana State University Press, 1982.

Cash, Wilbur J. *The Mind of the South.* 1941. Reprint, New York: Random House, 1991.

Cayleff, Susan. "Gender, Ideology and the Water Cure Movement." In *Other Healers: Unorthodox Medicine in America,* ed. Norman Gevitz, 82–98. Baltimore, Md.: Johns Hopkins University Press, 1988.

————. *Wash and Be Healed: The Water-Cure Movement and Women's Health.* Philadelphia: Temple University Press, 1987.

Cell, John. *The Highest Stage of White Supremacy: The Origins of Segregation in South Africa and the American South.* New York: Cambridge University Press, 1982.

Chafe, William. *The American Woman: Her Changing Social, Economic and Political Roles, 1920–1970.* New York: Oxford University Press, 1972.

Chalmers, David. *Hooded Americanism: The History of the Ku Klux Klan.* 2d ed. New York: New Viewpoints, 1981.

Clarke, E. H. *Sex in Education, or A Fair Chance for Girls.* Boston: J. R. Osgood & Co., 1873.

Clark-Lewis, Elizabeth. *Living In, Living Out: African American Domestics in Washington, D.C., 1910–1940.* Washington, D.C.: Smithsonian Institution Press, 1994.

Clayton, Bruce. *The Savage Ideal: Intolerance and Intellectual Leadership in the South, 1890–1914.* Baltimore, Md.: Johns Hopkins University Press, 1972.

Clements, William, ed. *100 Years of American Folklore Studies: A Conceptual History.* Washington, D.C.: American Folklore Society, 1988.

Clifford, James. *The Predicament of Culture: Twentieth-Century Ethnography, Literature, and Art.* Cambridge: Harvard University Press, 1988.

Clifford, James, and George Marcus, eds. *Writing Culture: The Poetics and Politics of Ethnography.* Berkeley: University of California Press, 1986.

Clinton, Catherine. *Fanny Kemble's Civil Wars.* New York: Simon and Schuster, 2000.

————. *The Plantation Mistress: Woman's World in the Old South.* New York: Pantheon, 1982.

————. *Tara Revisited: Women, War and the Plantation Legend.* New York: Abbeville Press, 1995.

Clinton, Catherine, and Nina Silber, eds. *Divided Houses: Gender and the Civil War.* New York: Oxford University Press, 1992.

Cole, Luella. *A History of Education: Socrates to Montessori.* New York: Rinehart, 1950.

Collins, Patricia Hill. *Black Feminist Thought: Knowledge, Consciousness, and the Politics of Empowerment.* Boston: Unwin Hyman, 1990.

Cooke, Blanche Wiesen. "Female Support Networks and Political Activism: Lillian Wald, Crystal Eastman, Emma Goldman." In *A Heritage of Her Own: Toward a New Social History of American Women,* ed. Nancy Cott and Elizabeth Pleck, 412–44. New York: Simon and Schuster, 1979.

Cooper, William. *The Conservative Regime, South Carolina, 1877–1890.* Baltimore, Md.: Johns Hopkins University Press, 1968.

Cott, Nancy. *The Bonds of Womanhood: "Women's Sphere" in New England, 1780–1835.* New Haven, Conn.: Yale University Press, 1977.

———. "'Across the Great Divide': Women in Politics before and after 1920." In *Women, Politics, and Change,* ed. Louise Tilly and Patricia Gurin, 153–76. New York: Russell Sage Foundation, 1990.

Cousins, Paul. *Joel Chandler Harris.* Baton Rouge: Louisiana State University Press, 1968.

Creel, Margaret Washington. *"A Peculiar People": Slave Religion and Community Culture among the Gullahs.* New York: New York University Press, 1988.

Daniel, Pete. *Lost Revolutions: The South in the 1950s.* Chapel Hill: University of North Carolina Press, 2000.

Davis, Gerald. "Afro-American Coil Basketry in Charleston County, South Carolina." In *American Folklife,* ed. Don Yoder, 151–84. Austin: University of Texas Press, 1976.

Degler, Carl. *At Odds: Women and Family in America from the Revolution to the Present.* New York: Oxford University Press, 1980.

Douglas, Ann. *The Feminization of American Culture.* New York: Knopf, 1977.

Doyle, Don. *New Men, New Cities, New South: Atlanta, Nashville, Charleston, Mobile, 1860–1910.* Chapel Hill: University of North Carolina Press, 1990.

Drago, Edmund. *Initiative, Paternalism, and Race Relations: Charleston's Avery Normal Institute.* Athens: University of Georgia Press, 1990.

DuBois, Ellen. *Feminism and Suffrage: The Emergence of an Independent Women's Movement in America, 1848–1869.* Ithaca: Cornell University Press, 1978.

Dudden, Faye. *Serving Women: Household Service in Nineteenth-Century America.* Middletown, Conn.: Wesleyan University Press, 1983.

Dunbar, Anthony. *Against the Grain: Southern Radicals and Prophets, 1929–1959.* Charlottesville: University of Virginia Press, 1981.

Edelstein, Tilden. *Strange Enthusiasm: A Life of Thomas Wentworth Higginson.* New Haven, Conn.: Yale University Press, 1968.

Edgar, Walter. *South Carolina: A History.* Columbia: University of South Carolina Press, 1998.

———. *South Carolina in the Modern Age.* Columbia: University of South Carolina Press, 1992.

Ellwood, Robert. "The American Theosophical Synthesis." In *The Occult in America: New Historical Perspectives,* ed. Howard Kerr and Charles Crow, 111–33. Urbana: University of Illinois Press, 1983.

Engs, Robert. *Educating the Disfranchised and Disinherited: Samuel Chapman Armstrong and Hampton Institute, 1839–1893.* Knoxville: University of Tennessee Press, 1999.

———. *Freedom's First Generation: Black Hampton, Virginia, 1861–1890.* Philadelphia: University of Pennsylvania Press, 1979.

Enstam, Elizabeth. "'They Called It Motherhood': Dallas Women and Public Life, 1895–1918." In *Hidden Histories of Women in the New South,* ed. Virginia Bernhard, Betty Brandon, Elizabeth Fox-Genovese, Theda Purdue, and Elizabeth Turner, 71–95. Columbia: University of Missouri Press, 1994.

Epstein, Barbara. *The Politics of Domesticity: Women, Evangelism and Temperance in Nineteenth Century America.* Middletown, Conn.: Wesleyan University Press, 1981.

Escott, Paul. "Clinton A. Cilley, a Yankee War Hero in the Postwar South: A Study in the Compatibility of Regional Values." *North Carolina Historical Review* 68, no. 4 (1991), 404–26.

Faust, Drew. "Clutching the Chains That Bind: Margaret Mitchell and *Gone with the Wind.*" *Southern Cultures* 5 (spring 1999): 6–20.

———. *James Henry Hammond and the Old South: A Design for Mastery.* Baton Rouge: Louisiana State University Press, 1982.

———. *Mothers of Invention: Women of the Slaveholding South in the American Civil War.* Chapel Hill: University of North Carolina Press, 1996.

Fields, Barbara. "Ideology and Race in American History." In *Region, Race and Reconstruction,* ed. J. Morgan Kousser and James McPherson, 143–78. New York: Oxford University Press, 1982.

Flexner, Eleanor. *Century of Struggle: The Women's Rights Movement in the United States.* 1959. Rev. ed. Cambridge: Harvard University Press, 1975.

Foner, Eric. *Reconstruction: America's Unfinished Revolution, 1863–1877.* New York: Harper and Row, 1988.

Foster, Frances Smith. *A Brighter Coming Day: A Frances Ellen Watkins Harper Reader.* New York: Feminist Press, 1990.

Fox-Genovese, Elizabeth. *Within the Plantation Household: Black and White Women of the Old South.* Chapel Hill: University of North Carolina Press, 1988.

Frankel, Noralee, and Nancy S. Dye, eds. *Gender, Class, Race and Reform in the Progressive Era.* Lexington: University Press of Kentucky, 1991.

Frankenberg, Ruth. *White Women, Race Matters: The Social Construction of Whiteness.* Minneapolis: University of Minnesota Press, 1993.

Fraser, Nancy. *Unruly Practices: Power, Discourse and Gender in Contemporary Social Theory.* Minneapolis: University of Minnesota Press, 1989.

Fraser, Walter. *Charleston! Charleston!: The History of a Southern City.* Columbia: University of South Carolina Press, 1989.

Fraser, Walter Jr., R. Frank Saunders Jr., and Jon Wakelyn, eds. *The Web of Southern Social Relations: Women, Family and Education.* Athens: University of Georgia Press, 1985.

Fredrickson, George. *The Black Image in the White Mind: The Debate on Afro-American Character and Destiny, 1817–1914.* New York: Harper and Row, 1972.

Friedman, Jean. *The Enclosed Garden: Women and Community in the Evangelical South, 1830–1900.* Chapel Hill: University of North Carolina Press, 1985.

Gaines, Kevin. *Uplifting the Race: Black Leadership, Politics and Culture in the Twentieth Century.* Chapel Hill: University of North Carolina Press, 1996.

Gaston, Paul. *The New South Creed: A Study in Southern Mythmaking.* New York: Knopf, 1970.

Gates, Henry Louis Jr., ed. *"Race," Writing, and Difference.* Chicago: University of Chicago Press, 1986.

————. *The Signifying Monkey: A Theory of African-American Literary Criticism.* New York: Oxford University Press, 1988.

Gates, Henry Louis Jr., and Nellie McKay, eds. *The Norton Anthology of African American Literature.* New York: W. W. Norton, 1997.

Gelston, Arthur. "Radical vs. Straight-Out in Post-Reconstruction Beaufort County." *South Carolina Historical Magazine* 75 (1974): 225–37.

Georgia Writer's Project. *Drums and Shadows.* 1940. Reprint, with foreword by Guy Johnson, Westport, Conn.: Greenwood Press, 1973.

Gilmore, Glenda. "Gender and Jim Crow: Sarah Dudley Pettey's Vision of the New South." *North Carolina Historical Review* 68 (July 1991): 261–85.

———. *Gender and Jim Crow: Women and the Politics of White Supremacy in North Carolina, 1896–1920.* Chapel Hill: University of North Carolina Press, 1996.

Ginzburg, Lori. *Women and the Work of Benevolence: Morality, Politics and Class in the Nineteenth Century United States.* New Haven, Conn.: Yale University Press, 1990.

Glatthaar, Joseph. *Forged in Battle: The Civil War Alliance of Black Soldiers and White Officers.* New York: Free Press, 1990.

Glenn, Evelyn Nakano, Grace Chang, and Linda Forcey, eds. *Mothering: Ideology, Experience, and Agency.* New York: Routledge, 1994.

Goings, Kenneth. *Mammy and Uncle Mose: Black Collectibles and American Stereotyping.* Bloomington: Indiana University Press, 1994.

Goldsmith, Barbara. *Other Powers: The Age of Suffrage, Spiritualism, and the Scandalous Victoria Woodhull.* New York: Knopf, 1998.

Gordon, Linda. "Black and White Visions of Welfare: Women's Welfare Activism, 1890–1945." In *"We Specialize in the Wholly Impossible": A Reader in Black Women's History,* ed. Darlene Clark Hine, Wilma King, and Linda Reed, 449–88. Brooklyn: Carlson, 1995.

Gossett, Thomas. *Race: The History of an Idea in America.* Dallas, Tex.: Southern Methodist University Press, 1963.

Grantham, Dewey. *Southern Progressivism: The Reconciliation of Progress and Tradition.* Knoxville: University of Tennessee Press, 1983.

Green, Elna. *Southern Strategies: Southern Women and the Woman Suffrage Question.* Chapel Hill: University of North Carolina Press, 1997.

Green, Harvey. *The Light of the Home: An Intimate View of the Lives of Women in Victorian America.* New York: Pantheon, 1983.

Greenwood, Janette Thomas. *Bittersweet Legacy: The Black and White "Better Classes" in Charlotte, 1850–1910.* Chapel Hill: University of North Carolina Press, 1994.

Griffith, Elisabeth. *In Her Own Right: The Life of Elizabeth Cady Stanton.* New York: Oxford University Press, 1984.

Habermas, Jurgen. *The Structural Transformation of the Public Sphere.* Translated by Thomas Burger. Cambridge: MIT Press, 1989.

Hale, Grace Elizabeth. *Making Whiteness: The Culture of Segregation in the South, 1890–1940.* New York: Vintage Books, 1998.

Hall, Jacquelyn Dowd. *Revolt against Chivalry: Jessie Daniel Ames and the Women's Campaign against Lynching.* New York: Columbia University Press, 1974.

Harlan, Louis. *Booker T. Washington: The Making of a Black Leader, 1856–1901.* Vol. 1 New York: Oxford University Press, 1972.

———. *Booker T. Washington: The Wizard of Tuskegee, 1901–1915.* Vol. 2. New York: Oxford University Press, 1983.

———. *Separate and Unequal: Public School Campaigns and Racism in the Southern Seaboard States.* 1958. Reprint, New York: Atheneum, 1968.

Harris, Barbara, and Jo Ann McNamara, eds. *Women and the Structure of Society: Papers from the Fifth Berkshire Conference on the History of Women.* Durham, N.C.: Duke University Press, 1984.

Harris, Julia Collier. *The Life and Letters of Joel Chandler Harris.* New York: Houghton & Mifflin, 1918.

Hedrick, Joan. *Harriet Beecher Stowe: A Life.* New York: Oxford University Press, 1994.

Heilbrun, Carolyn. *Writing a Woman's Life.* New York: Ballantine, 1988.

Helly, Dorothy, and Susan Reverby, eds. *Gendered Domains: Rethinking Public and Private in Women's History.* Ithaca: Cornell University Press, 1992.

Herskovits, Melville. *The Myth of the Negro Past.* 1941. Reprint, Boston: Beacon Press, 1958.

Hewitt, Nancy. "Politicizing Domesticity: Anglo, Black and Latin Women in Tampa's Progressive Movements." In *Gender, Class, Race and Reform in the Progressive Era,* ed. Noralee Frankel and Nancy Schrom Dye, 24–41. Lexington: University of Kentucky Press, 1991.

———. *Women's Activism and Social Change: Rochester, New York, 1822–1872.* Ithaca: Cornell University Press, 1984.

Hewitt, Nancy, and Suzanne Lebsock, eds. *Visible Women: New Essays in American Activism.* Urbana: University of Illinois Press, 1993.

Higginbotham, Evelyn Brooks. "African-American Women's History and the Metalanguage of Race." *Signs* 17 (winter 1992): 251–74.

———. *Righteous Discontent: The Women's Movement in the Black Baptist Church, 1880–1920.* Cambridge: Harvard University Press, 1993.

Hine, Darlene Clark. *Black Women in White: Racial Conflict and Cooperation in the Nursing Profession, 1890–1950.* Bloomington: Indiana University Press, 1989.

———. "'We Specialize in the Wholly Impossible': The Philanthropic Work of Black Women." In *Lady Bountiful Revisited: Women, Philanthropy and Power,* ed. Kathleen McCarthy, 70–93. New Brunswick: Rutgers University Press, 1990.

Hine, Darlene Clark, Wilma King, and Linda Reed, eds. *"We Specialize in the Wholly Impossible": A Reader in Black Women's History.* Brooklyn: Carlson, 1995.

History Committee, St. Helena Episcopal Church, Beaufort, S.C.. *History of the Parish Church of St. Helena.* Columbia, S.C.: R. L. Bryan Co., 1990.

Holt, Thomas. *Black Over White: Negro Political Leadership in South Carolina during Reconstruction.* Urbana: University of Illinois Press, 1979.

Horowitz, Helen Lefkowitz. *Alma Mater: Design and Experience in the Women's Colleges from Their Nineteenth Century Beginnings to the 1930s.* New York: Knopf, 1984.

Howe, Irving. *Socialism and America.* San Diego, Calif.: Harcourt, Brace, Jovanovich, 1985.

Huber, Richard. *The American Idea of Success.* New York: McGraw-Hill, 1971.

Hunter, Jane. "Inscribing the Self in the Heart of the Family: Diaries and Girlhood in Late Victorian America." *American Quarterly* 44, no. 1 (March 1992): 51–81.

———. "Politics and Culture in Women's History: A Symposium." *Feminist Studies* 6 (spring 1980): 26–64.

Hutchison, William. *The Transcendentalist Ministers: Church Reform in the New England Renaissance.* Boston: Beacon Press, 1959.

Iles, Teresa. *All Sides of the Subject: Women and Biography.* New York: Teachers College Press, 1992.

Jacob, Margaret. *Living the Enlightenment: Freemasonry and Politics in Eighteenth-Century Europe.* New York: Oxford University Press, 1991.

Jacoway, Elizabeth. *Yankee Missionaries in the South: The Penn School Experiment.* Baton Rouge: Louisiana State University Press, 1980.

James, William. *The Varieties of Religious Experience.* 1902. Reprint, New York: Longmans, Green, 1928.

Johnpoll, Bernard. *Pacifist's Progress: Norman Thomas and the Decline of American Socialism.* Chicago: Quadrangle, 1970.

Johnson, Guion. *A Social History of the Sea Islands with Special Reference to St. Helena Island, South Carolina.* Chapel Hill: University of North Carolina Press, 1930.

Johnson, Guy. *Folk Culture on St. Helena Island, South Carolina.* Chapel Hill: University of North Carolina Press, 1930.

Jones, Jacqueline. *Labor of Love, Labor of Sorrow: Black Women, Work and the Family, from Slavery to the Present.* New York: Random House, 1985.

———. *Soldiers of Light and Love: Northern Teachers and Georgia Blacks, 1865–1873.* Chapel Hill: University of North Carolina Press, 1980.

Jones-Jackson, Patricia. *When Roots Die: Endangered Traditions on the Sea Islands.* Athens: University of Georgia Press, 1987.

Joyner, Charles. *Down by the Riverside: A South Carolina Slave Community.* Urbana: University of Illinois Press, 1984.

———. "Introduction." In Elizabeth Allston Pringle, *A Woman Rice Planter,* xiii–lv. 1913. Reprint, Columbia: University of South Carolina Press, 1992.

Kantrowitz, Stephen. *Ben Tillman and the Reconstruction of White Supremacy.* Chapel Hill: University of North Carolina Press, 2000.

Karcher, Carolyn. *The First Woman in the Republic: A Cultural Biography of Lydia Maria Child.* Durham: Duke University Press, 1994.

Katzman, David. *Seven Days a Week: Women and Domestic Service in Industrializing America.* Urbana: University of Illinois Press, 1981.

Kaufman, Martin. *Homeopathy in America: The Rise and Fall of a Medical Heresy.* Baltimore, Md.: Johns Hopkins University Press, 1971.

Kelly, Joan. "Did Women Have a Renaissance?" In *Becoming Visible: Women in European History,* ed. Renate Bridenthal and Claudia Koonz, 2d ed., 175–202. Boston: Houghton Mifflin, 1987.

Kerber, Linda. "Separate Spheres, Female Worlds, Women's Place: The Rhetoric of Women's History." *Journal of American History* 75 (June 1988): 8–37.

Kerr, Andrea. *Lucy Stone: Speaking Out for Equality.* New Brunswick, N.J.: Rutgers University Press, 1992.

Kerr, Howard. *Mediums, and Spirit-Rappers, and Roaring Radicals: Spiritualism in American Literature, 1850–1900.* Urbana: University of Illinois Press, 1972.

Kirby, Jack Temple. *Rural Worlds Lost: The American South, 1920–1960.* Baton Rouge: Louisiana State University Press, 1987.

Kiser, Clyde. *Sea Island to City: A Study of St. Helena Islanders in Harlem and Other Urban Centers.* New York: Columbia University Press, 1932.

Knupfer, Anne Meis. *Toward a Tenderer Humanity and a Nobler Womanhood: African American Women's Clubs in Turn-of-the-Century Chicago.* New York: New York University Press, 1996.

Kolodny, Annette. *The Land before Her: Fantasy and Experience of the American Frontier, 1630–1860.* Chapel Hill: University of North Carolina Press, 1984.

Kousser Jr., Morgan. *The Shaping of Southern Politics: Suffrage Restriction and the Establishment of the One-Party South, 1880–1910.* New Haven, Conn.: Yale University Press, 1974.

Kousser Jr., Morgan, and James McPherson, eds. *Region, Race and Reconstruction: Essays in Honor of C. Vann Woodward.* New York: Oxford University Press, 1982.

Kraditor, Aileen. *The Ideas of the Woman Suffrage Movement, 1890–1920.* 1965; rev. ed. New York: W. W. Norton, 1981.

Kusmer, Kenneth. *A Ghetto Takes Shape: Black Cleveland, 1870–1930.* Urbana: University of Illinois Press, 1976.

Lane, Ann. *To Herland and Beyond: The Life and Work of Charlotte Perkins Gilman.* New York: Penguin, 1990.

Lears, T. J. Jackson. *No Place of Grace: Antimodernism and the Transformation of American Culture, 1880–1920.* New York: Pantheon Books, 1981.

Lebsock, Suzanne. *The Free Women of Petersburg: Status and Culture in a Southern Town, 1784–1860.* New York: W. W. Norton, 1984.

———. "Woman Suffrage and White Supremacy: A Virginia Case Study." In *Visible Women: New Essays in American Activism,* ed. Nancy Hewitt and Suzanne Lebsock, 62–100. Urbana: University of Illinois Press, 1993.

———. "Women and American Politics, 1880–1920." In *Women, Politics and Change,* ed. Louise Tilly and Patricia Gurin, 35–62. New York: Russell Sage, 1992.

Lemons, J. Stanley. *The Woman Citizen: Social Feminism in the 1920s.* Urbana: University of Illinois Press, 1973.

Leuchtenburg, William. *Franklin Roosevelt and the New Deal, 1932–1940.* New York: Harper and Row, 1963.

Levine, Lawrence. *Black Culture and Black Consciousness: Afro-American Folk Thought from Slavery to Freedom.* New York: Oxford University Press, 1977.

Lewis, David Levering. *W. E. B. Du Bois: Biography of a Race.* New York: Henry Holt, 1993.

Lincoln, C. Eric, and Lawrence Mamiya. *The Black Church in the African American Experience.* Durham: Duke University Press, 1990.

Littlefield, Daniel. *Rice and Slaves: Ethnicity and the Slave Trade in Colonial South Carolina.* Baton Rouge: Louisiana State University Press, 1981.

Loewenberg, Bert, and Ruth Bogin. *Black Women in Nineteenth-Century American Life: Their Words, Their Thoughts, Their Feelings.* University Park: Pennsylvania State University Press, 1976.

Logan, Rayford. *The Negro in American Life and Thought: The Nadir, 1877–1901.* New York: Dial Press, 1954.

Lott, Eric. *Love and Theft: Blackface Minstrelsy and the American Working Class.* New York: Oxford University Press, 1993.

Lystra, Karen. *Searching the Heart: Women, Men and Romantic Love in Nineteenth Century America.* New York: Oxford University Press, 1989.

Mack, Kibibi Voloria. *Parlor Ladies and Ebony Drudges: African American Women, Class, and Work in a South Carolina Community.* Knoxville: University of Tennessee Press, 1999.

MacLean, Nancy. *Behind the Mask of Chivalry: The Making of the Second Ku Klux Klan.* New York: Oxford University Press, 1994.

Mandle, Jay. *The Roots of Black Poverty: The Southern Plantation Economy after the Civil War.* Durham: Duke University Press, 1978.

McClintock, Anne. *Imperial Leather: Race, Gender and Sexuality in the Colonial Contest.* New York: Routledge, 1995.

McDowell, John Patrick. *The Social Gospel in the South: The Women's Home Mission Movement in the Methodist Episcopal Church, South, 1886–1939.* Baton Rouge: Louisiana State University Press, 1982.

McPherson, James. *Abolitionist Legacy: From Reconstruction to the NAACP.* Princeton: Princeton University Press, 1975.

Meier, August. *Negro Thought in America, 1880–1915: Racial Ideologies in the Age of Booker T. Washington.* Ann Arbor: University of Michigan Press, 1963.

Melton, J. Gordon. *The Encyclopedia of American Religions.* Vol. 2. Wilmington, N.C.: McGrath, 1978.

Meyer, Donald. *The Positive Thinkers: A Study of the American Quest for Health, Wealth, and Personal Power from Mary Baker Eddy to Norman Vincent Peale.* New York: Doubleday, 1965.

Miller, Edward Jr. *Gullah Statesman: Robert Smalls from Slavery to Congress, 1839–1915.* Columbia: University of South Carolina Press, 1995.

Mintz, Stephen, and Susan Kellogg. *Domestic Revolutions: A Social History of American Family Life.* New York: Macmillan, 1988.

Mixon, Wayne. *Southern Writers and the New South Movement, 1865–1913.* Chapel Hill: University of North Carolina Press, 1980.

———. "The Ultimate Irrelevance of Race: Joel Chandler Harris and Uncle Remus in Their Time." *Journal of Southern History* 56, no. 3 (August 1990): 457–80.

Moldow, Gloria. *Women Doctors in Gilded-Age Washington: Race, Gender and Professionalization.* Urbana: University of Illinois Press, 1987.

Montenyohl, Eric. "Joel Chandler Harris and American Folklore." *Atlanta Historical Review* 30 (fall–winter 1986–87): 70–88.

———. "Joel Chandler Harris and the Ethnologists: The Folk's View of Early American Folkloristics." *Southern Folklore* 47, no. 3 (1990): 227–37.

———. "The Origins of Uncle Remus." *Folklore Forum* 18 (spring 1986): 136–67.

Montgomery, Michael, ed. *The Crucible of Carolina: Essays in the Development of Gullah Language and Culture.* Athens: University of Georgia Press, 1994.

Morantz, Regina. "Nineteenth Century Health Reform and Women: A Program of Self-Help." In *Medicine without Doctors: Home Health Care in American History,* ed. Guenter Risse, Ronald Numbers, and Judith Walzer Leavitt, 73–93. New York: Science History Publications, 1977.

Morantz-Sanchez, Regina. *Sympathy and Science: Women Physicians in American Medicine.* New York: Oxford University Press, 1985.

Morgan, Philip. "Work and Culture: The Task System and the World of Lowcountry Blacks, 1700–1880." In *Material Life in America, 1600–1860,* ed. Robert St. George, 203–32. Boston: Northeastern University Press, 1988.

Mott, Luther. *A History of American Magazines.* Vols. 2–3. New York: D. Appleton & Co., 1938.

National Association for the Advancement of Colored People. *Thirty Years of Lynching in the United States, 1889–1918.* 1919. Reprint, New York: Negro Universities Press, 1969.

Neverdon-Morton, Cynthia. *Afro-American Women of the South and the Advancement of the Race, 1895–1925.* Knoxville: University of Tennessee Press, 1989.

Norton, Mary Beth, David Katzman, Paul Escott, Howard Chudacoff, Thomas Paterson, and William Tuttle Jr., eds. *A People and a Nation: A History of the United States.* 2d ed. Boston: Houghton Mifflin, 1986.

Numbers, Ronald. "Do-It-Yourself the Sectarian Way." In *Medicine without Doctors: Home Health Care in American History,* ed. Guenter Risse, Ronald Numbers, and Judith Walzer Leavitt, 49–72. New York: Science History Publications, 1977.

———. *Prophetess of Health: Ellen G. White and the Origins of Seventh Day Adventist Health Reform.* Rev. ed. Knoxville: University of Tennessee Press, 1992.

O'Neill, William. *Everyone Was Brave: The History of Feminism in America.* Chicago: Quadrangle, 1969.

Ownby, Ted. *Subduing Satan: Religion, Recreation and Manhood in the Rural South, 1865–1920.* Chapel Hill: University of North Carolina Press, 1990.

Painter, Nell. "Introduction." In *The Secret Eye: The Journal of Ella Gertrude Clanton Thomas, 1848–1889,* ed. Virginia Burr, 1–67. Chapel Hill: University of North Carolina Press, 1990.

———. *Sojourner Truth: A Life, A Symbol.* New York: W. W. Norton, 1996.

———. *Standing at Armageddon: The United States, 1877–1919.* New York: W. W. Norton, 1987.

Parker, Gail Thain. *Mind Cure in New England from the Civil War to World War I.* Hanover, N.H.: University Press of New England, 1973.

Pease, Jane, and William Pease. *Ladies, Women and Wenches: Choice and Constraint in Antebellum Charleston and Boston.* Chapel Hill: University of North Carolina Press, 1990.

Personal Narratives Group, eds. *Interpreting Women's Lives: Feminist Theory and Personal Narratives.* Bloomington: Indiana University Press, 1989.

Poovey, Mary. *Uneven Developments: The Ideological Work of Gender in Mid-Victorian England.* London: Virago Press, 1989.

Powell, Lawrence. *New Masters: Northern Planters during the Civil War and Reconstruction.* New Haven, Conn.: Yale University Press, 1980.

Rabinowitz, Howard. *Race Relations in the Urban South, 1865–1890.* 1978. Rev. ed., Urbana: University of Illinois Press, 1980.

Rabinowitz, Richard. *The Spiritual Self in Everyday Life: The Transformation of Personal Religious Experience in Nineteenth-Century New England.* Boston: Northeastern University Press, 1989.

Reynolds, Emily, and Joan Faunt, eds. *Biographical Directory of the Senate of South Carolina, 1776–1964.* Columbia: South Carolina Archives, 1964.

Rhiel, Mary, and David Suchoff, eds. *The Seductions of Biography.* New York: Routledge, 1996.

Roberts, John. *From Trickster to Badman: The Black Folk Hero in Slavery and Freedom.* Philadelphia: University of Pennsylvania Press, 1989.

———. "African American Diversity and the Study of Folklore." *Western Folklore* 52 (Apr., July, Oct. 1993): 157-71.

Robeson, Elizabeth. "The Ambiguity of Julia Peterkin." *Journal of Southern History* 61 (November 1995): 761–86.

Robinson, Carline, and William Dortch. *The Blacks in These Sea Islands, Then and Now.* New York: Vantage Press, 1985.

Roediger, David. *Towards the Abolition of Whiteness: Essays on Race, Politics, and Working Class History.* London and New York: Verso, 1994.

———. *The Wages of Whiteness: Race and the Making of the American Working Class.* London: Verso, 1991.

Rogers, Naomi. "Women and Sectarian Medicine." In *Women, Health and Medicine: A Historical Handbook,* ed. Rima Apple, 273–302. New Brunswick: Rutgers University Press, 1990.

Rollins, Judith. *Between Women: Domestics and Their Employers.* Philadelphia: Temple University Press, 1985.

Rose, Willie Lee. *Rehearsal for Reconstruction: The Port Royal Experiment.* New York: Vintage Books, 1964.

Rosenberg, Charles. "The Therapeutic Revolution." In *Explaining Epidemics and Other Studies in the History of Medicine,* 9–31, ed. Morris Vogel and Charles Rosenberg. Cambridge: Cambridge University Press, 1992.

Rosengarten, Dale. *Row upon Row: Sea Grass Baskets.* Columbia: McKissick Museum, University of South Carolina, 1986.

Rosengarten, Theodore. *Tombee: Portrait of a Cotton Planter with the Journal of Thomas B. Chaplin (1822–1890).* Edited and annotated with Susan W. Walker. New York: William Morrow, 1986.

Rothman, Ellen. *Hands and Hearts: A History of Courtship in America.* New York: Basic Books, 1984.

Rothman, Sheila. *Living in the Shadow of Death: Tuberculosis and the Social Experience of Illness in American History.* Baltimore, Md.: Johns Hopkins University Press, 1995.

Rouse, Jacqueline. *Lugenia Burns Hope: Black Southern Reformer.* Athens: University of Georgia Press, 1989.

Rowbotham, Sheila. *Woman's Consciousness, Man's World.* New York: Penguin, 1973.

Rowland, Lawrence, Alexander Moore, and George Rogers Jr., *The History of Beaufort County, South Carolina.* Vol. 1, 1514–1861. Columbia: University of South Carolina Press, 1996.

Ruddick, Sara. *Maternal Thinking: Toward a Politics of Peace.* Boston: Beacon Press, 1995.

Ruether, Rosemary, and Eleanor McLaughlin. *Women of Spirit: Female Leadership in the Jewish and Christian Traditions.* New York: Simon and Schuster, 1979.

Ruether, Rosemary, and Rosemary Keller, eds. *Women and Religion in America. Vol. 1: The Nineteenth Century.* San Francisco: Harper and Row, 1981.

Ruiz, Vicki, and Ellen Carol Dubois, eds. *Unequal Sisters: A Multi-Cultural Reader in U.S. Women's History.* 2d ed. New York: Routledge, 1994.

Ryan, Mary. *Women in Public: Between Banners and Ballots, 1825–1880.* Baltimore, Md.: Johns Hopkins University Press, 1990.

Scharf, Lois, and Joan Jensen, eds. *Decades of Discontent: The Woman's Movement, 1920–1940.* Westport, Conn.: Greenwood Press, 1983.

Schechter, Patricia. "Unsettled Business: Ida B. Wells against Lynching, or, How Antilynching Got Its Gender." In *Under Sentence of Death: Lynching in the South,* ed. W. Fitzhugh Brundage, 292–310. Chapel Hill: University of North Carolina Press, 1997.

———. *Ida B. Wells-Barnett and American Reform, 1880–1930.* Chapel Hill: University of North Carolina Press, 2001.

Schwalm, Leslie. *A Hard Fight for We: Women's Transition from Slavery to Freedom in South Carolina.* Urbana: University of Illinois Press, 1997.

Scott, Anne Firor. "Most Invisible of All: Black Women's Voluntary Associations." *Journal of Southern History* 56 (February 1990): 3–22.

———. *Natural Allies: Women's Associations in American History.* Urbana: University of Illinois Press, 1991.

———. *The Southern Lady: From Pedestal to Politics, 1830–1930.* Chicago: University of Chicago Press, 1970.

Scott, Anne Firor, and Andrew MacKay Scott. *One Half the People: The Fight for Woman Suffrage.* Urbana: University of Illinois Press, 1982.

Scott, James. *Domination and the Arts of Resistance: Hidden Transcripts.* New Haven, Conn.: Yale University Press, 1990.

Scott, Joan. *Gender and the Politics of History.* New York: Columbia University Press, 1988.

———. "Gender as a Useful Category of Historical Analysis." *American Historical Review* 91 (December 1986), 1053–75.

Seidler, Murray. *Norman Thomas: Respectable Rebel.* Binghamton: Syracuse University Press, 1961.

Shaw, Stephanie. "Black Club Women and the Creation of the National Association of Colored Women." In *"We Specialize in the Wholly Impossible": A Reader in Black Women's History,* ed. Darlene Clark Hine, Wilma King, and Linda Reed, 433–48. Brooklyn: Carlson, 1995.

———. *What a Woman Ought to Be and Do: Black Professional Women Workers during the Jim Crow Era.* Chicago: University of Chicago Press, 1996.

Shteir, Anne. "Linneaus's Daughters: Women and British Botany." In *Women and the Structure of Society: Papers from the Fifth Berkshire Conference on the History of Women,* ed. Barbara J. Harris and Jo Ann McNamara, 67–73. Durham: Duke University Press, 1984.

Silber, Nina. *The Romance of Reunion: Northerners and the South, 1865–1900.* Chapel Hill: University of North Carolina Press, 1993.

Simkins, Francis Butler. *Pitchfork Ben Tillman: South Carolinian.* Gloucester, Mass.: Peter Smith, 1964.

Sims, Anastatia. "Beyond the Ballot: The Radical Vision of the Antisuffragists." In *Votes for Women!: The Woman Suffrage Movement in Tennessee, the South, and the Nation,* ed. Marjorie Spruill Wheeler, 105–28. Knoxville: University of Tennessee Press, 1995.

———. *The Power of Femininity in the New South: Women's Organizations and Politics in North Carolina, 1880–1930.* Columbia: University of South Carolina Press, 1997.

Sklar, Kathryn Kish. *Catharine Beecher: A Study in American Domesticity.* New Haven, Conn.: Yale University Press, 1973.

———. *Florence Kelley and the Nation's Work: The Rise of Women's Political Culture, 1830–1900.* New Haven, Conn.: Yale University Press, 1995.

————. "Hull House Maps and Papers: Social Science as Women's Work in the 1890s." In *The Social Survey in Historical Perspective, 1880–1940,* ed. Martin Bulmer, Kevin Bales, and Kathryn Kish Sklar, 111–47. Cambridge: Cambridge University Press, 1991.

Smedley, Katherine. *Martha Schofield and the Re-Education of the South, 1839–1915.* Lewiston, N.Y.: Edwin Mellen Press, 1987.

Smith, Susan. *Sick and Tired of Being Sick and Tired: Black Women's Health Activism in America, 1890–1950.* Philadelphia: University of Pennsylvania Press, 1995.

Smith-Rosenberg, Carroll. *Disorderly Conduct: Visions of Gender in Victorian America.* New York: Oxford University Press, 1985.

Sosna, Morton. *In Search of the Silent South: Southern Liberals and the Race Issue.* New York: Columbia University Press, 1977.

Spivey, Donald. *Schooling for the New Slavery.* Westport, Conn.: Greenwood Press, 1978.

Steady, Filomina. *The Black Woman Cross-Culturally.* Cambridge, Mass.: Schenkman, 1981.

Stevenson, Brenda, ed. *The Journals of Charlotte Forten Grimke.* New York: Oxford University Press, 1989.

Stewart, James Brewer. *Holy Warriors: The Abolitionists and American Slavery.* New York: Hill and Wang, 1976.

St. George, Robert Blair, ed. *Material Life in America, 1600–1860.* Boston: Northeastern University Press, 1988.

Still, William. *The Underground Railroad.* 1872. Reprint, New York: Arno Press, 1968.

Stowe, Steven. *Intimacy and Power in the Old South: Ritual in the Lives of the Planters.* Baltimore, Md.: Johns Hopkins University Press, 1987.

Strickland, John. "Traditional Culture and the Moral Economy: Social and Economic Change in the South Carolina Low Country, 1865–1910." In *The Countryside in the Age of Capitalist Transformation,* ed. Steven Hahn and Jonathan Prude, 141–78. Chapel Hill: University of North Carolina Press, 1985.

Sutch, Richard. *One Kind of Freedom: The Economic Consequences of Emancipation.* New York: Cambridge University Press, 1977.

Swanberg, W. A. *Norman Thomas: The Last Idealist.* New York: Charles Scribner, 1976.

Talley, Thomas. *The Negro Traditions.* Edited by Charles Wolfe and Laura Jarmon. Knoxville: University of Tennessee Press, 1993.

Taylor, Antoinette Elizabeth. "South Carolina and the Enfranchisement of Women: The Early Years." *South Carolina Historical Magazine* 77, no. 2 (1976): 115–26.

———. "South Carolina and the Enfranchisement of Women: The Later Years." *South Carolina Historical Magazine* 80, no. 4 (1979): 298-310.

Terborg-Penn, Roslyn. *African American Women in the Struggle for the Vote, 1850–1920.* Bloomington: Indiana University Press, 1998.

———. "African American Women and the Woman Suffrage Movement." In *One Woman, One Vote: Rediscovering the Woman Suffrage Movement,* ed. Marjorie Spruill Wheeler, 135–56. Troutdale, Oreg.: NewSage Press, 1995.

———. "Discontented Black Feminists: Prelude and Postlude to the Passage of the Nineteenth Amendment." In *Decades of Discontent: The Women's Movement, 1920–1940,* ed. Lois Scharf and Joan Jensen, 261–78. Westport, Conn.: Greenwood Press, 1983.

Tetzlaff, Monica Maria. "Abigail Mandana Holmes Christensen." In *American Folklore: An Encyclopedia,* ed. Jan Brunvand, 142. New York: Garland Publishing, 1996.

———. "Shout." In *American Folklore: An Encyclopedia,* ed. Jan Brunvand, 667–68. New York: Garland Publishing, 1996.

Thomson, Robert Faris. *Flash of the Spirit: African and Afro-American Art and Philosophy.* New York: Vintage Books, 1983.

Tilly, Louise, and Patricia Gurin, eds. *Women, Politics, and Change.* New York: Russell Sage, 1990.

Tindall, George. *The Emergence of the New South, 1913–1945.* Baton Rouge: Louisiana State University Press, 1967.

———. *South Carolina Negroes: 1877–1900.* Columbia: University of South Carolina Press, 1952.

Tucker, Susan. *Telling Memories among Southern Women: Domestic Workers and Their Employers in the Segregated South.* Baton Rouge: Louisiana State University Press, 1988.

Turner, Lorenzo Dow. *Africanisms in the Gullah Dialect.* 1949. Reprint, New York: Arno Press, 1969.

Twining, Mary Arnold. "Movement and Dance on the Sea Islands." *Journal of Black Studies* 15 (June 1985): 463–79.

————. *Sea Island Roots: Studies in African Cultural Continuities*. Trenton, N.J.: Africa World Press, 1988.

Twining, Mary Arnold, and Keith Baird. "The Significance of Sea Island Culture." *Journal of Black Studies* 10 (June 1980), 379–86.

Tyson, Timothy. *Radio Free Dixie: Robert F. Williams and the Roots of Black Power*. Chapel Hill: University of North Carolina Press, 1999.

Vazquez, Josephina, and Lorenzo Meyer. *The United States and Mexico*. Chicago: University of Chicago Press, 1985.

Vlach, John Michael. *The Afro-American Tradition in Decorative Arts*. Cleveland: University of Cleveland Museum, 1978.

Walker, Alice. *In Search of Our Mothers' Gardens*. San Diego: Harcourt, Brace, Jovanovich, 1983.

————. "The Dummy in the Window: Joel Chandler Harris and the Invention of Uncle Remus." In *Living by the Word: Selected Writings, 1973–1987*. New York: Harcourt, Brace, Jovanovich, 1988.

Walker, S. S. "African Gods in the Americas—The Black Religious Continuum." *Black Scholar* 11, no. 8 (1980): 25–36.

Wallace, David Duncan. *South Carolina: A Short History, 1520–1948*. Columbia: University of South Carolina Press, 1966.

Walsh, Mary Roth. *Doctors Wanted. No Women Need Apply: Sexual Barriers in the Medical Profession, 1835–1975*. New Haven, Conn.: Yale University Press, 1977.

Ware, Vron. *Beyond the Pale: White Women, Racism and History*. London and New York: Verso, 1992.

Waters, Donald. *Strange Ways and Sweet Dreams: Afro-American Folklore from Hampton Institute*. Boston: G. K. Hall, 1983.

Welter, Barbara. "The Cult of True Womanhood, 1820–1860." *American Quarterly* 18 (summer 1966): 131–75.

Wheeler, Marjorie Spruill. *New Women of the New South: The Leaders of the Woman Suffrage Movement in the Southern States*. New York: Oxford University Press, 1993.

————, ed. *One Woman, One Vote: Rediscovering the Woman Suffrage Movement*. Troutdale, Oreg.: NewSage Press, 1995.

Whisnant, David. *All That Is Native and Fine: The Politics of Culture in an American Region*. Chapel Hill: University of North Carolina Press, 1983.

Wiebe, Robert. *The Search for Order: 1877–1920*. New York: Hill and Wang, 1967.

Wiener, Jonathan. *Social Origins of the New South: Alabama, 1860–1885.* Baton Rouge: Louisiana State University Press, 1978.

Wiggins, William. "Afro-Americans as Folk: From Savage to Civilized." In *One Hundred Years of American Folklore Studies: A Conceptual History,* ed. William Clements, 29–32. Washington, D.C.: American Folklore Society, 1988.

Williams, Susan Millar. *A Devil and a Good Woman, Too: The Lives of Julia Peterkin.* Athens: University of Georgia Press, 1997.

———. "Foreword." In Charles Colcock Jones Jr., *Gullah Folktales from the Georgia Coast,* xi–xxxv. Athens: University of Georgia Press, 2000.

Williamson, Joel. *After Slavery: The Negro in South Carolina during Reconstruction, 1861–1877.* Chapel Hill: University of North Carolina Press, 1965.

———. *The Crucible of Race: Black-White Relations in the American South since Emancipation.* New York: Oxford University Press, 1984.

Wolf, Kurt. "Laura M. Towne and the Freed People of South Carolina, 1862–1901." *South Carolina Historical Magazine* 98 (October 1997): 349–74.

Wood, Peter. *Black Majority: Negroes in Colonial South Carolina from 1670 through the Stono Rebellion.* New York: Knopf, 1974.

Woodward, C. Vann. *Origins of the New South, 1877–1913.* 1956. Reprint, Baton Rouge: Louisiana State University Press, 1967.

———. *The Strange Career of Jim Crow.* 3d ed. New York: Oxford University Press, 1974.

Woody, Thomas. *A History of Women's Education in the United States.* 1929. Reprint, New York: Octagon Books, 1966.

Wright, Gavin. *Old South, New South: Revolutions in the Southern Economy since the Civil War.* New York: Basic Books, 1986.

Wyatt-Brown, Bertram. *Southern Honor: Ethics and Behavior in the Old South.* New York: Oxford University Press, 1982.

Yates, Frances. *The Rosicrucian Enlightenment.* London: Routledge and Kegan Paul, 1972.

Yellin, Jean Fagin, and John Van Horne, eds. *The Abolitionist Sisterhood: Women's Political Culture in Antebellum America.* Ithaca: Cornell University Press, 1994.

Zahniser, Marvin. *Charles Cotesworth Pinckney, Founding Father.* Chapel Hill: University of North Carolina Press, 1967.

Zelizer, Viviana. *Pricing the Priceless Child: The Changing Social Value of Children.* New York: Basic Books, 1985.

Zikmund, Barbara Brown. "The Feminist Thrust of Sectarian Christianity." In *Women of Spirit: Female Leadership in the Jewish and Christian Traditions,* ed. Rosemary Ruether and Eleanor McLaughlin, 205–24. New York: Simon and Schuster, 1979.

Zumwalt, Rosemary. *American Folklore Scholarship: A Dialogue of Dissent.* Bloomington: Indiana University Press, 1988.

———. *Wealth and Rebellion: Elsie Clews Parsons, Anthropologist and Folklorist.* Urbana: University of Illinois Press, 1992.

Theses, Dissertations, and Unpublished Writings

Elliott, Florence. "Growing up White, Genteel and Female in a Changing South, 1865–1915." Ph.D. diss., University of California, Berkeley, 1992.

Guthrie, Patricia. "Catching Sense: The Meaning of Plantation Membership among Blacks on St. Helena Island, South Carolina." Ph.D. diss., University of Rochester, 1977.

Heyer, Kathryn. "Rootwork: Psychosocial Aspects of Malign Magical and Illness Beliefs in a South Carolina Sea Island Community." Ph.D. diss., University of Connecticut, 1981.

Johnson, Joan Marie. "'This Wonderful Dream Nation!': Black and White South Carolina Women and the Creation of the New South, 1898–1930." Ph.D. diss., University of California, Los Angeles, 1997.

McGuire, Mary Jennie. "Getting Their Hands on the Land: The Revolution in St. Helena Parish, 1861–1900." Ph.D. diss., University of South Carolina, 1985.

Shirley, William Harrison Jr. "A Black Republican Congressman during the Democratic Resurgence in South Carolina: Robert Smalls, 1876–1882." M.A. thesis, University of South Carolina, 1970.

Sims, Anastatia. "Sallie Southall Cotten and the North Carolina Federation of Women's Clubs." M.A. thesis. University of North Carolina, 1976.

Ulmer, Barbara Bellows. "Virginia Durant Young: New South Suffragist." M.A. thesis, University of South Carolina, 1979.

Index